# Law and the Environment

*A Multidisciplinary Reader*

# Law and the Environment

A Multidisciplinary Reader

EDITED BY

Robert V. Percival
and Dorothy C. Alevizatos

TEMPLE UNIVERSITY PRESS

PHILADELPHIA

Temple University Press, Philadelphia 19122
Copyright © 1997 by Temple University
All rights reserved
Published 1997
Printed in the United States of America

♾ The paper used in this publication meets the requirements of the American National Standard for Information Sciences—Permanence of Paper for Printed Library Materials, ANSI Z39.48-1984

Text design by Erin Kirk New

Library of Congress Cataloging-in-Publication Data
Law and the environment: a multidisciplinary reader / edited by
    Robert V. Percival, Dorothy C. Alevizatos.
        p.      cm.
     Includes index.
     ISBN 1–56639–523–2 (cloth : alk. paper). — ISBN 1–56639–524–0
(paper : alk. paper)
     1. Environmental law—United States.   2. Environmental policy—
United States.   3. Human ecology.   I. Percival, Robert V.
II. Alevizatos, Dorothy C. 1968–   .
KF3775.L38   1997
344.73'046—dc20
[347.30446]                                                    96–41366

To V. M. and S. V., whose love and courage have made the world a brighter place.
  R. V. P.

To my parents, with unbounded love and gratitude.
  D. C. A.

# Contents

# Part II: Environmental Law and Regulatory Policy 135

# Preface

One of the most remarkable developments of the twentieth century has been the worldwide growth of public concern for the environment. Efforts to translate that concern into effective public policy have posed formidable challenges for the legal system. Even as our understanding of environmental problems has improved, we have become acutely aware of the complexity and uncertainty that bedevil efforts to trace the effects of human activities on the environment.

In addition to confronting these uncertainties, environmental policy makers must also make decisions that involve profound ethical choices. Environmental regulation determines how much society is willing to invest to protect human life and health, and how fairly environmental risks will be distributed across society. It also reflects the kind of world we aspire to, and the condition in which we will leave it for future generations. As we seek to develop, improve, and refine tools for protecting the environment, our ability to use law to achieve these aims tests our capacity as a society to control our own destiny.

This book explores how the legal system has responded to environmental problems. It includes excerpts from some of the most important essays on environmental law, science, and policy written to date. Drawn from the most influential works in the field, the readings explore environmental policy problems in all their richness and complexity. Reflecting the multidisciplinary nature of the subject, the readings include works by scientists, ecologists, philosophers, legal scholars, economists, historians, and journalists. The readings include not only time-honored classics, but also some rare gems that are not widely known. We hope they will reignite enthusiasm for such important works and the valuable lessons they have to offer.

The process of selecting and editing the readings in this anthology gave us an opportunity to revisit the original works of what has become an astoundingly rich literature. This literature has had a major influence on the environmental law field, but it has generally been hard for students to access, particularly in courses pertaining to environmental law. The articles in this anthology have therefore been edited to make them more accessible for the reader. The original sources from which the material is drawn are listed in footnotes at the beginning of each reading. We have omitted virtually all footnotes that were contained in the original readings.

We would like to express our appreciation to all those who helped us with the manuscript, including research assistant Rachel Schowalter, the librarians and secretaries at the University of Maryland School of Law, copyeditor Sue Gleason, and the anonymous reviewers who made very helpful suggestions concerning our selection of articles. We also would like to express our appreciation to the contributors who were willing to forgo or reduce their normal permissions fees in order to enable us to incorporate such a rich collection of materials in this reader. Most of all, we are grateful to Laura Mrozek, Administrator of the Maryland Environmental Law Program, and to our editor, Doris Braendel of Temple University Press, for her unwavering faith in and support of the project.

# Introduction

This reader is divided into four parts. Part I introduces alternative perspectives on the nature and sources of environmental problems, including ecological, economic, and ethical perspectives. It considers why each of these disciplines provides strong support for pursuing some form of collective action to protect the environment. Chapter 1 considers scientists' concerns about the impact of human activity on the natural environment and how ecologists have fundamentally changed their conception of the natural state of the environment, with important implications for regulatory policy. Chapter 2 examines the classic economic explanation for environmental problems, as well as its criticisms and defenses. Chapter 3 considers the work of philosophers who have struggled to develop principles of environmental ethics that go beyond strictly human-centered perspectives. Chapter 4 examines the emerging environmental justice movement and how it has focused attention on inequities in the distribution of environmental burdens across socioeconomic groups.

Part I considers the diverse justifications for collective action to protect the environment; Part II examines how society has sought to use law to pursue this goal. The early history of environmental regulation is explored in Chapter 5, which reviews how society responded to environmental problems before the emergence of national regulatory programs. Chapter 6 examines the political forces that generated a burst of federal legislative activity to protect the environment during the 1970s and 1980s. Chapter 7 provides a nontechnical overview of the structure of current environmental law and an introduction to the debate over the efficiency and effectiveness of the current regulatory system. Chapter 8 examines the debate over the merits of alternative regulatory strategies, including technology-based regulation and economic incentive approaches.

Part III explores how law is translated into regulatory policy. The important roles of citizen groups and the public in influencing regulatory decisions are considered in Chapter 9. Chapter 10 identifies the forces that have made it extremely difficult for regulatory agencies to implement environmental laws. The growing use of risk assessment by regulatory agencies and efforts to use it to set regulatory priorities are covered in Chapter 11.

Part IV of the reader presents a global vision of the future of environmental law. Chapter 12 traces the rapid growth of international environmental law, which is generating numerous multilateral treaties and has become a major concern in the negotiation and implementation of international trade agreements. Chapter 13 considers diverse visions of the future of environmental law and policy and an assessment of why it is so difficult to reach consensus on environmental issues.

# Part I

## Perspectives on Environmental Problems

*Humans care deeply about the environment—for good reason. The quality of our lives ulti-mately depends on the quality of our surroundings, and the environment encompasses every-thing that surrounds us. The health of the environment is crucial to our own health, as well as to the productivity of our economy and to our capacity to derive aesthetic enjoyment and spiritual inspiration from our surroundings. How we feel about the environment helps define who we are; it reflects some of our deepest values and concerns, and it shapes the legacy we hope to leave future generations.*

*The four chapters comprising Part I of this reader explore different perspectives on the na-ture and sources of environmental problems—ecological, economic, and ethical. Read to-gether, they provide a powerful illustration of the importance of multidisciplinary perspec-tives in this field. No single discipline can provide the answers to environmental policy questions. Environmental policy makers often must make decisions that raise fundamental ethical concerns, and usually, even after consulting the best available information, they must act in the face of considerable uncertainty.*

*Scientists were among the first to sound the alarm about the effects of human activity on the health of ecosystems. As they gathered data that suggested frightening trends, they real-*

*ized the need to mobilize other disciplines in an effort to change public attitudes and policies toward the environment. Economists view environmental degradation as a product of market failures that imply that resources are not being used efficiently. They endorse collective action to supply public goods like clean air and clean water though they also caution against certain kinds of regulatory policies whose inefficiencies they decry. Environmental ethicists contend that the environment should be protected for its own sake as an ethical imperative with intrinsic value over and above human-centered concern for the impact of environmental degradation. The environmental justice movement has brought fairness to the forefront of policy debates by focusing on the disproportionate concentration of environmental risks in poor and minority communities. Despite the diversity of these views, the different disciplinary perspectives from which they spring, and the different policy advice they produce, each provides a strong rationale for some form of collective action to protect the environment, as explained in the chapters that follow. Although this consensus may be highly general, it has considerable importance for understanding the legal system's response to environmental concerns.*

# CHAPTER 1

---

# Ecological Perspectives

The readings in this chapter reflect the evolution of scientific concern over the effects of human actions on the environment. The authors revel in the beauty and complexity of the natural world, while worrying about the long-term effects of human activity. Recognizing the incredible complexity of ecosystems, they are reluctant to risk definitive predictions, but they have no doubt that anthropogenic activity is altering the natural world at an unprecedented and frightening pace.

The first two readings are the work of self-taught ecologists. George Perkins Marsh traveled extensively in Europe and Asia during the nineteenth century while serving as the U.S. ambassador to Turkey. His observations of environmental degradation in countries with long histories of natural resource exploitation inspired his 1864 work *Man and Nature; or, Physical Geography as Modified by Human Action.* Marsh presented an extraordinarily well-documented challenge to society's embrace of industrial progress by focusing on the environmental damage caused by industrial development. Marsh's work was surprisingly influential; in particular it boosted the late-nineteenth century campaign to establish national parks. A second edition of this work, entitled *The Earth as Modified by Human Action,* was published in 1874.

In the excerpt contained in this reader, Marsh describes how human activity has transformed the landscape around the world. He acknowledges that some human impact is inevitable and that many of these effects are beneficial, particularly from a human-centered perspective. But he argues that technology has so dramatically increased the scale of human ability to alter the environment that nature's limits can be readily exceeded, causing irreversible damage with severe consequences for humans. A visionary for his times, Marsh anticipates the possibility that human activity will cause climate change. His ideas embrace the concept of what today is known as "sustainable development," by stressing the importance of respecting the earth's carrying capacity.

Marsh concludes by warning against assuming that anything in nature is too small to be of significance. Contrasting this with the ancient legal maxim *de minimis non cu-*

*rat lex,* Marsh notes that, even if law does not concern itself with trifles, "in the vocabulary of nature, little and great are terms of comparison only; she knows no trifles, and her laws are as inflexible in dealing with an atom as with a continent or a planet." Thus, although humans may be unable to fully comprehend the range of their impact on the natural world, they "are never justified in assuming a force to be insignificant" just "because its measure is unknown, or even because no physical effect can now be traced to its origin."

Aldo Leopold's keen appreciation of the natural world was acquired in large part through his experience working as a national forest manager. Part of his job was to kill "bad" predators, such as wolves and mountain lions, which eventually helped him realize the folly of human efforts to manage the natural world. Leopold describes nature as a "biotic pyramid" and "a slowly augmented revolving fund of life." Leopold's field observations convinced him of the necessity of developing an entirely new ethic to govern humans' relationship with nature. Rejecting the prevailing model of humans as "conquerors" of the natural world, Leopold articulates his own "land ethic," which has become perhaps the quintessential statement of environmental consciousness. Published posthumously in *A Sand County Almanac,* Leopold's land ethic articulates a simple ethical principle focused on ecological impacts: "A thing is right when it tends to preserve the integrity, stability, and beauty of the biotic community. It is wrong when it tends otherwise."

The third reading in this chapter is an excerpt from Eugene Odum's classic ecology textbook. Odum emphasizes the importance of realizing that humans are part of a larger biotic community on which human welfare ultimately depends. He discusses the meaning and importance of resource conservation and the need to consider the environment holistically. Citing Leopold, Odum warns that tampering with any part of nature may affect the whole, an important lesson of ecology that he concedes is not yet widely appreciated.

Biologist Edward O. Wilson transports us to an Amazon rain forest as a violent thunderstorm approaches after dark. The jungle is teeming with life, though most of it cannot even be discerned by human senses. Wilson uses this particular storm to illustrate how nature's awesome violence renews and rejuvenates the jungle ecosystem. He describes the rain forest as a place of perpetual change, whose diversity and excitement can barely be appreciated by the human eye. It is a place where organisms compete for survival in a marathon that is "always beginning somewhere in the forest." Wilson observes that "it is diversity by which life builds and saturates the rain forest," as many organisms fail to survive but are replaced by others that thrive in the rich environment. He concludes that diversity holds the key to understanding why life has been carried far beyond the rain forest environment to survive in some of the harshest environments on earth.

Wilson contrasts the benificent violence of the rainstorm with the destructive violence wrought by human activity, which is rapidly depleting biodiversity. Wilson's deep appreciation for the diversity of life springs from his wonderment at the seemingly impossible odds of successfully threading the gauntlet of 3.8 billion years of evolutionary history. While he celebrates science's growing understanding of the incredible complexity of the rain forest, Wilson bemoans "the ultimate irony of organic evolution: that in the instant of achieving self-understanding through the mind of man, life has doomed its most beautiful creations." He reports that scientists have identified only 1.4 million of the 10 to 100 million species estimated to be on the planet. Yet one-fifth of these are expected to vanish in the next few decades due to human actions that are extinguishing species, like "caus[ing] lights to go out all over."

Dan Tarlock explains how science has changed our concept of nature in recent years, with the theory of a stable balance of nature being displaced by a "new ecology" that views the natural world as a chaotic, constantly changing set of ecosystems. Tarlock explores how the new ecology has undermined some of the assumptions on which environmental policy was founded. He explains that the demise of the "balance of nature" concept does not mean that human activity is just another factor to be tolerated regardless of its environmental effects. There are limits to the carrying capacity of ecosystems, and the new discipline of conservation biology is trying to understand what some of those limits are. Tarlock concludes that the "new ecology" and the demise of the equilibrium model of nature complicate the task policy makers must confront in making decisions in the face of considerable uncertainty. He maintains that management strategies should become more adaptive to facilitate changes in response to new scientific information.

*George Perkins Marsh*

---

# The Earth as Modified by
# Human Action (1877)

### Reaction of Man on Nature

. . . We cannot always distinguish between the results of man's action and the effects of purely geological or cosmical causes. The destruction of the forests, the drainage of lakes and marshes, and the operations of rural husbandry and industrial art have unquestionably tended to produce great changes in the hygrometric, thermometric, electric, and chemical condition of the atmosphere, though we are not yet able to measure the force of the different elements of disturbance, or to say how far they have been neutralised by each other, or by still obscurer influences; and it is equally certain that the myriad forms of animal and vegetable life, which covered the earth when man first entered upon the theatre of a nature whose harmonies he was destined to derange, have been, through his interference, greatly changed in numerical proportion, sometimes much modified in form and product, and sometimes entirely extirpated.

The physical revolutions thus wrought by man have not indeed all been destructive to human interests, and the heaviest blows he has inflicted upon nature have not been wholly without their compensations. Soils to which no nutritious vegetable was indigenous, countries which once brought forth but the fewest products suited for the sustenance and comfort of man—while the severity of their climates created and stimulated the greatest number and the most imperious urgency of physical wants—surfaces the most rugged and intractable, and least blessed with natural facilities of communication, have been brought in modern times to yield and distribute all that supplies the material necessities, all that contributes to the sensuous enjoyments and conveniences of civilized life. . . .

From George Perkins Marsh, *The Earth as Modified by Human Action* (New York: Scribner, Armstrong & Co., 1877).

## Destructiveness of Man

Man has too long forgotten that the earth was given to him for usufruct alone, not for consumption, still less for profligate waste. Nature has provided against the absolute destruction of any of her elementary matter, the raw material of her works; the thunderbolt and the tornado, the most convulsive throes of even the volcano and the earthquake, being only phenomena of decomposition and recomposition. But she has left it within the power of man irreparably to derange the combinations of inorganic matter and of organic life, which through the night of aeons she had been proportioning and balancing, to prepare the earth for his habitation, when in the fullness of time his Creator should call him forth to enter into its possession.

Apart from the hostile influence of man, the organic and the inorganic world are, as I have remarked, bound together by such mutual relations and adaptations as secure, if not the absolute permanence and equilibrium of both, a long continuance of the established conditions of each at any given time and place, or at least, a very slow and gradual succession of changes in those conditions. But man is everywhere a disturbing agent. Wherever he plants his foot, the harmonies of nature are turned to discords. The proportions and accommodations which insured the stability of exsting arrangements are overthrown. Indigenous vegetable and animal species are extirpated, and supplanted by others of foreign origin, spontaneous production is forbidden or restricted, and the face of the earth is laid bare or covered with a new and reluctant growth of vegetable forms, and with alien tribes of animal life. These intentional changes and substitutions constitute, indeed, great revolutions; but vast as is their magnitude and importance, they are, as we shall see, insignificant in comparison with the contingent and unsought results which have flowed from them.

The fact that, of all organic beings, man alone is to be regarded as essentially a destructive power, and that he wields energies to resist which Nature—that nature whom all material life and all inorganic substance obey—is wholly impotent, tends to prove that, though living in physical nature, he is not of her, that he is of more exalted parentage, and belongs to a higher order of existences, than those which are born of her womb and live in blind submission to her dictates.

There are, indeed, brute destroyers, beasts and birds and insects of prey—all animal life feeds upon, and, of course, destroys other life,—but this destruction is balanced by compensations. It is, in fact, the very means by which the existence of one tribe of animals or of vegetables is secured against being smothered by the encroachments of another; and the reproductive powers of species, which serve as the food of others, are always proportioned to the demand they are destined to supply. Man pursues his victims with reckless destructiveness; and, while the sacrifice of life by the lower animals is limited by the cravings of appetite, he unsparingly persecutes, even to extirpation, thousands of organic forms which he cannot consume.

The earth was not, in its natural condition, completely adapted to the use of man, but only to the sustenance of wild animals and wild vegetation. These live, multiply their kind in just proportion, and attain their perfect measure of strength and beauty, without producing or requiring any important change in the natural arrangements of surface, or in each other's spontaneous tendencies, except such mutual repression of excessive increases as may prevent the extirpation of one species by the encroachments of another. In short, without man, lower animal and spontaneous vegetable life would have been practically constant in type, distribution, and proportion, and the physical geography of the earth would have remained undisturbed for indefinite periods, and been subject to revolution only from slow development, from possible, unknown cosmical causes, or from geological action.

But man, the domestic animals that serve him, the field and garden plants the product of which supply him with food and clothing, cannot subsist and rise to the full development of their higher properties, unless brute and unconscious nature be effectually combated, and, in a great degree, vanquished by human art. Hence, a certain measure of transformation of terrestrial surface, of suppression of natural, and stimulation of artificially modified productivity becomes necessary. This measure man has unfortunately exceeded. He has felled the forests whose network of fibrous roots bound the mould to the rocky skeleton of the earth; but had he allowed here and there a belt of woodland to reproduce itself by spontaneous propagation, most of the mischiefs which his reckless destruction of the natural protection of the soil has occasioned would have been averted. He has broken up the mountain reservoirs, the percolation of whose waters through unseen channels supplied the fountains that refreshed his cattle and fertilized his fields; but he has neglected to maintain the cisterns and the canals of irrigation which a wise antiquity had constructed to neutralize the consequences of its own imprudence. While he has torn the thin glebe which confined the light earth of extensive plains, and has destroyed the fringe of semiaquatic plants which skirted the coast and checked the drifting of the sea sand, he has failed to prevent the spreading of the dunes by clothing them with artificially propagated vegetation. He has ruthlessly warred on all the tribes of animated nature whose spoil he could convert to his own uses, and he has not protected the birds which prey on the insects most destructive to his own harvests.

Purely untutored humanity, it is true, interferes comparatively little with the arrangements of nature, and the destructive agency of man becomes more and more energetic and unsparing as he advances in civilization, until the impoverishment, with which his exhaustion of the natural resources of the soil is threatening him, at last awakens him to the necessity of preserving what is left, if not of restoring what has been wantonly wasted. The wandering savage grows no cultivated vegetable, fells no forest, and extirpates no useful plant, no noxious weed. If his skill in the chase enables him to entrap numbers of the animals on which he feeds, he compensates this loss by destroying also the lion, the tiger, the wolf, the otter, the seal, and the eagle, thus indirectly protecting the feebler quadrupeds and fish and fowls, which would otherwise become the booty of beasts and birds of prey. But with stationary life, or at latest with the pastoral state, man at once commences an almost indiscriminate warfare upon all the forms of animal and vegetable existence around him, and as he ad-

vances in civilization, he gradually eradicates or transforms every spontaneous product of the soil he occupies. . . .

The ravages committed by man subvert the relations and destroy the balance
which nature had established between her organized and her inorganic creations,
and she avenges herself upon the intruder, by letting loose upon her defaced provinces
destructive energies hitherto kept in check by organic forces destined to be his best
auxiliaries, but which he has unwisely dispersed and driven from the field of action.
When the forest is gone, the great reservoir of moisture stored up in its vegetable
mould is evaporated, and returns only in deluges of rain to wash away the parched
dust into which that mould has been converted. . . . The earth is fast becoming an un-
fit home for its noblest inhabitant, and another era of equal human crime and human
improvidence, and of like duration with that through which traces of that crime and
that improvidence extend, would reduce it to such a condition of impoverished pro-
ductiveness, of shattered surface, of climatic excess, as to threaten the depravation,
barbarism, and perhaps even extinction of the species.

*Aldo Leopold*

# A Sand County Almanac (1949)

## The Community Concept

All ethics so far evolved rest upon a single premise: that the individual is a member of a community of interdependent parts. His instincts prompt him to compete for his place in the community, but his ethics prompt him also to co-operate (perhaps in order that there may be a place to compete for).

The land ethic simply enlarges the boundaries of the community to include soils, waters, plants, and animals, or collectively: the land.

This sounds simple: do we not already sing our love for and obligation to the land of the free and the home of the brave? Yes, but just what and whom do we love? Certainly not the soil, which we are sending helter-skelter downriver. Certainly not the waters, which we assume have no function except to turn turbines, float barges, and carry off sewage. Certainly not the plants, of which we exterminate whole communities without batting an eye. Certainly not the animals, of which we have already extirpated many of the largest and most beautiful species. A land ethic of course cannot prevent the alteration, management, and use of these 'resources,' but it does affirm their right to continued existence, and, at least in spots, their continued existence in a natural state.

In short, a land ethic changes the role of Homo sapiens from conqueror of the land-community to plain member and citizen of it. It implies respect for his fellow-members, and also respect for the community as such.

In human history, we have learned (I hope) that the conqueror role is eventually self-defeating. Why? Because it is implicit in such a role that the conqueror knows, *ex cathedra,* just what makes the community clock tick, and just what and who is valuable, and what and who is worthless, in community life. It always turns out that he knows neither, and this is why his conquests eventually defeat themselves.

In the biotic community, a parallel situation exists. Abraham knew exactly what the land was for: it was to drip milk and honey into Abraham's mouth. At the present moment, the assurance with which we regard this assumption is inverse to the degree of our education.

The ordinary citizen today assumes that science knows what makes the community clock tick; the scientist is equally sure that he does not. He knows that the biotic mechanism is so complex that its workings may never be fully understood. . . .

## Substitutes for a Land Ethic

. . . One basic weakness in a conservation system based wholly on economic motives is that most members of the land community have no economic value. Wildflowers and songbirds are examples. Of the 22,000 higher plants and animals native to Wisconsin, it is doubtful whether more than 5 per cent can be sold, fed, eaten, or otherwise put to economic use. Yet these creatures are members of the biotic community, and if (as I believe) its stability depends on its integrity, they are entitled to continuance.

When one of these non-economic categories is threatened, and if we happen to love it, we invent subterfuges to give it economic importance. At the beginning of the century songbirds were supposed to be disappearing. Ornithologists jumped to the rescue with some distinctly shaky evidence to the effect that insects would eat us up if birds failed to control them. The evidence had to be economic in order to be valid.

It is painful to read these circumlocutions today. We have no land ethic yet, but we have at least drawn nearer the point of admitting that birds should continue as a matter of biotic right, regardless of the presence or absence of economic advantage to us. . . .

## The Land Pyramid

An ethic to supplement and guide the economic relation to land presupposes the existence of some mental image of land as a biotic mechanism. We can be ethical only in relation to something we can see, feel, understand, love, or otherwise have faith in.

The image commonly employed in conservation eduction is "the balance of nature." For reasons too lengthy to detail here, this figure of speech fails to describe accurately what little we know about the land mechanism. A much truer image is the one employed in ecology: the biotic pyramid. . . .

Plants absorb energy from the sun. This energy flows through a circuit called the biota, which may be represented by a pyramid consisting of layers. The bottom layer is the soil. A plant layer rests on the soil, an insect layer on the plants, a bird and rodent layer on the insects, and so on up through various animal groups to the apex layer, which consists of the larger carnivores.

The species of a layer are alike not in where they came from, or in what they look like, but rather in what they eat. Each successive layer depends on those below it for food and often for other services, and each in turn furnishes food and services to those above. Proceeding upward, each successive layer decreases in numerical abundance. Thus, for every carnivore there are hundreds of his prey, thousands of their prey, millions of insects, uncountable plants. The pyramidal form of the system reflects this numerical progression from apex to base. Man shares an intermediate layer with the bears, raccoons, and squirrels which eat both meat and vegetables. . . .

Land, then, is not merely soil; it is a fountain of energy flowing through a circuit of soils, plants, and animals. Food chains are the living channels which conduct energy upward; death and decay return it to the soil. The circuit is not closed; some energy is dissipated in decay, some is added by absorption from the air, some is stored in soils, peats, and long-lived forests; but it is a sustained circuit, like a slowly augmented revolving fund of life. There is always a net loss by downhill wash, but this is normally small and offset by the decay of rocks. It is deposited in the ocean and, in the course of geological time, raised to form new lands and new pyramids.

The velocity and character of the upward flow of energy depend on the complex structure of the plant and animal community, much as the upward flow of sap in a tree depends on its complex cellular organization. Without this complexity, normal circulation would presumably not occur. Structure means the characteristic numbers, as well as the characteristic kinds and functions, of the component species. This interdependence between the complex structure of the land and its smooth functioning as an energy unit is one of its basic attributes.

When a change occurs in one part of the circuit, many other parts must adjust themselves to it. Change does not necessarily obstruct or divert the flow of energy; evolution is a long series of self-induced changes, the net result of which has been to elaborate the flow mechanism and to lengthen the circuit. Evolutionary changes, however, are usually slow and local. Man's invention of tools has enabled him to make changes of unprecedented violence, rapidity, and scope.

## Land Health and the A-B Cleavage

A land ethic, then, reflects the existence of an ecological conscience, and this in turn reflects a conviction of individual responsibility for the health of the land. Health is the capacity of the land for self-renewal. Conservation is our effort to understand and preserve this capacity.

Conservationists are notorious for their dissension. Superficially these seem to add up to mere confusion, but a more careful scrutiny reveals a single plane of cleavage common to many specialized fields. In each field one group (A) regards the land as soil, and its function as commodity-production; another group (B) regards the land as a biota, and its function as something broader. How much broader is admittedly in a state of doubt and confusion.

In my own field, forestry, group A is quite content to grow trees like cabbages, with cellulose as the basic forest commodity. It feels no inhibition against violence; its ideology is agronomic. Group B, on the other hand, sees forestry as fundamentally different from agronomy because it employs natural species, and manages a natural environment rather than creating an artificial one. Group B prefers natural reproduction on principle. It worries on biotic as well as economic grounds about the loss of species like chestnut, and the threatened loss of the white pines. It worries about a whole series of secondary forest functions: wildlife, recreation, watersheds, wilderness areas. To my mind, Group B feels the stirrings of an ecological conscience. . . .

## The Outlook

It is inconceivable to me that an ethical relation to land can exist without love, respect, and admiration for land, and a high regard for its value. By value, I of course mean something far broader than mere economic value; I mean value in the philosophical sense.

Perhaps the most serious obstacle impeding the evolution of a land ethic is the fact that our educational and economic system is headed away from, rather than toward, an intense consciousness of land. Your true modern is separated from the land by many middlemen, and by innumerable physical gadgets. He has no vital relation to it; to him it is the space between cities on which crops grow. Turn him loose for a day on the land and if the spot does not happen to be a golf links or a 'scenic' area, he is bored stiff. If crops could be raised by hydroponics instead of farming, it would suit him very well. Synthetic substitutes for wood, leather, wool, and other natural land products suit him better than the originals. In short, land is something he has 'outgrown.'

Almost equally serious as an obstacle to a land ethic is the attitude of the farmer for whom the land is still an adversary, or a taskmaster that keeps him in slavery. Theoretically, the mechanization of farming ought to cut the farmer's chains, but whether it really does is debatable.

One of the requisites for an ecological comprehension of land is an understanding of ecology, and this is by no means co-extensive with 'education'; in fact, much higher education seems deliberately to avoid ecological concepts. An understanding of ecology does not necessarily originate in courses bearing ecological labels; it is quite as likely to be labeled geography, botany, agronomy, history, or economics. This is as it should be, but whatever the label, ecological training is scarce.

The case for a land ethic would appear hopeless but for the minority which is in obvious revolt against these 'modern' trends.

The 'key-log' which must be moved to release the evolutionary process for an ethic is simply this: quit thinking about decent land-use as solely an economic problem. Examine each question in terms of what is ethically and esthetically right, as well as what is economically expedient. A thing is right when it tends to preserve the integrity, stability, and beauty of the biotic community. It is wrong when it tends otherwise. . . .

The evolution of a land ethic is an intellectual as well as emotional process. Conservation is paved with good intentions which prove to be futile, or even dangerous, because they are devoid of critical understanding either of the land, or of economic land-use. I think it is a truism that as the ethical frontier advances from the individual to the community, its intellectual content increases.

The mechanism of operation is the same for any ethic: social approbation for right actions: social disapproval for wrong actions.

By and large, our present problem is one of attitudes and implements. We are remodeling the Alhambra with a steam-shovel, and we are proud of our yardage. We shall hardly relinquish the shovel which after all has many good points, but we are in need of gentler and more objective criteria for its successful use.

*Eugene P. Odum*

# Fundamentals of Ecology (1959)

## The Biotic Community Concept

A biotic community is any assemblage of populations living in a prescribed area or physical habitat; it is a loosely organized unit to the extent that it has characteristics additional to its individual and population components. It is the living part of the ecosystem. . . .

The community concept is one of the most important principles in ecological thought and in ecological practice. It is important in ecological theory because it emphasizes the fact that diverse organisms usually live together in an orderly manner, not just haphazardly strewn over the earth as independent beings. Like an ameba, the biotic community is constantly changing its appearance (visualize the forest in autumn and in spring), but it has structures and functions which can be studied and described, and which are unique attributes of the group. . . .

The community concept is important in the practice of ecology because "as the community goes, so goes the organism." . . . Man's welfare, like that of the quail or mosquito, depends ultimately on the nature of the communities and ecosystems upon which he superimposes his culture. . . .

## Conservation of Natural Resources in General

Conservation in the broadest sense is probably the most important application of ecology. Unfortunately, the term "conservation" suggests "hoarding," as if the idea were simply to ration static supplies so that there would be some left for the future. The aim of good conservation is to insure a continuous yield of useful plants, animals, and materials, by establishing a balanced cycle of harvest and renewal. Thus, a "no

From Eugene P. Odum, *Fundamentals of Ecology*, 2nd ed. (Philadelphia: W. B. Saunders Co., 1959).

fishing" sign on a pond may not be as good conservation as a management plan which allows for removal of several hundred pounds of fish per acre year after year. The principle of the ecosystem, therefore, is the basic and most important principle underlying conservation.

It is customary to divide natural resources into two categories: renewable and non-renewable. Although it is true that coal, iron, and oil deposits are not renewable in the same sense as forests or fish, nevertheless nitrogen, iron, and energy sources are renewable just as much as living resources. Man need never lack vital materials so long as the biogeochemical cycles operate in such a way that materials as well as organisms are "reassembled" as fast as they are "dispersed."

Although "hoarding" may not be the long-time aim of good conservation, there are instances in which complete restriction of use constitutes good conservation. The setting aside of natural areas for study and esthetic enjoyment is an example. With the increase in human population, it becomes more important that adequate samples of all major natural communities be preserved undisturbed for study and enjoyment. Since man establishes his civilization and his food chains by modifying natural ecosystems (and not by creating completely new systems), it is important that we have samples of unmodified communities for study; only with such "controls" can the effects of man's modification be properly judged, and unwise practices avoided. No laboratory scientist would think of undertaking an experiment without an adequate control, yet the field ecologist is often called on to evaluate the effects of man's experiments without a control being available. In the United States such organizations as the Audubon societies, the Wilderness Society, the Nature Conservancy (which developed as an offshoot from the Ecological Society of America), and the National Park Service are doing important work in seeking out and preserving natural areas which will serve both as valuable study and as recreation areas. Thus, "natural areas" have a somewhat different function from "wildlife refuges." In the former, entire communities are preserved unmodified; in the latter, extensive modification of the environment may be undertaken in order to increase the production of some specific organism or group of organisms. Both constitute sound conservation practice so long as the basic difference in function is realized.

Probably the most important job in conservation for the immediate future is to establish the fact in the minds of the general public that man is a part of a complex environment which must be studied, treated, and modified as a whole and not on the basis of isolated "projects." To emphasize this point, we can do no better than quote from the writings of the late Aldo Leopold. Leopold not only was one of the most able research men in applied ecology produced by this country, but he was also a very profound thinker and a gifted writer. The passage quoted below refers to the relation of water to land, but expresses very well the general need for a sound philosophy and understanding of the ecosystem principle:

> Mechanized man, having rebuilt the landscape, is now rebuilding the waters. The sober citizen who would never submit his watch or his motor to amateur tamperings freely sub-

mits his lakes to drainings, fillings, dredgings, pollutions, stabilizations, mosquito control, algae control, swimmer's itch control, and the planting of any fish able to swim. So also with rivers. We constrict them with levees and dams, and then flush them with dredgings, channelizations and floods and silt of bad farming.

The willingness of the public to accept and pay for these contradictory tamperings with the natural order arises, I think, from at least three fallacies in thought. First, each of these tamperings is regarded as a separate project because it is carried out by a separate bureau or profession, and as expertly executed because its proponents are trained, each in his own narrow field. The public does not know that bureaus and professions may cancel one another, and that expertness may cancel understanding. Second, any constructed mechanism is assumed to be superior to a natural one. Steel and concrete have wrought much good, therefore anything built with them must be good. Third, we perceive organic behavior only in those organisms which we have built. We know that engines and governments are organisms; that tampering with a part may affect the whole. We do not yet know that this is true of soils and water.

Thus men too wise to tolerate hasty tinkering with our political constitution accept without a qualm the most radical amendment to our biotic constitution.

# Edward O. Wilson

## The Diversity of Life (1992)

The storm arrived, racing from the forest's edge, turning from scattered splashing drops into sheets of water driven by gusts of wind. It forced me back to the shelter of the corrugated iron roof of the open-air living quarters, where I sat and waited with the *mateiros*. The men stripped off their clothing and walked out into the open, soaping and rinsing themselves in the torrential rain, laughing and singing. In bizarre counterpoint, leptodactylid frogs struck up a loud and monotonous honking on the forest floor close by. They were all around us. I wondered where they had been during the day. I had never encountered a single one while sifting through the vegetation and rotting debris on sunny days, in habitats they are supposed to prefer.

Farther out, a kilometer or two away, a troop of red howler monkeys chimed in, their chorus one of the strangest sounds to be heard in all of nature, as enthralling in its way as the songs of humpback whales. A male opened with an accelerating series of deep grunts expanding into prolonged roars and was then joined by the higher-pitched calls of the females. This far away, filtered through dense foliage, the full chorus was machine-like: deep, droning, metallic.

Such raintime calls are usually territorial advertisements, the means by which the animals space themselves out and control enough land to forage and breed. For me they were a celebration of the forest's vitality: *Rejoice! The powers of nature are within our compass, the storm is part of our biology!*

For that is the way of the nonhuman world. The greatest powers of the physical environment slam into the resilient forces of life, and nothing much happens. For a very long time, 150 million years, the species within the rain forest evolved to absorb precisely this form and magnitude of violence. They encoded the predictable occurrence of nature's storms in the letters of their genes. Animals and plants have come to use heavy rains and floods routinely to time episodes in their life cycle. They threaten rivals, mate, hunt prey, lay eggs in new water pools, and dig shelters in the rain-softened earth.

On a larger scale, the storms drive change in the whole structure of the forest. The natural dynamism raises the diversity of life by means of local destruction and regeneration.

Somewhere a large horizontal tree limb is weak and vulnerable, covered by a dense garden of orchids, bromeliads, and other kinds of plants that grow on trees. The rain fills up the cavities enclosed by the axil sheaths of the epiphytes and soaks the humus and clotted dust around their roots. After years of growth the weight has become nearly unsupportable. A gust of wind whips through or lightning strikes the tree trunk, and the limb breaks and plummets down, clearing a path to the ground. Elsewhere the crown of a giant tree emergent above the rest catches the wind and the tree sways above the rain-soaked soil. The shallow roots cannot hold, and the entire tree keels over. Its trunk and canopy are downward like a blunt ax, shearing through smaller trees and burying understory bushes and herbs. Thick lianas coiled through the limbs are pulled along. Those that stretch to other trees act as hawsers to drag down still more vegetation. The massive root system heaves up to create an instant mound of bare soil. At yet another site, close to the river's edge, the rising water cuts under an overhanging bank to the critical level of gravity, and a 20-meter front collapses. Behind it a smaller section of forest floor slides down, toppling trees and burying low vegetation.

Such events of minor violence open gaps in the forests. The sky clears again and sunlight floods the ground. The surface temperature rises and the humidity falls. The soil and ground litter dries out and warms up still more, creating a new environment for animals, fungi, and microorganisms of a different kind from those in the dark forest interior. In the following months pioneer plant species take seed. They are very different from the young shade-loving saplings and understory shrubs of the prevailing old-stand forest. Fast-growing, small in stature, and short-lived, they form a single canopy that matures far below the upper crowns of the older trees all around. Their tissue is soft and vulnerable to herbivores. . . .

Climb into the tangle of fallen vegetation, tear away pieces of rotting bark, roll over logs, and you will see these creatures teeming everywhere. As the pioneer vegetation grows denser, the deepening shade and higher humidity again favor old-forest species, and their saplings sprout and grow. Within a hundred years the gap specialists will be phased out by competition for light, and the tall storied forest will close completely over.

In the succession, pioneer species are the sprinters, old-forest species the long-distance runners. The violent changes and a clearing of space bring all the species briefly to the same starting line. The sprinters dash ahead, but the prolonged race goes to the marathoners. Together the two classes of specialists create a complete mosaic of vegetation types across the forest which, by regular tree falls and landslides, is forever changing. If square kilometers of space are mapped over decades of time, the mosaic turns into a riotous kaleidoscope whose patterns come and go and come again. A new marathon is always beginning somewhere in the forest. The percentages of successional vegetation types are consequently more or less in a steady state, from earliest pioneer species through various mixes of pioneer and deep-forest trees to stands of the most mature physiognomy. Walk randomly on any given day for one or two kilometers through the forest, and you will cut through many of these successional stages and sense the diversity sustained by the passage of storms and the fall of forest giants.

It is diversity by which life builds and saturates the rain forest. And diversity has carried life beyond, to the harshest environments on earth. Rich assemblages of animals swarm in the shallow bays of Antarctica, the coldest marine habitats on earth. Perch-like notothenioid fishes swim there in temperatures just above the freezing point of salt water but cold enough to turn ordinary blood to ice, because they are able to generate glycopeptides in their tissues as antifreeze and thrive where other fish cannot go. Around them flock dense populations of active brittlestars, krill, and other invertebrate animals, each with protective devices of its own. . . .

Archaebacteria, one-celled microorganisms so different from ordinary bacteria as to be candidates for a separate kingdom of life, occupy the boiling water of mineral hot springs and volcanic vents in the deep sea. . . .

Life is too well adapted in such places, out to the edge of the physical envelope where biochemistry falters, and too diverse to be broken by storms and other ordinary vagaries of nature. But diversity, the property that makes resilience possible, is vulnerable to blows that are greater than natural perturbations. It can be eroded away fragment by fragment, and irreversibly so if the abnormal stress is unrelieved. This vulnerability stems from life's composition as swarms of species of limited geographical distribution. Every habitat, from Brazilian rain forest to Antarctic bay to thermal vent, harbors a unique combination of plants and animals. Each kind of plant and animal living there is linked in the food web to only a small part of the other species. Eliminate one species, and another increases in number to take its place. Eliminate a great many species, and the local ecosystem starts to decay visibly. Productivity drops as the channels of the nutrient cycles are clogged. More of the biomass is sequestered in the form of dead vegetation and slowly metabolizing, oxygen-starved mud, or is simply washed away. Less competent pollinators take over as the best-adapted bees, moths, birds, bats, and other specialists drop out. Fewer seeds fall, fewer seedlings sprout. Herbivores decline, and their predators die away in close concert.

In an eroding ecosystem life goes on, and it may look superficially the same. There are always species able to recolonize the impoverished area and exploit the stagnant resources, however clumsily accomplished. Given enough time, a new combination of species—reconstituted fauna and flora—will reinvest the habitat in a way that transports energy and materials somewhat move efficiently. The atmosphere they generate and the composition of the soil they enrich will resemble those found in comparable habitats in other parts of the world, since the species are adapted to penetrate and reinvigorate just such degenerate systems. They do so because they gain more energy and materials and leave more offspring. But the restorative power of the fauna and flora of the world as a whole depends on the existence of enough species to play that special role. They too can slide into the red zone of endangered species.

Biological diversity—"biodiversity" in the new parlance—is the key to the maintenance of the world as we know it. Life in a local site struck down by a passing storm springs back quickly because enough diversity still exists. Opportunistic species evolved for just such an occasion rush in to fill the spaces. They entrain the succession that circles back to something resembling the original state of the environment.

This is the assembly of life that took a billion years to evolve. It has eaten the storms—folded them into its genes—and created the world that created us. It holds the world steady. When I rose at dawn the next morning, Fazenda Dimona had not changed in any obvious way from the day before. The same high trees stood like a fortress along the forest's edge; the same profusion of birds and insects foraged through the canopy and understory in precise individual timetables. All this seemed timeless, immutable, and its very strength posed the question: how much force does it take to break the crucible of evolution? . . .

## The Environmental Ethic

The sixth great extinction spasm of geological time is upon us, grace of mankind. Earth has at last acquired a force that can break the crucible of biodiversity. I sensed it with special poignancy that stormy night at Fazenda Dimona, when lightning flashes revealed the rain forest cut open like a cat's eye for laboratory investigation. An undisturbed forest rarely discloses its internal anatomy with such clarity. Its edge is shielded by thick secondary growth or else, along the river bank, the canopy spills down to ground level. The nighttime vision was a dying artifact, a last glimpse of savage beauty. . . .

. . . If there is a danger in the human trajectory, it is not so much in the survival of our own species as in the fulfillment of the ultimate irony of organic evolution: that in the instant of achieving self-understanding through the mind of man, life has doomed its most beautiful creations. And thus humanity closes the door to its past.

The creation of that diversity came slow and hard: 3 billion years of evolution to start the profusion of animals that occupy the seas, another 350 million years to assemble the rain forests in which half or more of the species on earth now live. There was a succession of dynasties. Some species split into two or several daughter species, and their daughters split yet again to create swarms of descendants that deployed as plant feeders, carnivores, free swimmers, gliders, sprinters, and burrowers, in countless motley combinations. These ensembles then gave way by partial or total extinction to newer dynasties, and so on to form a gentle upward swell that carried biodiversity to a peak—just before the arrival of humans. Life had stalled on plateaus along the way, and on five occasions it suffered extinction spasms that took 10 million years to repair. But the thrust was upward. Today the diversity of life is greater than it was 100 million years ago—and far greater than 500 million years before that. . . .

Ninety-nine percent of all the species that ever lived are now extinct. The modern fauna and flora are composed of survivors that somehow managed to dodge and weave through all the radiations and extinctions of geological history. Many contemporary world-dominant groups, such as rats, ranid frogs, nymphalid butterflies, and plants of the aster family Compositae, attained their status not long before the

Age of Man. Young or old, all living species are direct descendants of the organisms that lived 3.8 billion years ago. They are living genetic libraries, composed of nucleotide sequences, the equivalent of words and sentences, which record evolutionary events all across that immense span of time. Organisms more complex than bacteria—protists, fungi, plants, animals—contain between 1 and 10 billion nucleotide letters, more than enough in pure information to compose an equivalent of the *Encyclopaedia Britannica*. Each species is the product of mutations and recombinations too complex to be grasped by unaided intuition. It was sculpted and burnished by an astronomical number of events in natural selection, which killed off or otherwise blocked from reproduction the vast majority of its member organisms before they completed their lifespans. Viewed from the perspective of evolutionary time, all other species are our distant kin because we share a remote ancestry. We still use a common vocabulary, the nucleic-acid code, even though it has been sorted into radically different hereditary languages.

Such is the ultimate and cryptic truth of every kind of organism, large and small, every bug and weed. The flower in the crannied wall—it *is* a miracle. If not in the way Tennyson, the Victorian romantic, bespoke the portent of full knowledge (by which "I should know what God and man is"), then certainly a consequence of all we understand from modern biology. Every kind of organism has reached this moment in time by threading one needle after another, throwing up brilliant artifices to survive and reproduce against nearly impossible odds.

Organisms are all the more remarkable in combination. Pull out the flower from its crannied retreat, shake the soil from the roots into the cupped hand, magnify it for close examinations. The black earth is alive with a riot of algae, fungi, nematodes, mites, springtails, enchytraeid worms, thousands of species of bacteria. The handful may be only a tiny fragment of one ecosystem, but because of the genetic codes of its residents it holds more order than can be found on the surfaces of all the planets combined. It is a sample of the living force that runs the earth—and will continue to do so with or without us.

We may think that the world has been completely explored. Almost all the mountains and rivers, it is true, have been named, the coast and geodetic surveys completed, the ocean floor mapped to the deepest trenches, the atmosphere transected and chemically analyzed. The planet is now continuously monitored from space by satellites; and, not least, Antarctica, the last virgin continent, has become a research station and expensive tourist stop. The biosphere, however, remains obscure. Even though some 1.4 million species of organisms have been discovered (in the minimal sense of having specimens collected and formal scientific names attached), the total number alive on earth is somewhere between 10 and 100 million. No one can say with confidence which of these figures is the closer. Of the species given scientific names, fewer than 10 percent have been studied at a level deeper than gross anatomy. The revolution in molecular biology and medicine was achieved with a still smaller fraction, including colon bacteria, corn, fruit flies, Norway rats, rhesus monkeys, and human beings, altogether comprising no more than a hundred species.

Enchanted by the continuous emergence of new technologies and supported by generous funding for medical research, biologists have probed deeply along a narrow sector of the front. Now it is time to expand laterally, to get on with the great Linnean enterprise and finish mapping the biosphere. The most compelling reason for the broadening of goals is that, unlike the rest of science, the study of biodiversity has a time limit. Species are disappearing at an accelerating rate through human action, primarily habitat destruction but also pollution and the introduction of exotic species into residual natural environments. I have said that a fifth or more of the species of plants and animals could vanish or be doomed to early extinction by the year 2020 unless better efforts are made to save them. . . . As the last forests are felled in forest strongholds like the Phillippines and Ecuador, the decline of species will accelerate even more. In the world as a whole, extinction rates are already hundreds or thousands of times higher than before the coming of man. They cannot be balanced by new evolution in any period of time that has meaning for the human race. . . .

In amnesiac revery it is also easy to overlook the services that ecosystems provide humanity. They enrich the soil and create the very air we breathe. Without these amenities, the remaining tenure of the human race would be nasty and brief. The life-sustaining matrix is built of green plants with legions of microorganisms and mostly small, obscure animals—in other words, weeds and bugs. Such organisms support the world with efficiency because they are so diverse, allowing them to divide labor and swarm over every square meter of the earth's surface. They run the world precisely as we would wish it to be run, because humanity evolved within living communities and our bodily functions are finely adjusted to the idiosyncratic environment already created. Mother Earth, lately called Gaia, is no more than the commonality of organisms and the physical environment they maintain with each passing moment, an environment that will destabilize and turn lethal if the organisms are disturbed too much. A near infinity of other mother planets can be envisioned, each with its own fauna and flora, all producing physical environments uncongenial to human life. To disregard the diversity of life is to risk catapulting ourselves into an alien environment. We will have become like the pilot whales that inexplicably beach themselves on New England shores.

Humanity coevolved with the rest of life on this particular planet; other worlds are not in our genes. Because scientists have yet to put names on most kinds of organisms, and because they entertain only a vague idea of how ecosystems work, it is reckless to suppose that biodiversity can be diminished indefinitely without threatening humanity itself. Field studies show that as biodiversity is reduced, so is the quality of the services provided by ecosystems. Records of stressed ecosystems also demonstrate that the descent can be unpredictably abrupt. As extinction spreads, some of the lost forms prove to be keystone species, whose disappearance brings down other species and triggers a ripple effect through the demographics of the survivors. The loss of a keystone species is like a drill accidentally striking a powerline. It causes lights to go out all over.

These services are important to human welfare. But they cannot form the whole foundation of an enduring environmental ethic. If a price can be put on something, that something can be devalued, sold, and discarded. It is also possible for some to dream that people will go on living comfortably in a biologically impoverished world. They suppose that a prosthetic environment is within the power of technology, that human life can still flourish in a completely humanized world, where medicines would all be synthesized from chemicals off the shelf, food grown from a few dozen domestic crop species, the atmosphere and climate regulated by computer-driven fusion energy, and the earth made over until it becomes a literal spaceship rather than a metaphorical one, with people reading displays and touching buttons on the bridge. Such is the terminus of the philosophy of exemptionalism: do not weep for the past, humanity is a new order of life, let species die if they block progress, scientific and technological genius will find another way. Look up and see the stars awaiting us.

But consider: human advance is determined not by reason alone but by emotions peculiar to our species, aided and tempered by reason. What makes us people and not computers is emotion. We have little grasp of our true nature, of what it is to be human and therefore where our descendants might someday wish we had directed Spaceship Earth. Our troubles, as Vercors said in *You Shall Know Them,* arise from the fact that we do not know what we are and cannot agree on what we want to be. The primary cause of this intellectual failure is ignorance of our origins. We did not arrive on this planet as aliens. Humanity is part of nature, a species that evolved among other species. The more closely we identify ourselves with the rest of life, the more quickly we will be able to discover the sources of human sensibility and acquire the knowledge on which an enduring ethic, a sense of preferred direction, can be built. . . .

The ethical imperative should therefore be, first of all, prudence. We should judge every scrap of biodiversity as priceless while we learn to use it and come to understand what it means to humanity. We should not knowingly allow any species or race to go extinct. And let us go beyond mere salvage to begin the restoration of natural environments, in order to enlarge wild populations and stanch the hemorrhaging of biological wealth. There can be no purpose more enspiriting than to begin the age of restoration, reweaving the wondrous diversity of life that still surrounds us.

The evidence of swift environmental change calls for an ethic uncoupled from other systems of belief. Those committed by religion to believe that life was put on earth in one divine stroke will recognize that we are destroying the Creation, and those who perceive biodiversity to be the product of blind evolution will agree. Across the other great philosophical divide, it does not matter whether species have independent rights or, conversely, that moral reasoning is uniquely a human concern. Defenders of both premises seem destined to gravitate toward the same position on conservation.

The stewardship of environment is a domain on the near side of metaphysics where all reflective persons can surely find common ground. For what, in the final analysis, is morality but the command of conscience seasoned by a rational examination of consequences? And what is a fundamental precept but one that serves all generations? An enduring environmental ethic will aim to preserve not only the health and freedom of our species, but access to the world in which the human spirit was born.

## A. Dan Tarlock

# The Nonequilibrium Paradigm in Ecology and the Partial Unraveling of Environmental Law (1994)

### The Power of the Equilibrium Paradigm in Ecology

Environmental law derives its political power and legitimacy from science. Ecology and toxicology have identified a wide range of harms potentially caused by human activities—such as waste discharges, energy production, and land use and development—but science has also provided strategies to remedy these harms. Driven by these two sciences, environmental law is now subdividing into two broad fields: pollution risk remediation and biodiversity protection. This Essay focuses on the relationship between the nonequilibrium paradigm, which dominates ecology, and the accepted scientific rationales for legal strategies, which prevent or mitigate human disturbance of land and water ecosystems to protect and promote biodiversity.

Ecology provides a justification for a wide range of prohibitions on human activities that alter "natural" land and water systems and, along with toxicology, form much of current pollution control regulation. Legislators, regulators, resource managers, and lawyers have derived a powerful and general lesson from ecology: Let nature be. The ur-text is Aldo Leopold's summary of his ecologically based land ethic: "A thing is right when it tends to preserve the integrity, stability, and beauty of the biotic community. It is wrong when it tends otherwise." This land ethic has gradually replaced the progressive conservation movement's ethic of multiple use as the dominant natural resource management strategy, although there are intense pockets of resistance, especially in the western United States.

The underlying ecological justification for the land ethic is the equilibrium para-

A. Dan Tarlock, The Nonequilibrium Paradigm in Ecology and the Partial Unraveling of Environmental Law, 27 Loyola L.A. L. Rev. 1121 (1994).

digm or, as it is crudely and popularly called, the balance of nature. Legislatures and lawyers enthusiastically embraced this paradigm because it seemed to be a neutral universal organizing principle potentially applicable to the use and management of all natural resources. Modern environmental law's contributions to the legal system, which are based on this paradigm, include the National Environmental Policy Act of 1969 (NEPA), the Endangered Species Act of 1973 (ESA), the Wilderness Act of 1964, and parts of the Clean Water Act, such as section 404. Twenty-five years after this paradigm was incorporated into law, it—and thus the basis for the core of biodiversity protection law—is now unraveling. In the twenty-five years since it has been enshrined in environmental law, the equilibrium paradigm has been rejected in ecology and replaced with a complex, stochastic nonequilibrium one.

Environmental law is just beginning to address this paradigm shift. The implications are profound and potentially impact environmental law on many levels from the basic question of its legitimacy to the modification of existing biodiversity protection strategies and the application of basic legal doctrines to biodiversity management. . . .

Environmental law took its basic principles from three disciplines: economics, engineering, and ecology. Each has made important and related contributions, but ecology remains the foundation of environmental law because it informed society about the adverse consequences of a wide range of human activity. Welfare economics's theory of externalities provided an explanation of environmental costs, such as pollution, and a justification for government intervention to limit emissions and other human activity. Engineering contributed the idea of technology-forcing performance standards to mandate pollution reduction levels. Each theory significantly contributed to environmentalism but ecology is *primes internus*. It provided the basic rationale for all environmental protection: Leave nature alone. Later, philosophers purported to raise a complex and controversial scientific theory to a Kantian and non-homocentric ethic. However, this effort has at best only reinforced science's claim that there are important utilitarian reasons to worry about the magnitude of human-caused ecosystem disturbance and to limit harmful activities to keep these systems "productive."

In the late 1960s the perceived teachings of ecology were incorporated into environmental law and management. The adoption of ecology as the defining norm of environmentalism and environmental law bears close examination because of dramatic changes in ecology since then. The application of science to natural resource management has a long and troubled history in this country. In 1968, however, ecology offered the hope of coherent and rational resource management that had eluded society in the past. . . .

In the late 1960s ecology was an underfunded, low-status science, but one with great appeal to policy makers. The most attractive idea was the theory of general equilibrium at both the population and ecosystem level. The ecologist Tansley had crystallized the concept of "relatively stable dynamic equilibrium" in 1935, and Aldo Leopold had popularized it in his posthumous *A Sand County Almanac*. In turn, these ideas drew on the image of a balanced nature, which was central to both the Christian and Enlightenment world views. For example, the idea of the balance of nature radically disturbed by human intervention was the message of Rachel Carson's indictment of chemical pesticides, *Silent Spring,* perhaps the book most responsible for the environmental movement. For the nonscientist seeking wisdom in the late 1960s, ecologist Eugene Odum's widely used textbook *Fundamentals of Ecology* provided the most authoritative scientific statement of equilibrium. . . .

In retrospect it is clear that ecology was not ready for its starring role. Odum's theory of ecosystem equilibrium is one of the last gasps of nineteenth-century deterministic science. The theory is a sophisticated and subtle extension of leading twentieth-century ecologist Clements's theory of plant communities as being stable superorganisms because they progress through a series of successional stages leading to a superorganistic permanent climax. In elite science, deterministic theories had already been replaced by probabilistic ones, but the shift came late to biology and even later to ecology. Ecologists reported varying levels of indeterminate results testing the paradigm, but many scientists glossed them over because of an extreme case of "physics-envy." The point for lawyers is that this internal debate was missed in the rush to implement Leopold's dictum to "think like a mountain" in the heady days of the rise of environmentalism.

Ecologists made it easy to ignore the debate, especially in the 1960s when ecology aspired to be a big, mathematically based science like physics or molecular biology. The profession enthusiastically suggested the regulatory implications of ecology, which represented its ability to deliver the requisite science to balance nature. . . .

Ecology's promise was embraced by Lynton K. Caldwell, a professor of public administration at Indiana University, Bloomington, who became the principal drafter of NEPA. In an influential article published in 1966, Caldwell suggested that qualitative environmental standards could provide the administrative coherence historically lacking in natural resources policy.


## The Nonequilibrium Paradigm Arrives

Since its incorporation into environmental law and policy, the equilibrium paradigm has undergone a Kuhnian revolution. The equilibrium paradigm was flawed from the start, but until recently many scientists and policy makers believed the problem was the lack of necessary data rather than the paradigm itself. The alternative paradigm was neither clearly articulated nor widely accepted until the 1980s. It has, however, with pockets of resistance, been replaced with the more hard-edged probabilistic theories of nonequilibrium. These theories undermine much of the law's approach to resources management, or in modern terms, biodiversity preservation strategies of classic environmental law. Nonequilibrium ecology rejects the vision of a balance of nature. Further, it rejects the romantic idea that nature should be a place without humans, and returns to the problem posed in Genesis: How should one manage the Garden of Eden after it has been invaded by humans?

In a path-breaking book, Daniel Botkin has "deconstructed" the equilibrium paradigm as a misguided effort to match science to theological and scientific visions of a perfect universe. His basic argument is that the images of nature that have influenced ecology are static when, in fact, the kinds of problems we face require a dynamic view of nature. This view starts from the premises that human action is one of the principal forces operating on ecosystems and that system disturbances are both predictable and random. Ecosystems are patches or collections of conditions that exist for finite periods of time. Further, the accelerating interaction between humans and the natural environment makes it impossible to return to an ideal state of nature. At best, ecosystems can be managed, but not restored or preserved. Management will be a series of calculated risky experiments: "Nature moves and changes and involves risks and uncertainties and . . . our own judgments of our actions must be made against this moving target."

Most ecologists now reject any idea of a *balance* of nature, and the nonequilibrium paradigm is now the organizing principle of modern ecology. As one ecologist recently commented, "the idea of a balance of nature makes good poetry but bad science." The best evidence of this paradigm shift is a short but extremely influential list of twenty great ecological ideas for the 1990s published by Eugene P. Odum,[1] the distinguished ecologist who is most responsible for implanting in the minds of lawyers and policy makers the idea that natural systems tended toward equilibrium if left undisturbed. The first and over-arching great idea states that "an ecosystem is a thermodynamically open, far from equilibrium system." The other ideas are either a specific application of the nonequilibrium principle or policy prescriptions to implement good management, commentary as it were on the first principle.

The nonequilibrium paradigm does not undermine the case for biodiversity protection because it accepts the principal lesson of ecology: Unregulated, humans harm ecosystems and the magnitude of human intervention is often too great. In many instances, it strengthens the scientific case for ecosystem management, while exacerbating the politics of that management. The scale of management is larger and the emphasis is on the maintenance of processes that produced undisturbed systems. This new paradigm can also serve as the basis for the argument that since nature is in flux, human change is just another "flux" to be tolerated. However, ecologists reject this argument because it undermines the functional, historical, and evolutionary limits of nature.

## The Science of the Nonequilibrium Paradigm

Adherents to the nonequilibrium paradigm have pioneered a sophisticated new applied science, conservation biology, to protect ecosystems from human insults. To date the science has been stimulated by the need to match protected natural habitats with the survival of listed endangered and threatened species. Conservation biology is a regulatory science that seeks to develop scientific standards that can be applied to regulatory criteria and then to develop the management strategies to meet those standards. For example, endangered species protection first requires the determina-

---

[1]Eugene P. Odum, Great Ideas for Ecology for the 1990s, 42 Bioscience 542 (1992).

tion of an "effective population size" for species viability. After this is calculated, a habitat reserve system must be designed, taking into account existing land use patterns and land uses that will preserve the species. Existing laws and the politics of endangered species protection require only that *minimum* necessary habitats be preserved. Not surprisingly, conservation biology is concerned with the relationship between species extinction and habitat fragmentation. The basic objective . . . is to manage nature to mimic natural systems. . . .

## The Legal Implications of the Nonequilibrium Paradigm

The legal implications of the nonequilibrium paradigm are substantial over space and time. This paradigm shift affects the fundamental justifications for environmental law, the strategies we have used to promote environmental values, the relationship between law and scientific research, and the rules that structure environmental decision making. Environmental law is, to a greater extent than other areas of law, a product of external values not rooted in the environment of human dignity and thus it is difficult to integrate into our legal system. The Constitution, for example, is not a source of environmental rights and duties because the values that environmentalism promotes are not exclusively those of the Enlightenment. Environmentalism carries forward the Enlightenment faith in science, but the nonhuman values captured in Aldo Leopold's land ethic flow from the romantic reaction to the end product of the Enlightenment—the French Revolution.

## Uncertainty and the Nonequilibrium Paradigm

The "experimental" nature of the science of nonequilibrium ecology exacerbates the existing problem of making decisions from conditions of extreme uncertainty. The tension between the limits of science to provide information about the magnitude of environmental insults and established standards of causation has been an enduring problem in environmental law. The law has resolved this uncertainty problem in several creative ways. Risk was substituted for cause-in-fact and issues were recast as ethical rather than purely scientific. However, the legitimacy of standards of proof that depart from common-law causation requirements is always contingent and these initial strategies may not work as well in the future. Based, as it is, on probabilistic science, the nonequilibrium paradigm is merely another example of the pervasive problem of scientific uncertainty. However, the time horizons involved in the application of the nonequilibrium paradigm to resource management intensify the existing uncertainty problems, making it more difficult to employ past strategies to navigate around the constraints on environmental management raised by uncertainty.

In the 1970s the federal government began to enact laws to prevent unsafe levels of exposure to toxic chemicals by mandated risk assessments. Risk assessment calls for unavailable information and thus, risk minimization legislation required administrators to make decisions on the frontiers of science under extreme uncertainty. The federal government first enacted laws to control gross forms of air and water pollution but, after the DDT controversy, cancer risk became a proxy for almost all environmental health risks. The net result was that the line between scientific inference and the more rigorous legal standard for cause-in-fact has blurred in the regulatory arena.

When regulators and lawyers began to implement NEPA, the Clean Air Act, the Clean Water Act . . . , and other environmental statutes, they had to confront what scientists had always known: Most environmental decisions must be made under extremely uncertain conditions. The regulated community seized on the pervasive uncertainty to argue that decisions should wait until "good science" provided conclusive evidence of harm.

Environmentalists, led by the first administrator of the federal Environmental Protection Agency (EPA), William Ruckelshaus, successfully argued that the establishment of a risk of future harm was a legitimate substitute for more traditional scientific and legal standards of cause and effect. The use of what is now know as risk assessment and risk management was also shielded from judicial review by two principles. First, the New Deal–based principle of deference to expertise was applied to scientific uncertainty, despite several efforts to develop a "hard look" theory of review of the scientific evidence. Second, courts have widely endorsed the argument of scientists and engineers that risk assessments must err on the side of loss prevention by the incorporation of wide margins of safety. This has been carried over from toxic substances law to biodiversity protection.

Lawyers have also dealt with uncertainty in a much more problematic way. Risk assessment data usually provides wide, and sometimes meaningless, ranges of risk. To justify the use of risk to limit discharges of toxic chemicals and to preserve ecological integrity, many commentators argue that risk assessment and management are not purely scientific matters but questions of public policy and ethics. Nonequilibrium ecology undermines this effort because it strips away both the pretense of the divine and mechanical. Contrary to much contemporary wisdom that sees environmentalism as grounded in an emerging ethic that attributes rights to nature, I argue that science remains the central explanation and justification for environmentalism. Without the scientific foundation, environmentalism would be the marginal aesthetic movement that it was between the progressive conservation era and the late 1960s. Without science, the central economic concept of externalities would remain an empty shell and the central premise of the environmental ethic, respect for nature, would be equally empty. . . .

## Adaptive Management: The Theory

The major institutional change necessitated by the nonequilibrium paradigm is the need to apply adaptive management to biodiversity protection. Students of organizational behavior have always counseled the need for feedback loops to reassess policy as new information accumulates; however, this has never been taken seriously in environmental law and policy. We favor management consistent with the core idea of the rule of law—consistent application of fixed rules to yield a single, final decision. Our environmental laws accept a scientific premise and then require its continued application regardless of subsequent research findings and thinking. For example, the Clean Water Act of 1977 requires that all coastal sewage discharges receive secondary treatment, although there is considerable evidence that this may not always be necessary to achieve environmental objectives. Adaptive management, in contrast, is premised on the assumption that management strategies should change in response to new scientific information. All resource management is an ongoing experiment. . . .

## Conclusion

The first part of a mountain climb is usually the easiest and the rapidity of the ascent may create a false sense that the effort will continue to be easy. A great deal of progress can be made by walking in a straight line. Progress becomes more difficult as the slope increases and the irregularity of landscape requires more sophisticated strategies to continue the ascent. Environmentalism and environmental law are now moving from a gentle to a steep slope. The scientific landscape is beginning to change from a simple, linear landscape to a complex, stochastic one. To balance the legal system's traditional promotion of individual fairness with the continued protection of the environment, it must now adapt to this new landscape, in part, by concepts that provide for the continuous integration of science and policy making. Resource management decisions will continue to be made "under conditions of uncertainty," but we need new strategies to reduce data gaps over time. In the future, we must pay as much attention to the implementation and monitoring of management policies as we do to their formation so that newly collected information can be used to modify policies as necessary. There can never be a final decision in science-based management.

# CHAPTER 2

## Economic Perspectives

Economics views environmental problems as involving situations in which resources are not used efficiently because market failures prevent them from being allocated in a way that maximizes human satisfaction. These situations arise when resources such as air or water are not privately owned, but rather are part of a commons to which access is unrestricted. Environmental problems occur because individuals using the commons do not bear the full social costs of their actions. The polluter who fouls the air or water or the herder who grazes her sheep on common pasture does not have to pay to use these resources. As a result, the commons is polluted or overgrazed beyond the socially efficient level, imposing costs (called environmental externalities) on society. Efforts to provide clean air or clean water generally require government intervention because the benefits of such "public goods" accrue so widely that they cannot be restricted only to those who agree to pay for their production (what is known as the "free rider" problem).

Economics provides strong support for some form of collective action to correct market failures and to provide public goods like environmental protection. Government regulation is the principal approach that has been used to pursue these goals, though economists caution that some approaches to regulation can be highly inefficient. As discussed in more detail in Chapter 8, greater effort is being devoted to promoting more efficient regulatory tools, including the use of economic incentive approaches such as marketable emissions allowances. These efforts have not been without controversy. Some question whether creating tradeable rights to pollute will reduce the moral force of environmental protection policy. Other critics of economics stress the difficulty, if not the impossibility, of placing a monetary value on environmental amenities such as clean air, clean water, and wilderness preservation. They also argue that economics cannot answer difficult questions of intergenerational equity that so often are implicated by environmental policy.

The readings in this chapter begin with Scott Gordon's classic analysis of the depletion of the fisheries—the quintessential illustration of the problems of managing a commons. Though written more than four decades ago, Gordon's article has con-

siderable contemporary force now that so many important fisheries have become severely depleted throughout the world. He explains why the absence of property
rights in the fisheries leads to overfishing when the commons is open to unregulated
private exploitation. Gordon notes the difficulty of determining what restrictions will
keep catches at sustainable levels because of uncertainty concerning the true size of
fish stocks and the external influence of weather, pollution, and natural fluctuations
in fish populations. He concludes that the solution may require privatization of the
commons or stringent government regulation.

Gordon discusses why it is necessary to limit access to common resources, a phenomenon later to be highlighted by Garrett Hardin's famous article, "The Tragedy of
the Commons." Rather than including Hardin's article, we have opted instead to use
Art McEvoy's refinement of it, which focuses on fisheries to illustrate Hardin's
"tragedy." McEvoy explains that each fisher has an incentive to take fish from the
commons rather than to conserve the resource, ultimately producing overfishing and
depletion of the resource. Restricting access to the commons can help correct this
problem, but it is very difficult for biologists to determine the resource's "maximum
sustainable yield," the level of harvest that does not impair the fishery's long-term
productivity. McEvoy stresses the importance of social and cultural influences in
managing common resources, noting that many traditional societies have evolved social norms that result in successful management without resort to formal regulation.

Ronald Coase examines pollution problems from the perspective of an economist.
His classic article "The Problem of Social Cost" illustrates how an economist's approach may differ from that employed by the legal system under the common law of
nuisance. Whereas the legal system deals with entitlements and rights, economics focuses on maximizing social welfare. Coase stresses that pollution problems are reciprocal in nature, as pollution is harmful because some person or property is exposed to
it. In what has become known as "Coase's theorem," he posits that, if polluters and victims could costlessly bargain with one another to resolve nuisance disputes, efficient
outcomes would be achieved regardless of how law initially allocates rights. Coase argues that the party that has the most to gain will be able to compensate the other party
either by the victims' paying to induce the polluter to stop polluting or by the polluter
paying the victims to accept it or to move to avoid the harm. Coase concludes that
courts should promote efficient outcomes by considering whether the gain from enjoining pollution is greater than the loss that would be suffered by the polluter.

Environmental philosopher Mark Sagoff is sharply critical of the way in which
economists approach environmental problems. His extensive writings are summarized in his book *The Economy of the Earth.* Sagoff argues that economists err by focusing on maximizing consumer preferences and by analyzing how much individuals are willing to pay for environmental amenities. He maintains that there is a sharp
distinction between our individual preferences as consumers and our public-inter-
ested values that we express as citizens concerned about the environment. Sagoff argues that environmental policy disputes should be approached from the standpoint
of ethics rather than economics. Carol Rose, in a review of Sagoff's book, rejects

Sagoff's attempt to distinguish between our roles as citizens and consumers and questions why public policy should not try to satisfy voter preferences—whether for consumer goods or environmental protection. Rose does not believe that the difficulties of placing valuations on environmental amenities justifies discarding economics from environmental policy debates, though she agrees that it is important to consider noneconomic values as well.

Environmental protection is motivated in large part by concern over the quality of life to be experienced by future generations. How willing should the current generation be to make sacrifices to ensure that future generations have a healthy environment? That is a question that economists find extremely difficult to answer. Because economists like to compare the costs and benefits of alternative policies, policies that have effects stretching into the future require some mechanism for comparing the values of different streams of costs and benefits that accrue over an extended period of time. Discount rates are employed to reflect a preference for benefits that accrue sooner rather than later. The chapter concludes with an article by Professors Daniel Farber and Paul Hemmersbaugh which examines different approaches for deciding what environmental legacy we should leave to future generations. They conclude that we should be cautious about discounting future benefits and thus employ a low discount rate in analyzing alternative environmental policies.

# H. Scott Gordon

# The Economic Theory of a Common-Property Resource: The Fishery (1954)

. . . Fishery resources are unusual in the fact of their common-property nature; but they are not unique, and similar problems are encountered in other cases of common-property resource industries, . . . where natural resources are owned in common and exploited under conditions of individualistic competition. . . .

The most vivid thread that runs through the biological literature is the effort to determine the effect of fishing on the stock of fish in the sea. This discussion has had a very practical orientation, being part of the effort to design regulative policies of a "conservation" nature. . . .

. . . In the sea fisheries the natural resource is not private property; hence the rent it may yield is not capable of being appropriated by anyone. The individual fisherman has not legal title to a section of ocean bottom. Each fisherman is more or less free to fish wherever he pleases. The result is a pattern of competition among fishermen which culminates in the dissipation of the rent of the intramarginal grounds. . . .

This is why fishermen are not wealthy, despite the fact that the fishery resources of the sea are the richest and most indestructible available to man. By and large, the only fisherman who becomes rich is one who makes a lucky catch or one who participates in a fishery that is put under a form of social control that turns the open resource into property rights. . . .

The theory advanced above is substantiated by important developments in the fishing industry. For example, practically all control measures have, in the past, been designed by biologists, with sole attention paid to the production side of the problem and none to the cost side. The result has been a wide-open door for the frustration of the purposes of such measures. The Pacific halibut fishery, for example, is often hailed as a great achievement in modern fisheries management. Under international agreement between the United States and Canada, a fixed-catch limit was established during the early thirties. Since then, catch-per-unit-effort indexes, as usually interpreted, show a significant rise in the fish population. . . . Actually, careful study of the statistics indicates that the estimated recovery of halibut stocks could not have been due principally to the control measures, for the average catch was, in fact, greater during the recovery years than during the years of decline. The total amount of fish taken was only a small fraction of the estimated population reduction for the years prior to regulation. Natural factors seem to be mainly responsible for the observed change in population, and the institution of control regulations almost a coincidence. Such coincidences are not uncommon in the history of fisheries policy, but they may be easily explained. If a long-term cyclical fluctuation is taking place in a commercially valuable species, controls will likely be instituted when fishing yields have fallen very low and the clamor of fishermen is great; but it is then, of course, that stocks are about due to recover in any case. The "success" of conservation measures may be due fully as much to the sociological foundations of public policy as to the policy's effect on the fish. Indeed, Burkenroad argues that biological statistics in general may be called into question on these grounds. Governments sponsor biological research when the catches are disappointing. If there are long-term cyclical fluctuations in fish populations, as some think, it is hardly to be wondered why biologists frequently discover that the sea is being depleted, only to change their collective opinion a decade or so later.

Quite aside from the biological argument on the Pacific halibut case, there is no clear-cut evidence that halibut fishermen were made relatively more prosperous by the control measures. Whether or not the recovery of the halibut stocks was due to natural factors or to the catch limit, the potential net yield this could have meant has been dissipated through a rise in fishing costs. Since the method of control was to halt fishing when the limit had been reached, this created a great incentive on the part of each fisherman to get the fish before his competitors. During the last twenty years, fishermen have invested in more, larger, and faster boats in a competitive race for fish. In 1933 the fishing season was more than six months long. In 1952 it took just twenty-six days to catch the legal limit in the area from Willapa Harbor to Cape Spencer, and sixty days in the Alaska region. What has been happening is a rise in the average cost of fishing effort, allowing no gap between average production and average cost to appear, and hence no rent.

Essentially the same phenomenon is observable in the Canadian Atlantic Coast lobster-conservation program. The method of control here is by seasonal closure. The result has been a steady growth in the number of lobster traps set by each fisherman. Virtually all available lobsters are now caught each year within the season, but at much greater cost in gear and supplies. At a fairly conservative estimate, the same quantity of lobsters could be caught with half the present number of traps. In a few places the fishermen have banded together into a local monopoly, preventing entry and controlling their own operations. By this means, the amount of fishing gear has been greatly reduced and incomes considerably improved.

That the plight of fishermen and the inefficiency of fisheries production stems from the common-property nature of the resources of the sea is further corroborated by the fact that one finds similar patterns of exploitation and similar problems in other cases of open resources. Perhaps the most obvious is hunting and trapping. Unlike fishes, the biotic potential of land animals is low enough for the species to be destroyed. Uncontrolled hunting means that animals will be killed for any short-range human reason, great or small: for food or simply for fun. Thus the buffalo of the western plains was destroyed to satisfy the most trivial desires of the white man, against which the long-term needs of the aboriginal population counted as nothing. Even in the most civilized communities, conservation authorities have discovered that a bag-limit *per man* is necessary if complete destruction is to be avoided.

The results of anthropological investigation of modes of land tenure among primitive peoples render some further support to this thesis. In accordance with an evolutionary concept of cultural comparison, the older anthropological study was prone to regard resource tenure in common, with unrestricted exploitation, as a "lower" stage of development comparative with private and group property rights. However, more complete annals of primitive cultures reveal common tenure to be quite rare, even in hunting and gathering societies. Property rights in some form predominate by far, and most important, their existence may be easily explained in terms of the necessity for orderly exploitation and conservation of the resource. Environmental conditions make necessary some vehicle which will prevent the resources of the community at large from being destroyed by excessive exploitation. Private or group land tenure accomplishes this end in an easily understandable fashion. Significantly, land tenure is found to be "common" only in those cases where the hunting resource is migratory over such large areas that it cannot be regarded as husbandable by the society. In cases of group tenure where the numbers of the group are large, there is still the necessity of co-ordinating the practices of exploitation, in agricultural, as well as in hunting or gathering, economies. Thus, for example, Malinowski reported that among the Trobriand Islanders one of the fundamental principles of land tenure is the co-ordination of the productive activities of the gardeners by the person possessing magical leadership in the group. Speaking generally, we may say that stable primitive cultures appear to have discovered the dangers of common-property tenure and to have developed measures to protect their resources. Or, if a more Darwinian explanation be preferred, we may say that only those primitive cultures have survived which succeeded in developing such institutions.

Another case, from a very different industry, is that of petroleum production. Although the individual petroleum producer may acquire undisputed lease or ownership of the particular plot of land upon which his well is drilled, he shares, in most cases, a common pool of oil with other drillers. There is, consequently, set up the same kind of competitive race as is found in the fishing industry, with attending over-expansion of productive facilities and gross wastage of the resource. In the United States, efforts to regulate a chaotic situation in oil production began as early as 1915. Production practices, number of wells, and even output quotas were set by governmental authority; but it was not until the federal "Hot Oil" Act of 1935 and the development of interstate agreements that the final loophole (bootlegging) was closed through regulation of interstate commerce in oil.

Perhaps the most interesting similar case is the use of common pasture in the medieval manorial economy. Where the ownership of animals was private but the resource on which they fed was common (and limited), it was necessary to regulate the use of common pasture in order to prevent each man from competing and conflicting with his neighbors in an effort to utilize more of the pasture for his own animals. Thus the manor developed its elaborate rules regulating the use of the common pasture, or "stinting" the common: limitations on the number of animals, hours of pasturing, etc., designed to prevent the abuses of excessive individualistic competition.

There appears, then, to be some truth in the conservative dictum that everybody's property is nobody's property. Wealth that is free for all is valued by none because he who is foolhardy enough to wait for its proper time of use will only find that it has been taken by another. The blade of grass that the manorial cowherd leaves behind is valueless to him, for tomorrow it may be eaten by another's animal; the oil left under the earth is valueless to the driller, for another may legally take it; the fish in the sea are valueless to the fisherman, because there is no assurance that they will be there for him tomorrow if they are left behind today. A factor of production that is valued at nothing in the business calculations of its users will yield nothing in income. Common-property natural resources are free goods for the individual and scarce goods for society. Under unregulated private exploitation, they can yield no rent; that can be accomplished only by methods which make them private property or public (government) property, in either case subject to a unified directing power.

*Arthur F. McEvoy*

# The Fisherman's Problem: Ecology and Law in the California Fisheries, 1850–1980 (1986)

The commercial development of California's lush and varied fisheries has followed a repetitive pattern of boom and bust, one typical of fisheries the world over. Usually, after a few pioneers demonstrate a fishery's profitability, capital and labor rush into it, and the harvest increases exponentially for a time. At some point, unable to bear the strain of exploitation indefinitely without sacrificing its ability to replenish itself, the resource begins to yield less and less to economic effort. As depletion erodes its productivity, a fishing industry may even improve its technical ability to find and catch fish, thereby sustaining profits for a time but drawing ever more effort into the harvest and even more life out of the stock of fish. Ultimately, harvesting so depletes the resources as to cripple it.

A stock of fish is a renewable resource: It sustains itself by breeding or "recruiting" enough new adults to balance its losses to predators and other causes from year to year. A fishing industry is simply another predator added to the environment. According to the so-called sustained yield theory, the amount of fish that any given level of harvesting effort will yield over the long term is a function of both the intensity of fishing and the capacity of the stock to reproduce. At some maximum sustainable yield (MSY), fishers take exactly as many fish as the stock recruits in a season and so do not impair the resource's long-term productivity. Less fishing, of course, will produce fewer fish. A higher level of effort, however, will also produce fewer fish in the long run by leaving fewer adults to breed. The task of fishery management under this rudimentary model, then, is to calculate each stock's MSY and limit the take to that point.

Developed gradually over the first half of the twentieth century, the sustained yield model guided most scientific thinking about fisheries, game animals, timber, and other living resources until the 1960s. It represented a considerable improvement over earlier thinking, which held that oceanic fisheries at least were so vast in relation to the harvest as to be practically inexhaustible. If certain grounds lost productivity from time to time, fishers would simply move to new ones and give them time to replenish. Regulating the harvest in that case simply made no sense. This idea, perfectly in keeping with late nineteenth-century laissez-faire ideology, made the very important assumption that there existed a radical dichotomy between the fishing industry and the ecology of its resources: Nature, in the form of the stock of fish, was a passive object to be exploited at will and without significant consequences either for the resource or for the industry itself.

For its part, the sustained-yield theory rested on the important postulate that the stock of fish existed in isolation from its environment; that is, that the only influence on its productivity was the number of breeding adults left after harvest. Most fisheries, however, do not behave as neatly as the theory suggested because, like any other biological resource, fish live in a complex and constantly changing environment. Thus, for a given level of fishing effort, any stock's sustainable yield shifts constantly and for all practical purposes at random in response to conditions in its habitat. Targeting a conservative yield from a real fishery is thus a problem in stochastic, or random-variable, analysis—more like predicting the weather or the outcome of an election than, say, the sustainable yield of guppies from a well-maintained aquarium.

Some species reproduce less efficiently at lower levels of population, so that recruitment is not a simple algebraic function of breeding stock. It only takes two whales of the appropriate sex, for example, to make more whales, but if there were only two in an entire ocean they might not be able to find each other. Similarly, a schooling fish like the sardine must spread its spawn over a large expanse of ocean to ensure that enough offspring find conditions favorable to their survival. A fishery under intensive harvesting pressure may thus be more brittle and vulnerable to collapse than an unexploited one.

Some environmental changes that impinge on the productivity of fisheries occur in nature without reference to human activity, as when currents shift or the weather changes. Fish are much more sensitive to such changes than are organisms that live in the air. Scientists now believe, for example, that environmental conditions during the first year of life have a larger role in the recruitment of sardine and other herring-like fishes than does the size of the parent stock, although, again, environmentally induced recruitment failure will have a much more catastrophic effect on a heavily fished stock than on an abundant one. A sudden drop in temperature can blanket a coast with tides of dead sardines or anchovies. The Spanish explorer Vizcaino observed this phenomenon at the southern end of Baja California in 1602; Monterey newspapers reported another such incident the last week of May 1858. More subtle shifts in climate may drastically influence the migration and survival of larger fish such as albacore or salmon as well.

In general, the effects of climate or other ecological change will be more pronounced if a fishery is under stress and more so at the margins of the stock's range than near its center. California fisheries are the more responsive to ecological change, then, because many species taken on either side of the climatic boundary at Point Conception live near the limits of their tolerance for heat or cold. Very slight shifts in conditions will cause wide fluctuations in the behavior of many of California's fishes, with dramatic economic consequences for the industries that harvest them. Such remote events as the El Nino–Southern Oscillation, a complex oceanic-atmospheric interaction that takes place in the equatorial Pacific every six years or so, can have a significant impact on fisheries in California waters. . . .

A self-preserving fishing industry would respect the biological limits of its resource's productivity, limiting its seasonal take to some safe minimum so as to guarantee future harvests. Fishing industries, however, do not generally manage their affairs in such a rational way. This is primarily because fishery stocks are "common property" resources; that is, although many different individuals or firms may compete with each other for fish, no one of them owns the resource so as to keep others away from it. As a result, everyone has an incentive to keep fishing so long as there is any money to be made in the effort, whereas no one has an individual incentive to refrain from fishing so as to conserve the stock. Every harvester knows that if he or she leaves a fish in the water someone else will get it, and the profit, instead. This is what economists call "the fisherman's problem": In a competitive economy, no market mechanism ordinarily exists to reward individual forbearance in the use of shared resources.

It falls to government to consider the interrelated environmental effects of economic activity, to set safe standards for resource use, and to regulate the behavior of resource users so as to protect the community's long-term interest in its natural endowment. One of the first scholars to point out the importance of legal and institutional arrangements for fishery conservation was an economist, H. Scott Gordon. In a 1954 article criticizing the sustained-yield theory of fishery management, Gordon analyzed fishery problems as the inevitable result of the industry's legal and economic organization rather than in terms of biology or population dynamics. The sustained-yield theory, he wrote, "overlooked essential elements of the problem" by neglecting the powerful incentives to overfish that operated in a common-property regime. . . .

In Gordon's model, if the industry lowers its cost of fishing by developing more efficient gear, it produces more income for a time but only draws more effort into the harvest until total yields again equal total costs. By fishing the stock harder, it also produces fewer and fewer fish in the long run. Such economic irrationalities as subsidies designed to keep fishers solvent or hungry people fed and the traditional reluctance of fishers to leave their chosen line of work can push a fishery well past the point at which earnings no longer cover costs and on toward commercial or even biological extinction. Gordon's idea was that market forces, properly channeled under a limited-entry rather than a common-property regime, would tend to reward ecologically prudent behavior and thus automatically work to conserve the resource. He concluded that imposing such a regime on a fishery would require making it "private property or public (government) property, in either case subject to a unified directing power" able to exclude outsiders and adjust harvesting effort to maximum advantage.

Although he used the fisheries as a model, Gordon thought his conclusions "applicable generally to all cases where natural resources are owned in common but exploited under conditions of individualistic competition." In 1968 the biologist Garrett Hardin fit the theory to a wide range of environmental issues in a popular article whose title, "The Tragedy of the Commons," subsequently became an inclusive symbol of environmental problems generally. Hardin cast the fisherman's problem in terms of a group of farmers grazing cows on a common pasture. Because no one farmer owns the pasture, each finds it more profitable to graze one more cow than the pasture can feed in the long run because all the profit from the extra cow goes to the individual farmer, while each bears only an average share of the cost of ruining the pasture. Eventually, everyone goes broke. Collectively and inevitably—tragically, to Hardin's mind—industry degrades and eventually destroys resources owned in common but used competitively. The model Hardin believed applied not only to rangeland and to fish and other wildlife. It also applied to national parks and the air and water that citizens "own" in common but pollute as competitors to underground aquifers, which collapse because competing users draw out more water than natural flow can replenish, and even to the planet's ultimate capacity to support the ever-increasing numbers of new people that individual families produce.

Hardin asserted that the fisherman's problem had "no technical solution." He observed that throughout history, as human population had increased and environmental degradation proceeded apace, some form of private property had supplanted "the commons" in one resource area after another. By itself, however, privatization was no answer: Pointing to Coase's "social cost" problem, Hardin allowed that the Anglo-American concept of private property actually encouraged people to pollute their neighbors' air and water. Concluding his article, Hardin could only point to what he called "mutual coercion mutually agreed upon" to restrain people from destroying the planet. Nature ran a closed economy, he reasoned, so that the utilitarian notion of providing "the greatest good for the greatest number" was ecologically absurd. It was simply not possible to maximize both environmental values and the satisfaction of human wants. In order to save the future of the species, the wants of many people in the here and now would have to be denied. Hardin admitted that the kinds of coercion that his "lifeboat ethics" would require might be Draconian and at times unjust, as the privatization of property in land had been in the early days of capitalism. The alternative, however, was "too horrifying to contemplate." "Injustice," he wrote, "is preferable to total ruin."

During the 1960s and 1970s, Hardin's formulation of the problem defined the terms in which most scientists, environmentalists, and policymakers understood environmental issues, of which, again, the fisheries offered the laboratory case. The great contribution made by the Gordon-Hardin analysis was to emphasize that environmental problems arose from the interaction between human activity and a responsive Nature. The sustained-yield theory had posited an abstract mathematical model of the resource, in isolation from its environment. Likewise, "the ecosystem of the fisheries biologist," Gordon observed, was one in which "man is regarded as an exogenous factor," and not as a variable element, along with the fish, in "a system of mutual interdependence." Property rights and market structure, as Gordon showed, had much to do with the ways in which people behaved.

Yet there were those who believed that even the Gordon-Hardin line of thinking failed to integrate environment and society sufficiently in addressing the fisherman's problem. Some economists pointed to situations in which, given a high enough interest rate, even a private owner might find it economically rational to turn all her fish into cash at once and invest the proceeds in a bank: "to clean up now and let future generations eat soybeans," as one put it. S. V. Ciriacy-Wantrup, a noted California agricultural economist, criticized Hardin's characterization of private property and common-property regimes, pointing to traditional societies that had managed commonly owned resources successfully and to privatized economies that had utterly wasted theirs.

Taking a fresh look at precapitalist societies during the 1960s and 1970s anthropologists drew attention to the "unified directing power" side of Gordon's equation; they suggested that the competitive individualism that Hardin believed led to "the tragedy of the commons" might not be a generic failing of the human species but rather the specific historical consequence of the social changes that followed the advent of modern capitalist modes of production and social organization. "Indeed," wrote one anthropologist, it signified a breakdown of "one of the most important ecological functions of human social systems," that of integrating individuals' perception of their short-term personal advantage with that of the community as a whole over the long run. Ciriacy-Wantrup agreed. Hardin's analysis, he argued, treated the institution of private property and commons as exogenous factors in the economy-environment interaction, in much the same way that Gordon had criticized the fishery biologists' earlier treatment of economic forces and the biologists, in turn, had criticized the laissez-faire theory's treatment of Nature itself.

Forms of property and other legal and social institutions, too, are not immutable, rather, they are creatures of history, evolving in response to their social and natural environments even as they mediate the interaction between the two. Confronting the problem of environment, then, requires analysis of the interaction among three elements—ecology, production, and legal process—each of which changes on its own while interacting with the other two. . . .

Modern U.S. culture is preeminently a legal one; U.S. society as a whole relies on legal forms and legal processes to order its social and natural environments, to bring problems to its corporate attention, and to make choices among alternative means of addressing them. Other cultures in other places and times have relied on tradition or charismatic authority to bring meaning and order to their social lives. That U.S. culture is what Weber termed a "legal-rational" one does not mean that the symbols and ideologies that knit it together are any less historically contingent than legal or economic institutions themselves. In particular, people's perceptions of what is "fair" or "just," on the one hand, and what is necessary evil, part of the "natural" order of things, or "tragic," on the other, change over time in tandem with the social and material conditions of life. What was done to Chinese and Indian fishers during the late nineteenth century, for example, or indeed even to whales or salmon, would be unconscionable a century later. The farmers on Hardin's common pasture, then, are not tragic in the sense that their undoing flows from some flaw in their inherent nature; rather, they are products of a particular culture with a particular history and a particular view of the world.

As important to resource ecology as are market forces and the legal rules that guide them are the social and cultural factors that lead people to use resources, to perceive resource problems, and to respond to those problems in the ways that they do. All three processes, ecological, economic, and cultural, are dynamic in themselves. Yet they are holocoenotic, that is, interdependent parts of a coherent, indivisible whole. The product of their interaction over time is the history of human industry in relation to the "natural" world. When policymaking proceeds on an ideological or theoretical foundation that posits fundamental dichotomies among any of the three, as it has in the California fisheries for most of the state's history, it ignores the fundamentally ecological character of human experience. From the gap between policy and reality, in this case, springs what we perceive as "the tragedy of the commons."

Again, although Hardin wrote primarily with regard to the problem of overpopulation, he based his thinking on economic models of the fishing industry propounded by Gordon and others. Fisheries simply provide a laboratory example of the problem of environment because they are ecologically volatile and because in most cases it is impossible to consign their husbandry to private owners as if they were cropland or stands of timber. "The fisheries," wrote one economist, "present in one form or another all of the major causes of market-mechanism failure that call for public intervention."

*Ronald H. Coase*

# The Problem of Social Cost (1960)

This paper is concerned with those actions of business firms which have harmful effects on others. The standard example is that of a factory the smoke from which has harmful effects on those occupying neighbouring properties. The economic analysis of such a situation has usually proceeded in terms of a divergence between the private and social product of the factory, in which economists have largely followed the treatment of Pigou in *The Economics of Welfare*. The conclusion to which this kind of analysis seems to have led most economists is that it would be desirable to make the owner of the factory liable for the damage caused to those injured by the smoke, or alternatively, to place a tax on the factory owner varying with the amount of smoke produced and equivalent in money terms to the damage it would cause, or finally, to exclude the factory from residential districts (and presumably from other areas in which the emission of smoke would have harmful effects on others). It is my contention that the suggested courses of action are inappropriate, in that they lead to results which are not necessarily, or even usually, desirable.

## The Reciprocal Nature of the Problem

The traditional approach has tended to obscure the nature of the choice that has to be made. The question is commonly thought of as one in which A inflicts harm on B and what has to be decided is: how should we restrain A? But this is wrong. We are dealing with a problem of a reciprocal nature. To avoid the harm to B would inflict harm on A. The real question that has to be decided is: should A be allowed to harm B or should B be allowed to harm A? The problem is to avoid the more serious harm. I instanced in my previous article the case of a confectioner the noise and vibrations from whose machinery disturbed a doctor in his work. To avoid harming the doctor would inflict harm on the confectioner. The problem posed by this case was essentially whether it was worth while, as a result of restricting the methods of production which could be used by the confectioner, to secure more doctoring at the cost of a reduced supply of confectionary products. Another example is afforded by the problem of straying cattle which destroy crops on neighbouring land. If it is inevitable that some cattle will stray, an increase in the supply of meat can only be obtained at the expense of a decrease in the supply of crops. The nature of the choice is clear: meat or crops. What answer should be given is, of course, not clear unless we know the value of what is obtained as well as the value of what is sacrificed to obtain it. To give another example, Professor George J. Stigler instances the contamination of a stream. If we assume that the harmful effect of the pollution is that it kills the fish, the question to be decided is: is the value of the fish lost greater or less than the value of the product which the contamination of the stream makes possible. It goes almost without saying that this problem has to be looked at in total *and* at the margin.

## The Pricing System with Liability for Damage

I propose to start my analysis by examining a case in which most economists would presumably agree that the problem would be solved in a completely satisfactory manner: when the damaging business has to pay for all damage caused *and* the pricing system works smoothly (strictly this means that the operation of a pricing system is without cost).

A good example of the problem under discussion is afforded by the case of straying cattle which destroy crops growing on neighbouring land. Let us suppose that a farmer and a cattle-raiser are operating on neighbouring properties. Let us further suppose that, without any fencing between the properties, an increase in the size of the cattle-raiser's herd increases the total damage to the farmer's crops. . . .

I think it is clear that if the cattle-raiser is liable for damage caused and the pricing system works smoothly, the reduction in the value of production elsewhere will be taken into account in computing the additional cost involved in increasing the size of the herd. This cost will be weighed against the value of the additional meat production and, given perfect competition in the cattle industry, the allocation of resources in cattle-raising will be optimal. What needs to be emphasized is that the fall in the value of the production elsewhere which would be taken into account in the costs of the cattle-raiser may well be less than the damage which the cattle would cause to the crops in the ordinary course of events. This is because it is possible, as a result of market transactions, to discontinue cultivation of the land. . . . Whether the cattle-raiser pays the farmer to leave the land uncultivated or himself rents the land by paying the land-owner an amount slightly greater than the farmer would pay (if the farmer was himself renting the land), the final result would be the same and would maximize the value of production. . . .

## The Pricing System with No Liability for Damage

I now turn to the case in which, although the pricing system is assumed to work smoothly (that is, costlessly), the damaging business is not liable for any of the damage which it causes. This business does not have to make a payment to those damaged by its actions. I propose to show that the allocation of resources will be the same in this case as it was when the damaging business was liable for damage caused. . . .

[Coase explains that the farmer should be willing to pay the cattle-raiser not to increase his herd an amount up to the amount of damage the farmer would suffer from the increased herd. He then concludes that, as a result,] the size of the herd will be the same whether the cattle-raiser is liable for damage caused to the crop or not. . . .

It is necessary to know whether the damaging business is liable or not for damage caused since without the establishment of this initial delimitation of rights there can be no market transactions to transfer and recombine them. But the ultimate result (which maximizes the value of production) is independent of the legal position if the pricing system is assumed to work without cost.

## The Legal Delimitation of Rights and the Economic Problem

. . . The problem which we face in dealing with actions which have harmful effects is not simply one of restraining those responsible for them. What has to be decided is whether the gain from preventing the harm is greater than the loss which would be suffered elsewhere as a result of stopping the action which produces the harm. In a world in which there are costs of rearranging the rights established by the legal system, the courts, in cases relating to nuisance, are, in effect, making a decision on the economic problem and determining how resources are to be employed. It was argued that the courts are conscious of this and that they often make, although not always in a very explicit fashion, a comparison between what would be gained and what lost by preventing actions which have harmful effects. But the delimitation of rights is also the result of statutory enactments. Here we also find evidence of an appreciation of the reciprocal nature of the problem. While statutory enactments add to the list of nuisances, action is also taken to legalize what would otherwise be nuisances under the common law. The kind of situation which economists are prone to consider as requiring corrective Government action is, in fact, often the result of Government action. Such action is not necessarily unwise. But there is a real danger that extensive Government intervention in the economic system may lead to the protection of those responsible for harmful effects being carried too far.

*Mark Sagoff*

---

# The Economy of the Earth (1988)

According to many economists, . . . social regulation, particularly public policy concerning natural resources and the environment, should create or simulate (through questionnaires and other methods of data-gathering) markets for unowned and unpriced resources so that markets—or if that is impossible, the government—can charge for these resources prices that reflect their value to society. "As far as economists are concerned," George Eads and Michael Fix observe, "the problems of environmental pollution, excessive levels of workplace hazards, or unsafe consumer products exist largely because 'commodities' like environmental pollution, workplace safety, and product safety do not trade in markets."

In this book, I . . . argue against the use of the efficiency criterion in social regulation, and against the idea that workplace, consumer-product, and environmental problems exist largely because "commodities" like environmental pollution, workplace safety, and product safety are not traded in markets. I . . . argue, in contrast, that these problems are primarily moral, aesthetic, cultural, and political and that they must be addressed in those terms. The notion of allocatory efficiency and related concepts in the literature of resource economics . . . have become academic abstractions and serve today primarily to distract attention from the moral, cultural, aesthetic, and political purposes on which social regulation is appropriately based. . . .

## The Citizen and the Consumer

In *The Presentation of Self in Everyday Life,* Erving Goffman describes a variety of roles each individual plays and a variety of attitudes, values, beliefs, and expectations each person brings to those roles. This variety is familiar to us all: Each of us recognizes that he or she acts in different ways and expresses different thoughts in different roles and situations—with strangers or with close friends, with family members or with fellow professionals, and so on. The desires and purposes a person pursues in one role often conflict with those appropriate to another, for example, when as a professional one might want to go to the office on a weekend, but as a parent one knows one should help with the children. When what we want to do in one role conflicts with what we want to do in another, we are sometimes unsure about the priority to give to each.

In this book, I [am] concerned with two rather abstract social roles we all play, namely, the role of citizen and the role of consumer. As a *citizen*, I am concerned with the public interest, rather than my own interest; with the good of the community, rather than simply the well-being of my family. Thus, as a citizen, I might oppose a foreign adventure, like the Vietnam War, because I think it is tragic from the point of view of the nation as a whole. As a consumer or producer of goods and services, however, I might at the same time look at the war as a good thing for me if, for example, neither I nor my children must serve and I have a lot of investments in war-related industries.

In my role as a *consumer*, in other words, I concern myself with personal or self-regarding wants and interests; I pursue the goals I have as an individual. I put aside the community-regarding values I take seriously as a citizen, and I look out for Number One instead. I act upon those preferences on which my personal welfare depends; I may ignore the values that are mine only insofar as I consider myself a member of the community, that is, as *one of us*.

. . . [I] contend that social regulation should reflect the community-regarding values we express through the political process and not simply or primarily the self-regarding preferences we seek to satisfy in markets. . . . [T]he interests, goals, or preferences we entertain as citizens with respect to social regulation, moreover, differ *logically* from those we seek to satisfy as individuals.

When an individual states his or her personal preference, he or she may say, "I want (desire, prefer. . . . ) x." When the individual states a view of what is right or best for the community—what the government should do—he or she may say, "*We* want (prefer, desire) x." Sentences that express the interest or preference of the community make a claim to intersubjective agreement—they are correct or mistaken—since they take the community ("we" rather than "I") as their logical subject. This is the logical difference between consumer and citizen preferences.

## Values and Motives

In an important essay on the nature of human freedom, Gary Watson distinguishes between the valuational and motivational systems of a person. *"The valuational system* of an agent," Watson writes, "is that set of considerations which, when combined with his factual beliefs . . . , yields judgments of the form: the thing for me to do in these circumstances, all things considered, is *a*. . . . The motivational system of an agent is that set of considerations which move[s] him to actions."

We may use this distinction to divide among preferences, desires, or wants in the following way. All preferences, however well or ill considered, however autonomous or heteronomous, however altruistic, self-regarding, or malevolent, may lead a person to action. Real and hypothetical markets, at least in principle, can measure the strength or intensity of these preferences in terms of willingness to pay, and thus, at least in theory, markets can rank these preferences in a quantitative way.

Some of these preferences—we shall call them "values"—reflect a considered judgment the individual makes about what is right or good or appropriate in the circumstances. We can measure the intensity of these values, but we may also inquire about their justification; that is, we can ask the individual why he or she holds these values or views. Thus, officials might respond to these "preferences" by inquiring how much citizens are willing to pay to satisfy them. Alternatively, officials might respond to the reasons and arguments citizens offer to justify their opinions.

To see this difference, imagine a public hearing like the one at which [an economist] testified. Representatives of environmental and other public interest groups testified as well. How should the views of groups such as these enter into the policy-making process? Should officials determine the intensity of the preferences involved, for instance, by asking how much public interest groups collect in dues? (Should the committee have asked [the economist] how much analysts such as he are willing to pay to vindicate their theories? Would this constitute a "breakthrough" in quantifying the importance of these beliefs?) When should public officials balance interests? When should they deliberate about ideas?

It is plausible to think that public officials ought to consider citizen values—the judgments citizens defend and the reasons they give—on the merits rather than to try to price them, as it were, at the margin. . . . [E]conomic analysts who seek to find quasi-market prices for citizen values (which they sometimes call "intangibles" or fragile values") commit what philosophers call a "category mistake." They ask of objective convictions and beliefs a question that is appropriate only for subjective wants and desires.

In making this criticism, I rely, of course, on the idea that the political process involves deliberation or judgment going to the merits of proposals; government does not act, then, mechanically as an extension of, or as a prophylactic on, markets. . . .

This book defends a positive and a negative thesis. The negative thesis can be stated simply: Market failure is not the basis of social regulation. This thesis should not be surprising. The statutes that give authority to agencies like EPA and OSHA generally instruct them to achieve stated ethical, aesthetic, and cultural objectives such as a cleaner environment and a safer workplace. These laws do not, as a rule, instruct these agencies to improve, ensure, simulate, or attend to the efficiency of markets. Although we may construe some environmental, public health, and public safety problems to a limited extent in terms of market failures, to do so consistently requires a willing suspension of disbelief. Attempts to explain or justify popular social policies—for example, the protection of endangered species—as necessary to "correct" market failures are often so implausible that they must bring into disrepute either the policy or the explanation.

Consider worker and consumer safety and health. These "commodities" *are* traded in markets. At the turn of the century, for example, workers voluntarily took jobs, knowing the risks, in sweatshops and on railroads where an egregious number were injured or killed. Almost a million young children labored under cruel conditions; thousands "hurried" coal in mines. Mining companies saved money by digging narrow shafts to accommodate small children and by paying the children lower wages. Thus, private ownership, freedom, and the profit motive . . . directed resources to those uses where they were the most productive, given individual preferences for goods and services and the income of the population.

The transactions that led to child labor, the sixteen-hour workday, and hideous workplace conditions were largely voluntary and informed; no centralized bureaucracy in Washington told workers how old they had to be or what minimum they had to be paid; labor markets were efficient. The resulting levels of death, misery, and disease, even if "optimal" or "efficient" from an economic point of view, cannot be tolerated in any civilized nation.

Similarly, the food and drug industries a century ago could fairly be described as murderous; not just the conditions, such as the availability of product information, but the consequences of market transactions, such as death and injury, have been the appropriate concern of the government. Today the government licenses physicians, inspects meat, sets standards for tires, and so on; regulation of this sort prevents mayhem by constraining free market transactions.

Social regulation of safety in consumer products, the workplace, and the environment historically responds to a need to make markets more humane, not necessarily to make them more efficient. These laws—whether statutory or judge-made—strive primarily to prevent injury, grief, misery, and death, not to correct market failures or to compensate for unequal bargaining power. Although I approve paternalistic regulations of this sort on utilitarian grounds, I wish to mention two arguments that may be offered against them.

First, many libertarians believe that when the government engages in humanitarian regulation it overrides freedoms and rights (e.g., freedom of contract and choice) that are even more important than the lives it saves or the mayhem it prevents. Libertarians generally understand that a free market system can lead to very nasty results, as it did in the United States before the era of regulation. Libertarians defend the free market, however, because of the rights and liberties it comprises, not because of the kind of allocation in which it results. I have no argument to make for or against libertarianism in this book. I merely wish to observe that libertarians take rights, especially property rights, very seriously. Like me, they reject the use of the efficiency criterion as a justification or as a pretext for governmental intervention in markets.

Second, one may reject paternalistic or humanitarian legislation, no matter how many lives it saves or injuries it prevents, if it inhibits markets from reaching a certain outcome, namely, an efficient allocation of resources. One might make this argument if one believed, for example, that an efficient allocation of resources maximizes social welfare. One may then contend that humanitarian policies, because they impede efficiency, reduce welfare. This conception of "welfare," however, is a highly academic and theoretical notion, with no basis in utilitarian goods like health and happiness. . . . [C]oncepts like "welfare" and "well-being," when they occur within the confines of a theory, lose the meanings they have in ordinary language and common sense.

The positive thesis of this book is that social regulation expresses what we believe, what we are, what we stand for as a nation, not simply what we wish to buy as individuals. Social regulation reflects public values we choose collectively, and these may conflict with wants and interests we pursue individually. It is essential to the liberty we cherish, of course, that individuals are free to try to satisfy their personal preferences under open and equitable conditions. It is also part of our cherished conception of liberty that we are free to choose societal ideals together and free to accomplish these ideas in ways consistent with personal and political rights through the rule of law.

Social regulation most fundamentally has to do with the identity of a nation—a nation committed historically, for example, to appreciate and preserve a fabulous natural heritage and to pass it on reasonably undisturbed to future generations. This is not a question of what we *want;* it is not exactly a question of what we *believe in;* it is a question of what we *are.* There is no theoretical way to answer such a question; the answer has to do with our history, our destiny, and our self-perception as a people. And there is no methodology for making "hard decisions" and "trade-offs." We have to rely on the virtues of deliberation—open-mindedness, attention to detail, humor, and good sense.

*Carol M. Rose*

# Environmental Faust Succumbs to Temptations of Economic Mephistopheles, or, Value by Any Other Name Is Preference (1989)

## Values vs. Preferences, Citizen vs. Consumer

. . . Sagoff rails at economists for failing to take environmental "values" into account, and then he turns around and rails at them even more when they try to do just that. The poor economists: First everybody said they ignored nonmarket goods, like wildlife and mountainous scenery; and now here is Sagoff telling them they are imbeciles and rogues for trying to translate those nonmarket goods into a cost-benefit calculation for decisionmakers. What's going on here?

What's going on, Sagoff says, is that economists want to talk about environmental matters as if they were (private) "preferences," when they really are (public) "values." When people talk about the environment, he says, they aren't talking about what they prefer for private consumption; they are talking, as citizens, about the things that have value for the whole community. So you can't just do a cost-benefit analysis of environmental values, as if you were adding up what people say they would pay for a pastrami sandwich. With the environment, they are talking about what is valuable for the community as a whole, not their private preferences.

Now, get ready, because here comes the clincher: Mixing up these discourses, Sagoff says, is a "category mistake." "Category mistake"? My Irish grandfather, who

Carol M. Rose, Environmental Faust Succumbs to Temptations of Economic Mephistopheles, or, Value by Any Other Name Is Preference. Reprinted from *Michigan Law Review*, May 1989, Vol. 87, no. 6, p. 1631.

sold liquor, would have said, "Darlin', when they say somethin' fancy like that, close the cash register." But I will take the risk of leaving the register open for the time being, and take up the point.

The point is, I don't know where this alleged category mistake happens. Or if there is some mistake, it is a mistake that is thoroughly embedded in ordinary discourse; and this makes it a little harder to see as a mistake in the first place, at least for somebody like Sagoff, who professes to reject dogmatic versions of knowledge in favor of Richard Rorty's kibbitzing approach.

Let me unpack this:

(i) Just for starters, why does Sagoff seem to think that public values are a matter of discussion, while private preferences aren't, and are just hanging there like lurking components of an idiot id? Surely preferences—including consumer preferences—are educable. Once educated, we may start to call preferences "tastes," but the point remains: One can educate one's preference for movies, beer, music, and all the rest. Moreover, people routinely do so through discussion with other people.

For argument's sake, let's go along with Sagoff's view that one's liking for ski areas is a private or consumer "preference," as opposed to the public "value" in one's yen for wilderness. Surely people can educate their liking for *either* ski areas *or* wildernesses, and surely they can learn to like one more than the other. It hardly seems a "category mistake" to see both consumer preferences and so-called public values as learned, and educable, *desiderata*.

(ii) More generally, why does he think there is some qualitative difference between public values and private preferences? People mix up private and civic concerns all the time, and put them all in the same hopper. Sagoff's students, who valiantly chose wilderness despite their fondness for ski resorts, may well have wanted both wilderness and ski areas, but they may just have wanted wilderness more, and chose wilderness when they knew they couldn't have both in one place. But they are still considering the two not as qualitatively separate categories, but as alternative good things.

It is no big secret that people think and talk about a lot of public and private matters as alternative goods. Take for example a citizen's reaction to a proposal for a new sidewalk assessment. She thinks, in rapid succession: (1) Gee, a new sidewalk would look great in front of the house; and (2) it would make the whole block look spiffier, and give the neighborhood a boost; but (3) it does sound kind of expensive for my budget; and (4) it is really going to take a bite out of old Mrs. Jones' pension.

This is an entirely normal progression of thinking about civic decisions. Does anyone except Sagoff really think that there is some sharp divider between the "public" and the "private" aspects of these reflections, or that some of these aspects are inappropriate to the citizenry's deliberations on matters of public importance?

(iii) To illustrate the supposed category mistake in mixing preferences with values, Sagoff occasionally poses a cute hypothetical: Someone who is promoting a particular public policy is asked how much he would pay to have his policy put into place. The very question is supposed to illustrate that it is ridiculous to mix preference-talk with value-talk.

Well, one can agree that this would normally be an odd sort of question, but one still wouldn't have to concede that there is some absurdity in policymakers' consideration of preferences. For one thing, sad to say, sometimes policymakers are thinking about how much they would pay, or to put it on the other side of the Coase theorem, how much they are getting paid for taking particular public policy positions. That is to say, they are thinking about their own consumer preferences when they support certain public policies, because someone is going to pay them for supporting those public policies.

Naturally, we think this is wrong. But it isn't wrong because the legislators are thinking about preferences as such. It is wrong because they are thinking about the *wrong people's* preferences—they are supposed to be thinking about their constituents' preferences and not their own. As Susan Rose-Ackerman has argued, the legislator who accepts a bribe violates an agency relationship with his constituents, because he is supposed to be thinking about the constituents' preferences, and instead he is thinking about his own. But the legislator still should be thinking about preferences—that is, those of his constituents. If he isn't, he may not be in office too long, because those constituents are certainly considering consumer preferences when they think about, say, whether they want a bond issue to fund the public schools, or whether they want to clean up the roadsides at the expense of paying a bottle deposit, and how they want their representative to vote on those matters. This is not to say that private consumption preferences are the only thing that citizens (or their representatives) think about with respect to public affairs, but it is one of the things they think about. What we really may want from our political leaders is some education of our preferences in matters relating to public affairs; after all, they are in office, and are supposed to have the time to think about these things and explain them to the rest of us working stiffs. But citizens and policymakers don't take a vacation from preferences and utility maximization just because they are talking about public issues.

So where's the category mistake in mixing up citizens' values and consumers' preferences? I think I've lost it. Moreover, I think most people never dreamed of it. Ordinary language mixes these up, and treats all of them as appropriate grist in the political "deliberation" or "conversation" about public decisions, whether they be environmental or something else.

Despite all this, Sagoff is clearly right that there probably is one important sense in which community goals may diverge from the sum of individual preferences. Take public health, for example: Individual health has repercussions beyond the healthy individual, not only because the healthy person doesn't infect others, but also because she holds a job, plays on the neighborhood softball team, acts cheerful, and in general passes on some nice positive externalities to others. But because some of these good things are externalities, she might be tempted to scrimp on expenditures for her own health. And the same goes for everyone else in the community: taken in the aggregate, individuals might not put enough resources into things that are beneficial not just to themselves, but to everybody else too. But the community as a whole will be better off with a higher level of expenditure. The more general point is that the community as a whole has objectives that may differ from the sum of individual wishes; perhaps this was what Rousseau had in mind with all the pluses and minuses in the "general will." On these matters, we want citizens and legislators to pay attention to common goods and evils, which do diverge from aggregated individual preferences.

This is not news in the literature from economics and economics-influenced branches of political science. On the contrary, there is a whole body of work out there about public goods and positive sum cooperative "games," and though not all of it is written by creepy neo-classical economists, economists have certainly had some influence on the discussion. It is a pity that Sagoff does not seem to have addressed this work, for two reasons. First, some of this literature offers some reasons for the public preservation of the environmental goods that Sagoff rightly thinks are so important. And second, this literature poses very important political questions about how people might get over the impulses they have to act self-interestedly, under circumstances where narrow self-interest is inappropriate, and why they might cooperate instead for a greater common good—questions that seem to me to be central to Sagoff's interest in public values. . . . .

So what is ailing our Faust, anyway? Why does he burn so hotly about economics, when he concedes so much? I think that what's getting to Sagoff is the rhetoric of economic discussion, not its category mistakes.

Sagoff does not say this in so many words, but he implies that one aspect of economic rhetoric is me-first-ism. For all the supposed indifference to goals in economics, preference-talk has the sound of an irreducible egotism, and implies that preference bearers, in their endless pulse-checking for their own preferences, really don't give two hoots about what their neighbors might want or need. Now, maybe this is a mistaken notion of what economists think, but mistaken or not, the rhetoric matters: If all this preference-talk gives you the idea that you are alone in caring about the neighbors, you may be less willing to act in their behalf. Why be the sucker when the rest of them are all out for themselves? That sort of attitude, of course, leads everybody down the primrose path to the old Prisoner's Dilemma, the ultimate noncooperative end to what should be a cooperative game, the point where me-first-ism impoverishes all the players.

Environmental problems are often commons problems, and thus they present just such Prisoner's Dilemma "games"; and insofar as this is true, as I mentioned earlier, the big task is to induce people to cooperate for the common good. In that task, it doesn't always help to have a very powerful rhetoric suggesting that charity and fellow-feeling, while just as good as any other preferences, are really not to be expected—so get yours while you can.

That is one rhetorical aspect of economic talk that may be getting under Sagoff's skin. I am less tentative about saying that he is bothered by a second rhetorical aspect: that is, the purported economic agnosticism about goals, which suggests that goals are all alike and that there is not really much point in talking about them. So you like wilderness? says our economic poll-taker. Great—but let's not talk about why. Sagoff, on the other hand, wants to say that you can talk about these matters, and that there is something you can say to shape goals.

On this point, although I disagree with Sagoff's sharp opposition between preferences and values, I think he is on to something. People do talk about the things they want; they change their minds as a result of discussion; they have informed views on what is desirable and why; they talk about traditions and practicalities—and this discussion puts them into a kind of fellowship with other participants in it, including those with whom they disagree on any particular issue. In this sense, Sagoff is not just being trendy in his appeal to Rorty and "deliberation" or "persuasion." When I want to sell my pollution rights to the plastics factory, maybe Sagoff and I can talk it over, and maybe he can talk me out of it.

But how is he going to do that? The book is more than a bit frustrating on the things that go into our deliberation: What do we deliberate about, and especially, what kinds of topics will withstand the economic rhetoric that suggests we won't really deliberate at all? . . .

One route Sagoff touches upon is the somewhat amorphous work that has been classed as "deep ecology"—a set of writings characterized by their urging that we acknowledge a kind of feeling-in and feeling-with nature. This is not preference-talk, but kinship-talk. Sagoff's interesting chapter on the history of environmentalism brings up this way of talking, pointing out the symbolic impact of nature in our cultural history.

It takes a lot of nerve to get into a discussion of kinship with nature, as the ideas can be easily pooh-poohed; besides, it is not altogether clear that the concept—or feel—of deep ecology can be conveyed adequately by argumentative discourse at all. As Sagoff suggests in his discussion of American literature, this kind of insight may only come through experience, or through artistic and narrative renditions of experience—which may be the reason why people like the photographer Ansel Adams and the storyteller Edward Abbey are so important in environmental history. Sagoff's discussion of an aesthetic or a narrative counter-rhetoric is an important contribution to the environmental "discussion"—and in my view considerably more provocative than his preferred argumentative rhetoric of "ethics."

A second route or counter-rhetoric is an expanded version of rights. Sagoff mentions this route in his nods to libertarianism on the one hand and to animal-rights advocates on the other. Rights-talk is tricky, though, because rights and entitlements are very much a part of the neoclassical economic baggage: Fixed and firm entitlements, one might think, are only there in order to assist in investment, trade, and all those Pareto-optimal moves in the Me-First universe. Maybe this explains why Sagoff himself is leery of rights-talk.

But rights-talk has another rhetorical face as well. As Martha Minow has pointed out, by applying rights-talk to such unexpected subjects as children and the mentally disabled, one invites the listener to take seriously their condition. These unorthodox subjects are not at all the usual rights-bearers, who defend their own entitlements. But the very metaphoric quality of rights-rhetoric, on behalf of those who are somehow rights-disabled, bridges a gap to the more ordinary rights-holder, and adds drama to the plea to consider their situation, as *if* they could stand up for rights in a more conventional way. Thus rights-talk may borrow the neoclassical rhetoric of entitlement, but may turn that rhetoric around to lend gravity to the discussion of novel subjects. Minow uses this rhetorical turn for children, but one could do the same for animals and plants and places of breathtaking beauty.

The turn-around in the rhetoric of rights suggests still another kind of counter-rhetoric, one that Sagoff eschews, though I think perhaps too hastily. It is the counter-rhetoric of cost-benefit analysis, which seems to me to have done a good deal to get us off the mark in thinking about the desirable qualities of the natural environment. Sagoff feels a monumental fury about the "shadow-pricing" of environmental benefits. He is right in a way; it does seem jarring to cost out, say, the scenery at Mt. Whitney.

But why shouldn't we see that shock as the same kind of shock that comes with the discussion of trees having rights? Why not see it as an effort to bridge a gap, to dramatize the value of things that are too easily ignored, to invite a discussion of the things we value, even though the neoclassical market rhetoric seems deaf and dumb about them? So what if we borrow that market language? We have to use what we have, and this talk may help to disarm those who would simply ignore environmental values. More important, the very pirating of market-talk adds to its metaphoric power when we use that talk to dramatize things that are not bought and sold at all. It's a dangerous game, to be sure, but the imaginative use of rhetoric may open up some minds that would otherwise be closed.

The major problem of environmentalism is that we live in an imperfect world of limited resources: There just isn't enough of everything to have all we would like, or even all we think would be good for us. But in talking about the environment, we realize that we live in a limited rhetorical world, too. We can't talk about the natural surroundings as we no doubt romantically dream that the Native Americans did in olden times—with ease, grace, and transparent understanding of the awe and loveliness of the earth and its creatures. Instead, we have all this pinched yakking about what's mine, and what's yours, and how much you are going to have to pay me if you want to get what's mine. But there are ways to build on this rhetoric, ways to move out from under its limitations.

Sagoff's book gropes toward a different rhetoric, and while he concentrates on his sharp distinctions between ethics and economics, I think he makes a much more substantial contribution with his brief discussion of narrative and artistic renderings of the experience of nature. Still, my chief concern is that he is neglecting the rhetorical resources that are available in other standard ways of talking. On the subject of economics in particular, his book sends the very mixed—but still rather conventional—signals of sin and salvation. A less belligerent exploration, on the other hand, might have opened up some more creative rhetorical possibilities in the language of rights, entitlements, and even costs and benefits. But whatever the price the book pays to its own Manicheanism, it does make some important contributions, and I have to hand it to Sagoff: What he has done better than anybody else so far is to point out that the way we talk about the environment is going to influence the way we think about it, and the things we do about it.

*Daniel A. Farber and*
*Paul A. Hemmersbaugh*

# The Shadow of the Future: Discount Rates, Later Generations, and the Environment (1993)

Discounting favors regulations that confer benefits in the present or near future over regulations whose benefits society realizes at a later date. One might even say that the purpose of discounting is to favor present benefits over future benefits. Discounting also will generally favor regulations that produce short-term benefits and long-term costs. Even a modest discount rate will favor small benefits conferred today over much larger benefits conferred in the distant future. . . .

One argument in favor of discounting benefits to future generations is that, without discounting, the present generation would sacrifice all consumption, because the total benefits to infinite future generations will always exceed any cost to a single current generation. However, that argument proves persuasive only if society intends to maximize net benefits over time, i.e., intergenerational efficiency. Society may also prefer to distribute benefits equitably among generations. If, instead of intergenerational efficiency, society cares about intergenerational equity, it does not need discounting to protect the legitimate interests of the present generation against the claims of the future.

An intermediate position might attempt to integrate the goals of efficiency and equity. One possibility is for society to discount future benefits but limit the total discount that it could apply to any future benefit. This method would prevent discounting from diminishing benefits below a certain level and avoid the . . . trivialization of distant future effects. . . .

Daniel A. Farber and Paul A. Hemmersbaugh, The Shadow of the Future: Discount Rates, Later Generations, and the Environment, 46 Vand. L. Rev. 267 (1993).

Another argument that supporters of discounting future benefits sometimes advance is that future generations will be wealthier; thus, our descendants will value any marginal unit of benefit less because it will represent a smaller portion of their total wealth. That "diminishing marginal utility" argument provides little support, however, for discounting future lives saved by regulation. The assumption that future generations will have greater wealth seems somewhat less assured today than as recently as thirty years ago. Even assuming that present conditions justify such optimism, little evidence exists of an inverse relationship between wealth and the value accorded to life and health. The reverse is probably true: future generations may place a higher monetary value on human health relative to other goods if their standard of living increases. The higher environmental, health, and safety standards in wealthy developed countries suggest that such a relationship exists between societies in the current generation.

We do not find any of the conventional arguments strongly persuasive. Without pretending to provide a definitive statement regarding duties toward future generations, however, we do think that agreement on some basic points may facilitate progress toward a practical resolution. . . .

As a practical matter, members of the current generation probably are unwilling to make greater sacrifices for anonymous members of future generations than they are for their own personal descendants. Thus, feelings of obligations toward descendants provide an upward *practical* bound on obligations toward future generations as a whole. If everyone in the current generation had equal wealth, each would undertake to save enough for her own descendants in order to provide this level of future welfare.

With respect to private goods, intergenerational effects raise no special problems because the decisions of individuals to save for their descendants satisfies society's obligation to future generations. As to public goods such as environmental quality, the situation is more complex. Each member of the current generation likely would be willing to sacrifice some current consumption in order to assure his descendants' access to public goods. As usual in public good situations, however, each member cannot do this without providing a free ride—in this situation, to other peoples' descendants. The optimum social decision requires the current generation as a whole to sacrifice the collective consumption needed to provide the desired level of public goods in the future. In other words, with respect to public goods, we can no longer consider each family separately but must consider each generation collectively. However, the objective remains to approximate the level of sacrifice that each family individually would undertake willingly, in the absence of a free ride, to provide the benefits of public goods to their descendants alone. The aggregate of those individual sacrifices would provide the necessary collective sacrifice required of the current generation.

Unfortunately, empirical measurement of the amounts individuals are willing to sacrifice for a future public good would encounter all the difficulties—perception, imperfect information, etc.—inherent in the estimation of individuals' risk and time preferences and individual valuations of human life. These practical measurement difficulties seem to necessitate the use of a proxy measure. As a practical matter, the responsibility to provide for personal descendants probably provides the best benchmark for this generation's obligations to future generations.

This benchmark enables us to invoke some widely shared intuitions. First, whether the language of "moral obligation" is appropriate when considering unborn descendants is not clear. If your great-grandparents squandered the family fortune, you may feel that they acted reprehensibly, but you would have difficulty charging them with violating a personal obligation toward you or with violating a "right" that you possessed. For this reason, we think the language of "responsibility" rather than "obligation" is more appropriate: mature individuals behave responsibly with respect to the interests of their descendants, but do not necessarily owe a "duty" to as-yet nonexistent individuals. Our point is not that the interests of future generations place no constraints on the current generation, but that "rights talk" is a problematic way of discussing the ethical issues.

Second, nothing requires members of the current generation to maximize the income of their descendants, with or without a discount factor. They are not even required to ensure future income levels equal to their own: we would not necessarily consider it irresponsible for extremely rich parents to leave their children only moderately rich. For this reason, the current generation is not truly a trustee with a moral obligation to preserve the entire corpus for future generations. Responsible individuals do attempt, however, to ensure that their descendants can enjoy a decent standard of living, at least if they can do this without extreme self-sacrifice. You would have grounds for complaint if your great-grandparents had taken actions that consigned you to poverty in order for them to live a life of luxury. Again, it might be improper to say that they had violated the "rights" of their future descendants, but they clearly would have acted irresponsibly.

Third, whether or not it is rationally defensible, we think that members of the current generation are felt to have a more compelling obligation toward the next generation (and perhaps at least to young grandchildren) than to later generations. Members of the current generations would be subject to criticism if they did not give the long-term welfare of their children substantial weight; any large discount factor significantly undercuts this responsibility.

Thus, in weighing extremely long-term benefits (more than about one generation in the future), discounting is not a particularly useful technique. This generation's responsibility to later generations seems to involve a side constraint necessary to ensure them a minimum level of welfare, rather than weighing their welfare against our own as part of a maximization problem. As a practical matter, we probably cannot project benefits with even minimal confidence over long periods such as over a century. Even if we could predict some benefits with a degree of accuracy over such long periods, today's generation likely would refuse to make severe sacrifices simply to create marginal improvements in the welfare of distant future generations. We can, however, realistically attempt to avoid substantial risks of future disaster to remote descendants. With few exceptions, these risks will pose dangers to the next generation as well, so our concern for the next generation will usually subsume these very long-term effects.

A maximization approach may have more relevance to decisions affecting the next generation or so, meaning that we might reasonably apply some discount factor. Arguably, we should weigh the welfare of our (collective) children equally with our own. In any event, society cannot set the discount factor too high, since it must accord significant weight to the interests of the next generation. In particular, the discount rate even for economic benefits cannot significantly exceed the expected long-term rate of economic growth; otherwise, we would discount even the destruction of most future Gross Domestic Product to a low present value over periods of only decades. Practically, these considerations require a discount rate no greater than one or two percent.

# CHAPTER 3

---

# Ethical Perspectives

Environmental ethics explores why we should protect the environment on the basis of moral philosophy. Philosophers have tried to develop consistent sets of ethical principles to govern environmental protection policy based on moral or religious obligations of respect for nature and for future generations, as well as on the role of nature in providing spiritual inspiration for humans. The ethical values that environmental philosophers have articulated are frequently referenced in environmental policy debates, but they can be difficult to apply in practice because they work better at a high level of generality than as guides for developing specific policy prescriptions.

Considerable controversy has raged over the question of whether the teachings of Western religions have contributed to environmental problems by encouraging humans to subdue nature. The materials that follow include Lynn White's influential essay "The Historical Roots of Our Ecologic Crisis," in which he argues that much of the blame for environmental degradation rests with the biblical account of the Creation, in which God set humans apart from the rest of creation and gave them dominion over nature. White provides a historical perspective on the pervasiveness of human-induced changes in the environment. He shows how changes in technology had unanticipated, adverse consequences for the natural world. While attributing the relatively recent emergence of the concept of "ecology" to dramatic changes in the scale of human impact on the environment, White notes that "[h]uman ecology is deeply conditioned by beliefs about our nature and destiny—that is, by religion." And White observes that the prevailing attitude toward nature deriving from Western religious traditions is one of superiority or contemptuousness. He concludes by arguing that we must reexamine our fundamental ideas about the man-nature relationship and suggests Saint Francis of Assisi as an appropriate role model because of his belief in the virtue of humility for man as a species.

White's analysis was supported soon thereafter in John Passmore's *Man's Responsibility for Nature* (1974). More recently, religious organizations have been active in promoting the notion that the biblical tradition of stewardship requires morally concerned individuals to participate actively in environmental protection efforts. For example, in an encyclical entitled "Peace With All Creation," Pope John Paul II warned that world peace is threatened "by a lack of due respect for nature, by the plundering of natural resources and by a progressive decline in the quality of life."

Environmental philosophers have wrestled long and hard to develop principles for respecting nature that go beyond its instrumental value to humans. As the first generation of environmental laws was being enacted, law professor Laurence Tribe wrote an important article criticizing the ethical foundations of this legislation, using plastic trees as a metaphor. Tribe argues that the growing capacity to satisfy human needs through artificial means makes it increasingly difficult to justify protection of wilderness or endangered species through policies "treating individual human need and desire as the ultimate frame of reference" and "assuming that human goals and ends must be taken as externally 'given' . . . rather than generated by reason." While conceding that it may be possible to develop analytical techniques to take into account "soft" values, such as respect for future generations or for the "rights" of plants or animals, Tribe argues for the development of a new ethical construct that rejects human domination over other modes of being.

Although many environmental philosophers believe in the moral worth of non-human organisms, there is considerable disagreement over the precise sources of this belief. Peter Singer and others have argued for an animal welfare ethic based on the capacity of animals to experience pleasure, pain, and other utilitarian notions (Peter Singer, *Animal Liberation,* 2nd ed., 1990). Tom Regan rejects the utilitarian approach. He finds instead support for animal rights in the idea that living beings who have the capacity to experience life in certain qualitative ways (including having beliefs and desires, perceptions, memory, and a sense of the future) possess inherent value that gives them a right to respect, independent of any pleasures or pains they experience. In the reading reproduced below, Regan argues that it is fundamentally wrong to view animals as resources for humans. After exploring problems with theories of contractarianism and utilitarianism, Regan advocates the inherent value principle. He maintains that it is impossible rationally to confine this principle to humans alone. Although he is uncertain whether such a principle should be extended to "rocks and rivers, trees and glaciers," Regan passionately defends a relatively absolutist position in defense of the rights of those animals he deems to possess inherent value.

J. Baird Callicott is sharply critical of Regan's position, particularly when its more general implications for environmental policy are considered. In a review of Regan's work that is reproduced below, Callicott notes that, because Regan's theory of inherent value extends only to mammals, Regan would countenance the extermination of endangered species of plants in order to prevent the death of one common rabbit. Moreover, Regan rejects Aldo Leopold's "land ethic" because it is holistic, focusing on entire ecosystems, collections of things to which Regan does not believe rights can meaningfully be extended. Callicott argues that it *is* possible to assert rights meaningfully on behalf of ecosystems. He maintains that Regan's focus on the rights of every individual member of an ecosystem "would be an attempt to stop practically all trophic processes beyond photosyntehsis," which are "at the heart of evolution-ary and ecological processes."

Like Callicott, other environmental philosophers focus on protection of ecosystems. For example, Paul Taylor argues that humans should view other species as integral elements of the biota, each pursuing its own good in its own way, requiring humans to respect nature and to act "out of consideration and concern for the good of wild living things" (Paul Taylor, Respect for Nature 84, 1986). Despite their substantial disagreements, philosophers generally remain committed to the pursuit of an environmental ethic that extends beyond considerations of instrumental value to humans. As Callicott explains, they seek to articulate "not an ethic for the *use* of the environment, a 'management ethic,' but an ethic *of* the environment" (J. Baird Callicott, The Case Against Moral Pluralism, 12 Environmental Ethics 99, 1990).

The branch of environmental philosophy that made the greatest effort to articulate an alternative, nonhuman-centered conception of ethics is called "deep ecology." Deep ecologists argue that respect for nature requires a fundamental transformation of values and social organization. They view protection of the nonhuman environment as having an intrinsic value independent of its usefulness for human purposes. As outlined in the statement of principles from Arne Naess that is reproduced below, deep ecologists believe that humans have no right to deplete the richness and diversity of the natural world except to satisfy vital needs. Stressing that their followers should "question everything," deep ecologists reject the agenda pursued by most of the large national environmental organizations. They envision an earth with a much smaller human population and a higher quality of life as a result of fundamental changes in the structure of society.

*Lynn White, Jr.*

# The Historical Roots of Our Ecologic Crisis (1967)

All forms of life modify their contexts. The most spectacular and benign instance is doubtless the coral polyp. By serving its own ends, it has created a vast undersea world favorable to thousands of other kinds of animals and plants. Ever since man became a numerous species he has affected his environment notably. The hypothesis that his fire-drive method of hunting created the world's great grasslands and helped to exterminate the monster mammals of the Pleistocene from much of the globe is plausible, if not proved. For six millennia at least, the banks of the lower Nile have been a human artifact rather than the swampy African jungle which nature, apart from man, would have made it. The Aswan Dam, flooding 5000 square miles, is only the latest stage in a long process. In many regions terracing or irrigation, overgrazing, the cutting of forests by Romans to build ships to fight Carthaginians or by Crusaders to solve the logistics problems of their expeditions, have profoundly changed some ecologies. Observation that the French landscape falls into two basic types, the open fields of the north and the *bocage* of the south and west, inspired Marc Bloch to undertake his classic study of medieval agricultural methods. Quite unintentionally, changes in human ways often affect nonhuman nature. It has been noted, for example, that the advent of the automobile eliminated huge flocks of sparrows that once fed on the horse manure littering every street. . . .

People, then, have often been a dynamic element in their own environment, but in the present state of historical scholarship we usually do not know exactly when, where, or with what effects man-induced changes came. As we enter the last third of the 20th century, however, concern for the problem of ecologic backlash is mounting feverishly. Natural science, conceived as the effort to understand the nature of things, had flourished in several eras and among several peoples. Similarly there has been an age-old accumulation of technological skills, sometimes growing rapidly, sometimes slowly. But it was not until about four generations ago that Western Europe and North America arranged a marriage between science and technology, a union of the theoretical and the empirical approaches to our natural environment. The emergence in widespread practice of the Baconian creed that scientific knowledge means technological power over nature can scarcely be dated before about 1850, save in the chemical industries, where it is anticipated in the 18th century. Its acceptance as a normal pattern of action may mark the greatest event in human history since the invention of agriculture, and perhaps in nonhuman terrestrial history as well.

Almost at once the new situation forced the crystallization of the novel concept of ecology; indeed, the word ecology first appeared in the English language in 1873. Today, less than a century later, the impact of our race upon the environment has so increased in force that it has changed in essence. When the first cannons were fired, in the early 14th century, they affected ecology by sending workers scrambling to the forests and mountains for more potash, sulfur, iron ore, and charcoal, with some resulting erosion and deforestation. Hydrogen bombs are of a different order: a war fought with them might alter the genetics of all life on this planet. By 1285 London had a smog problem arising from the burning of soft coal, but our present combustion of fossil fuels threatens to change the chemistry of the globe's atmosphere as a whole, with consequences which we are only beginning to guess. With the population explosion, the carcinoma of planless urbanism, the now geological deposits of sewage and garbage, surely no creature other than man has ever managed to foul its nest in such short order.

There are many calls to action, but specific proposals, however worthy as individual items, seem too partial, palliative, negative: ban the bomb, tear down the billboards, give the Hindus contraceptives and tell them to eat their sacred cows. The simplest solution to any suspect change is, of course, to stop it, or, better yet, to revert to a romanticized past: make those ugly gasoline stations look like Anne Hathaway's cottage or (in the Far West) like ghost-town saloons. The "wilderness area" mentality invariably advocates deep-freezing an ecology, whether San Gimignano or the High Sierra, as it was before the first Kleenex was dropped. But neither atavism or prettification will cope with the ecologic crisis of our time.

What shall we do? No one yet knows. Unless we think about fundamentals, our specific measures may produce new backlashes more serious than those they are designed to remedy.

As a beginning we should try to clarify our thinking by looking, in some historical depth, at the presuppositions that underlie modern technology and science. Science was traditionally aristocratic, speculative, intellectual in intent; technology was lower-class, empirical, action-oriented. The quite sudden fusion of these two, towards the middle of the 19th century, is surely related to the slightly prior and contemporary democratic revolutions which, by reducing social barriers, tended to assert a functional unity of brain and hand. Our ecologic crisis is the product of an emerging, entirely novel, democratic culture. The issue is whether a democratized world can survive its own implications. Presumably we cannot unless we rethink our axioms. . . .

## Medieval View of Man and Nature

Until recently, agriculture has been the chief occupation even in "advanced" societies; hence, any change in methods of tillage has much importance. Early plows, drawn by two oxen, did not normally turn the sod but merely scratched it. Thus, cross-plowing was needed and fields tended to be squarish. In the fairly light soils and semiarid climates of the Near East and Mediterranean, this worked well. But such a plow was inappropriate to the wet climate and often sticky soils of northern Europe. By the latter part of the 7th century after Christ, however, following obscure beginnings, certain northern peasants were using an entirely new kind of plow, equipped with a vertical knife to cut the line of the furrow, a horizontal share to slice under the sod, and a moldboard to turn it over. The friction of this plow with the soil was so great that it normally required not two but eight oxen. It attacked the land with such violence that cross-plowing was not needed, and fields tended to be shaped in long strips.

In the days of the scratch-plow, fields were distributed generally in units capable of supporting a single family. Subsistence farming was the presupposition. But no peasant owned eight oxen: to use the new and more efficient plow, peasants pooled their oxen to form large plow-teams, originally receiving (it would appear) plowed strips in proportion to their contribution. Thus, distribution of land was based no longer on the needs of a family but, rather, on the capacity of a power machine to till the earth. Man's relation to the soil was profoundly changed. Formerly man had been part of nature; now he was the exploiter of nature. Nowhere else in the world did farmers develop any analogous agricultural implement. Is it coincidence that modern technology, with its ruthlessness toward nature, has so largely been produced by descendants of these peasants of northern Europe?

This same exploitive attitude appears slightly before A.D. 830 in Western illustrated calendars. In older calendars the months were shown as passive personifications. The new Frankish calendars, which set the style for the Middle Ages, are very different: they show men coercing the world around them—plowing, harvesting, chopping trees, butchering pigs. Man and nature are two things, and man is master.

These novelties seem to be in harmony with larger intellectual patterns. What people do about their ecology depends on what they think about themselves in relation to things around them. Human ecology is deeply conditioned by beliefs about our nature and destiny—that is, by religion. To Western eyes this is very evident in, say, India or Ceylon. It is equally true of ourselves and of our medieval ancestors.

The victory of Christianity over paganism was the greatest psychic revolution in the history of our culture. It has become fashionable today to say that, for better or worse, we live in "the post-Christian age." Certainly the forms of our thinking and language have largely ceased to be Christian, but to my eye the substance often remains amazingly akin to that of the past. Our daily habits of action, for example, are dominated by an implicit faith in perpetual progress which was unknown either to Greco-Roman antiquity or to the Orient. It is rooted in, and is indefensible apart from, Judeo-Christian teleology. The fact that Communists share it merely helps to show what can be demonstrated on many other grounds: that Marxism, like Islam, is a Judeo-Christian heresy. We continue today to live, as we have lived for about 1700 years, very largely in a context of Christian axioms.

What did Christianity tell people about their relations with the environment?

While many of the world's mythologies provide stories of creation, Greco-Roman mythology was singularly incoherent in this respect. Like Aristotle, the intellectuals of the ancient West denied that the visible world had had a beginning. Indeed, the idea of a beginning was impossible in the framework of their cyclical notion of time. In sharp contrast, Christianity inherited from Judaism not only a concept of time as nonrepetitive and linear but also a striking story of creation. By gradual stages a loving and all-powerful God had created light and darkness, the heavenly bodies, the earth and all its plants, animals, birds, and fishes. Finally, God had created Adam and, as an afterthought, Eve to keep man from being lonely. Man named all the animals, thus establishing his dominance over them. God planned all of this explicitly for man's benefit and rule: no item in the physical creation had any purpose save to serve man's purposes. And, although man's body is made of clay, he is not simply part of nature: he is made in God's image.

Especially in its Western form, Christianity is the most anthropocentric religion the world has seen. As early as the 2nd century both Tertullian and Saint Irenaeus of Lyons were insisting that when God shaped Adam he was foreshadowing the image of the incarnate Christ, the Second Adam. Man shares, in great measure, God's transcendence of nature. Christianity, in absolute contrast to ancient paganism and Asia's religions (except, perhaps, Zoroastrianism), not only established a dualism of man and nature but also insisted that it is God's will that man exploit nature for his proper ends.

At the level of the common people this worked out in an interesting way. In Antiquity every tree, every spring, every stream, every hill had its own *genius loci*, its guardian spirit. These spirits were accessible to men, but were very unlike men; centaurs, fauns, and mermaids show their ambivalence. Before one cut a tree, mined a mountain, or dammed a brook, it was important to placate the spirit in charge of that particular situation, and to keep it placated. By destroying pagan animism, Christianity made it possible to exploit nature in a mood of indifference to the feelings of natural objects. . . .

When one speaks in such sweeping terms, a note of caution is in order. Christianity is a complex faith, and its consequences differ in differing contexts. What I have said may well apply to the medieval West, where in fact technology made spectacular advances. But the Greek East, a highly civilized realm of equal Christian devotion, seems to have produced no marked technological innovation after the late 7th century, when Greek fire was invented. The key to the contrast may perhaps be found in a difference in the tonality of piety and thought which students of comparative theology find between the Greek and the Latin Churches. The Greeks believed that sin was intellectual blindness, and that salvation was found in illumination, orthodoxy—that is, clear thinking. The Latins, on the other hand, felt that sin was moral evil, and that salvation was to be found in right conduct. Eastern theology has been intellectualist. Western theology has been voluntarist. The Greek saint contemplates; the Western saint acts. The implications of Christianity for the conquest of nature would emerge more easily in the Western atmosphere.

The Christian dogma of creation, which is found in the first clause of all the Creeds, has another meaning for our comprehension of today's ecologic crisis. By revelation, God had given man the Bible, the Book of Scripture. But since God had made nature, nature also must reveal the divine mentality. The religious study of nature for the better understanding of God was known as natural theology. In the early Church, and always in the Greek East, nature was conceived primarily as a symbolic system through which God speaks to men: the ant is a sermon to sluggards; rising flames are the symbol of the soul's aspiration. This view of nature was essentially artistic rather than scientific. While Byzantium preserved and copied great numbers of ancient Greek scientific texts, science as we conceive it could scarcely flourish in such an ambience.

However, in the Latin West by the early 13th century natural theology was following a very different bent. It was ceasing to be the decoding of the physical symbols of God's communication with man and was becoming the effort to understand God's mind by discovering how his creation operates. The rainbow was no longer simply a symbol of hope first sent to Noah after the Deluge: Robert Grosseteste, Friar Roger Bacon, and Theodoric of Freiberg produced startlingly sophisticated work on the optics of the rainbow, but they did it as a venture in religious understanding. From the 13th century onward, up to and including Leibnitz and Newton, every major scientist, in effect, explained his motivations in religious terms. Indeed, if Galileo had not been so expert an amateur theologian he would have got into far less trouble; the professionals resented his intrusion. And Newton seems to have regarded himself more as a theologian than as a scientist. It was not until the late 18th century that the hypothesis of God became unnecessary to many scientists.

It is often hard for the historian to judge, when men explain why they are doing what they want to do, whether they are offering real reasons or merely culturally acceptable reasons. The consistency with which scientists during the long formative centuries of Western science said that the tasks and the reward of the scientist was "to think God's thoughts after him" leads one to believe that this was their real motivation. If so, then modern Western science was cast in a matrix of Christian theology. The dynamism of religious devotion, shaped by the Judeo-Christian dogma of creation, gave it impetus.

## An Alternative Christian View

We would seem to be headed toward conclusions unpalatable to many Christians. Since both science and technology are blessed words in our contemporary vocabulary, some may be happy at the notions, first, that, viewed historically, modern science is an extrapolation of natural theology and, second, that modern technology is at least partly to be explained as an Occidental, voluntarist realization of the Christian dogma of man's transcendence of, and rightful mastery over, nature. But, as we now recognize, somewhat over a century ago science and technology—hitherto quite separate activities—joined to give mankind powers which, to judge by many of the ecologic effects, are out of control. If so, Christianity bears a huge burden of guilt.

I personally doubt that disastrous ecologic backlash can be avoided simply by applying to our problems more science and more technology. Our science and technology have grown out of Christian attitudes toward man's relation to nature which are almost universally held not only by Christians and neo-Christians but also by those who fondly regard themselves as post-Christians. Despite Copernicus, all the cosmos rotates around our little globe. Despite Darwin, we are not, in our hearts, part of the natural process. We are superior to nature, contemptuous of it, willing to use it for our slightest whim. The newly elected Governor of California, like myself a churchman but less troubled than I, spoke for the Christian tradition when he said (as is alleged), "when you've seen one redwood tree, you've seen them all." To a Christian a tree can be no more than a physical fact. The whole concept of the sacred grove is alien to Christianity and to the ethos of the West. For nearly two millennia Christian missionaries have been chopping down sacred groves, which are idolatrous because they assume spirit in nature.

What we do about ecology depends on our ideas of the man-nature relationship. More science and more technology are not going to get us out of the present ecologic crisis until we find a new religion, or rethink our old one. The beatniks, who are the basic revolutionaries of our time, show a sound instinct in their affinity for Zen Buddhism, which conceives of the man-nature relationship as very nearly the mirror image of the Christian view. Zen, however, is as deeply conditioned by Asian history as Christianity is by the experience of the West, and I am dubious of its viability among us.

Possibly we should ponder the greatest radical in Christian history since Christ: Saint Francis of Assisi. The prime miracle of Saint Francis is the fact that he did not end at the stake, as many of his left-wing followers did. He was so clearly heretical that a General of the Franciscan Order, Saint Bonaventura, a great and perceptive Christian, tried to suppress the early accounts of Franciscanism. The key to an understanding of Francis is his belief in the virtue of humility—not merely for the individual but for man as a species. Francis tried to depose man from his monarchy over creation and set up a democracy of all God's creatures. With him the ant is no longer simply a homily for the lazy, flames a sign of the thrust of the soul toward union with God; now they are Brother Ant and Sister Fire, praising the Creator in their own ways as Brother Man does in his.

Later commentators have said that Francis preached to the birds as a rebuke to men who would not listen. The records do not read so: he urged the little birds to praise God, and in spiritual ecstasy they flapped their wings and chirped rejoicing. Legends of saints, especially the Irish saints, had long told of their dealings with animals but always, I believe, to show their human dominance over creatures. With Francis it is different. The land around Gubbio in the Apennines was being ravaged by a fierce wolf. Saint Francis, says the legend, talked to the wolf and persuaded him of the error of his ways. The wolf repented, died in the odor of sanctity, and was buried in consecrated ground.

What Sir Steven Ruciman calls "the Franciscan doctrine of the animal soul" was quickly stamped out. Quite possibly it was in part inspired, consciously or unconsciously, by the belief in reincarnation held by the Cathar heretics who at that time teemed in Italy and southern France, and who presumably had got it originally from India. It is significant that at just the same moment, about 1200, traces of metempsychosis are found also in western Judaism, in the Provencal *Cabbala*. But Francis held neither to transmigration of souls nor to pantheism. His view of nature and of man rested on a unique sort of pan-psychism of all things animate and inanimate, designed for the glorification of their transcendent Creator, who, in the ultimate gesture of cosmic humility, assumed flesh, lay helpless in a manger, and hung dying on a scaffold.

I am not suggesting that many contemporary Americans who are concerned about our ecologic crisis will be either able or willing to counsel with wolves or exhort birds. However, the present increasing disruption of the global environment is the product of a dynamic technology and science which were originating in the Western medieval world against which Saint Francis was rebelling in so original a way. Their growth cannot be understood historically apart from distinctive attitudes toward nature which are deeply grounded in Christian dogma. The fact that most people do not think of these attitudes as Christian is irrelevant. No new set of basic values has been accepted in our society to displace those of Christianity. Hence we shall continue to have a worsening ecologic crisis until we reject the Christian axiom that nature has no reason for existence save to serve man.

The greatest spiritual revolutionary in Western history, Saint Francis, proposed what he thought was an alternative Christian view of nature and man's relation to it: he tried to substitute the idea of the equality of all creatures, including man, for the idea of man's limitless rule of creation. He failed. Both our present science and our present technology are so tinctured with orthodox Christian arrogance toward nature that no solution for our ecologic crisis can be expected from them alone. Since the roots of our trouble are so largely religious, the remedy must also be essentially religious, whether we call it that or not. We must rethink and refeel our nature and destiny. The profoundly religious, but heretical, sense of the primitive Franciscans for the spiritual autonomy of all parts of nature may point a direction. I propose Francis as a patron saint for ecologists.

*Laurence H. Tribe*

# Ways Not to Think about Plastic Trees: New Foundations for Environmental Law (1974)

Baudelaire's *Rêve Parisien* paints what is quite literally a still life—a dreamscape of a metallic city where groves of colonnades stand in the place of trees and, in the place of water, pools of lead. More prosaic but no less unnerving was the recent decision by Los Angeles County officials to install more than 900 plastic trees and shrubs in concrete planters along the median strip of a major boulevard. The construction of a new box culvert, it seemed, had left only 12 to 18 inches of dirt on the strip, insufficient to sustain natural trees. County officials decided to experiment with artificial plants constructed of factory-made leaves and branches wired to plumbing pipes, covered with plastic and "planted" in aggregate rock coated with epoxy. Although a number of the trees were torn down by unknown vandals and further plantings were halted, the tale may not be over. For an article in *Science* suggested recently that, just as advertising can lead people to value wilderness and nature, so too it can "create plentiful substitutes." "The demand for rare environments is . . . learned," the *Science* article observes, and "conscious public choice can manipulate this learning so that the environments which people learn to use and want reflect environments that are likely to be available at low cost. . . . Much more can be done with plastic trees and the like to give most people the feeling that they are experiencing nature."

While so explicit an acknowledgment of the acceptability of artificial environments may be unusual, the attitude it expresses toward the natural order is far from uncommon. Increasingly, artificial objects and settings supplant those supplied by nature. Durable Astroturf replaces grass in football stadiums and around swimming

Reprinted by permission of The Yale Law Journal Company and Fred B. Rothman & Company from *The Yale Law Journal*, Vol. 83, pages 1315–1348.

pools. Guests at the Hyatt Regency Hotel in San Francisco walk among more than 100 natural trees growing in the 20-story lobby but listen to recorded bird calls broadcast from speakers hidden in the tree branches. And Walt Disney World offers a multitude of visitors what one *Newsweek* writer described as "a programmed paradise."

I do not focus on Astroturf and the plastic trees of Los Angeles as harbingers of our most urgent environmental problems. Although the long-term prospects in this regard are probably more troublesome, I claim no imminent risk that we will too cleverly engineer ourselves into a synthetic hell. Quite apart from any such danger, I believe that such "natural surrogates" provide an illuminating metaphor through which to expose and criticize certain premises which underlie most current discussions of environmental thought, law, and policy.

While it might appear initially that nature surrogates would be antithetical to the ecological concern embodied in present environmental legislation and policy, a closer analysis leads to precisely the opposite conclusion. The perpetually green lawn and the plastic tree, far from representing the outcroppings of some inexplicable human perversion, are expressions of a view of nature fully consistent with the basic assumptions of present environmental policy. These assumptions, which are implicit in developing uses of policy analysis as well as in emerging institutional structures, make all environmental judgments turn on calculations of how well human wants, discounted over time, are satisfied. . . .

Despite occasional probes in less familiar directions, the emerging field of environmental law is being built on the basic platform of analytic sophistication in the service of human need. Statutes and judicial decisions typically mandate "systematic" and "interdisciplinary" attempts to "insure that presently unquantified environmental amenities and values may be given appropriate consideration in decisionmaking along with economic and technical considerations." Public interest challenges to decisions alleged to be environmentally unsound are diverted by the pressures of doctrine and tradition from claims about the value of nature as such into claims about interference with human use, even when the real point may be that a particular wilderness area, for example, should be "used" by no-one. . . .

Policy analysts typically operate within a social, political and intellectual tradition that regards the satisfaction of individual human wants as the only defensible measure of the good, a tradition that perceives the only legitimate task of reason to be that of consistently identifying and then serving individual appetite, preference, or desire. This tradition is echoed as well in environmental legislation which protects nature not for its own sake but in order to preserve its potential value for man.

By treating individual human need and desire as the ultimate frame of reference, and by assuming that human goals and ends must be taken as externally "given" (whether physiologically or culturally or both) rather than generated by reason, environmental policy makes a value judgment of enormous significance. And, once that judgment has been made, any claim for the continued existence of threatened wilderness areas or endangered species must rest on the identification of human wants and needs which would be jeopardized by a disputed development. As our capacity increases to satisfy those needs and wants artificially, the claim becomes tenuous indeed.

Consider again the plastic trees planted along a freeway's median strip by Los Angeles county officials. If the most sophisticated application of the techniques of policy analysis could unearth no human need which would, after appropriate "education," be better served by natural trees, then the environmental inquiry would be at an end. The natural trees, more costly and vulnerable than those made of plastic, would offer no increment of satisfaction to justify the added effort of planting and maintaining them.

To insist on the superiority of natural trees in the teeth of a convincing demonstration that plastic ones would equally well serve human purposes may seem irrational. Yet the tendency to balk at the result of the analysis remains. There is a suspicion that some crucial perspective has been omitted from consideration, that the conclusion is as much a product of myopia as of logic.

## Beyond Human Wants: A New Rationale for Environmental Policy

What has been omitted is, at base, an appreciation of an ancient and inescapable paradox: We can be truly free to pursue our ends only if we act out of obligation, the seeming antithesis of freedom. To be free is not simply to follow our ever-changing wants wherever they might lead. To be free is to choose what we shall want, what we shall value, and therefore what we shall be. But to make such choices without losing the thread of continuity that integrates us over time and imparts a sense of our wholeness in history, we must be able to reason about what to choose—to choose in terms of commitments we have made to bodies of principle which we perceive as external to our choices and by which we feel bound, bodies of principle that can define a coherent and integrative system even as they evolve with our changing selves.

To deny the existence of such bodies of principle is fashionable, but it is not inevitable. However obvious, it is worth recalling that most of the great philosophical systems of our own past—those of Plato and Aristotle, of Aquinas and the Scholastics, of Hegel and the Idealists—were grounded in the view that the highest purpose of human reason is to evolve a comprehensive understanding of mankind's place in the universe, not merely to serve as a detector of consistency and causality and thus as an instrument for morally blind desire. "The emphasis," as Horkheimer reminds us, "was on ends rather than on means." It is only recently that the concept of reason as calculation without content became central in the West—that reason began to liquidate itself "as an agency of ethical, moral, and religious insight." Unless we are to remain in the shadow of that intellectual eclipse, we cannot simply assume that we must stand mute when confronting the ultimate question of whether we want our children, and their children's children, to live in, and *enjoy*, a plastic world. . . .

Theoretically at least, policy analyses and legislative provisions can be so calibrated as to be sensitive to, and then to accommodate, whatever values individuals are capable of discerning. Yet it does not follow, simply because all values susceptible to human perception may thus be formally "included" in our designs, that an institutional system or an analytic technique which relentlessly treats all such values as manifestations of individual human preference will prove satisfactory. To reach such a conclusion would require another premise: that the act of characterizing all values as expressions of human preference does not affect their content or distort their perception. It is a premise that does not withstand scrutiny. Treating all values as based on personal preferences results in a major shift of focus: Attention is no longer directed to the ostensible content of the value but rather to the fact that it is a more or less abstracted indicium of self-interest. Even if one ultimately chooses the same actions under such a shift of focus, one may well end with the feeling that one has chosen them not out of obligation or for their own sake, but because their opportunity cost in terms of one's range of personal interest was low enough, thereby distorting the meaning of the choice and of the actions chosen.

To offer a simple illustration, suppose a person feels an obligation to protect a wilderness area from strip mining. The initial perception of that obligation is likely to take the form of sympathy for the wildlife and vegetation which would be destroyed or displaced. Indeed, the perceived obligation may display at least the rudiments of an internal structure: Killing "higher" animal life may seem unjustifiable except for compelling reasons (to sustain, or to avert a direct threat to, human life, for instance); destroying plant life may seem improper if destruction can be avoided without "undue" cost. Certain categories of harm which might leave human civilization intact while threatening the global eco-system as a whole—severe radioactive contamination of the oceans, for instance—may seem wrong regardless of the strength of the countervailing human interest.

If the sense of obligation prompts the individual to undertake some concrete effort on behalf of the environment, such as making an adverse response to an environmental survey, initiating a suit to enjoin the strip mining, or advancing an argument in favor of preservation, a subtle transformation is likely to be occasioned by the philosophical premises of the system in which the effort is undertaken. The felt obligation will be translated into the terminology of human self-interest: It may be said that future generations will be deprived of contact with wildlife; that the aesthetic satisfaction of certain individuals will be diminished; that other recreational areas will become overcrowded. Like Kant, proponents of environmental protection will, at best, couch their disapproval of human mistreatment of nature in terms of the indirect consequences for mankind.

While the environmentalist may feel somewhat disingenuous in taking this approach, he is likely to regard it as justified by the demands of legal doctrine and the exigencies of political reality. What the environmentalist may not perceive is that, by couching his claim in terms of human self-interest—by articulating environmental goals wholly in terms of human needs and preferences—he may be helping to legitimate a system of discourse which so structures human thought and feeling as to erode, over the long run, the very sense of obligation which provided the initial impetus for his own protective efforts.

This metamorphosis of obligation into self-interest and personal preference ironically echoes aspects of Mill's utilitarian theory. Mill argued that the sense of moral obligation was a subjective feeling developed through learning and association from the primary responses of pain aversion and pleasure maximization. He discounted the possibility that obligation, when perceived as an accretion of such responses, might ultimately lose its compelling force and dissolve into unmitigated self-aggrandizement; in Mill's view, the impulse toward conformity and other social pressures would insulate ethical feelings from any such reductionist tendency. However justifiable Mill's faith in the efficacy of communal reinforcement in the context of interpersonal obligation, the phenomenon clearly plays a less important role when the occasion of an ethical impulse is not a member of the human community but a natural object. Despite impassioned efforts by ecologists to suggest the contrary, the best interests of individual persons (and even of future human generations) are not demonstrably congruent with those of the natural order as a whole, even if such a congruence can be established as between individuals and the human communities in which they live. Indeed, individually or communally defined human interests may often be at odds with the primal ethical impulse—the sense of duty beyond self—that gives passion and conviction to many who see elements of the inviolable in nature. In this situation, communal reinforcement, far from impeding the transformation of ethical obligation into a category of self-interest, may actually accelerate the process.

To return to our example, once obligation has been transformed into a mere matter of personal preference, the tendency is inevitable to compare the value of wilderness with the value of strip mined coal in terms of self-interest. From there, it is but a short step to an even more blatantly reductionist approach: In order to insure that the comparison is "rational," the two values will almost certainly be translated into smoothly exchangeable units of satisfaction, such as dollars. While certain discontinuities may still be recognized—destruction of *all* wilderness areas may not be deemed worth even an infinite supply of coal—they will tend to be gradually eroded by the pressure toward analytic uniformity.

The translation of all values into homocentric terms thus creates two distortions: First, an inchoate sense of obligation toward natural objects is flattened into an aspect of self-interest; second, value discontinuities tend to be foreshortened. It is important to emphasize again that these distortions do not follow as a necessary result from the theoretical premises of policy analysis. Although Aaron Wildavsky suggested in a 1966 critique that cost-benefit techniques structurally presuppose the individualistic premise that only personal preferences matter, it is obviously possible to compute the costs of an activity in any terms one wishes or to impose whatever nonindividualistic constraint is deemed important. There is nothing in the logic of analytic techniques (or, for that matter, the logic of interest identification which precedes legislative enactment) that limits the use of such methods to the tradition of liberal individualism in any of its diverse forms.

The distortion occurs rather because the process of interest identification, as it is presently employed, interacts in a crucial way with the content of the interest being identified. The identification takes place in the context of a system of attitudes and assumptions which treat human want satisfaction as the only legitimate referent of policy analysis and choice. These assumptions, and the desire for analytic clarity which accompanies them, together exert an enormous reductionist pressure on all values which would otherwise seem incommensurable with a calculus of individual human wants. Thus the distortion results not from a logical flaw in the techniques of policy analysis but rather from what I have elsewhere described as the ideological bias of the system in which such analysis is imbedded, a system that has come to treat the human will and its wants as the center around which reason as calculation must revolve. . . .

Like Schiller's mechanics who dare not let the wheels run down while they repair "the living clockwork of the State," or Neurath's sailors who must rebuild their ship on the open sea without discerning its ideal design, we are condemned to toil in the dimmest light as we feel our way toward the evolution of our conceptions and ideals of the natural order. But, if, as we have concluded, the spiral that traces such evolution is to reject human domination over other modes of being, then at least its first turns seem within our grasp. At a minimum, we must begin to extricate our nature-regarding impulses from the conceptually oppressive sphere of human want satisfaction, by encouraging the elaboration of perceived obligations to plant and animal life and to objects of beauty in terms that do not falsify such perceptions from the very beginning by insistent "reference to human interests." Thus environmental impact surveys and statements might make explicit reference to obligations felt toward nature. Resources might be devoted to improving our technical capacity to incorporate such felt obligations in policy analyses. And legislation might be enacted to permit the bringing of claims directly on behalf of natural objects without imposing the requirement that such claims be couched in terms of interference with human use. . . .

But we might plausibly hope for more. At least so long as we remain within empathizing distance of the objects whose rights we seek to recognize, it seems reasonable to expect the acknowledgement of such rights to be regarded as more than fictitious. Thus, protecting cats and dogs from torture on the basis of their desire to be free from pain and hence their right not to be mistreated seems less jarring conceptually than protecting a forest from clear-cutting on the theory that the threatened trees have an inherent "right to life."

It is not surprising that one of the few pieces of existing federal law aimed unambiguously at protecting nonhuman interests—the Federal Laboratory Animal Welfare Act—limits its protection to mammals, whose perceptions of pain and discomfort we presume to be similar to our own. In addition to supporting a general hypothesis that the needs of creatures close to man on the evolutionary scale are easier to assimilate into contemporary value systems than are the needs of our more distant relatives, the legislative history of the 1970 amendments to the Act also provides a graphic illustration of the process of anthropomorphic validation: The House committee report proclaims that the purpose of the legislation is to ensure that animals are "accorded the basic *creature comforts* of adequate housing, ample food and water, reasonable handling, *decent sanitation* . . . and adequate veterinary care including the appropriate use of *pain*-killing drugs. . . . The statutory terms reveal an obvious transference of human values to the nonhuman rights-holders: The words "comfort," "decent sanitation" and indeed "pain" refer to human experiences and perceptions. By incorporating such terms into legislation protecting animals, the draftsmen are equating the perceptions of animals with those of humans; the terminology subliminally reinforces our sympathy for the plight of mistreated animals by evoking images of human suffering. As a result, the propriety of legal protection in the interest of the animals themselves becomes more apparent.

As the evolutionary distance between man and nonhuman rights-holders increases, the difficulty of analogizing to human experiences mounts. Torturing a dog evokes a strong sympathetic response; dismembering a frog produces a less acute but still unambiguous image of pain; even pulling the wings off a fly may cause a sympathetic twinge; but who would flinch at exterminating a colony of protozoa?

When legal protection is sought for plant life, the obstacles to convincing analogy are greater still. Yet even here the prospects are not altogether hopeless. Humans share certain fundamental needs with plants. Humans and plants both require water, oxygen and nutrition; both grow and reproduce; both die. A set of basic reference points for analogizing plant requirements to human needs thus exists. Some research even suggests that plants exhibit electrical and chemical reactions which are functionally analogous to pain. And, once the bases for empathy are thus established, biologists and ecologists can obviously enrich our understanding of what "needs" exist for the other life forms with whom we have begun to feel new kinship.

What is crucial to recognize is that the human capacity for empathy and identification is not static; the very process of recognizing *rights* in those higher vertebrates with whom we can already empathize could well pave the way for still further extensions as we move upward along the spiral of moral evolution. It is not only the human liberation movements—involving first blacks, then women, and now children—that advance in waves of increased consciousness. The inner dynamic of every assault on domination is an ever broadening realization of reciprocity and identity. Viewed from a slightly different perspective, new possibilities for respect and new grounds for community elevate both master and slave simultaneously, reaffirming the truth that the oppressor is among the first to be liberated when he lifts the yoke, that freedom can be realized only in fidelity to obligation.

A passage in Faulkner's *Absalom, Absalom!* may hold the key: "Maybe happen is never once but like ripples maybe on water after the pebble sinks, the ripples moving on, spreading, the pool attached by a narrow umbilical water-cord to the next pool . . . . " But there are some shores too remote for even these concentric circles to reach in the foreseeable future. When it is urged that legal protection be extended to nonliving entities like canyons and cathedrals, not for our sake but for theirs, it may be precisely such distant shores at which we are asked to gaze. Saint Francis of

Assisi could embrace Brother Fire and Sister Water, but Western societies in the last third of this century may be unable to entertain seriously the notion that a mountain or a seashore has intrinsic needs and can make independent moral claims upon our design.

Still we can try. We can set aside resources and create public authorities for the specific purpose of preserving intact at least some major areas of real wilderness while we convert others into more Walt Disney Worlds and Coney Islands. The very process of treating some places with such respect may itself reveal and even create conceptual possibilities beyond our present capacities. If, as I have argued elsewhere, certain choices do not merely implement but radically alter the value systems within which they are made, then choosing to accord nature a fraternal rather than an exploited role—even when the resulting institutions resolve in particular cases not to forego certain human opportunities "for nature's sake"—might well make us different persons from the manipulators and subjugators we are in danger of becoming.

*Tom Regan*

# The Case for Animal Rights (1983)

I regard myself as an advocate of animal rights—as a part of the animal rights movement. That movement, as I conceive it, is committed to a number of goals, including:

1. the total abolition of the use of animals in science
2. the total dissolution of commercial animal agriculture
3. and the total elimination of commercial and sport hunting and trapping.

There are, I know, people who profess to believe in animal rights who do not avow these goals. Factory farming, they say, is wrong—violates animals' rights—but traditional animal agriculture is all right. Toxicity tests of cosmetics on animals violates their rights; but not important medical research—cancer research, for example. The clubbing of baby seals is abhorrent; but not the harvesting of adult seals. I used to think I understood this reasoning. Not anymore. You don't change unjust institutions by tidying them up.

What's wrong—what's fundamentally wrong—with the way animals are treated isn't the details that vary from case to case. It's the whole system. The forlornness of the veal calf is pathetic—heart wrenching; the pulsing pain of the chimp with electrodes planted deep in her brain is repulsive; the slow, torturous death of the raccoon caught in the leg hold trap, agonizing. But what is fundamentally wrong isn't the pain, isn't the suffering, isn't the deprivation. These compound what's wrong. Sometimes—often—they make it much worse. But they are not the fundamental wrong.

The fundamental wrong is the system that allows us to view animals as *our resources*, here for us—to be eaten, or surgically manipulated, or put in our cross hairs for sport or money. Once we accept this view of animals—as our resources—the rest is as predictable as it is regrettable. Why worry about their loneliness, their pain, their death? Since animals exist for us, here to benefit us in one way or another, what harms them really doesn't matter—or matters only if it starts to bother us, makes us feel a trifle uneasy when we eat our veal scampi, for example. So, yes, let us get veal calves out of solitary confinement, give them more space, a little straw, a few companions. But let us keep our veal scampi.

But a little straw, more space, and a few companions don't eliminate—don't even touch—the fundamental wrong, the wrong that attaches to our viewing and treating these animals as our resources. A veal calf killed to be eaten after living in close confinement is viewed and treated in this way: but so, too, is another who is raised (as they say) "more humanely." To right the fundamental wrong of our treatment of farm animals requires more than making rearing methods "more human"—requires something quite different—requires the total dissolution of commercial animal agriculture. . . .

How to proceed? We begin by asking how the moral status of animals has been understood by thinkers who deny that animals have rights. Then we test the mettle of their ideas by seeing how well they stand up under the heat of fair criticism. If we start our thinking in this way we soon find that some people believe that we have no duties directly to animals—that we owe nothing *to them*—that we can do nothing that *wrongs them*. Rather, we can do wrong acts that involve animals, and so we have duties regarding them, though none to them. Such views may be called indirect duty views. By way of illustration:

Suppose your neighbor kicks your dog. Then your neighbor has done something wrong. But not to your dog. The wrong that has been done is a wrong to you. After all, it is wrong to upset people, and your neighbor's kicking your dog upsets you. So you are the one who is wronged, not your dog. Or again: by kicking your dog your neighbor damages your property. And since it is wrong to damage another person's property, your neighbor has done something wrong—to you, of course, not to your dog. Your neighbor no more wrongs your dog than your car would be wronged if the windshield were smashed. Your neighbor's duties involving your dog are indirect duties to you. More generally, all of our duties regarding animals are indirect duties to one another—to humanity.

How could someone try to justify such a view? One could say that your dog doesn't feel anything and so isn't hurt by your neighbor's kick, doesn't care about the pain since none is felt, is as unaware of anything as your windshield. Someone could say this but no rational person will since, among other considerations, such a view will commit one who holds it to the position that no human being feels pain either—that human beings also don't care about what happens to them. A second possibility is that though both humans and your dog are hurt when kicked, it is only human pain that matters. But, again, no rational person can believe this. Pain is pain wheresoever it occurs. If your neighbor's causing you pain is wrong because of the pain that is caused, we cannot rationally ignore or dismiss the moral relevance of the pain your dog feels.

Philosophers who hold indirect duty views—and many still do—have come to understand that they must avoid the two defects just noted—avoid, that is, both the view that animals don't feel anything as well as the idea that only human pain can be morally relevant. Among such thinkers the sort of view now favored is one or another form of what is called *contractarianism*.

Here, very crudely, is the root idea: morality consists of a set of rules that individuals voluntarily agree to abide by—as we do when we sign a contract (hence the name: contractarianism). Those who understand and accept the terms of the contract are covered directly—have rights created by, and recognized and protected in, the contract. And these contractors can also have protection spelled out for others who, though they lack the ability to understand morality and so cannot sign the contract themselves, are loved or cherished by those who can. Thus young children, for example, are unable to sign and lack rights. But they are protected by the contract nonetheless because of the sentimental interests of others, most notably their parents. So we have, then, duties involving these children, duties regarding them, but no duties to them. Our duties in their case are indirect duties to other human beings, usually their parents.

As for animals, since they cannot understand the contract, they obviously cannot sign; and since they cannot sign, they have no rights. Like children, however, some animals are the objects of the sentimental interest of others. You, for example, love your dog . . . or cat. So these animals—those enough people care about: companion animals, whales, baby seals, the American bald eagle—these animals, though they lack rights themselves, will be protected because of the sentimental interests of people. I have, then, according to contractarianism, no duty directly to your dog or any other animal, not even the duty not to cause them pain or suffering; my duty not to hurt them is a duty I have to those people who care about what happens to them. As for other animals, where no or little sentimental interest is present—farm animals, for example, or laboratory rats—what duties we have grow weaker and weaker, perhaps to the vanishing point. The pain and death they endure, though real, are not wrong if no one cares about them.

Contractarianism could be a hard view to refute when it comes to the moral status of animals if it was an adequate theoretical approach to the moral status of human beings. It is not adequate in this latter respect, however, which makes the question of its adequacy in the former—regarding animals—utterly moot. For consider: morality, according to the (crude) contractarianism position before us, consists of rules people agree to abide by. What people? Well, enough to make a difference—enough, that is, so that collectively they have the power to enforce the rules that are drawn up in the contract. That is very well and good for the signatories—but not so good for anyone who is not asked to sign. And there is nothing in contractarianism of the sort we are discussing that guarantees or requires that everyone will have a chance to participate equitably in framing the rules of morality. The result is that this approach to ethics could sanction the most blatant forms of social, economic, moral, and political injustice, ranging from a repressive caste system to systematic racial or sexual discrimination. Might, on this theory, does make right. Let those who are the victims of injustice suffer as they will. It matters not so long as no one else—no contractor, or too few of them—cares about it. Such a theory takes one's moral breath away . . . as if, for example, there is nothing wrong with apartheid in South Africa if too few white South Africans are upset by it. A theory with so little to recommend it at the level of the ethics of our treatment of our fellow humans cannot have anything more to recommend it when it comes to the ethics of how we treat our fellow animals. . . .

Indirect duty views, then, including the best among them, fail to command our rational assent. Whatever ethical theory we rationally should accept, therefore, it must at least recognize that we have some duties directly to animals, just as we have some duties directly to each other. The next two theories I'll sketch attempt to meet this requirement.

The first I call the cruelty-kindness view. Simply stated, this view says that we have a direct duty to be kind to animals and a direct duty not to be cruel to them. Despite the familiar, reassuring rings of these ideas, I do not believe this view offers an adequate theory. To make this clearer, consider kindness. A kind person acts from a certain kind of motive—compassion or concern, for example. And that is a virtue. But there is no guarantee that a kind act is a right act. If I am a generous racist, for example, I will be inclined to act kindly toward members of my own race, favoring their interests above others. My kindness would be real and, so far as it goes, good. But I trust it is too obvious to require comment that my kind acts may not be above moral reproach—may, in fact, be positively wrong because rooted in injustice. So kindness, notwithstanding its status as a virtue to be encouraged, simply will not cancel the weight of a theory of right action.

Cruelty fares no better. People or their acts are cruel if they display either a lack of sympathy for or, worse, the presence of enjoyment in, seeing another suffer. Cruelty in all its guises *is* a bad thing—*is* a tragic human failing. But just as a person's being motivated by kindness does not guarantee that they do what is right, so the absence of cruelty does not assure that they avoid doing what is wrong. Many people who perform abortions, for example, are not cruel, sadistic people. But that fact about their character and motivation does not settle the terribly difficult question about the morality of abortion. The case is no different when we examine the ethics of our treatment of animals. So, yes, let us be for kindness and against cruelty. But let us not suppose that being for the one and against the other answers questions about moral right and wrong.

Some people think the theory we are looking for is *utilitarianism.* The first is a principle of equality: everyone's interests count, and similar interests must be counted as having similar weight or importance. White or black, male or female, American or Iranian, human or animal: everyone's pain or frustration matter and matter equally with the like pain or frustration of anyone else. The second principle a utilitarian accepts is the principle of utility: do that act that will bring about the best balance of satisfaction over frustration for everyone affected by the outcome.

As a utilitarian, then, here is how I am to approach the task of deciding what I morally ought to do: I must ask who will be affected if I choose to do one thing rather than another, how much each individual will be affected, and where the best results are most likely to lie—which option, in other words, is most likely to bring about the best results, the best balance of satisfaction over frustration. That option, whatever it may be, is the one I ought to choose. That is where my moral duty lies.

The great appeal of utilitarianism rests with its uncompromising *egalitarianism:* everyone's interests count and count equally with the like interests of everyone else. The kind of odious discrimination some forms of contractarianism can justify—discrimination based on race or sex, for example—seems disallowed in principle by utilitarianism, as is speciesism—systematic discrimination based on species membership.

The sort of equality we find in utilitarianism, however, is not the sort an advocate of animal or human rights should have in mind. Utilitarianism has no room for the equal moral rights of different individuals because it has no room for their equal inherent value or worth. What has value for the utilitarian is the satisfaction of an individual's interests, not the individual whose interests they are. A universe in which you satisfy your desire for water, food, and warmth, is, other things being equal, better than a universe in which these desires are frustrated. And the same is true in the case of an animal with similar desires. But neither you nor the animal have any value in your own right. Only your feelings do. . . .

Serious problems arise for utilitarianism when we remind ourselves that it enjoins us to bring about the best consequences. What does this mean? It doesn't mean the best consequences for me alone, or, for my family or friends, or any other person taken individually. No, what we must do is, roughly, as follows: we must add up—somehow!—the separate satisfactions and frustrations of everyone likely to be affected by our choice, the satisfactions in one column, the frustrations in the other. We must total each column for each of the options before us. That is what it means to say the theory is aggregative. And then we must choose that option which is most likely to bring about the best balance of totaled satisfactions over totaled frustrations. Whatever act would lead to this outcome is the one we morally ought to perform—is where our moral duty lies. And that act quite clearly might not be the same one that would bring about the best results for me personally, or my family or friends, or a lab animal. The best aggregated consequences for everyone concerned are not necessarily the best for each individual.

That utilitarianism is an aggregative theory—that different individual's satisfactions or frustrations are added, or summed, or totaled—is the key objection to this theory. My Aunt Bea is old, inactive, a cranky, sour person, though not physically ill. She prefers to go on living. She is also rather rich. I could make a fortune if I could get my hands on her money, money she intends to give me in any event, after she dies, but which she refuses to give me now. In order to avoid a huge tax bite, I plan to donate a handsome sum of my profits to a local children's hospital. Many, many children will benefit from my generosity, and much joy will be brought to their parents, relatives, and friends. If I don't get the money rather soon, all these ambitions will come to naught. The once-in-a-life-time-opportunity to make a real killing will be gone. Why, then, not really kill my Aunt Bea? Oh, of course I *might* get caught. But I'm no fool and, besides, her doctor can be counted on to cooperate (he has an eye for the same investment and I happen to know a good deal about his shady past). The deed can be done . . . professionally, shall we say. There is *very* little chance of getting caught. And as for my conscience being guilt ridden, I am a resourceful sort of fellow and will take more than sufficient comfort—as I lie on the beach at Acapulco—in contemplating the joy and health I have brought to so many others.

Suppose Aunt Bea is killed and the rest of the story comes out as told. Would I have done anything wrong? Anything immoral? One would have thought that I had. But not according to utilitarianism. Since what I did brought about the best balance of totaled satisfaction over frustration for all those affected by the outcome, what I did was not wrong, indeed, in killing Aunt Bea the physician and I did what duty required.

This same kind of argument can be repeated in all sorts of cases, illustrating, time after time, how the utilitarian's position leads to results that impartial people find morally callous. It *is* wrong to kill my Aunt Bea in the name of bringing about the best results for others. A good end does not justify an evil means. Any adequate moral theory will have to explain why this is so. Utilitarianism fails in this respect and so cannot be the theory we seek.

What to do? Where to begin anew? The place to begin, I think, is with the utilitarian's view of the value of the individual—or, rather, lack of value. In its place suppose we consider that you and I, for example, do have value as individuals—what we'll call *inherent value.* To say we have such value is to say that we are something more than, something different from, mere receptacles. Moreover, to insure that we do not pave the way for such injustices as slavery or sexual discrimination, we must believe that all who have inherent value have it equally, regardless of their sex, race, religion, birthplace, and so on. Similarly to be discarded as irrelevant are one's talents or skills, intelligence and wealth, personality or pathology, whether one is loved and admired—or despised and loathed. The genius and the retarded child, the prince and the pauper, the brain surgeon and the fruit vendor, Mother Theresa and the most unscrupulous used car salesman—all have inherent value, all possess it equally, and all have an equal right to be treated with respect, to be treated in ways that do not reduce them to the status of things, as if they exist as resources for others. My value as an individual is independent of my usefulness to you. Yours is not dependent on your usefulness to me. For either of us to treat the other in ways that fail to show respect for the other's independent value is to act immorally—is to violate the individual's rights.

Some of the rational virtues of this view—what I call the rights view—should be evident. Unlike (crude) contractarianism, for example, the rights view *in principle* denies the moral tolerability of any and all forms of racial, sexual, or social discrimination; and unlike utilitarianism, this view *in principle* denies that we can justify good results by using evil means that violate an individual's rights—denies, for example, that it could be moral to kill my Aunt Bea to harvest beneficial consequences for others. That would be to sanction the disrespectful treatment of the individual in the name of the social good, something the rights view will not—categorically will not—ever allow.

The rights view—or so I believe—is rationally the most satisfactory moral theory. It surpasses all other theories in the degree to which it illuminates and explains the foundation of our duties to one another—the domain of human morality. On this score, it has the best reasons, the best arguments, on its side. Of course, if it were possible to show that only human beings are included within its scope, then a person like myself, who believes in animal rights, would be obliged to look elsewhere than to the rights view.

But attempts to limit its scope to humans only can be shown to be rationally defective. Animals, it is true, lack many of the abilities humans possess. They can't read, do higher mathematics, build a bookcase, or make *baba ghanoush*. Neither can many human beings, however, and yet we don't say—and shouldn't say—that they (these humans) therefore have less inherent value, less of a right to be treated with respect, than do others. It is the *similarities* between those human beings who most clearly, most noncontroversially have such value—the people reading this, for example—it is our similarities, not our differences, that matter most. And the really crucial, the basic similarity is simply this; we are each of us the experiencing subject of a life, each of us a conscious creative being having an individual welfare that has importance to us whatever our usefulness to others. We want and prefer things; believe and feel things; recall and expect things. And all these dimensions of our life, including our pleasure and pain, our enjoyment and suffering, our satisfaction and frustration, our continued existence or our untimely death—all make a difference to the quality of our life as lived, as experienced by us as individuals. As the same is true of those animals who concern us (those who are eaten and trapped), for example, they, too, must be viewed as the experiencing subjects of a life with inherent value of their own.

There are some who resist the idea that animals have inherent value. "Only humans have such value," they profess. How might this narrow view be defended? Shall we say that only humans have the requisite intelligence, or autonomy, or reason? But there are many, many humans who will fail to meet these standards and yet who are reasonably viewed as having value above and beyond their usefulness to others. Shall we claim that only humans belong to the right species—the species Homosapiens? But this is blatant speciesism. Will it be said, then, that all—and only—humans have immortal souls? Then our opponents more than have their work cut out for them. I am myself not ill-disposed to there being immortal souls. Personally, I profoundly hope I have one. But I would not want to rest my position on a controversial ethical issue on the even more controversial question about who or what has an immortal soul. That is to dig one's hole deeper, not climb out. Rationally, it is better to resolve moral issues without making more controversial assumptions than are needed. The question of who has inherent value is such a question, one that is more rationally resolved without the introduction of the idea of immortal souls than by its use.

Well, perhaps some will say that animals have some inherent value, only *less* than we do. Once again, however, attempts to defend this view can be shown to lack rational justification. What could be the basis of our having more inherent value than animals? Will it be their lack of reason, or autonomy, or intellect? Only if we are willing to make the same judgment in the case of humans who are similarly deficient. But it is not true that such humans—the retarded child, for example, or the mentally deranged—have less inherent value than you or I. Neither, then, can we rationally sustain the view that animals like them in being the experiencing subjects of a life have less inherent value. All who have inherent value have *it equally*, whether they be human animals or not.

Inherent value, then, belongs equally to those who are the experiencing subjects of a life. Whether it belongs to others—to rocks and rivers, trees and glaciers, for example—we do not know. And may never know. But neither do we need to know, if we are to make the case for animal rights. We don't need to know how many people, for example, are eligible to vote in the next presidential election before we can know whether I am. Similarly, we do not need to know *how many* individuals have inherent value before we can know that some do. When it comes to the case for animal rights, then what we need to know is whether the animals who in our culture are routinely eaten, hunted, and used in our laboratories, for example, are like us in being subjects of a life. And we *do* know this. We do *know* that many—literally, billions and billions—of these animals are the subjects of a life in the sense explained and so have inherent value if we do. And since, in order to have the best theory of our duties to one another, we must recognize our equal inherent value, as individuals, reason—not sentiment, not emotion—reason compels us to recognize the equal inherent value of these animals. And, with this, their equal right to be treated with respect.

# J. Baird Callicott

# Review of Tom Regan, The Case for Animal Rights (1985)

Over the last decade Tom Regan has contributed numerous essays to animal welfare ethics. . . . *The Case for Animal Rights* . . . is a magnificent professional achievement by one of our ablest colleagues. . . . I concentrate in this review on . . . the implications of Regan's theory of animal rights for environmental ethics and policy. . . .

Not all animals have moral rights. Regan's moral base class is more restricted than Peter Singer's—his chief internecine rival in the field of animal welfare ethics—who doesn't regard *all* animals as equal either. Singer called for equal consideration of the diverse interests of all *sentient* animals. According to Regan, however, only those animals who have "inherent value" have rights. And only those animals who meet the "subject-of-a-life criterion" have inherent value. To be a subject-of-a-life involves, among other things, being self-conscious and having the capacity to believe, desire, conceive the future, entertain goals, and act deliberately. The only animals Regan is sure meet all these qualifications are "mentally normal mammals of a year or more."

The case for animal rights turns out to be, thus, the case for mammal rights. Nevertheless, Regan insists on using the word *animal* throughout his discussion, even though what he really means, as he himself notes, is "mammal," on the grounds of "economy of expression." This is puzzling since both words contain six letters. Why wasn't this book called *The Case for Mammal Rights?* Biologically literate readers with broader concerns (as well as philosophers concerned with precision, no less than economy, of expression) will immediately be put on the alert.

## II

Regan tells us "how [and how not] to worry about endangered species." His discussion of endangered species is astounding for two reasons—its candor and its naiveté. Regan to his credit does not hedge or attempt to disguise the fact that the

J. Baird Callicott, Review of Tom Regan, The Case for Animal Rights, 7 Envt'l Ethics 365 (1985).

"rights view" he recommends provides no rights (nor, for that matter, any discernible moral status whatever) for species *per se:* "Species are not individuals [contrary to David Hull and others who have thought deeply about this matter], and the rights view does not recognize the moral rights of species to anything, including survival."

Perhaps some attempt could be made to adapt the rights view so that it might more positively address what has emerged as the primary and most desperate environmental concern of our time—biocide: abrupt, massive, wholesale anthropogenic species extinction. Perhaps it could by analogy with "minority rights," special rights which attach, not to minority groups *per se,* but which devolve upon individuals by virtue of their being members of minority groups. An individual member of a minority, many people think, has a right to be hired, for example, in preference to an equally qualified member of a non-minority group. Similarly, perhaps a member of a rare and endangered species, like the black-footed ferret, might have a right, an individual right, to analogous preferential treatment in circumstances of direct conflict of interest with a member of an abundant species, like the domestic sheep. Regan expressly denies that his theory can be so amplified:

> That an individual animal is among the last remaining members of a species confers no further right on that animal, and its rights not to be harmed must be weighed equitably with the rights of any others who have this right. If, in a prevention situation, we had to choose between saving the last two members of an endangered species [the last two Furbish louseworts, let us say] or saving another individual [e.g., a cotton-tail rabbit] who belonged to a species that was plentiful but whose death would be a greater prima facie harm to that individual than the harm that death would be to the two [plants], then the rights view requires that we save that individual [the rabbit].

So much for affirmative action in the area of species conservation. Adding insult to injury, Regan goes on to say that even if it were a matter of sacrificing "the last thousand or million members" of a species, members who do not qualify for rights, to prevent grave harm to a single individual mammal, then according to this theory, such a sacrifice would be mandated.

Regan is not opposed to saving endangered species so long as we do so for the right reason, which is, ironically, not to save species, but to prevent harm befalling individual rights-holding members of species. Thus, the Greenpeace effort to "save the whales" (my example, not his) is morally worthwhile and laudable from Regan's rights point of view, not as a desperate struggle against the extinction of whales, which apparently is of no moral consequence whatever, but because it prevents individual whales from being brutally harpooned and dying slow agonizing deaths. Species conservation should be regarded essentially as a non-moral aesthetic and ecosystemic bonus following upon the protection of mammals' rights.

What is biologically naive in this indirect ethic for species conservation is Regan's inattention to the fact that the vast majority of endangered species are not comprised of rights-holding mammals. The vast majority are plants and invertebrates. Regan bubbles along talking about how "any and all harm done to rare or endangered animals . . . is wrong" without so much as mentioning rare and endangered plants or, for that matter, even apparently thinking about all the animals (his persistent use of "animals" to refer only to furry creatures does, I admit, consistently irritate me because I think it is consistently misleading)—butterflies, beetles, mollusks, crustaceans, birds, fish, and amphibians—that fall outside his very restrictive qualifications for rights bearers.

## III

Regan's moral zeal does not generally dispose him to rhetorical temperance in condemning widespread and wholesale disregard of "animal" rights. But when he comes to consider Aldo Leopold's holistic land ethic, which would override an animal's rights to deal more directly and effectively with such pressing moral issues as biocide, he pulls all stops, drops rational argument altogether, and resorts to name calling. Because it is holistic, the land ethic, according to Regan, "might be fairly dubbed 'environmental fascism.'" And, "[e]nvironmental fascism and the rights view are like oil and water: they don't mix." Well, who would ever want to be an environmental fascist?! So much then for the seminal and classic paradigm for all subsequent *environmental* ethics.

As an alternative to Leopold's fascist approach to environmental ethics, Regan recommends that "environmentalists" take the rights view a step or two further than he has taken it. He toys with the idea that "collections or systems of natural objects might have inherent value" and thus the primary qualification, according to his theory, for holding rights. But he suggests that it would be pretty far-fetched to imagine that wholes have rights, that is, that "moral rights could be meaningfully attributed to the *collection* of trees or the ecosystem."

Regan, of course, has bought into the myth of the real existence of rights—a confusion, as Wittgenstein might have diagnosed it, arising from language mesmerization. "Rights(s)" is a noun. So we are tempted to ask what real, but metaphysical, *thing(s)* it labels. Like shoes, teeth, feathers, souls, and other things, some beings seem to have them and others don't. To construct a theory of moral rights, from this point of view, is to attempt to discover the true nature of rights and to identify the entities which naturally possess them. But "right(s)" is actually an expressive locution masquerading as a substantive. (That is the secret of its talismanic power.) "Rights(s)" formulations are used to *state* claims. As opposed to mineral rights, water rights, property rights, civil rights, legal rights, etc., "moral rights" is used to claim moral consideration—for oneself or for other less articulate beings.

Even though "paradigmatic right-holders are individuals," it is not difficult *meaningfully* to assert moral rights on behalf of wholes like the whooping crane or the Bridger wilderness. People meaningfully assert all the time that non-individuals— unions, corporations, states (as in "states' rights"), nations, sports teams, species, and ecosystems—have various rights, including moral rights. Only the occasional philosopher pretends to be puzzled about what is meant.

Upon the strength of such brief and facile considerations, Regan goes on to suggest that the most promising approach to environmental ethics is to make "the case that individual inanimate natural objects (e.g., *this* redwood) have inherent value and a basic moral right to treatment respectful of that value . . . . Were we to show proper respect for the rights of the individuals who make up the biotic community, would not the *community* be preserved?"

As Mark Sagoff recently remarked, "this is an empirical question, the answer to which is 'no.'" To take an illustration familiar to almost everyone, if the right of individual whitetail deer to live unmolested were respected, the biotic communities which they help to make up would not be preserved. On the contrary, without some provision for "thinning the herd"—a euphemism for killing deer—plant members of some communities would be seriously damaged, some beyond recovery. Regan might object that I have missed his point in singling out one species among the myriad that compose a biotic community. Perhaps he means that if the rights of *each* individual of *every* species were *simultaneously* respected, then the community would be preserved. But to attempt to safeguard the rights of each and every individual member of an ecosystem would be to attempt to stop practically all trophic processes beyond photosynthesis—and even then we would somehow have to attempt to deal ethically with the individual life-threatening and hence rights-violating competition among plants for sunlight.

Nature, as Sagoff points out, is not fair: it does not respect the rights of individuals. An ethic for the preservation of nature, therefore, could hardly get off on the right foot if at the start it condemns as unjust and immoral the trophic asymmetries lying at the heart of evolutionary and ecological processes. An environmental ethic, therefore, could not be generated, as it were, by an invisible hand, from a further extension of rights (on the basis of some yet-to-be-worked-out theory) to "individual inanimate natural objects."

## IV

. . . Regan's permission of animal predation . . . stands in direct contradiction to his theory of animal rights. He says, "Since animals can pose innocent threats and because we are sometimes justified in overriding their rights when they do . . ., one cannot assume that all hunting and trapping are wrong." "Pose innocent threats" to whom? To people, as he explains. But Regan's whole case for animal rights turns on the principle that basic moral rights are enjoyed equally by all who are entitled to them: "As a matter of strict justice, then, we are required to give equal respect to those individuals who have equal inherent value . . . whether they be humans or animals." And "all who possess [basic moral] rights possess them equally." Since some animals can and do pose innocent threats to other (rights holding) animals, as a matter of strict justice, we ought to deal with such threats no differently than we would if they were threats to (rights holding) humans. If we ought to protect humans' rights not to be preyed upon by both human and animal predators, then we ought to protect animals' rights not to be preyed on by both human and animal preditors. In short, then, Regan's theory of animal rights implies a policy of humane predator extermination, since predators, however innocently, violate the rights of their victims.

Regan appears to recognize that the Achilles' heel of his elaborate case for animal rights is just this issue—predator policy. He is not willing to embrace the implications of his theory regarding predators and, as Steve Sapontzis actually does, recommend *as a morally better world*, a world purged of carnivores, a world of plants and herbivores. Somewhat desperately Regan concludes that "wildlife managers should be principally concerned with *letting animals be*, keeping human predators out of their affairs, allowing these 'other nations' to carve out their own destiny."

Regan's allusion to Henry Beston's reconfiguration of our image of animals is ironic in this context. Beston's point is that we have incorrectly cast animals in our own image and then condescendingly judged them imperfect or incomplete: "We *patronize* them for their incompleteness, for their tragic fate of having taken form so far below ourselves." But this is precisely what animal liberation and animal rights has now for more than a decade persisted in doing. The primary moral fulcrum of animal liberation/rights has been the "argument from marginal cases," as Regan has called it. If marginal human beings (e.g., the severely retarded) are entitled to equal consideration and/or basic moral rights, as most people think, then so are animals who are at a similar mental level. This argument quite directly and deliberately equates animals with imbeciles, with imperfect and incomplete humans.

Animal rights, à la Regan, does nothing if it does not draw some animals (mammals) into a single community with humans. Either they are members of other nations with their own lives to live and laws to live by or they are honorary mentally deficient and morally incompetent members of the human community, entangled, to both their benefit and peril, with such human artifices as rights and correlative restraints. (Beston, to whom Regan approvingly refers, takes the former alternative: "[Do not] expect Nature to answer to your human values as to come into your house and sit in a chair [like domestic cats and dogs]. The economy of nature . . . *has an ethic of its own*.")

*Arne Naess*

# The Deep Ecological Movement:
# Some Philosophical Aspects (1986)

## Basic Principles

1. The well-being and flourishing of human and non-human Life on Earth have value in themselves (synonyms: intrinsic value, inherent worth). These values are independent of the usefulness of the non-human world for human purposes.
2. Richness and diversity of life forms contribute to the realization of these values and are also values in themselves.
3. Humans have no right to reduce this richness and diversity except to satisfy vital needs.
4. The flourishing of human life and cultures is compatible with a substantial decrease of the human population. The flourishing of non-human life *requires* a smaller human population.
5. Present human interference with the non-human world is excessive, and the situation is rapidly worsening.
6. Policies must therefore be changed. These policies affect basic economic, technological, and ideological structures. The resulting state of affairs will be deeply different from the present.
7. The ideological change will be mainly that of appreciating life quality (dwelling in situations of inherent value) rather than adhering to an increasingly higher standard of living. There will be a profound awareness of the difference between bigness and greatness.
8. Those who subscribe to the foregoing points have an obligation directly or indirectly to try to implement the necessary changes.

Arne Naess, The Deep Ecological Movement: Some Philosophical Aspects, 8 Philosophical Inquiry (Thessaloniki, Greece: Aristotelian University, 1986), D.Z. Andriopoulis (ed.).

## Comments on the Eight Points of the Platform

RE(1): This formulation refers to the biosphere, or more professionally, to the eco-sphere as a whole (this is also referred to as "ecocentrism"). This includes individuals, species, populations, habitat, as well as human and non-human cultures. Given our current knowledge of all-pervasive intimate relationships, this implies a fundamental deep concern and respect.

The term "life" is used here in a more comprehensive non-technical way also to refer to what biologists classify as "non-living": rivers (watersheds), landscapes, ecosystems. For supporters of deep ecology, slogans such as "let the river live" illustrate this broader usage so common in many cultures.

Inherent value, as used in (1), is common in deep ecology literature (e.g., "The presence of inherent value in a natural object is independent of any awareness, interest, or appreciation of it by any conscious being").

RE(2): The so-called simple, lower, or primitive species of plants and animals contribute essentially to the richness and diversity of life. They have value in themselves and are not merely steps toward the so-called higher or rational life forms. The second principle presupposes that life itself, as a process over evolutionary time, implies an increase of diversity and richness.

Complexity, as referred to here, is different from complication. For example, urban life may be more complicated than life in a natural setting without being more complex in the sense of multifaceted quality.

RE(3): The term "vital need" is deliberately left vague to allow for considerable latitude in judgment. Differences in climate and related factors, together with differences in the structures of societies as they now exist, need to be taken into consideration.

RE(4): People in the materially richest countries cannot be expected to reduce their excessive interference with the non-human world overnight. The stabilization and reduction of the human population will take time. Hundreds of years! Interim strategies need to be developed. But in no way does this excuse the present complacency. The extreme seriousness of our current situation must first be realized. And the longer we wait to make the necessary changes, the more drastic will be the measures needed. Until deep changes are made, substantial decreases in richness and diversity are liable to occur: the rate of extinction of species will be ten to one hundred or more times greater than in any other short period of earth history.

RE(5): This formulation is mild. For a realistic assessment, see the annual reports of the Worldwatch Institute in Washington, D.C.

The slogan of "non-interference" does not imply that humans should not modify some ecosystems, as do other species. Humans have modified the earth over their entire history and will probably continue to do so. At issue is the *nature and extent* of such interference. The per capita destruction of wild (ancient) forests and other wild ecosystems has been excessive in rich countries; it is essential that the poor do not imitate the rich in this regard.

The fight to preserve and extend areas of wilderness and near-wilderness ("free

Nature") should continue. The rationale for such preservation should focus mainly on the ecological functions of these areas (one such function: large wilderness areas are required in the biosphere for the continued evolutionary speciation of plants and animals). Most of the present designated wilderness areas and game reserves are not large enough to allow for such speciation.

RE(6): Economic growth as it is conceived of and implemented today by the industrial states is incompatible with points (1) through (5). There is only a faint resemblance between ideal sustainable forms of economic growth and the present policies of industrial societies.

Present ideology tends to value things because they are scarce and because they have a commodity value. There is prestige in vast consumption and waste (to mention only several relevant factors).

Whereas "self-determination," "local community," and "think globally, act locally," will remain key terms in the ecology of human societies, nevertheless the implementation of deep changes requires increasingly global action: Action across borders.

Governments in Third World countries are mostly uninterested in Deep Ecological issues. When institutions in the industrial societies try to promote ecological measures through Third World governments, practically nothing is accomplished (e.g., with problems of desertification). Given this situation, support for global action through non-governmental international organizations becomes increasingly important. Many of these organizations are able to act globally "from grassroots to grassroots" thus avoiding negative governmental interference.

Cultural diversity today requires advanced technology, that is, techniques that advance the basic goals of each culture. So-called soft, intermediate, and alternative technologies are steps in this direction.

RE(7): Some economists criticize the term "quality of life" because it is supposedly vague. But, on closer inspection, what they consider to be vague is actually the non-quantifiable nature of the term. One cannot quantify adequately what is important for the quality of life as discussed here, and there is no need to do so.

RE(8): There is ample room for different opinions about priorities: what should be done first; what next? What is the most urgent? What is clearly necessary to be done, as opposed to what is highly desirable but not absolutely pressing? The frontier of the environmental crisis is long and varied, and there is a place for everyone. . . .

## Deep Versus Shallow Ecology

A number of key terms and slogans from the environmental debate will clarify the contrast between the shallow and the deep ecology movements.

### Pollution

Shallow Approach: Technology seeks to purify the air and water and to spread pollution more evenly. Laws limit permissible pollution. Polluting industries are preferably exported to developing countries.

Deep Approach: Pollution is evaluated from a biospheric point of view, not focusing exclusively on its effects on human health, but rather on life as a whole, including the life conditions of every species and system. The shallow reaction to acid rain, for example, is to tend to avoid action by demanding more research, and the attempt to find species of trees which will tolerate high acidity, etc. The deep approach concentrates on what is going on in the total ecosystem and calls for a high priority fight against the economic conditions and the technology responsible for producing the acid rain. The long-range concerns are one hundred years, at least.

The priority is to fight the deep causes of pollution, not merely the superficial, short-range effects. The Third and Fourth World countries cannot afford to pay the total costs of the war against pollution in their regions; consequently they require the assistance of the First and Second World countries. Exporting pollution is not only a crime against humanity, it is a crime against life in general.

*Resources*

Shallow Approach: The emphasis is upon resources for humans, especially for the present generation in affluent societies. In this view, the resources of the earth belong to those who have the technology to exploit them. There is confidence that resources will not be depleted because, as they get rarer, a high market price will conserve them, and substitutes will be found through technological progress. Further, plants, animals, and natural objects are valuable only as resources for humans. If no human use is known, or seems likely ever to be found, it does not matter if they are destroyed.

Deep Approach: The concern here is with resources and habitats for all life-forms for their own sake. No natural object is conceived of solely as a resource. This leads, then, to a critical evaluation of human modes of production and consumption. The question arises: to what extent does an increase in production and consumption foster ultimate human values? To what extent does it satisfy vital needs, locally or globally? How can economic, legal and educational institutions be changed to counteract destructive increases? How can resource use serve the quality of life rather than the economic standard of living as generally promoted by consumerism? From a deep perspective, there is an emphasis upon an ecosystem approach rather than the consideration merely of isolated life-forms or local situations. There is a long-range maximal perspective of time and place. . . .

## But Why a "Deep" Ecology?

The decisive difference between a shallow and a deep ecology, in practice, concerns the willingness to question, and an appreciation of the importance of questioning, every economic and political policy in public. This questioning is both "deep" and public. It asks "why" insistently and consistently, taking nothing for granted!

Deep ecology can readily admit to the practical effectiveness of homocentric arguments:

> It is essential for conservation to be seen as central to human interests and aspirations. At the same time, people—from heads of state to the members of rural communities—will most readily be brought to demand conservation if they themselves recognize the contribution of conservation to the achievement of their needs as perceived by them, and the solution of their problems, as perceived by them.[1]

There are several dangers in arguing solely from the point of view of narrow human interests. Some policies based upon successful homocentric arguments turn out to violate or unduly compromise the objectives of deeper argumentation. Further, homocentric arguments tend to weaken the motivation to fight for necessary social change, together with the willingness to serve a great cause. In addition, the complicated arguments in human-centered conservation documents such as the World Conservation Strategy go beyond the time and ability of many people to assimilate and understand. They also tend to provoke interminable technical disagreements among experts. Special interest groups with narrow short-term exploitive objectives, which run counter to saner ecological policies, often exploit these disagreements and thereby stall the debate and steps toward effective action.

When arguing from deep ecological premises, most of the complicated proposed technological fixes need not be discussed at all. The relative merits of alternative technological proposals are pointless if our vital needs have already been met. A focus on vital issues activates mental energy and strengthens motivation. On the other hand, the shallow environmental approach, by focusing almost exclusively on the technical aspects of environmental problems, tends to make the public more passive and disinterested in the more crucial non-technical, lifestyle-related, environmental issues.

Writers within the deep ecology movement try to articulate the fundamental presuppositions underlying the dominant economic approach in terms of value priorities, philosophy, and religion. In the shallow movement, questioning and argumentation comes to a halt long before this. The deep ecology movement is therefore "the ecology movement which questions deeper." A realization of the deep changes which are required, as outlined in the deep ecology eight point platform, makes us realize the necessity of "questioning everything."

---

[1]IUCN, World Conservation Strategy: Living Resource Conservation for Sustainable Development (Gland, Switzerland, 1980), section 13 (concluding paragraph).

# CHAPTER 4

# Environmental Justice

One of the most important recent developments in environmental policy has been the rise of the environmental justice movement. Linking environmental concerns with a broader agenda for social justice, this movement seeks to combat disparities in the distribution of environmental risks across society. Arguing that low-income and minority communities bear a disproportionate burden of pollution and locally undesirable land uses, the movement challenges policy makers to broaden their focus to consider not only overall levels of environmental risk but also how fairly those risks are distributed. The environmental justice movement seeks to promote fairness as an explicit policy goal.

There is powerful evidence that environmental risks are indeed disproportionately concentrated in poor and minority communities, as discussed in the article by Robert Bullard, a scholar who has done some of the pioneering work in this area. Bullard argues that environmental racism is a product of an imbalance of power in society, which results in public policies that benefit whites while shifting costs to people of color. He reviews many of the studies that have confirmed that people of color and low-income groups experience much higher levels of lead poisoning and live in communities where toxic waste dumps and other environmentally undesirable facilities are concentrated. Bullard traces the emergence of the grassroots environmental justice movement and calls for national policy to incorporate the movement's concerns in official decision making.

Bullard's concerns are echoed in the subsequent article by a seemingly unlikely source for championing the cause of environmental justice, conservative columnist George Will. Will's little-known article "The Poison Poor Children Breathe" was written shortly after the Reagan administration abandoned a potentially disastrous proposal to repeal all limits on the amount of lead in gasoline. Studies showed that this proposal would have dramatically increased lead poisoning among young children, which already was disproportionately concentrated in low-income and minority communities. Will's concluding admonition to conservatives who favor equal opportunity that this goal will remain elusive so long as environmental risks are distributed unequally remains a powerful insight for public policy today. For, even though the United States has dramatically reduced the incidence of lead poisoning by banning lead additives in gasoline, environmental injustice is far from being eradicated.

Although the disproportionate distribution of environmental risks is well documented, the causes of this phenomenon are not entirely clear, making it difficult to formulate corrective strategies. Robert Collin, a professor of urban and environmental planning, explores some of the factors that have contributed to the disproportionate concentration of environmentally hazardous land uses in low-income and minority communities. Collin examines how zoning policies, the economics of land acquisition costs, and procedures for reviewing facility siting decisions have either contributed to the problem or failed to correct it. He identifies a number of trends, such as increasingly stringent regulation of solid and hazardous waste disposal facilities, that are likely to exacerbate the problem unless environmental policy successfully responds to environmental justice concerns.

Vicki Been questions the assumption that disproportionate exposure of minorities to locally undesirable land uses (LULUs) reflects racism in facility siting. She notes that, even if LULUs are sited neutrally, market dynamics may later result in concentrations of minorities near such facilities. Based on empirical analysis, Been concludes that "while siting decisions do disproportionately affect minorities and the poor, market dynamics also play a very significant role in creating the uneven distribution of the burdens LULUs impose." She argues that policies to promote environmental justice should focus not only on the siting process, but also on the market forces that help surround LULUs with people of color and the poor.

Environmental justice is an important goal because fairness undoubtedly should play a major role in the development and implementation of policy. The question of how best to promote environmental justice is more controversial. In 1991 the United Church of Christ's Commission for Racial Justice convened the First National People of Color Environmental Leadership Summit. This summit adopted seventeen "Principles of Environmental Justice," which are reproduced in this chapter, and recommended that they be pursued through grassroots social and political action.

The chapter concludes with an article by Richard Lazarus, who explores the meaning of environmental justice and the tools available for promoting it. Professor Lazarus argues that much can be accomplished under existing laws, particularly if federal agencies exercise their discretion to promote distributional fairness. President Clinton has issued an executive order directing each federal agency to "make achieving environmental justice part of its mission" and to develop a strategy for accomplishing this. While public policy is now responding to environmental justice concerns, the effectiveness of this response remains a subject of considerable debate.

*Robert D. Bullard*

# The Threat of Environmental Racism (1993)

Communities consisting primarily of people of color continue to bear a disproportionate burden of this nation's air, water, and waste problems. Even in today's society, race influences the likelihood of exposure to environmental and health risks as well as accessibility to health care. People of color are more likely than their white counterparts to live near freeways, sewage treatment plants, municipal and hazardous waste landfills, incinerators, and other noxious facilities. Disparate siting and land-use patterns result in elevated health risks to nearby inhabitants.

The charge of environmental racism has heightened the debate surrounding social inequities that exist in the larger society. Environmental racism exacerbates existing social inequities. Environmental racism refers to any policy, practice, or directive that differentially affects or disadvantages (whether intended or unintended) individuals, groups, or communities based on race or color. It also includes exclusionary and restrictive practices that limit participation by people of color in decision-making boards, commissions, and regulatory bodies.

Environmental racism exists within local zoning boards as well as the U.S. Environmental Protection Agency (EPA). Recently, the EPA acknowledged the problems faced by communities of color and the poor. After some prodding from outside academicians and activists, the agency created the Work Group on Environmental Equity. A final report of this work group, *Environmental Equity: Reducing Risks to All Communities,* was released in February 1992. The products of this effort included the creation of an Office of Environmental Equity and an Environmental Equity Cluster. These are first steps in placing environmental justice issues on the national agenda.

Environmental racism is also present in nongovernmental organizations such as the nation's mainstream environmental and conservation groups. In 1990, groups representing people of color sent letters to the "Big Ten" environmental groups challenging their hiring practices and participation by people of color on their boards. A flurry of activity was undertaken to diversify, yet it became apparent that environmental racism was institutionalized and would not likely disappear with attempts by the mainstream groups to "color coordinate" their staffs and boards.

Environmental racism combines with public policies and industry practices to provide *benefits* for whites while shifting *costs* to people of color. Many of the at-risk communities are victims of land-use decisionmaking that mirrors the power arrangements of the dominant society. Historically, exclusionary zoning has been a subtle form of using government authority and power to foster and perpetuate discriminatory practices. Generally, planning and zoning commissions are not known for their racial and ethnic diversity.

## Who Pays and Who Benefits?

The question of who *pays* and who *benefits* from current urban land-use policies is central to any analysis of environmental racism. A form of illegal "exaction" forces disenfranchised communities to pay costs of environmental benefits for the public at large. In the United States, race interpenetrates class and creates special vulnerabilities for locally unwanted land uses (LULUs). Race can also operate independently of class in explaining the distribution of air pollution, the location of municipal landfills and incinerators, abandoned toxic waste dumps, and lead poisoning in children.

The nation's lead problem typifies a subpopulation at risk: African-American children. Even when income is held constant, African-American children are two to three times more likely than their white counterparts to suffer from lead poisoning. These wide disparities hold up for African-American children who live inside and outside central cities.

The Agency for Toxic Substances [and] Disease Registry (ATSDR) in its 1988 report to Congress, *The Nature and Extent of Lead Poisoning in Children in the United States*, reveals that lead is the "number one environmental health problem in children." Lead affects between three to four million children in the United States—most of whom are African-Americans and Latinos who live in urban areas. The ATSDR found that for families earning less than $6,000 annually, 68 percent of African-American children had lead poisoning compared with 36 percent for white children. In families with annual income exceeding $15,000, more than 38 percent of African-American children suffer from lead poisoning compared with 12 percent of whites. The Environmental Defense Fund, using the 1991 lead statistics, estimated that 85 percent of African-American families with annual incomes above $15,000 had unsafe amounts of lead in their blood, compared to 47 percent of white families with similar incomes.

Why are so many African-American children at risk of becoming lead poisoned? Why has so little been done to rid the nation of this *preventable* disease? Race, housing, land use, and residential patterns play a large part in explaining this disparity.

African-Americans continue to be the most segregated racial minority group in the United States. No matter what their educational or occupational achievement or income level, African-Americans are exposed to lower-quality neighborhoods and greater environmental threats because of their race.

The ability of an individual to escape a health-threatening physical environment is usually correlated with income. However, housing discrimination, redlining, and residential segregation make it difficult for some individuals to buy their way out of health-threatening physical environments. An African-American family that has an annual income of $50,000 can be as residentially segregated as an African-American family on welfare.

Residential apartheid and skewed development policies limit mobility, reduce neighborhood options, diminish job opportunities, and decrease environmental choices for millions of Americans. Residential apartheid is alive and well in the United States. Why do some communities get dumped on and others do not? Waste generation is directly correlated with per capita income. However, few waste facilities are proposed and fewer are actually built in the white middle-class suburbs.

Garbage dumps and incinerators are not randomly scattered across the landscape. These facilities are often located in communities that have high percentages of poor, elderly, young, and minority residents. The 1979 case of *Bean v. Southwestern Waste,* 482 F. Supp. 673 (S.D. Tex.), was the civil rights challenge to the siting of a waste disposal facility. The lawsuit was brought in Houston, Texas, the only major American city without zoning. Data collected in support of the *Bean* challenge comprised the first empirical study that linked municipal solid waste siting with the race of the surrounding residents. From the early 1920s to the late 1970s, all of the city-owned municipal landfills, and six of its eight garbage incinerators in this area of Houston were located in African-American neighborhoods.

From 1970 to 1978, three of the four privately owned landfills used to dispose of Houston's garbage were located in African-American neighborhoods. Although African-Americans make up only 28 percent of Houston's population, 82 percent of the municipal landfill sites (public and private) were located in African-American neighborhoods.

Waste facility siting inequity was identified by the U.S. General Accounting Office (GAO) as early as 1983—nearly a decade ago. After protests sparked by plans to site a PCB landfill in the most African-American county of Warren, North Carolina, the GAO initiated its own investigation into hazardous waste facility siting in EPA's Region IV. The GAO found a strong relationship between the location of off-site hazardous waste landfills and race and socio-economic status of the surrounding communities in the region.

The GAO identified four off-site hazardous waste landfills in Region IV. The four sites were the Chemical Waste Management site (Sumter County, Alabama); the SCA Services site (Sumter County, South Carolina); the Industrial Chemical Company site (Chester County, South Carolina); and the Warren County PCB landfill (Warren County, North Carolina). African-Americans made up the majority of the population in three of the four communities where these off-site hazardous waste landfills were located. In 1983, African-Americans were clearly overrepresented in communities with waste sites since they made up only about one-fifth of the region's population; however, three-fourths of the landfills were located in African-American communities. These siting imbalances uncovered in 1983 have not disappeared. In 1992, African-Americans comprise about one-fifth of the population in Region IV; however, the two remaining operating off-site hazardous waste landfills in the region are located in zip codes where African-Americans comprise a majority of the population.

The Commission for Racial Justice's landmark study *Toxic Wastes and Race,* found race to be the single most important siting factor—more important than income, home ownership rate, and property values—in the location of abandoned toxic waste sites. The study also found that:

- three out of five African-Americans live in communities with abandoned toxic waste sites;
- 60 percent (15 million) of African-Americans live in communities with one or more abandoned toxic waste sites;
- three of the five largest commercial hazardous waste landfills are located in predominately African-American or Latino communities and account for 40 percent of the nation's total estimated landfill capacity; and
- African-Americans are heavily overrepresented in the population of cities with the largest number of abandoned toxic waste sites, which include Memphis, St. Louis, Houston, Cleveland, Chicago, and Atlanta.

Communities with hazardous waste incinerators also generally have large minority populations, low incomes, and low property values. A 1990 Greenpeace report, *Playing with Fire,* discovered the following:

- The minority portion of the population in communities with existing incinerators is 89 percent higher than the national average;
- Communities where incinerators are proposed have minority populations 60 percent higher than the national average;
- The average income in communities with existing incinerators is 15 percent less than the national average;
- Property values in communities that actually host incinerators are 38 percent lower than the national average; and
- In communities where incinerators are proposed, average property values are 35 percent lower than the national average.

## Dumping in Dixie

The southern United States is rapidly becoming the dumping ground for household garbage and hazardous waste. Historically, the South has scored at or near the bottom on almost all indicators of well-being, such as education, income, economic development, environmental quality, and health care. The region has a long history of exploiting land and people, especially African-Americans, dating back to times of slavery.

There is a clear link between the region's ecological policies and race relations. The findings in my book, *Dumping in Dixie* (1990), reveal that African-Americans in the South bear a disparate burden in siting hazardous waste landfills and incinerators, lead smelters, petrochemical plants, and a host of other noxious facilities. Disparate noxious facility siting is epitomized in South Louisiana's "Cancer Alley," an eighty-five mile stretch along the Mississippi River from Baton Rouge to New Orleans, and Alabama's "blackbelt." For example, the nation's largest commercial hazardous waste landfill, dubbed the "Cadillac of dumps," is located in Emelle, Alabama. Emelle is a rural community in the heart of Alabama's blackbelt. African-Americans make up over 90 percent of the population in Emelle and 75 percent of the residents in Sumter County. The Emelle landfill receives wastes from Superfund sites from all forty-eight contiguous states. . . .

Environmental racism is not unique to the southern United States. The resulting problems are national and international in scope. Some urban neighborhoods have become "sacrifice zones." A classic example of such a sacrifice zone is the land-use pattern that has evolved in Chicago's southside neighborhoods. Chicago is the nation's third largest city and one of the most racially segregated big cities in the country with just under 90 percent of the city's 1.1 million African-Americans residing in racially segregated areas. The Altgeld Gardens housing project, located on the city's southeast side, is one of these segregated enclaves. The Chicago neighborhood is home to 150,000 residents: 70 percent African-American and 11 percent Latino. Altgeld Gardens is encircled by a host of polluting industries including fifty active or closed commercial hazardous waste landfills, one hundred factories (including seven chemical plants and five steel mills), and over one hundred abandoned toxic waste dumps. Hazel Johnson, an environmental activist from Altgeld Gardens, has dubbed her neighborhood a "toxic doughnut."

In California, Latino and African-American communities are especially vulnerable to environmental racism. For example, the mostly African-American South Central Los Angeles and Latino East Los Angeles neighborhoods were targeted for a municipal solid waste incinerator and a hazardous waste incinerator, respectively. The small rural farmworker community of Kettleman City (located in California's agriculturally rich Central Valley) has been proposed for a hazardous waste incinerator. . . .

As environmental regulations have become more stringent in recent years, Native Americans' lands have become prime targets for "dirty" industries. Some groups have called the practice "garbage imperialism." More than one hundred proposals have been made to locate waste (household garbage, hazardous waste, and low-level nuclear waste) facilities on reservations. Nearly all of these proposals have been defeated or are under review. Native Americans' lands pose a special case for environmental protection.

Few reservations have environmental regulations or the infrastructure to handle the threat posed by these industries. Because of the special quasi-sovereign status of Indian nations, some waste disposal companies have attempted to circumvent regulations by siting on Indian lands. The threat to Native Americans' lands exists from Maine to California. . . .

A new form of grassroots environmental activism has emerged in the United States. Much of this activism is centered on securing environmental justice for communities of color. Environmental racism is seen as a major barrier to achieving equitable distribution of "healthy" physical environments and equal protection against the ravages of industrial pollution.

Environmental justice activists have begun to seek changes in discriminatory land-use practices, redlining, housing patterns, and destructive industrial production processes that threaten public safety. Through their grassroots networks, they have begun to build a national environmental justice movement with mainstream environmentalists, social justice activists, academicians, and lawyers.

A national policy is needed to begin addressing environmental inequities that exist in people of color, working class, and low-income communities. State and local decisionmakers need to incorporate environmental justice goals into their planning and development models to ensure that no one segment of society should have to bear a disparate burden of the rest of society's environmental problems.

*George F. Will*

# The Poison Poor Children Breathe
# (1982)

A synonym for "leaden" is "dull," but the problem of lead in the environment is fascinating. It is a childhood health problem that illustrates how society's hazards are often distributed regressively—persons lowest on the social ladder have special handicaps for climbing.

Recently the Reagan administration moved to strengthen restrictions on lead additives in gasoline. Although different refiners have different interests, this was basically a victory for environmentalists over industry. One refinery blamed the decision on "politics." Well, yes: politics is the assignment of social values and costs in accordance with a concept of equity. The Republican role in God's plan may generally be to lighten regulations, but this case illustrates how strong government can serve conservative values.

America uses 1.3 million tons of lead annually, 600,000 tons of this useful, ubiquitous and toxic metal are released into the environment. Because of high metabolism rates, children are especially susceptible to lead poisoning, which can cause retardation, brain damage, anemia, seizures, hyperactivity and death. Analysis of polar ice layers suggests that lead in the environment has increased 200-fold since industrialism began.

People are exposed to lead from food, household dust and the air. Burning a tankful of gasoline emits, according to one study, up to two ounces of lead. Upwards of 28 million buildings have lead-based paint, which tastes sweet to children. A flake the size of a fingernail can be damaging. Some pre-1950 houses have paint with 100 times more lead than is now permitted. Lead in paint is the most dangerous source, but reduce lead in gasoline and you will reduce lead in children. The mean blood-level of lead in children has declined 25 percent since the beginning of restrictions on lead in gasoline.

George F. Will, "The Poison Poor Children Breathe," *Washington Post*, 16 September 1982, p. A23. © 1982, Washington Post Writers Group. Reprinted with permission.

According to one study, 4 percent of preschool children have excessive levels of lead in their blood. That would be dismaying enough even if the distribution were geographically, and hence socially, even. But high lead concentrations are among the things that say, Shaker Heights and downtown Cleveland do not share equally. The percentage of black preschoolers with excessive lead levels is six times that of white preschoolers. Other studies indicate excessive levels in one-fifth of black children from low-income families.

Children often are deficient in iron, calcium and zinc. Poor children are especially apt to be deficient. The more deficient children are, the more apt they are to absorb lead. Federal budget cutting and recession-related reductions of local revenues have reduced programs for screening for lead poisoning in children, and for removing lead-based paint from old buildings. Philadelphia's health commissioner says that if the city loses 10 percent of its lead-poisoning detection funds, that means 200 fewer homes visited, and five more cases of retardation. Studies have found correlations between even relatively low elevations of lead blood-levels and measurable reductions of IQ.

Any childhood disease that threatened affluent children as lead poisoning threatens poor children would produce public action faster than you can say "swine flu." As things are, government spends upward of $1 billion annually on children with lead poisoning, 80 percent on special education for the learning-disabled.

Conservatives dissolve in admiration for this insight: "There is no free lunch." It means someone must pay for anything that has costs. That, although hardly a sunburst, is true enough. So is this: society shall pay (for example, with slightly higher energy costs) for reducing lead use; and society shall continue to pay a lot (for injuries to its human capital) if it does not reduce lead use.

In Saul Bellow's most recent novel, *The Dean's December*, a scientist offers "the real explanation of what goes on" in slums. "Millions of tons of intractable lead residues poisoning the children of the poor. . . . Crime and social disorganization in inner-city populations can all be traced to the effects of lead. It comes down to the nerves, to brain damage."

The dean thinks: "Direct material causes? Of course. Who could deny them? But what was odd was that no other causes were conceived of." The dean is properly dubious about thoroughgoing materialism, that neglects society's cultural, spiritual ingredients. But the body is not just a temple in which the mind rattles about; the mind is not a ghost in a machine.

Mind is grounded in matter, woven into our physical constitutions. Conservatives who rightly prefer equality of opportunity to equality of outcome as a social goal, have yet to come to terms with how complex and elusive their goal is in light of all that we are learning about social influences on human capacity.

*Robert W. Collin*

# Environmental Equity: A Law and Planning Approach to Environmental Racism (1992)

## Land Use Planning, Environmental Regulation and Race

Tremendous economic growth after World War II and a concomitant increase in waste production have contributed greatly to problems of environmental inequity in the United States. As land available for waste siting has decreased while waste production has increased, communities of color have come to bear a disproportionate share of society's burden in accommodating the by-products of growth.

Several economic phenomena have led to a land use dilemma. First, the petrochemical industry began an era of rapid expansion: From 1950 to 1980, synthetic organic compound production increased from less than ten billion pounds to more than 350 billion pounds per year. Wastes produced were often toxic and hazardous. Also, municipal waste production increased dramatically, although it is difficult to develop historically accurate estimates of the degree of increase because landfill regulation is a recent phenomenon and because "midnight dumping" practices are untraceable. Recent data indicate, nevertheless, that regular waste output continues to increase. The United States disposes of 179.6 million tons of municipal waste annually: 73% is buried in landfills; 13% is recycled; and 14% is incinerated. Furthermore, landfill capacity to accommodate additional waste at existing sites has become increasingly scarce. In 1990, it was estimated that about one-third of existing landfills would close within two years and that 80% would close in the next twenty years. Finally, making sites safer compounds the problem of site selection and expansion, be-

Robert W. Collin, Environmental Equity: A Law and Planning Approach to Environmental Racism, 11 Va. Envt'l L. J. 495 (1992).

cause if landfills are airtight and watertight, their contents require more time to degrade.

Industrial and municipal wastes have outgrown existing landfills. Recent history suggests that society has resolved the dilemma by meeting the demand for new and enlarged waste sites in communities of color.

### Minority Neighborhoods: To Plunder or Protect?

Zoning is the regulation of land use to control growth and development for the health, safety and welfare of the community. Originally, zoning was advocated by planners and social reformers as a way to restrict the use of land in order to keep out "nuisances." Generally considered a public mechanism for promoting and stabilizing land development, zoning decreases risk in property development and protects the quality of life in single-family residential neighborhoods. Although approaches to land use control by zoning differ greatly by state and community, in general practice, the land use control framework determines where unwanted land uses are permitted.

Many early land use practices systematically excluded people on the basis of race, though today such an exclusionary practice is illegal. Indeed, land use ordinances that have the effect of discriminating on the basis of race have been subject to strict judicial scrutiny. Race-based exclusionary practices, however, can take forms other than official zoning laws. For example, the enforcement of racially restrictive covenants, racially discriminatory site selection, tenant distribution procedures in public housing and the enactment of many urban renewal policies have also effectively excluded certain people from living in certain areas.

Zoning can be more than exclusionary; it can be expulsive. Expulsive zoning often designates black residential areas for industrial or commercial uses, a practice which results in the eventual displacement of blacks from these areas. As noted by Professor [Yale] Rabin,

> [b]ecause it appears that such areas were mainly black, and because whites who may have been similarly displaced were not subject to racially determined limitations in seeking alternative housing, the adverse impacts of expulsive zoning on blacks were far more severe and included, in addition to accelerated blight, increases in overcrowding and racial segregation.

Expulsive zoning may have provided the original mechanism in land use law that has led to the current racially disproportionate distribution of environmentally hazardous land uses. It is possible that the roots of environmental inequity lie partially in these traditional race-based zoning practices. Before environmental regulation, many industrial and commercial facilities located in minority communities on account of zoning and may have disposed of waste either on-site or nearby because of the lower cost of doing so.

Many communities have excluded locally unwanted land uses (LULUs) from their neighborhoods by means of a well-documented process and philosophy that has been characterized as the "not-in-my-backyard" (NIMBY) syndrome. As a general proposition, a landfill is one of the most unwanted land uses, especially if that landfill will contain toxic and hazardous waste. Professor Bullard maintains that these unwanted land uses are sited in politically and economically disenfranchised neighborhoods in a process he calls "PIBBY," or "place-in-blacks'-backyards."

As the need for new landfill sites increases, and as communities become aware of the potential hazards of landfills, the siting process becomes a decisive battleground. In general, the greater the known or suspected physical effects of an unwanted land use are, the greater the residential resistance will be. The concern over possible property devaluation deepens in communities with a higher ratio of homeowners to renters. Even if the drop in monetary land value is illusory, most communities simply do not want environmentally hazardous land uses located nearby; however great the economic anxieties, residents are often concerned that siting locally unwanted land uses near residential areas may reduce their quality of life. In other words, residents recognize that neighborhood value includes an element of psychic value that exceeds the sum of the values of the individual parcels. This attitude is particularly strong in minority and lower-income communities where residents have limited mobility and rely a great deal on the neighborhood as a source of information and mutual aid.

The debate extends beyond neighborhood borders in cases where wastes are so toxic and so hazardous that they have the potential to affect entire regions. For this reason alone, the site selection process may interest more than just the communities of racial minorities that are located near site areas. Initially, it was assumed that if the land uses were dangerous, they were dangerous only to those who lived nearby. However, landfills, toxic and hazardous waste and waste transfer stations are now known to affect airsheds, watersheds and the carrying capacity of land.

## Hazardous Waste Site Selection: State Supervision, Local Resistance and Private Enterprise

Because the states are responsible for implementing the Resource Conservation and Recovery Act (RCRA) and other EPA regulations, they effectively control the siting of toxic and hazardous waste landfills. Unfortunately, state control of the siting process has not diminished the NIMBY problem. States generally take one of three broad approaches to site selection: super review; site designation; or local control.

Under the super review approach, the developer of the hazardous waste facility selects a possible site and applies for a land use permit from the state authorizing agency. The agency then reviews the application and evaluates the environmental impact. If the state decides to issue the permit, it then appoints a special administrative body to allow the public to participate in the site selection. These administrative bodies encourage public participation in order to decrease community resistance and "to minimize the issue of political expediency and emphasize environmental safety." All of the states that use this approach have preemption clauses that permit the siting despite community resistance.

Because private developers initiate the site selection process, the costs of acquiring the land and assembling the site influence decisions in the early phases of site selection. Unfortunately, low land cost and easy site assembly do not necessarily lead to the best site for waste transfer or disposal. Low-income and racial minority communities are often in areas with lower land values. With relatively few sites chosen in the initial phase of site selection, subsequent phases often place a final site in a minority neighborhood, due in large part to the lower community resistance that often accompanies minority sitings. The super review approach, then, probably does not alleviate inequitable distribution of waste disposal sites.

Under the site designation approach, the state, not a private developer, creates an inventory of possible sites. Techniques for developing the inventory vary from state to state. Because this approach lessens the cost incentive in site selection, it may lead to a more equitable distribution of waste sites. Furthermore, it provides the state with a statewide data gathering mechanism that can inform environmental decision-making in the future.

The third approach basically defers to local land use control. Here, the state does not exercise its right to preempt the authority of the locality to regulate toxic or hazardous wastes. This approach allows those communities that do not want a toxic or hazardous waste facility to simply prohibit that type of land use. As such, it does little but facilitate the NIMBY practice.

It is very difficult for any of these state siting approaches to overcome entrenched, well-funded community resistance. In wealthier communities, this resistance can take the form of protracted litigation. In site selection approaches that are developer-driven, the threat and reality of a lawsuit can increase the cost of the site and the site preparation process. Therefore, communities that cannot afford to litigate will be more vulnerable to site selection. Wealthier communities may also have better access to informal networks in the state government.

Full public participation requires that communities have adequate notice, accurate information and an understanding of the communal and individual risks involved. The increase in public knowledge about the nature of transfer and storage facilities for toxic and hazardous waste has also been part of the evolution of public recognition of environmental equity. An increasing number of states and municipalities have adopted community right-to-know statutes and ordinances. Public participation in state and federal environmental impact studies, together with community right-to-know statutes, have given poor and minority communities greater exposure to, although not necessarily greater influence over, the site selection process. Furthermore, when outside environmentalists or citizens from other communities in the region participate in the process, the public is further exposed to the disproportionate distribution of environmental hazards and can better understand their true dimensions.

## The Downside of Environmental Regulation: Unexpected Pressures on Minority Communities

In addition to statutory site selection procedures, other environmental regulations governing land use, recycling and waste toxicity have made waste disposal sites more difficult to acquire and thus more likely to locate in minority communities.

To protect fragile elements of the environment, land use regulation can either completely prohibit residential development in environmentally sensitive areas or drastically limit the density of development on each site. When regulation removes certain land from the supply available for building, demand increases for what remains. These measures can drive up the cost of housing so that only middle- and upper-income individuals can afford the environmental amenity. In this manner, the poor and racial minorities may not only be on the receiving end of the waste disposal but also may not be able to afford to live in an area benefitted by sound environmental regulation. . . .

Zoning and building codes that address recycling also increase the cost of land development and thus encourage development in areas with inexpensive land and a small or uninformed population. At the federal level, the EPA wants the nation to divert 25% of its waste stream to recycling by 1992. Many states currently require that a portion of each municipal waste stream be recycled, with a planned increase in recycling to occur within the next several years. For example, the California Integrated Waste Management Act requires each city and county to have reduced its current solid waste stream by 25% in 1995 and by 50% in 2000. The Act directs these jurisdictions to adopt a comprehensive integrated solid waste management plan that includes not only recycling and source reduction requirements, but also any building code or zoning ordinance amendments necessary to ensure adequate storage space for source-separated materials. One jurisdiction, the City of Sacramento, has enacted a zoning ordinance that specifies the mandatory location, size and design features of recycling containers for new and existing commercial buildings and for residential developments with five or more units. Environmentalists espouse these recycling measures and applaud them. However, such regulation inevitably subjects waste siting decisions and site assembly to greater economic pressure. In turn, such economic pressure can strengthen the incentive to place waste sites in minority areas where not only is land less expensive but also site assembly costs are lower because of ineffectual community resistance.

EPA regulations that define toxic chemicals and address the identification and disposal of hazardous waste also make site selection more difficult. The EPA published its final ruling on toxicity characteristics in 1990. Twenty-five new organic chemical compounds have been added to an official inventory of toxic constituents that can cause waste to be classified as hazardous. If a solid waste has the ability to leach any of these compounds at levels above EPA specified limits, it is classified and regulated as hazardous under the Resource Conservation and Recovery Act. The rules apply to both large and small quantity solid waste and waste water generators. Also, newly regulated generators must notify the EPA and acquire an EPA identification number.

The EPA predicts that this rule will increase the amount of waste classified as hazardous roughly three-fold. These regulations will increase the complexity and cost of hazardous waste disposal and thereby increase development pressure on communities that are unable to resist siting decisions.

## Economic Efficiency Versus Political Will

By simple economics, waste disposal facilities frequently locate where the land and site assembly costs are lower. Less expensive land will often be targeted for waste siting; likewise, areas with existing landfills will already have lowered property values and thus will more likely be targets for new landfills. As governments have developed and promulgated regulations to control the ecological costs of toxic and hazardous wastes, the development pressure on those communities that already have a disproportionate share of waste transfer and disposal sites has increased. Some states have pursued siting approaches that impose the social costs only on the community with the hazardous waste facility while the entire state enjoys the benefit. In other states, however, the developer or the state itself must pay the host community for these social costs.

In sheer market terms, increased hazardous waste generation and large profit margins have greatly increased demand for sites. Hazardous waste generation is increasing at an estimated rate of 5.5% per year. Estimated revenues from remediation and waste cleanup alone were $3.25 billion in 1990 and are expected to grow 115% by 1996. Certain communities, largely "poor, rural, and minority communities," are targeted for these new waste sites based on their perceived inability to resist a site. These economic dynamics, including the lower property values that are often characteristic of minority neighborhoods, lead to the inequitable distribution of waste sites. Achieving equitable distribution of waste sites, then, becomes an act of political will and moral justice and not an exercise in economic efficiency. People of color often lack the political will to overcome these problems because they have not yet garnered sufficient support from mainstream environmental organizations.

Part of the explanation of how the problem of environmental inequity developed lies in the ambivalence of traditionally white environmental groups to the issues of race and equity. Mainline environmental organizations have few minority members on their staffs or on their boards of directors. The supervisory, managerial and executive work force at the EPA also is made up of mainly non-minority males.

The post–World War II migration to the suburbs by whites shaped many of the traditional American environmental values of open space, biodiversity and things green. In many ways, this migration helped to encapsulate the earlier conservation basis of environmentalism into neat, isolated islands of residential oneness with nature. Unfortunately, the problems of pollution are ecologically based in regional systems of air, land and water and do not observe human geo-political boundaries. In the 1970s, groundwater, pollution, acid rain and holes in the ozone finally brought troubling issues of pollution home to the suburbs. The Audubon Society noted "[n]ow the environmental groups are looking hard at toxic waste facilities and garbage incinerators. And, as they squint across decades of indifference to the plight of the cities, they are seeing the wreckage left behind when their parents and grand-parents fled."

The racial stratification of the environmental movement occurred despite the pleas of poor and racial minority communities for some relief from the burden of a dis-proportionate amount of waste. The inclusion of these previously environmentally disenfranchised groups is one of the major changes necessary in American Environ-mentalism. It is also one of its greatest challenges.

*Vicki Been*

# Locally Undesirable Land Uses in Minority Neighborhoods: Disproportionate Siting or Market Dynamics? (1994)

The environmental justice movement contends that people of color and the poor are exposed to greater environmental risks than are whites and wealthier individuals. The movement charges that this disparity is due in part to racism and classism in the siting of environmental risks, the promulgation of environmental laws and regulations, the enforcement of environmental laws, and the attention given to the cleanup of polluted areas. To support the first charge—that the siting of waste dumps, polluting factories, and other locally undesirable land uses (LULUs) has been racist and classist—advocates for environmental justice have cited more than a dozen studies analyzing the relationship between neighborhoods' socioeconomic characteristics and the number of LULUs they host. The studies demonstrate that those neighborhoods in which LULUs are located have, on average, a higher percentage of racial minorities and are poorer than non-host communities.

That research does not, however, establish that the host communities were disproportionately minority or poor at the time the sites were selected. Most of the studies compare the *current* socioeconomic characteristics of communities that host various LULUs to those of communities that do not host such LULUs. This approach leaves open the possibility that the sites for LULUs were chosen fairly, but that subsequent events produced the current disproportion in the distribution of LULUs. In other words, the research fails to prove environmental justice advocates' claim that the dis-

Reprinted by permission of The Yale Law Journal Company and Fred B. Rothman & Company from *The Yale Law Journal*, Vol. 103, pages 1383–1422.

proportionate burden poor and minority communities now bear in hosting LULUs is the result of racism and classism in the *siting process* itself.

In addition, the research fails to explore an alternative or additional explanation for the proven correlation between the current demographics of communities and the likelihood that they host LULUs. Regardless of whether the LULUs originally were sited fairly, it could well be that neighborhoods surrounding LULUs became poorer and became home to a greater percentage of people of color over the years following the sitings. Such factors as poverty, housing discrimination, and the location of jobs, transportation, and other public services may have led the poor and racial minorities to "come to the nuisance"—to move to neighborhoods that host LULUs—because those neighborhoods offered the cheapest available housing. Despite the plausibility of that scenario, none of the existing research on environmental justice has examined how the siting of undesirable land uses has subsequently affected the socioeconomic characteristics of host communities. Because the research fails to prove that the siting process causes any of the disproportionate burden the poor and minorities now bear, and because the research has ignored the possibility that market dynamics may have played some role in the distribution of that burden, policymakers now have no way of knowing whether the siting process is "broke" and needs fixing. Nor can they know whether even an ideal siting system that ensured a perfectly fair initial distribution of LULUs would result in any long-term benefit to the poor or to people of color. . . .

## Market Dynamics and the Distribution of LULUs

The residential housing market in the United States is extremely dynamic. Every year, approximately 17% to 20% of U.S. households move to a new home. Some of those people stay within the same neighborhood, but many move to different neighborhoods in the same city, or to different cities. Some people decide to move, at least in part, because they are dissatisfied with the quality of their current neighborhoods. Once a household decides to move, its choice of a new neighborhood usually depends somewhat on the cost of housing and the characteristics of the neighborhood. Those two factors are interrelated because the quality of the neighborhood affects the price of housing.

The siting of a LULU can influence the characteristics of the surrounding neighborhood in two ways. First, an undesirable land use may cause those who can afford to move to become dissatisfied and leave the neighborhood. Second, by making the neighborhood less desirable, the LULU may decrease the value of the neighborhood's property, making the housing more available to lower income households and less attractive to higher income households. The end result of both influences is likely to be that the neighborhood becomes poorer than it was before the siting of the LULU.

The neighborhood also is likely to become home to more people of color. Racial discrimination in the sale and rental of housing relegates people of color (especially African-Americans) to the least desirable neighborhoods, regardless of their income level. Moreover, once a neighborhood becomes a community of color, racial discrimination in the promulgation and enforcement of zoning and environmental protection laws, the provision of municipal services, and the lending practices of banks may cause neighborhood quality to decline further. That additional decline, in turn, will induce those who can leave the neighborhood—the least poor and those least subject to discrimination—to do so.

The dynamics of the housing market therefore are likely to cause the poor and people of color to move to or remain in the neighborhoods in which LULUs are located, regardless of the demographics of the communities when the LULUs were first sited. As long as the market allows the existing distribution of wealth to allocate goods and services, it would be surprising indeed if, over the long run, LULUs did not impose a disproportionate burden upon the poor. And as long as the market discriminates on the basis of race, it would be remarkable if LULUs did not eventually impose a disproportionate burden upon people of color.

By failing to address how LULUs have affected the demographics of their host communities, the current research has ignored the possibility that the correlation between the location of LULUs and the socioeconomic characteristics of neighborhoods may be a function of aspects of our free market system other than, or in addition to, the siting process. It is crucial to examine that possibility. Both the justice of the distribution of LULUs and the remedy for any injustice may differ if market dynamics play a significant role in the distribution.

If the siting process is primarily responsible for the correlation between the location of LULUs and the demographics of host neighborhoods, the process may be unjust under current constitutional doctrine, at least as to people of color. Siting processes that result in the selection of host neighborhoods that are disproportionately poor (but not disproportionately composed of people of color) would not be unconstitutional because the Supreme Court has been reluctant to recognize poverty as a suspect classification. A siting process motivated by racial prejudice, however, would be unconstitutional. A process that disproportionately affects people of color also would be unfair under some statutory schemes and some constitutional theories of discrimination.

On the other hand, if the disproportionate distribution of LULUs results from market forces which drive the poor, regardless of their race, to live in neighborhoods that offer cheaper housing because they host LULUs, then the fairness of the distribution becomes a question about the fairness of our market economy. Some might argue that the disproportionate burden is part and parcel of a free market economy that is, overall, fairer than alternative schemes, and that the costs of regulating the market to reduce the disproportionate burden outweigh the benefits of doing so. Others might argue that those moving to a host neighborhood are compensated through the market for the disproportionate burden they bear by lower housing costs, and therefore that the situation is just. Similarly, some might contend that while the poor suffer lower quality neighborhoods, they also suffer lower quality food, housing, and medical care, and that the systemic problem of poverty is better addressed through income redistribution programs than through changes in siting processes.

Even if decisionmakers were to agree that it is unfair to allow post-siting market dynamics to create disproportionate environmental risk for the poor or minorities, the remedy for that injustice would have to be much more fundamental than the remedy for unjust siting *decisions*. Indeed, if market forces are the primary cause of the correlation between the presence of LULUs and the current socioeconomic characteristics of a neighborhood, even a siting process radically revised to ensure that LULUs are distributed equally among all neighborhoods may have only a short-term effect. The areas surrounding LULUs distributed equitably will become less desirable neighborhoods, and thus may soon be left to people of color or the poor, recreating the pattern of inequitable siting. Accordingly, if a disproportionate burden results from or is exacerbated by market dynamics, an effective remedy might require such reforms as stricter enforcement of laws against housing discrimination, more serious efforts to achieve residential integration, changes in the processes of siting low and moderate income housing, changes in programs designed to aid the poor in securing decent housing, greater regulatory protection for those neighborhoods that are chosen to host LULUs, and changes in production and consumption processes to reduce the number of LULUs needed.

Information about the role market dynamics play in the distribution of LULUs would promote a better understanding of the nature of the problem of environmental injustice and help point the way to appropriate solutions for the problem. Nonetheless, market dynamics have been largely ignored by the current research on environmental justice.

## The Evidence of Disproportionate Siting

Several recent studies have attempted to assess whether locally undesirable land uses are disproportionately located in neighborhoods that are populated by more people of color or are more poor than is normal. The most important of the studies was published in 1987 by the United Church of Christ Commission for Racial Justice (CRJ). The CRJ conducted a cross-sectional study of the racial and socioeconomic characteristics of residents of the zip code areas surrounding 415 commercial hazardous waste facilities and compared those characteristics to those of zip code areas which did not have such facilities. The study revealed a correlation between the number of commercial hazardous waste facilities in an area and the percentage of the "nonwhite" population in the area. Areas that had one operating commercial hazardous waste facility, other than a landfill, had about twice as many people of color as a percentage of the population as those that had no such facility. Areas that had more than one operating facility, or had one of the five largest landfills, had more than three times the percentage of minority residents as areas that had no such facilities.

Several regional and local studies buttress the findings of the nationwide CRJ study. The most frequently cited of those studies, which is often credited for first giving the issue of environmental justice visibility, was conducted by the United States General

Accounting Office (GAO). The GAO examined the racial and socioeconomic characteristics of the communities surrounding four hazardous waste landfills in the eight southeastern states that make up EPA's Region IV. The sites studied include some of the largest landfills in the United States.

The results of the study are summarized in Table A. In short, three of the four communities where such landfills were sited were majority African-American in 1980; African-Americans made up 52%, 66%, and 90% of the population in those three communities. In contrast, African-Americans made up between 22% and 30% of the host states' populations. The host communities were all disproportionately poor, with between 26% and 42% of the population living below the poverty level. In comparison, the host states' poverty rates ranged from 14% to 19%.

Another frequently cited local study was conducted by sociologist Robert Bullard and formed important parts of his books, *Invisible Houston* and *Dumping in Dixie*. Professor Bullard found that although African-Americans made up only 28% of the Houston population in 1980, six of Houston's eight incinerators and mini-incinerators and fifteen of seventeen landfills were located in predominantly African-American neighborhoods.

With one exception, described below, none of the existing studies addressed the question of which came first—the people of color and the poor, or the LULU. As noted by the CRJ, the studies "were not designed to show cause and effect," but only to explore the relationship between the current distribution of LULUs and host communities' demographics. The evidence of disproportionate siting is thus incomplete: it does not establish that *the siting process* had a disproportionate effect upon minorities or the poor.

Professor James T. Hamilton of Duke University has performed the only research to date that has addressed the "which came first" question. Professor Hamilton recently examined how the planned capacity changes for hazardous waste processing facilities in 1987, correlated with the political power (measured by voter registration) of the facilities' host counties as of the 1980 census. In the course of his study, Professor Hamilton also examined correlations between planned capacity changes and county demographics. Because Professor Hamilton's analysis examined decisions about whether to expand or contract facilities that were made five or six years after the census from which data on the county's socioeconomic characteristics were derived, and because decisions to expand or contract capacity share some of the same characteristics as initial siting decisions, his analysis is probative of whether there is a correlation between siting decisions and the characteristics of affected communities near the time of those decisions. Professor Hamilton concluded that when other factors were controlled, the race and income of the county at the time of the expansion decisions were not significant predictors of expansion plans. Race was a statistically significant determinant of the facilities' plans to reduce capacity, however; as the percentage of a county's minority population increased, it was less likely that the facility planned to reduce its capacity.

In addition, Professor Hamilton compared 1970 census data regarding the counties in which surveyed facilities were sited in the 1970's and early 1980's to census data for all counties in the United States. Professor Hamilton found that both race and

TABLE A.   Summary of GAO's Findings

| Landfill | Population | Mean Family Income | | Population Below Poverty Level |
| --- | --- | --- | --- | --- |
| | % African-American | All Races | African-American | % |
| Chemical Waste | 90 | $11,198 | $10,752 | 42 |
| SCA Services | 38 | 16,372 | 6,781 | 31 |
| Ind. Chem. | 52 | 18,996 | 12,941 | 26 |
| Warren Cty. PCB | 66 | 10,367 | 9,285 | 32 |

median household income were statistically significant predictors of sitings during the 1970's and early 1980's. Professor Hamilton's study has several limitations: the sample did not include facilities that went out of business before the 1987 survey; the data examined was for entire counties rather than the tracts or county subdivisions in which the facility was actually located; and the 1970 census data was used even for siting decisions made in the early 1980's. The study nevertheless provides important evidence that the siting process itself has had a disproportionate effect on low income communities and communities of color. Professor Hamilton did not examine whether the socioeconomic characteristics of host communities changed once the facilities were sited, however, so his study does not provide any evidence about the role that market dynamics may play in the distribution of LULUs.

In summary, with the exception of Professor Hamilton's study, the existing research fails to focus on the characteristics of communities at the time LULUs were sited, and therefore cannot establish whether the correlation between a neighborhood's current demographics and the number of LULUs it hosts was caused by the siting process. None of the existing research examines how market dynamics affected the socioeconomic characteristics of host neighborhoods. The literature therefore sheds little light on whether the current distribution of LULUs resulted from siting processes that had a disproportionate effect upon minorities and the poor, or from market dynamics, or both.

## Did the Siting Disparities Revealed by the GAO and Professor Bullard Result from Siting Practices, Market Dynamics or Both?

To begin to fill the gaps in the literature, this Part expands the GAO and Bullard studies described above. First, it adds to those studies data regarding the socioeconomic characteristics of the host communities at the time the siting decisions were made.

Second, it traces changes in the demographics of the host communities since the sitings took place.

### The GAO Study

... [A]n examination of the characteristics of the host communities at issue in the GAO's study at the time the facilities were sited shows that the host communities were home to a considerably larger percentage of African-Americans and were somewhat poorer than other communities within the host states. The analysis therefore suggests that the siting process had a disproportionate effect on the poor and people of color. At the same time, the analysis provides no support for the theory that the location of LULUs in poor or minority communities is a result of the dynamics of the housing market.

### The Bullard Study

... [E]xamining the data for the census closest to the date of each siting decision shows that the siting process had a disproportionate effect upon African-Americans. In addition, such an analysis provides considerable support for the theory that market dynamics contribute to the disproportionate burden LULUs impose upon people of color and the poor. As the argument that LULUs change a neighborhood's demographics by driving down property values would predict, the data reveal that the homes surrounding the landfill sites in most of the host neighborhoods became less valuable properties relative to other areas of Harris County after the landfills were sited, and the host communities became increasingly populated by African-Americans and increasingly poor. ...

## Conclusion

... The preliminary evidence derived from this extension of two of the leading studies of environmental justice, along with evidence offered by Professor Hamilton's study of capacity expansion plans, shows that research examining the socioeconomic characteristics of host neighborhoods at the time they were selected, then tracing changes in those characteristics following the siting, would go a long way toward answering the question of which came first—the LULU or its minority or poor neighbors. Until that research is complete, proposed "solutions" to the problem of disproportionate siting run a substantial risk of missing the mark.

*First National People of Color*
*Environmental Leadership Summit*

# Principles of Environmental Justice (1991)

We, the People of Color, are gathered together at this First National People of Color Environmental Leadership Summit, to begin to build a national movement of all peoples of color to fight the destruction of our lands and communities, do hereby reestablish our spiritual interdependence to the sacredness of our Mother Earth; we respect and celebrate each of our cultures, languages and beliefs about the natural world and our roles in healing ourselves; to insure environmental justice; to promote economic alternatives which would contribute to the development of environmentally safe livelihoods; and to secure our political, economic and cultural liberation that has been denied for over 500 years of colonization and oppression, resulting in the poisoning of our communities and land and the genocide of our peoples, do affirm and adopt these Principles of Environmental Justice.

1. Environmental justice affirms the sacredness of Mother Earth, ecological unity and the interdependence of all species, and the right to be free from ecological destruction.
2. Environmental justice demands that public policy be based on mutual respect and justice for all peoples, free from any form of discrimination or bias.
3. Environmental justice mandates the right to ethical, balanced and responsible uses of land and renewable resources in the interest of a sustainable planet for humans and other living things.
4. Environmental justice calls for universal protection from extraction, production and disposal of toxic/hazardous wastes and poisons that threaten the fundamental right to clean air, land, water and food.
5. Environmental justice affirms the fundamental right to political, economic, cultural and environmental self-determination to all peoples.

6. Environmental justice demands the cessation of the production of all toxins, hazardous wastes, and radioactive substances, and that all past and current producers be held strictly accountable to the people for detoxification and the containment at the point of production.

7. Environmental justice demands the right to participate as equal partners at every level of decision-making including needs assessment, planning, implementation, enforcement and evaluation.

8. Environmental justice affirms the right of all workers to a safe and healthy work environment, without being forced to choose between an unsafe livelihood and unemployment It also affirms the right of those who work at home to be free from environmental hazards.

9. Environmental justice protects the rights of victims of environmental injustice to receive full compensation and reparations for damages as well as quality health care.

10. Environmental justice considers governmental acts of environmental injustice a violation of international law, the Universal Declaration on Human Rights, and the United Nations Convention on Genocide.

11. Environmental justice recognizes the special legal relationship of Native Americans to the U.S. government through treaties, agreements, compacts, and covenants affirming their sovereignty and self-determination.

12. Environmental justice affirms the need for an urban and rural ecology to clean up and rebuild our cities and rural areas in balance with nature, honoring the cultural integrity of all our communities, and providing fair access for all to the full range of resources.

13. Environmental justice calls for the strict enforcement of principles of informed consent, and a halt to the testing of experimental reproductive and medical procedures and vaccinations on people of color.

14. Environmental justice opposes the destructive operations of multi-national corporations.

15. Environmental justice opposes military occupations, repression and exploitation of lands, peoples and cultures.

16. Environmental justice calls for the education of present and future generations which emphasizes social and environmental issues, based on our experience and an appreciation of our diverse cultural perspectives.

17. Environmental justice requires that we, as individuals, make personal and consumer choices to consume as little of Mother Earth's resources and to produce as little waste as possible; and make the conscious decision to challenge and reprioritize our lifestyles to insure the health of the natural world for present and future generations.

*Richard J. Lazarus*

# The Meaning and Promotion of Environmental Justice (1994)

## What Is "Environmental Justice"?

"Environmental Justice" focuses on the distribution of environmental hazards across society and seeks a fair distribution of those hazards. Environmental justice includes within its purview the distributional implications of the environmental protection laws designed to redress those hazards, which have their own distinct set of benefits and burdens.

The origins of the environmental justice movement are illustrative. The beginning of the environmental justice movement is usually traced to the 1982 protests against the siting of a PCB landfill in a predominantly African American community in Warren County, North Carolina. At the First National People of Color Environmental Leadership Conference held in Washington, D.C., in October 1991, the Warren County protests were frequently discussed and celebrated. One of the most telling moments at the Conference, however, was when an unidentified person from Emelle, Alabama, rose to speak. She commended those active in the Warren County protests for their work, but she explained that the result of their efforts was that waste destined for Warren County, North Carolina, had instead ended up being transported and incinerated in Emelle, Alabama. The population of Emelle is approximately 80 percent African American. The environmental risks associated with environmental protection (the incineration of PCBs) were reduced, but they also were redistributed geographically. And, in a pattern that seems to have been repeated throughout the nation, those new risks finally were located in a racial minority community.

What "environmental justice" teaches is that environmental policymakers need to be concerned about more than the two basic issues of (1) what is the "correct" amount

Richard J. Lazarus, The Meaning and Promotion of Environmental Justice, 5 Md. J. Contemp. Legal Issues 1 (1994).

of pollution (the laws of thermodynamics suggest the foolhardiness of assuming that answer is always zero); and (2) what is the most economically efficient way to meet that standard (e.g., command and control regulations and standards versus market incentives). These are critical inquiries, to be sure, but they should not be the exclusive focus of policymakers.

During the past twenty-five years of the modern environmental law era, however, environmental policymakers largely ignored the distributional consequences of their actions. Consideration of distributional consequences was characterized as raising "social" issues that had little to do with the kinds of "technical" and "scientific" judgments considered central to the establishment of environmental protection programs. Distribution of hazards was not an independent public interest consideration in the formation of environmental policy.

Presumably, most policymakers simply assumed that it was safe not to focus on distribution. At worst, they may have assumed that environmental protection would result in a neutral distribution of the benefits and burdens (including environmental risks) created by environmental protection programs—certainly, there was no reason to believe that there would be an unfair distributional skewing. At best, the resulting distribution would likely be progressive—minority and low income communities appeared to be the disproportionate victims of environmental pollution, and therefore, should be the disproportionate beneficiaries of cleanup efforts. Accordingly, Congress, the Environmental Protection Agency (EPA), and the environmental public interest community gave very little consideration to distributional issues, particularly as they pertained to either income or race.

In making these assumptions, policymakers ignored several countervailing factors, which have proven quite significant. The first was that even a notion as basic as "environmental protection" is replete with distributional implications. The most significant factor is the potential for risk aggregation. An environmental cleanup, for instance, does not eliminate pollution; it reduces the associated environmental risks. The cleanup of a hazardous waste site, therefore, may reduce the environmental risks from 100 to 20 residual units of risk. The same is true for air and water pollution control. Neither eliminates all risk (or pollution). They instead seek to minimize risk consistent with applicable health, safety, technological, and economic standards.

In reducing overall societal risk (the benefit), moreover, the laws generally convert environmental risks of one kind or at one location to residual risks of another kind or at another location (the burden). As one commentator succinctly put it, "[t]he present regime concentrates on moving pollution from one place to another. . . . The initial destination of pollutants may be altered, but the pollutants ultimately reenter the flow of material in the environment."

The problem of aggregation is realized when the residual risks from a series of distinct cleanup activities are all brought together in one place. Thus, the 20 units of residual risk from a host of hazardous waste cleanup activities might all be brought to the same disposal site. The obvious problem is that the geographical location of the new site for residual risks is worse off, as are those who reside in that community. To be sure, because the total amount of environmental risk will be significantly lower than before, society as a whole is far better off. But that does not mean that those exposed to the site of aggregation of residual risks are better off. Indeed, they may be far worse off.

There are good theoretical reasons to expect that such aggregation would occur in racial minority communities. First, there is no reason to assume that all of those responsible for making the relevant decisions are immune from racist attitudes or, at the very least, from relying on the kinds of racially stereotypical judgments that might produce aggregation in such communities, e.g., minorities care less about environmental protection than others. It also cannot be denied that the vestiges of decades of *de jure* racist policies in this country, while now unlawful, are self-perpetuating. Racial minorities have fewer of the economic and political resources necessary to influence the legislative or regulatory priorities that determine whether and where risk aggregation is likely to occur.

Finally, many minority communities are unlikely to be in an effective position to protect themselves from the aggregation of the environmental risks. The environmental quality promised by environmental protection laws is not self-executing. Its realization ultimately depends on effective enforcement at the ground level. This includes enforcement during the siting process to ensure that those facilities that are sited are regulated to the full extent necessary, or, at the very least, that the maximum economic rent is extracted on behalf of the locality, as well as subsequent enforcement to ensure actual compliance with all applicable requirements.

Government resources dedicated to compliance monitoring and enforcement, however, have never been anywhere near commensurate to the level of regulated activities. Congress has never appropriated the funds necessary for the actual accomplishment of all of the ambitious programs provided for in the federal environmental laws. Environmental protection laws regulate literally hundreds of thousands of sources of pollution. To enforce compliance with all applicable pollution control standards would require a federal and state effort several orders of magnitude greater than that which presently exists.

Hence, it is often EPA's own allocation of its scarce enforcement resources that determines which communities are in fact most protected from environmental risks. The kinds of factors that affect how EPA's enforcement resources are generally allocated on a day-to-day basis (which occurs mostly at the level of regional agency offices) have likely worked against the interest of many minority communities. Agency personnel naturally respond more readily to individuals who have the access, clout, or basic know-how of agency operations necessary to command their attention. The cumulative effect of factors as basic as whether EPA inspectors prefer to spend their time inspecting a facility in the suburbs rather than in poor urban ghettos can skew enforcement efforts. A conscious racial motivation is not required to produce a disproportionate result.

One example of how enforcement-related factors can produce disparate environmental results is the case of the Anacostia and Potomac Rivers. Both run through and near Washington, D.C., and both are subject to the Clean Water Act's pollution control program. However, the polluted Anacostia, which runs through poorer, minority communities, compares very unfavorably with the cleaner Potomac, which runs through wealthier, nonminority communities.

To be sure, Congress anticipated the federal and state environmental enforcement shortfall and, for that reason, included generous citizen suit provisions in virtually all of the federal environmental protection laws. Those provisions, along with rigorous reporting requirements, are designed to allow adversely affected private citizens to make up for the shortfall in available government enforcement resources. But, given the sheer complexity (indeed seeming impenetrability) of much environmental protection law, such supplemental enforcement has been realized only by either those communities with the economic resources required to hire environmental law experts or those fortunate enough to be associated with national environmental law public interest group citizen suit programs. According to those in many racial minority communities, however, until quite recently, national environmental organizations had little interest in representing their communities.

A very real danger therefore exists that the worst environmental hazards will be found or placed in localities where there is also the least effective monitoring and enforcement. Particularly vulnerable in this respect are those communities whose members are not in a good position to resist the siting of undesirable facilities, to ensure that those facilities that are permitted are required to comply with stringent health and safety requirements, or to ensure that, once sited, those facilities actually comply with such limitations on their operation. Such communities are likewise not in the best position to ensure that they receive their fair share of the economic benefits of the facility through, for instance, permitting exactions.

## How Can We Achieve Environmental Justice?

The first step toward achieving environmental justice is to recognize that distributional injustice exists and that race is a contributing factor to this injustice. Socioeconomics, too, is plainly important. But socioeconomics is neither unrelated to race, nor is it likely the exclusive factor. While widely condemned, racist attitudes and stereotypical judgments are also widely held and known to influence private and public decisionmaking in a wide range of areas. The significance of environmental justice lies in part in its ability to educate about how far the problem of race discrimination extends.

A second important threshold step is to recognize that equity is relevant to environmental law policymaking. Whether in the distribution of the benefits or the burdens created by environmental protection laws, equity has intrinsic value. It is worthy of resource expenditure, independent of (and sometimes at the expense of) allocation efficiency objectives.

Heightened emphasis on distributional fairness is also likely to promote greater allocation efficiency. By focusing on distributional factors, government officials are more likely to identify those areas where the biggest problems are presented, i.e., where environmental risks are aggregated and noncompliance is greatest. Those same areas are, of course, where enforcement resources can have their greatest return. A distributional focus, therefore, promotes more efficient enforcement.

There are also a series of concrete measures that environmental policymakers can take to further environmental justice goals. For instance, Congress could amend existing laws to require an accounting of distributional concerns. Unlike environmental protection laws, natural resources laws have long contained provisions that address—and in many cases redress—the distributional implications of the laws themselves. The substantive provisions of environmental protection law could similarly account for such concerns. They could do so merely by requiring that such matters be considered, leaving the agency with the discretion to determine how best to strike the balance, or, going even further, the law could dictate how the balance should be struck.

The proposed Environmental Justice Act of 1992, co-sponsored by Representative John Lewis (D-Ga.) and then-Senator Al Gore (D-Tenn.) provides an example of an approach. That bill, if enacted, would have required the EPA to identify areas of aggregated environmental risk and then to allocate enforcement resources to such areas. The bill further called for a moratorium on the siting of facilities that would impose further environmental risks in such pre-existing "environmental high impact areas" under certain prescribed circumstances.

Legislation currently under consideration by Congress ranges from structural reform, like the Senate-passed proposal to create a sub-cabinet level Office of Environmental Justice, to more substantive, mandatory provisions being debated in the House; one proposal would create an advisory council that could represent "environmentally disadvantaged groups" and provide citizens with enforceable rights; another proposal would allow residents of an "environmentally disadvantaged community" to challenge the siting of a new waste facility in their community.

Significant reform is also possible in the absence of statutory amendment. For instance, the President could issue an executive order requiring federal agency consideration of the distributional implications of environmental protection (and/or other federal policies and programs) for low income persons and racial minorities. President Reagan did as much for allocation efficiency goals in Executive Order No. 12291. Distributional fairness certainly deserves its own emphasis.

EPA also has significant unexercised authority to promote distributional fairness. Title VI of the Civil Rights Act of 1964 is one potential source of authority that, as I have explained elsewhere, has not yet been fully tapped. Indeed, the United States Commission on Civil Rights recently began to investigate EPA's compliance with Title VI. The White House is reportedly in the process of drafting an executive order that admonishes all federal agencies to comply strictly with Title VI to ensure that the burdens and benefits of federally-funded pollution control programs are distributed in a nondiscriminatory fashion. And, finally, EPA is currently considering the merits of at least two Title VI administrative complaints filed against state environmental agencies based on the discriminatory effects of those states' administration of federally-funded environmental protection programs.

EPA can also accomplish much under existing environmental protection laws. For instance, EPA could use the nonattainment provisions of the Clean Air Act to promote a more progressive and environmentally protective distribution of federal transportation funds. Federal funds for highway construction tend to subsidize individuals who choose to commute into the city from wealthier suburbs; they also increase vehicular miles travelled (VMTS) in contravention of clean air goals. By contrast, mass transit can be consistent with both air quality requirements (by reducing VMTS) and environmental justice goals (by subsidizing modes of transportation used by lower income persons). While EPA has not yet focused on the potential for mass transit to harmonize the agency's environmental justice and clean air goals, the agency has recently indicated a willingness to consider environmental equity in developing and choosing among options for meeting Clean Air Act requirements.

EPA and the states could also revisit some of the assumptions underlying their environmental protection standards that fail to account for the differences in communities. In particular, those setting standards purporting to protect public health may fail to provide adequate protection to certain racial minority communities by not accounting for how many community differences, whether cultural or socioeconomic, may cause some persons to be exposed more frequently than assumed or to be more sensitive to specified levels of pollution than assumed. For example, existing EPA modeling techniques for the setting of water pollution control standards may have disadvantaged African American urban communities by not considering the fact that many members of those communities may consume larger than average amounts of fish caught from polluted urban waterways.

Federal and state environmental protection agencies can also strive to level the playing field for communities that possess relatively few of the resources necessary to protect their interests in the processes related to the siting of environmentally risky facilities. Such facilities may have to be sited somewhere; and, to the extent that the facilities lower property values, there may be some merit to the argument that siting in certain low income areas is unavoidable. But even assuming the necessity for such siting, government remains responsible for ensuring that procedural safeguards are in place, that strict substantive standards are imposed, and, when applicable, that the affected communities receive their proportionate share of the economic benefits of the sited facilities.

Presently, the possible economic advantages are typically proffered to justify the siting of a particular facility in a minority community. However, the economic benefits (unlike the burdens) are not necessarily enjoyed by those in the immediate locale. Instead, persons from distant commuting communities often tend to gain from the newly-created employment. The host communities generally have not extracted significant transfer payments from industries in exchange for the burdens imposed on them by the facility.

Federal and state environmental protection agencies also need to enhance the ability of host communities to protect their interests through citizen suit enforcement when necessary. Congress intended such suits as an important supplement to federal and state efforts. The government could promote such lawsuits by providing technical and legal assistance—perhaps something akin to the EPA's National Enforcement Training Institute, which now provides training for government enforcement personnel.

At the very least, much could be achieved by simply lending training support to legal services offices. These offices are often the primary provider of legal services for many persons in low income communities. Presumably because of a lack of familiarity with environmental protection laws, legal services have not, historically, viewed such laws as especially relevant to their clients' lives. With the recent challenge to that view, some legal service offices have begun to initiate environmental lawsuits. Rather than discourage such efforts, federal and state environmental agencies should embrace their initiatives.

The United States Department of Justice could also play an important role. Although the Department is not a major environmental policymaker, it could send an important message. The Department's Environment and Natural Resources Division could create an environmental equity enforcement initiative by bringing a coordinated series of enforcement actions in those communities where environmental hazards are aggregated and where historically there has been minimal enforcement. An environmental equity initiative would send a clear message to the regulated community: Compliance with environmental protection laws is expected, and facilities in low income and racial minority communities are no different.

Finally, the environmental public interest community needs to rethink its own priorities or risk becoming irrelevant. The problems of the urban poor, including the unhealthy environment in which they live, should be a primary item on the agenda of environmentalists. But at the same time, as the national environmental organizations rush to embrace environmental justice concerns, these organizations must be careful not to exploit the issue to its detriment. In particular, they must take care not to exploit the environmental justice issue in their own fund-raising efforts at the expense of local community organizations.

For all those, like myself, who have been involved in the teaching and formulation of environmental law during the past two decades, this is an unsettling time. Environmental justice challenges the status quo. It questions the wisdom and, indeed, the fundamental fairness of much of the significant gains accomplished by the environmental movement. This is no doubt the reason why many involved in the movement have not readily embraced the basic teachings of environmental justice.

But just such an embracing is now warranted. Environmental justice invites environmentalists to return to the roots of environmental law: to look past its important allocation efficiency justifications, and to include distributional fairness between disparate communities, as well as between generations. Environmental justice invites the reintroduction of human health into the ecological equation. That challenge to environmental protection law is not incidental, but it is exciting and ultimately compelling.

# Part II

## Environmental Law and Regulatory Policy

*This part of the book reviews how environmental law and regulatory policy have evolved, tracing their history and examining the political forces that generated the federal regulatory statutes that dominate the field today. The readings provide a structural overview of current law, and they discuss some of the major criticisms of existing approaches to environmental regulation.*

*Chapter 5 explores the early history of environmental regulation. It explains why the common law, despite struggling mightily to adapt to changed circumstances, ultimately proved inadequate to arrest accelerating environmental degradation in the wake of the Industrial Revolution. Although pollution control was primarily a state and local responsibility until after World War II, federal officials were, from an early date, involved in major battles over natural resource policies. The chapter examines the history of an intense battle over the construction of a dam near Yosemite National Park, which marked a major turning point in the history of the conservation movement. It also considers the public health controversy over the introduction of tetraethyl lead additives in gasoline during the 1920s, prior to the advent of comprehensive federal health and safety legislation, when regulatory decisions were made by convening expert panels who tried to reach consensus. The chapter concludes with a discussion of the impact of Rachel Carson's* Silent Spring, *widely credited with spawning the modern environmental movement.*

*Chapter 6 examines the political forces that led to creation of the current federal regulatory infrastructure. It explores the factors that generated a veritable explosion of federal environmental legislation during the 1970s and 1980s. The readings in this chapter consider the roles played by citizen groups, the courts, legislators, and federal agencies in erecting and implementing the laws on the books today. They explore why the enactment of laws is only the first step in a complex process by which laws are translated into regulations designed to affect individual and corporate behavior.*

*Chapter 7 provides a structural overview of the current regulatory system. It provides a nontechnical introduction to the major environmental laws and the types of regulation that they authorize. The readings in the chapter consider the roles of federal and state authorities in implementing and enforcing environmental laws, and the capabilities of courts and agencies to umpire environmental disputes.*

*Chapter 8 reviews the principal approaches to regulation and resource management embodied in the environmental laws. It explores the controversy between advocates of economic incentive approaches and defenders of technology-based, command-and-control regulation. The chapter concludes by considering efforts to reinvent regulation to make it more flexible and efficient, as well as proposals for new strategies to protect the environment.*

# CHAPTER 5

---

# Environmental Regulation in Historical Perspective

To understand our complex system of environmental laws it is important to consider its historical antecedents. Long before federal regulatory legislation came to dominate the field, common law courts struggled to resolve environmental conflicts. Much of our understanding of law and legal history is shaped by celebrated decisions rendered by appellate courts. But, as Lawrence Friedman has demonstrated, focus on appellate decisions tends to obscure understanding of what transpires in the trial courts, where the vast bulk of the legal system's business is processed with far less visibility. In the first reading in this chapter, Joel Brenner describes how common law courts responded to pollution problems generated by the Industrial Revolution. At the dawn of the eighteenth century, English courts articulated the famous legal principle of *sic utere tuo ut alienum non laedas,* that "every man must so use his own as not to damnify another." However, focusing on what typically happened in private nuisance actions in late-nineteenth-century England, Brenner concludes that the law simply "was not being applied in industrial towns," because lawsuits were unpopular and prohibitively expensive. Fearful of discouraging industrialization, courts applied longstanding legal doctrines in a manner that tolerated industrial pollution, holding factories liable only in the rare cases in which wealthy landowners had suffered unusual damage.

The conflicts between environmental and economic interests in late-nineteenth-century England that Brenner highlights persisted in the new world. The second reading focuses on one of the most historically significant natural resource management disputes, which occurred in the United States in the early twentieth century. Environmental historian Roderick Nash describes the impassioned national debate over a proposal to build a dam on the Tuolumne River that would flood Yosemite National Park's magnificent Hetch Hetchy Valley. Nash highlights how the conflict exacerbated the split between the preservationist and conservationist movements in the United States. Preservationist John Muir, founder of the Sierra Club, sought to provoke outrage that such spiritually important wilderness would be destroyed for economic gain. Conservationists Gifford Pinchot and President Theodore Roosevelt maintained that the dam was essential to supply water to earthquake-ravaged San Francisco. Although Muir ultimately lost the battle, the public fury he generated helped validate wilderness preservation as an important public value. Recognition that the American public now cared deeply about preserving the natural environment eventually helped generate a flood of environmental legislation.

Although battles over natural resource management have a long history, efforts to use the law to protect public health from environmental risks have become important only relatively recently. Concern about the long-term health effects of exposure to environmental toxins has generated widespread public support for preventive regulation. But prior to the advent of federal health and safety legislation, public concern over potentially significant health risks rarely generated a regulatory response. Instead, conferences of experts were convened to make reccomendations about how to respond to such concerns. David Rosner and Gerald Markowitz describe how this procedure was used during the public health controversy over the introduction of leaded gasoline in the 1920s. Their article illustrates the difficulty of predicting harm to public health from exposure to environmental toxins until after such exposures have become so widespread that harm becomes manifest. Rosner and Markowitz conclude that societal judgments concerning levels of acceptable risk inevitably involve more than scientific issues; they also embrace political and economic concerns.

The chapter closes with a discussion of the impact of Rachel Carson's *Silent Spring*. This book, widely credited with spawning the modern environmental movement, warned that use of chemical pesticides ultimately would produce grave environmental damage. Carson argued that persistent pesticides like DDT were accumulating in the foodchain and poisoning song birds, leading to a time when spring would no longer be heralded by the sounds of birds. Carson's warning about the coming of this "silent spring" galvanized public concern for the environment that produced an explosion of environmental legislation during the late 1960s and early 1970s.

*Joel Franklin Brenner*

# Nuisance Law and the Industrial Revolution (1974)

The story may be picked up in 1608, when William Aldred brought an action at the Norfolk Assizes against his neighbor Thomas Benton for building a pig sty adjacent to Aldred's house and creating a stink. By "property" English law refers not only to the physical attributes and productive capacity of a thing, but also to a nexus of rights and duties, privileges and obligations which inhere in it. One of those obligations was not to foul the neighbors' air. In arrest of judgment against him, Benton argued that "the building of the house for hogs was necessary for the sustenance of man: and one ought not to have so delicate a nose, that he cannot bear the smell of hogs. . . ." But the plea was thrown out, and Aldred got his judgment. This is not to imply that a mere unpleasant odor from a neighbor's yard would have been good ground for an action. The air and streets in most seventeenth century towns were notoriously foul, and when a plaintiff won such an action we may be sure that the smell was truly wretched. Ordinary comfort and necessity, not fastidious taste, was the criterion. Ruining the view would create no cause of action, explained Wray, C.J., "for prospect . . . is a matter of only of delight, and not of necessity." But if the defendant had blocked the plaintiff's light or created a terrible stink, an action would lie, for both light and clean air are necessary for wholesome habitation.

*Aldred's case* shows how different are the questions appropriate to nuisance from the kind of analysis typical of negligence actions. In negligence the plaintiff must prove that the defendant was under a duty to take care, but in nuisance this is unnecessary. All he must show is that he has been injured by the defendant's conduct, and it is up to the defendant to excuse himself if he can.

One such excuse in an action in negligence is that the defendant's conduct was reasonable. But while reasonableness is not irrelevant in nuisance, its relevance is primarily to the gravity of the plaintiff's alleged injury in light of predominant standards of comfort rather then to the characterization of the defendant's activity. In 1628, for instance, a brewer was told that it was no answer to a nuisance action that beer was necessary. The issue was whether his works gave off offensive smells too close to the plaintiff's house. A tannery was also necessary, said Hide, C.J., since everybody wears shoes, but still it could actually be pulled down if it were a nuisance. If the plaintiff's goods were spoiled and his house rendered uninhabitable, his action would lie.

The reason for the rule, explained Lord Holt in 1705, was the "every man must so use his own as not to damnify another." In the case before him, the wall that separated the defendant's privy from the plaintiff's house had fallen into disrepair—with disgusting consequences for the plaintiff. This must have been a common nuisance in those days, but here the defendant refused to fix the wall. Lord Holt decided against him: "And as every man is bound to look to his cattle, as to keep them out of his neighbour's ground; so he must keep in the filth of his house of office, that it may not flow in upon and damnify his neighbour."

The import of this doctrine is more apparent if we go a step beyond the vocabulary of neighborly relations. Nuisance is the common law of competing land use. In insisting that certain lawful and necessary trades, such as soapboiling, brewing, brick-burning, and calendering, could be closed down and forced to move elsewhere if they were nuisances to the neighborhood, the courts were saying in effect that certain land uses were to be preferred over others. Nuisance therefore had a zoning function, and this function of allocating activities to appropriate areas was explicitly recognized. In the seventeenth century a brewery on Ludgate Hill was closed down by the court and directed "to another use; for that such trades ought not to be in the principal parts of the city, but in the outskirts." Blackstone used similar language. The perpetrator of a nuisance may be enjoined, he said, even if the nuisance arises from a lawful act, "for it is incumbent on him to find some other place to do that act, where it will be less offensive."

By Blackstone's time, however, very few nuisance actions were brought for abatement, with the possible exceptions of those arising from obstruction of light. Most plaintiffs brought actions on the case, which by then had become pretty much the sole remedy. The assize of nuisance and the action *quod permittat posternere* were not actually abolished until 1833, but by then they had long been antiquarian relics. In spite of the fact that it lay only for damages and not for abatement, case was preferred because of its simpler process and because there was no requirement that the parties be freeholders. If a stubborn defendant refused to abate, the plaintiff had to seek an injunction in equity.

Yet not until after 1850 are there reports of plaintiffs seeking to enjoin industrial polluters. The huge expense and great delay involved in equity proceedings can be only part of the explanation of this surprising fact. Potential plaintiffs must have known that courts which rarely granted damage awards against industrial defendants would be unlikely to order a factory to abate. In one case where a copper-smelting works had polluted the air so badly that much of the vegetation and some of the animals in the area had died, the smelting was enjoined. Equitable relief was also granted in two water pollution cases, where the circumstances of the dumping of wastes were altered but the dumping not prevented by the court. But these cases seem to have been unusual because the pollution was particularly serious and its source easily identifiable. On the whole, injunctions or abatement orders were rare indeed. The general rule was that equity courts would "not intervene by way of mandatory injunction, except in cases in which extreme, or at all events, very serious damage will arise from its interference being withheld." Most plaintiffs therefore preferred to seek common law relief in damages. . . .

The primary reason why the common law of nuisance had so little effect either in hampering the pace of industrialization or in preventing the deterioration of the environment was that, while the black-letter law changed little, the field of its applicability became relatively narrower. Two assertions are being made here and deserve to be separated. The first is that the pace of industrialization in England was by nineteenth-century standards extremely rapid and that an attendant consequence was the pollution of the air and water. In general the law tended to facilitate industrialization, and nuisance certainly did not hamper it. The second assertion is that the main explanation of the irrelevance of nuisance to industrialization lies not in the doctrine itself but rather in the fact that it was not applied precisely to those classes of parties who were most responsible for economic growth and pollution.

The argument proceeds in two ways. The first is to look at the law and the way the courts applied it. I will show (1) that during a crucial period in the 1850's and 1860's the law of nuisance was invaded by a standard of care; (2) that the law was applied differently to factories than to private individuals; (3) that nuisance law was hardly applied at all to quasi-public enterprises such as railways, by virtue of their statutory authorization; and (4) that there was no systematic prosecution of public nuisances. A thorough investigation of the records of Quarter Sessions might disclose that there were many more prosecutions than the reports would lead one to believe, but I doubt it.

The second method is to look not at the law but at the state of the environment. To this end I have examined the seriousness of air and river pollution in the last century and have tried to gauge public consciousness of it. But no attempt is made to present a systematic ecological study of nineteenth century England, and even the investigation of air and river pollution is indicative and not exhaustive. One response to material of this kind is always, "Yes, but couldn't it have been worse?" As the answer to that must *always* be, "Of course it could have been worse," the question is not very enlightening. The country was not a legal anarchy and neither did it welcome industrial pollution. But the legislature, the courts, and substantial segments of the public did favor industrialization, and they were anxious not to burden industry with damage actions. A deterioration of the quality of the water and air and a much higher noise level were prices they were willing to pay.

If any course of conduct produces unreasonable interference with a neighbor's use or enjoyment of his property, then that conduct constitutes a legal nuisance. The doctrine of lawfulness is therefore contingent on what the courts at any given time believe to be unreasonable, and we are right to suspect that a change in the application of this branch of the law between the seventeenth century and the nineteenth is in part due to a change in expectations which accompanied the transition from a rural to an urban society. That transition brought with it dramatic changes in the size and distribution of the population. At the beginning of the eighteenth century London had a population of over half a million, but only some 35,000 people lived in the second largest city, Edinburgh, and only two other towns, Bristol and Norwich, had more than 20,000. England, Wales, and Scotland together had a population of about seven million; by 1801 it was about 10.5 million. In the next fifty years that figure doubled, and at the same time the migration to the cities ensured that this vastly increased population lived in more compressed circumstances than ever before. Between 1801 and 1841 London's population grew from 864,845 to 1,873,676, while from 1801 to 1861 the percentage of the country's population living in towns with a population of 20,000 and over increased from just under 17 per cent to more than 38 per cent; that is, it more than doubled. Meanwhile, as the population became urbanized, the nation's economic base shifted rapidly from agriculture to industry, and factories became an established feature of national life. In these circumstances one could expect that the judicial response to reasonable interferences with an occupier's comfort would change significantly. *De facto* changes in nuisance law did not, therefore, require *de jure* changes; a drastically different socio-economic milieu and new levels of tolerance of noise and smoke could accomplish the same thing.

But under the guise of semantic continuity, an actual change in the law itself did occur, at least for a time. What happened was that the notion of reasonableness was applied in a different role. As long as every alleged annoyance was not remediable at law, a court had to evaluate the plaintiff's complaint by striking a balance between his suffering and the general standard of amenity. A plaintiff, said Vice-Chancellor Bruce in 1851, was not entitled to completely "untainted" and "unpolluted" air, but to "air not rendered to an important degree less compatible, or at least not rendered incompatible, with the physical comfort of human existence. . . ." The defendant's brick kiln interfered with this right of the plaintiff's, and his brick burning was enjoined. Levels of comfort change over time, but the element of reasonableness was always there. The vice-chancellor continued:

> ought this inconvenience to be considered in fact as more than fanciful, more than one of mere delicacy or fastidiousness, as an inconvenience materially interfering with the ordinary comfort physically of human existence, not merely according to elegant or dainty modes and habits of living, but according to plain and sober and simple notions among the English people?

This was the balance traditionally implied by "reasonable." The complaint was weighed against general and minimal standards of comfort.

Another kind of balance was also possible. The reasonableness of the standard of amenity could be evaluated in light of the importance of the offending activity and the manner in which the defendant carried it on. This was the balance struck in the mid-nineteenth century, at least temporarily. The case that introduced the change was *Hole* v. *Barlow* in 1858. The Common Pleas ruled that a jury had been properly directed that a nuisance action would not lie if the offending activity was legal, reasonable, and carried on in a convenient place. "[I]t is not everybody," Byles, J., had said at the trial,

> whose enjoyment of life and property is rendered uncomfortable by the carrying on of an offensive or noxious trade in the neighbourhood that can bring an action. If that were so . . . the neighbourhood of Birmingham and Wolverhampton and the other great manufacturing towns of England would be full of persons bringing actions for nuisances arising from the carrying on of noxious or offensive trades in their vicinity, to the great injury of the manufacturing and social interests of the community. I apprehend the law to do this, that no action lies for the use, the reasonable use, of a lawful trade in a convenient and proper place even though some one may suffer annoyance from its being carried on.

The Common Pleas approved this direction. The common law right to clean air, said Willes, J., must be qualified: "necessities may arise for an interference with that right pro bono publico . . . private convenience must yield to public necessity." By comparison with such high-powered legal ammunition, the facts of the case were rather paltry. The plaintiff was the occupant of a house next to the defendant's field. The defendant was going to build some houses on the field and had excavated clay for brick-burning, which was a smelly enterprise because of the lime involved. This was held no nuisance. The right to burn bricks, said Willes, in a moment of fancy, was analogous to the Queen's right to take land compulsorily; both activities were necessary.

*Hole* v. *Barlow* was a radical departure from previous law. Part of the decision's logic may have lain in the modern association of nuisance with the action on the case, which was being transformed into an action for negligence. But the doctrine was nonetheless novel. I have found only one earlier instance where an English court was willing to allow the convenience of the offending activity to be the deciding factor in an action, and that was a case of overriding and obvious public interest. Moreover, it was a decision in equity, not law, where an injunction was sought to prevent the building of a hospital for infectious diseases, on the grounds that the neighborhood would be endangered. The injunction was refused because the hospital was a matter of great public need and benefit and because a hospital is of no use to anyone if it is moved out of town.

The necessity of the offense may also be inferred in one other situation. I have seen no case in modern reports—and heard of none of the Year Books or even in manorial court records—where a nuisance action was brought in respect of smoke coming from a *domestic* fire. Until relatively recently, if a person wanted to cook food or to keep warm in winter he had to build a fire. Without fire, and therefore smoke, these essential human activities were impossible, and there was no question of a court's enjoining or penalizing them simply because they made some smoke. Before *Hole* v. *Barlow*, in other words, the only times the courts had been willing to weigh the importance of the offending activity was when that activity was absolutely indispensable to human life and society: medical care, sustenance, heat.

Under *Hole* v. *Barlow,* the successful plaintiff would probably have had to show that the defendant had acted unreasonably in doing him damage, and the liability would have come to resemble negligence, as it does in America. As it happened, the courts departed from the case rather quickly, although technicalities were found to avoid for a few years the task, which courts always find unpleasant, of having to overturn it. In a case from 1861, for instance, arsenic from the works of calico printers was found to be polluting the town reservoir eleven miles downstream. The question put to the jury was whether the defendant's occupation was a lawful trade, necessary or useful to the community, and carried on in a reasonable and proper manner and place. To such a direction the jury could only answer yes. On appeal, however, the Court of Exchequer reversed the decision, in effect ruling that the jury had been misdirected. Yet they declined to overturn *Hole* v. *Barlow,* because the defendants had produced no evidence to show that their trade was reasonable and had therefore failed to make out an affirmative defense irrespective of the direction.

In the following year the Exchequer Chamber confronted the problem squarely and *Hole* v. *Barlow* was thrown out—but not without several qualifications and a strenuous dissent by Pollock, C.B. As in the previous case, *Hole* had been followed at *nisi prius,* and the Queen's Bench had refused to reverse the decision. The suit again involved fumes from a brick kiln—an annoyance which the defendant said was only temporary while he built his house. But Bramwell, B., said that the nuisance was substantial and that it was the defendant's duty to excuse himself. As for its being temporary, he said that if the defendant burned bricks only until he had exhausted the brick earth, that too would be "temporary." Being temporary did not mitigate the plaintiff's suffering and was no excuse. The most succinct statement of the law came from Mellish, Q.C. for the plaintiff, who took care to distinguish private purposes from public benefit. "It may be that for the sake of trade in towns, or for the public benefit," he said, "a nuisance is sometimes justified, such as a tallow chandler's factory; but the nuisance in the present case was created by the defendant for a private purpose, vis., burning bricks for a house for himself, and the extent of the advantage or convenience to the defendant cannot justify the creation of such a nuisance to the plaintiff."

While some if not all the judges were ready to see that persons did not ruin their neighbors' amenity in the name of convenience, they were not willing to extend a similar protection to persons suffering personal discomfort from industrial nuisances. The dearth of reported nuisance actions against factories suggests that this dual standard had been long operating before it was effectively ratified by the House of Lords in *St. Helen's Smelting Co.* v. *Tipping* in 1865. This is arguably the most important nuisance case of the era.

Mr. Tipping had four years earlier purchased a 1300-acre estate in the Mersyside town of St. Helen's. It was not clear from the evidence whether the defendants' copper-smelting works were then in operation, and the point was thought to be immaterial. In 1863 Tipping brought his action to recover damages (1) for injuries to trees, hedges, fruit, and cattle, and (2) for substantial personal discomfort. Mellor, J. told the jury that the law did not regard "trifling inconveniences" and that where noxious vapors were concerned "the injury to be actionable must be such as visibly to diminish the value of the property and the comfort and enjoyment of it." Locality had to be considered; those in industrial areas could not stand on extreme rights, or the business of the whole country would suffer. The jury returned a verdict with damages for Tipping.

The Lords upheld the Exchequer Chamber's ruling that the company was liable for any physical damage it caused, but not for the deterioration of the plaintiff's comfort. The decision seemed almost to measure nuisances by a trespass standard. "The word 'suitable,'" said Lord Westbury "unquestionably cannot carry with it the consequence, that a trade may be carried on in a particular locality, the consequence of which trade may be injury and destruction of the neighbouring property." The affairs of life require compromises about standards of comfort, but if a person damaged the property of another he would be liable: "the submission which is required from persons living in society to that amount of discomfort which may be necessary for the legitimate and free exercise of the trade of their neighbours, would not apply to circumstances the immediate result of which is sensible injury to the *value* of their property."

By ruling against Tipping on the personal discomfort count, the Lords were making an explicit distinction between nuisance actions for physical injury to property and nuisance actions in respect of personal discomfort. This came perilously close to obscuring the fact that, in either case, nuisance was a remedy for injury to land and that a serious interference with the possessor's comfort was *per se* such an injury.

*St. Helen's* made actions in respect of discomfort virtually impossible in the industrial Midlands and in regions such as Swansea and Cardiff. This is not to say that a successful action in respect of discomfort caused by an industrial nuisance was no longer *conceivable* in an industrial town, but the discomfort would have had to be direct, immediate, and obviously physical as in trespass. An eye put out by a cinder would have done, but not severe personal discomfort. As for property damage, the plaintiff had to prove that the *value* of his property had *visibly* diminished, else he could not recover. In other words, a decline in property value would not itself support a nuisance action. There also had to be actual, physical damage. In Tipping's case, his property damage was so severe that he eventually had the copper smelting enjoined, but damage to comfort and health commanded no such protection. In this case, where the physical damage allowed Tipping to recover his lost property value, the distinction may not have been significant—assuming that the declining market value was an accurate reflection of the valued amenity. But in cases where there was no physical damage, the distinction was crucial.

Another factor that tended to make nuisance liability less onerous was the emphasis on locality. Stated abstractedly, it might mean no more than that neighbors had to be reasonable and tolerant of one another's activities. This was nothing new. After the 1850s, however, the zoning function of nuisance law became more apparent as the importance of locality came to the fore. It was common to hear a judge say that life in factory towns required more forebearance than life elsewhere; or that an annoyance which was a nuisance on a quiet residential street might not be a nuisance elsewhere. It is difficult to assess the extent to which this aspect of nuisance doctrine has actually changed, for the early reports are fragmentary. But it is certain that the milieu in which the law operated changed radically after 1800, and this change had important consequences. In the thirteenth century, when the worst nuisance in a town might be a brick kiln or a chandler, and in the nineteenth, when whole towns could be built, demographic patterns altered, occupations eliminated and created, and skies blackened, all by factories—in such incomparable circumstances the same law could be greatly different in its import. Somehow we do not associate sociological and environmental metamorphosis with brick kilns, chandlers, and privies, annoying though they may have been to those few close by. It was one thing to close down a smelly tannery and to tell the tanner to move elsewhere or to find another occupation. It was quite another to close down two or three objectionable factories in a Merseyside town, when the consequences could be disastrous for hundreds or even thousands of people. So what the Lords meant when they said that location was a factor to be weighed in evaluating the plaintiff's complaint was that they were going to be more forthright in striking a balance between comfort and health on the one hand and economic interests on the other.

What the Lords did in effect in the *St. Helen's* case was not to bury *Hole* v. *Barlow*, as they seemed to be doing, but rather to apply it discriminatorily. While they were unwilling to recognize the case as good law and thereby to dilute formal nuisance liability, they were also unwilling to apply the "Every man must so use his own" rule to large industrial concerns as well as to ordinary private persons, except in the most extreme cases. They compromised. Strict nuisance liability would apply to John Doe down the street, but Doe Manufacturing Co., Ltd. would be judged by a more lenient rule. In Lancashire above all, said Lord Wensleydale, "where great works have been created and carried on, and are the means of developing the national wealth, you must not stand on extreme rights and allow a person to say, 'I will bring an action against you for this and that, and so on.' Business could not go on if it were so." . . .

If a man of substance such as Tipping could not win in nuisance except for actual physical damage of his property, then a lesser man was unlikely to make out at all against an industrial opponent. There was a number of reasons why nuisance law did him no good, some legal, some social. First was the exclusion of nearly all injuries except actual, physical damage to property from legal redress under the obscuring phrase, "trifling inconvenience." Second was the ruling, also from the *St. Helen's* case, that damage to property was not actionable unless it involved visible, actual injury *and* a fall in the property's value. No matter what kinds of damage qualified as legal injuries, the measure of damages was strictly the property's market value. Damage to the occupier's health and comfort was no longer a property injury *per se*. Since property values in the most contaminated areas often rose rather than fell (though in either case there is no logical connection between the value of the property and the right of its occupier to clean air and water), unhealthy conditions were doubly excluded from the scope of a nuisance remedy. The Royal Commission on Noxious Vapours noted in 1878 that both land values and tenant rents rose in the area of works, "and this increase fully compensated for such damage as was to some extent inevitable." This is a confusing and misleading statement. An occupier did not benefit from an increased land value unless he were also the owner. Tenants certainly did not benefit from having their rents raised. But nuisance is an occupier's remedy. A reversioner cannot bring nuisance unless he can demonstrate a clear and permanent physical injury to the property, and he has no remedy for noise, smoke, or other impermanent irritations, even if they drive away his tenants and reduce his rents. Rising land values and higher rents were no substitute for actions at law.

A third reason why an average British workingman did not bring nuisance actions was simply the prohibitive cost of justice. Taking a local smelting company to court was out of the question for most people.

A fourth reason lay in the requirement that the "state of the neighbourhood" be taken into account in evaluating the nuisance. In one sense it could not be otherwise. But the state of many neighborhoods in factory towns was so bad that the requirement militated against the recognition by the common law of minimum standards of comfort and health. It is not surprising to learn that a specially commissioned investigation into industrial nuisances in 1882 found no correlation between the frequency of complaints and the extent and intensity of nuisances.

## Public Regulation: The Common Law

The oldest method of public regulation of offensive activities is the indictment of public nuisance.

Flooded mill ponds, stinking privies, smoking chimneys: these are private nuisances and are the subject of civil litigation. Public nuisances, by contrast, are offenses against the public authority and are indictable as misdemeanors. The earliest and also the most common public nuisances were cases of encroachment on the royal domain or obstruction of the public's right of way along the king's highway, but by the mid-thirteenth century the category had been expanded to include a variety of transgressions which included keeping a brothel, interfering with a market, emitting noxious vapors, or fouling common water.

Indictments of public nuisances were not of great importance in the nineteenth century. One does find scattered indictments throughout the period, but the number of reported cases does not suggest that indictments played a significant regulatory role. Nor, when indictments did occur, were the courts eager to find large enterprises guilty of public nuisances, because they feared the economic consequences of a policy of strict enforcement. In an indictment against a private gas company, for example, the polluting of a river, the destruction of the fish, and the consequent unemployment of many fisherman were held inadequate to sustain a prosecution. Otherwise, said Denman, C.J., "every successful speculation in trade might be the subject of a prosecution." Such results evidenced a complete turnabout from the policy followed before the Industrial Revolution, when polluting tradesmen were indicted and convicted without worry that the courts were endangering large economic ventures. An exhaustive search of the treatises and manuals on both local government law and nuisance law for the period suggests that local authorities did not concern themselves with pollution prevention. Where nuisances are mentioned in these works at all, they are usually highway obstructions (often parking offenses). Local authorities also had statutory control over such matters as sewers and drains, paving, and lighting, but if London is in any way typical of other local jurisdictions, this control did not lead to the prosecution of many nuisances, except obstructions.

Insofar as polluting enterprises were public and quasi-public works, such as docks and railways, indictments were of course useless. These enterprises had statutory authorization and were therefore protected from indictments for public nuisances. The only means of recourse against them, unless they had been negligent or *ultra vires*, was under statutory provision, if any. Such provisions were narrowly construed. . . .

## Conclusion

By the mid-nineteenth century the courts had restricted the common law of nuisance so that it could have only little effect on the quality of the environment or the progress of industrialization. Partly for this reason, and partly because various legislative actions created novel situations where nuisance law was inapplicable, the common law was rendered incompetent to deal with the already serious problems of air and water pollution. Statutory regulation was neither a systematic nor a satisfactory substitute.

There were three reasons, in addition to the inherent difficulty of regulating through case law, for the inapplicability of the common law. One: the law was temporarily invaded by a standard of care which was alien to nuisance. Two: the law was applied differently to industrial enterprises than to private individuals. To win a nuisance action against an industrial firm one practically had to prove trespass to land. And three: quasi-public enterprises with statutory authorization were not liable in tort unless they had acted *ultra vires* or negligently. This meant that many serious interferences with enjoyment of land could not be remedied in nuisance at all: "since the legislature had thought fit to authorize the use of locomotive engines on railways," said Williams, J., "the companies who under that authority use on their lines these engines, calculated as they are to interfere in some respects with the ordinary rights of enjoyment of property by others, are yet not responsible for the consequences of so using them, provided they are not guilty of any negligence."

Other factors were also important. Suits were expensive and slow. Proving the source and amount of the damage was often difficult or impossible. Public nuisances were not systematically prosecuted. . . .

We may conclude that the law did not prevent, or even diminish significantly, the level of air and water pollution in nineteenth-century England. But could it have been otherwise? The extensive pollution that I have described was a product of the industrialization that was the basis of English power and prosperity and it is impossible to imagine the courts stopping or seriously interfering with that industrialization, even had they wished to, which they did not. The story told here is only a small part of a broad narrative of the transformation of England from an agricultural to an industrial society. A judge with his books may help to regulate such a transformation, but he does not stop or start it. For the first time in history a society was faced with the necessity of making grave trade-offs; dirty air in return for factory employment and consumer goods, dirty water in return for towns which had gutters and sewers. Few people even today would venture to say that the choices they made were basically wrong. Legislative attempts to improve the environment had of course only mixed results; they have only mixed results today. But when modern statutory regulation of nuisances began in the 1840s, the problem was still only a few decades old and no legislature anywhere had previously faced a regulatory problem of comparable scope and complexity. The care with which information was gathered, the persistence with which one act was followed with another, are impressive even by our standards. If air and water pollution were not immediately the highest priority, it is because more serious threats to health and amenity had to be dealt with first: cholera, flooded cesspools, city streets without sewers or lights.

To conclude that the decision to industrialize was economically right, and that the courts were right not to obstruct it, is not however to conclude that the process of industrialization was equitable. Nor need one conclude that industrial defendants required the extent of protection that was given them. Nor, given the flexibility of the doctrines they inherited, did the courts need to empty the nuisance standard of nearly all its contents of minimum decency. My point, however, is that even if the courts had done better, it is unlikely that the situation would have been much altered.

*Roderick Nash*

# Wilderness and the American Mind (1982)

### Hetch Hetchy

As to my attitude regarding the proposed use of Hetch Hetchy by the city of San Francisco . . . I am fully persuaded that . . . the injury . . . by substituting a lake for the present swampy floor of the valley . . . is altogether unimportant compared with the benefits to be derived from its use as a reservoir.
GIFFORD PINCHOT, 1913

These temple destroyers, devotees of ravaging commercialism, seem to have a perfect contempt for Nature, and instead of lifting their eyes to the God of the Mountains, lift them to the Almighty Dollar.
JOHN MUIR, 1912

Situated on a dry, sandy peninsula, the city of San Francisco faced a chronic freshwater shortage. In the Sierra, about one hundred and fifty miles distant, the erosive action of glaciers and the Tuolumne River scooped the spectacular, high-walled Hetch Hetchy Valley. As early as 1892, city engineers pointed out the possibility of damming its narrow, lower end to make a reservoir. They also recognized the opportunity of using the fall of the impounded water for the generation of hydroelectric power. In 1890, however, the act creating Yosemite National Park designated Hetch Hetchy and its environs a wilderness preserve. Undaunted, San Francisco's mayor James D. Phelan applied for the valley as a reservoir site shortly after the turn of the century. Secretary of the Interior Ethan A. Hitchcock's refusal to violate the sanctity of a national park was only a temporary setback, because on April 18, 1906, an earthquake and fire devastated San Francisco and added urgency and public sympathy to the search for an adequate water supply. The city immediately reapplied for

Hetch Hetchy, and on May 11, 1908, Secretary James R. Garfield approved the new application. "Domestic use," he wrote, "is the highest use to which water and available storage basins . . . can be put."

John Muir, Robert Underwood Johnson, and those whom they had won to the cause of wilderness preservation disagreed. Secretary Garfield's approval stimulated them to launch a national protest campaign. Given the flourishing cult of wilderness on the one hand and the strength of traditional assumptions about the desirability of putting undeveloped natural resources to use on the other, the battle over Hetch Hetchy was bound to be bitter. Before Congress and President Woodrow Wilson made a final decision in 1913, the valley became a *cause célèbre*. The principle of preserving wilderness was put to the test. For the first time in the American experience the competing claims of wilderness and civilization to a specific area received a thorough hearing before a national audience.

When the preservationists first learned of San Francisco's plans for Hetch Hetchy, Theodore Roosevelt occupied the White House, and the choice of reservoir or wilderness placed him in an awkward position. There were few Americans so committed to a belief in the value of wild country. Yet Roosevelt appreciated the importance of water, lumber, and similar commodities to national welfare and as President felt responsible for providing them. The result of this ambivalence was inconsistency in Roosevelt's early policy statements. In 1901 he declared in his first annual message that "the fundamental idea of forestry is the perpetuation of forest by use. Forest protection is not an end in itself; it is a means to increase and sustain the resources of our country and the industries which depend on them." But later in the message, he revealed his hope that some of the forest reserves could be made "preserves for the wild forest creatures." The same uncertainty appeared two years later in an address on the goal of forestry: "primarily the object is not to preserve forests because they are beautiful—though that is good in itself—not to preserve them because they are refuges for the wild creatures of the wilderness—though that too is good in itself—but the primary object of forest policy . . . is the making of prosperous homes, is part of the traditional policy of homemaking in our country."

In this seesaw manner Roosevelt hoped to hold the two wings of the conservation movement together on a united front. The task was formidable: Muir already had found his position incompatible with Gifford Pinchot's. But after 1905 Pinchot was Chief Forester and the principal spokesman of the utilitarian conception of conservation. Moreover, he enjoyed a close friendship with Roosevelt. According to Johnson, the President went so far as to declare that "in all forestry matters I have put my conscience in the keeping of Gifford Pinchot." And Pinchot favored converting Hetch Hetchy into a reservoir. Yet Roosevelt had camped in Yosemite with Muir and appreciated the growing political strength of the preservationist position. Early in September 1907, he received a letter from Muir that brought the issue to a head. Reminding the President of their 1903 trip into the Sierra wilderness, Muir expressed his desire that the region "be saved from all sorts of commercialism and marks of man's works." While acknowledging the need for an adequate municipal water supply, he maintained that it could be secured outside "our wild mountain parks." Concluding the letter, Muir expressed his belief that over ninety percent of the American people would oppose San Francisco's plans if they were apprised of their consequences.

Roosevelt's initial reaction, made even before Muir's communication, was to seek advice from engineers about alternative reservoir sites. The report, however, was that Hetch Hetchy offered the only practical solution to San Francisco's problem. Reluctantly Roosevelt made up his mind. While assuring Muir that he would do everything possible to protect the national parks, the President reminded him that if these reservations "interfere with the permanent material development of the State instead of helping . . . the result will be bad." Roosevelt ended with an expression of doubt that the great majority would take the side of wilderness in a showdown with the material needs of an expanding civilization. . . .

In spite of his doubts Roosevelt had made a choice, and in the spring of 1908 the Garfield permit opened the way for the development of the valley. Muir was discouraged but not defeated. He believed it still was possible to arouse a national protest and demonstrate to federal authorities that Roosevelt was mistaken in his judgment about the lack of public sentiment for keeping Hetch Hetchy wild. But Muir fully realized that "public opinion is not yet awakened." The first task of the preservationists was to capitalize on the wilderness cult and replace ignorance with anger. Telling arguments against the reservoir were needed. As the basis for their protest, the friends of wilderness turned to the old Romantic case against "Mammon." They made Hetch Hetchy into a symbol of ethical and aesthetic qualities, while disparaging San Francisco's proposal as tragically typical of American indifference toward them. This line of defense took advantage of national sensitivity to charges of being a culture devoted entirely to the frantic pursuit of the main chance. It criticized the commercialism and sordidness of American civilization, while defending wilderness.

John Muir opened the argument for the Valley on aesthetic grounds with an article in *Outlook*. After describing its beauties, he declared that its maintenance as a wilderness was essential, "for everybody needs beauty as well as bread, places to play in and pray in where Nature may heal and cheer and give strength to body and soul alike." Others took up the same theme in the national press. Writing in *Century*, which he now edited, Robert Underwood Johnson charged that only those who had not advanced beyond the "pseudo-'practical' stage" could favor San Francisco. The presence of these individuals in the nation, he added, "is one of the retarding influences of American civilization and brings us back to the materialistic declaration that 'Good is only good to eat.'" As a self-appointed spokesman for culture and refinement, Johnson took it upon himself to defend intangibles. In a brief submitted at the first Congressional hearing on the Hetch Hetchy question in December 1908, he made his protest "in the name of all lovers of beauty . . . against the materialistic idea that there must be something wrong about a man who finds one of the highest uses of nature in the fact that it is made to be looked at."

As president of the American Civic Association, J. Horace McFarland took every opportunity to preach the desirability, indeed the necessity, of maintaining some element of beauty in man's environment. He believed the aesthetic should have a place in the conservation movement, and in 1909 expressed his displeasure at its concentration on utilitarian aims. In the same year he told Pinchot that "the conservation movement is now weak, because it has failed to join hands with the preservation of scenery." For McFarland, Hetch Hetchy was a test case, and he spoke and wrote widely in its defense. If even national parks were to be given over to utilitarian purposes, there was no guarantee that ultimately all the beauty of unspoiled nature would be destroyed. Speaking before the Secretary of the Interior on the Hetch Hetchy question, McFarland contended that such undeveloped places would become increasingly valuable for recreation as more and more Americans lived in cities. Yet when the preservation of wilderness conflicted with "material interests," those financially affected cried: "that is sentimentalism; that is aestheticism; that is pleasure-loving; that is unnecessary; that is not practical." Usually such resistance carried the day and wildness was sacrificed. McFarland objected because "it is not sentimentalism, Mr. Secretary; it is living." Elsewhere he elaborated on his ideas: "the primary function of the national forests is to supply lumber. The primary function of the national parks is to maintain in healthful efficiency the lives of the people who must use that lumber. . . . The true ideal of their maintenance does not run parallel to the making of the most timber, or the most pasturage, or the most water power."

Lyman Abbott, the editor of *Outlook,* also felt it was a mistake "to turn every tree and waterfall into dollars and cents." His magazine found most of its readers among a class of people concerned over what they thought was the eclipse of morality, refinement, and idealism by urbanization, industrialization, and an emphasis on business values. The defense of wilderness attracted them because it permitted making a positive case—they could be for something (wilderness) rather than merely against amorphous forces. . . .

The same disparaging reference to American tastes and values appeared in the statements of preservationists in early 1909 at the House and Senate hearings in regard to Hetch Hetchy. One man, who had camped in the valley, pointedly asked: "is it never ceasing; is there nothing to be held sacred by this nation; is it to be dollars only; are we to be cramped in soul and mind by the lust after filthy lucre only; shall we be left some of the more glorious places?" Others joined him in pleading that "loftier motives" than saving money for San Francisco be taken into consideration. "May we live down our national reputation for commercialism," one letter concluded. . . .

Another tactic of the preservationists emphasized the spiritual significance of wild places and the tendency of money-minded America to ignore religion. Hetch Hetchy became a sanctuary or temple in the eyes of the defenders. John Muir, for one, believed so strongly in the divinity of wild nature that he was convinced he was doing the Lord's battle in resisting the reservoir. . . .

Using these arguments, and the especially effective one (unrelated to wilderness) that the valley as part of Yosemite National Park was a "public playground" which should not be turned over to any special interest, the preservationists were able to arouse considerable opposition to San Francisco's plans. . . .

San Francisco was bewildered and incensed at the public unwillingness that it should have Hetch Hetchy as a reservoir. Was not supplying water to a large city a worthy cause, one that certainly took priority over preserving wilderness? The San Francisco *Chronicle* referred to the preservationists as "hoggish and mushy aesthetes," while the city's engineer, Marsden Manson, wrote in 1910 that the opposition was largely composed of "short-haired women and long-haired men." San Francisco argued that the beauties of wilderness were admirable, but in this case human health, comfort, and even human life were the alternatives. . . .

At every opportunity the proponents of the dam expressed their belief that a lake in Hetch Hetchy would not spoil its beauty but, rather, enhance it. A prominent engineer reported on the City's behalf that roads and walks could be built which would open the region for public recreation in the manner of European mountain-lake resorts. Since the preservationists frequently based their opposition on the need to maintain a "scenic wonder" or "beauty spot," and on the desirability of maintaining a public playground, the claims of San Francisco were difficult to dismiss. If, instead, more attention had been paid specifically to the wilderness qualities of Hetch Hetchy—which *any* man-made construction would have eliminated—San Francisco's point about the scenic attraction of an artificial lake could have been more easily answered. As it was, this tactical error cost the preservationists considerable support.

The Hetch Hetchy controversy entered its climactic stage on March 4, 1913, when the Woodrow Wilson administration took office. San Francisco's hopes soared, because the new Secretary of the Interior, Franklin K. Lane, was a native, a former attorney for the city, and a proponent of the reservoir. But Lane upheld the policy of previous Secretaries that in cases involving national parks Congress must make the final decision. . . .

On June 25 the House Committee on the Public Lands opened hearing on the Hetch Hetchy issue, with Gifford Pinchot as the star witness. Pinchot simplified the question into "whether the advantage of leaving this valley in a state of nature is greater than . . . using it for the benefit of the city of San Francisco." He admitted that the idea of preserving wilderness appealed to him "if nothing else were at stake," but in this case the need of the city seemed "overwhelming." . . .

Since the House hearings were called on short notice, Edmund D. Whitman of the Appalachian Mountain Club was the only preservationist to testify. He attempted to show that the reservoir would substantially reduce the value of Yosemite National Park as a public recreation ground and beauty spot. But Whitman did not bring out the fact that wilderness was at stake in Hetch Hetchy. As a result Phelan's rejoinder that San Francisco would cover the dam with moss, vines, and trees and would build picnic spots and trails around the reservoir seemed to answer his objections. Whitman concluded his testimony more effectively with a quotation from a Robert Underwood Johnson letter on the danger that without unspoiled nature to provide a "touch of idealism," life degenerated into "a race for the trough."

On the basis of the June hearings, the Committee submitted a report unanimously endorsing the reservoir plans. When the bill reached the floor of the House on August 29, 1913, strong support immediately developed for its passage. Applying the time-honored utilitarian yardstick to the problem, Representative Raker of California asserted that the "old barren rocks" of the valley have a "cash value" of less than $300,000 whereas a reservoir would be worth millions. But most proponents of the dam were not so positive. They prefaced their support of the dam with a declaration of their love of wilderness and reluctance to have it destroyed. . . .

As the consideration of the Hetch Hetchy question in the House continued into September 1913, the sentiments of William Kent and other supporters of San Francisco encountered stiffer opposition. Halvor Steenerson of Minnesota declared it was nonsense to claim that an artificial lake would add to the beauty of the valley. "You may as well improve upon the lily of the field by handpainting it," he pointed out, and added that all the city offered was a power plant making a "devilish hissing noise" and a "dirty muddy pond." Concluding his remarks, Steenerson spoke in the agrarian tradition, deploring the tendency of Americans to live in cities, and in the Romantic manner, hoping that some day a poet would use the "pristine glory" of Hetch Hetchy "to produce something more valuable than money." . . . But Martin Dies of Texas rose to say the final word before the House vote. He felt that natural resources should serve civilization. "I want them to open the reservations in this country," Dies declared. "I am not for reservations and parks." Applause and cries of "Vote!" greeted the conclusion of Dies' remarks.

On September 3 the House passed the Hetch Hetchy bill 183 to 43, with 203 Representatives not voting. No Congressman from a Western state voted against it. Most of its support came from the Southern and Middle Western Democrats. In fact, the bill was rumored to be an administration measure, connected, in some minds, with the votes California had given to Wilson in the recent election.

The Senate still had to decide on San Francisco's application, and in preparation the preservationists worked frantically. Their plan was "to flood the Senate with letters from influential people." In addition, the Society for the Preservation of National Parks and the newly organized National Committee for the Preservation of the Yosemite National Park, published several pamphlets which called on Americans to write or wire their President and Congressmen and suggested arguments against the dam. Thousands of copies circulated, and the public responded. Between the time of the House passage and early December when the Senate began its debate, the destruction of the wilderness qualities of Hetch Hetchy Valley became a major national issue. Hundreds of newspapers throughout the country, including such opinion leaders as the New York *Times*, published editorials on the question, most of which took the side of preservation. Leading magazines, such as *Outlook, Nation, Independent*, and *Collier's*, carried articles protesting the reservoir. A mass meeting on behalf of the valley took place at the Museum of Natural History in New York City. Mail poured into the offices of key Senators: Reed Smoot of Utah estimated late in November that he had received five thousand letters in opposition to the bill, and other Senators were likewise besieged. The protests came from women's groups, outing and sportsmen's clubs, scientific societies, and the faculties of colleges and universities as well as from individuals. The American wilderness had never been so popular before. . . .

A decision had been made to vote on December 6, and when the Senators entered their chamber that morning they found copies of a "Special Washington Edition" of the San Francisco *Examiner* on their desks. Skillful drawings showed how the valley might appear as a man-made lake with scenic drives for automobiles and boating facilities for happy family groups. The *Examiner* also published experts' testimony justifying the grant in a variety of ways. In comparison, the preservationists' campaign literature was considerably less impressive.

At three minutes before midnight on December 6, the Senate voted. Fifty-three favored the grant, twenty-nine did not vote or were absent. Eighteen votes from Southern Democrats were the decisive factor, and suggested, as in the case of the House, that the Wilson administration was behind San Francisco. Only nine of the "yeas" came from Republicans.

A Presidential veto was the last hope of the preservationists. After the Senate passage, Wilson received numerous letters calling upon him to defend Yosemite National Park. Robert Underwood Johnson wrote, characteristically, that "God invented courage for just such emergencies. The moral effect of a veto would be immense." He even called in person on the President, but when he left the office, William Kent was waiting to enter! On December 19, 1913, Wilson approved the Hetch Hetchy grant. In signing he declared that "the bill was opposed by so many public-spirited men . . . that I have naturally sought to scrutinize it very closely. I take the liberty of thinking that their fears and objections were not well founded."

The preservationists had lost the fight for the valley, but they had gained much ground in the larger war for the existence of wilderness. A deeply disappointed John Muir took some consolation from the fact that "the conscience of the whole country has been aroused from sleep." Scattered sentiment for wilderness preservation had, in truth, become a national movement in the course of the Hetch Hetchy controversy. Moreover, the defenders of wilderness discovered their political muscles and how to flex them by arousing an expression of public opinion, and in Hetch Hetchy they had a symbol which, like the *Maine,* would not easily be forgotten. . . .

Indeed the most significant thing about the controversy over the valley was that it occurred at all. One hundred or even fifty years earlier a similar proposal to dam a wilderness river would not have occasioned the slightest ripple of public protest. Traditional American assumptions about the use of undeveloped country did not include reserving it in national parks for its recreational, aesthetic, and inspirational values. The emphasis was all the other ways—on civilizing it in the name of progress and prosperity. Older generations conceived of the thrust of civilization into the wilderness as the beneficent working out of divine intentions, but in the twentieth century a handful of preservationists generated widespread resistance against this very process. What had formerly been the subject of national celebration was made to appear a national tragedy.

Muir, Johnson, and their colleagues were able to create a protest because the American people were ready to be aroused. Appreciation of wild country and the desire for its preservation had spread in the closing decades of the nineteenth century from a small number of literati to a sizeable segment of the population. The extent and vigor of the resistance to San Francisco's plans for Hetch Hetchy constituted tangible evidence for the existence of a wilderness cult. Equally revealing was the fact that very few favored the dam *because* they opposed wilderness. Even the partisans of San Francisco phrased the issue as not between a good (civilization) and an evil (wilderness) but between two goods. While placing material needs first, they still proclaimed their love of unspoiled nature. Previously most Americans had not felt compelled to rationalize the conquest of wild country in this manner. For three centuries they had chosen civilization without any hesitation. By 1913 they were no longer so sure.

*David Rosner and Gerald Markowitz*

# A "Gift of God"?: The Public Health Controversy over Leaded Gasoline during the 1920s (1985)

. . . [A]s early as the 1920s public health experts, government officials, scientists, corporate leaders, labor, and the public were acutely aware of the dangers posed by the introduction of lead into gasoline. The depth of concern was manifested by the fact that leaded gasoline was banned in New York City for over three years and in many states and other municipalities for shorter periods of time. In 1925, the production of leaded gasoline was halted for over nine months.

During the 1920s, the petrochemical and automobile industries emerged as the corporate backbone of the United States. Because the acceptance or rejection of leaded gasoline had profound implications for these industries, a spirited and often heated controversy arose. Public health professionals found themselves under intense pressure to sanction and minimize the hazards associated with the manufacture and use of this new potentially toxic substance and the pages of the *American Journal of Public Health* were compromised during the months and years when the fate of leaded gasoline was being decided. The debates of that era centered on issues of health and public policy that remain current today. Numerous questions arose regarding the evaluation of health hazards associated with new and potentially harmful substances, including: How can scientists evaluate the relative importance of acute and chronic effects of toxic substances? What should constitute adequate proof of safety or harm? What business, professional, or government agencies should be responsible for evaluating possibly dangerous substances? How does one study potentially toxic substances while protecting the right to health of human subjects? Does industry have to

David Rosner and Gerald Markowitz, A "Gift of God"?: The Public Health Controversy over Leaded Gasoline during the 1920s, 75 AJPH 344 (1985).

prove a new substance safe or do public health experts have to prove it dangerous? In the face of scientific uncertainty concerning the safety or dangers posed by leaded gasoline, and the perceived need for this substance by the automobile industry, the broader question became: What was the level of acceptable risk that society should be willing to assume for industrial progress? . . . [A]t every stage of the debate, the political, economic and scientific issues were inextricably intertwined. . . .

## Leaded Gasoline Developed

. . . Central to the creation of powerful and large automobiles was the development of a more efficient fuel capable of driving cars at greater speed. In 1922, Thomas Midgley and co-workers at the General Motors Research Laboratory in Dayton, Ohio discovered that adding tetraethyl lead to gasoline raised the compression and hence, speed, by eliminating the engine "knock." This allowed for the development of the "modern" automobile produced over the next 50 years.

General Motors, which had an interlocking directorship with the DuPont Chemical Company, quickly contracted with DuPont and Standard Oil of New Jersey to produce tetraethyl lead. Leaded gasoline was placed on sale in selected markets on February 1, 1923. In 1924, DuPont and General Motors created the Ethyl Corporation to market and produce its final product. This was done in spite of the fact that industrial hygienists such as Alice Hamilton had long since identified lead as an industrial toxin.

In the very year that Midgley and his co-workers at General Motors Research Corporation heralded the discovery of this powerful anti-knock compound, scientists in and outside of government warned that tetraethyl lead might be a potent threat to the public's health. William Mansfield Clark, a professor of chemistry, wrote to A. M. Stimson, Assistant Surgeon General at the Public Health Service, in October of 1922 warning of "a serious menace to the public health." He noted that in the early production of tetraethyl lead, "several very serious cases of lead poisoning have resulted." He feared that its use in gasoline would result in environmental pollution, theorizing that "on busy thoroughfares it is highly probable that the lead oxide dust will remain in the lower stratum." . . .

## Oil Company Disaster

The industry's assurances of the safety of leaded gasoline were undermined by a horrifying disaster that occurred in the Standard Oil Company's experimental laboratories in Elizabeth, New Jersey. Between October 26 and October 30, 1924, five workers died and 35 others experienced severe palsies, tremors, hallucinations, and other serious neurological symptoms of organic lead poisoning. Thus, of 49 workers in the tetraethyl lead processing plant, over 80 percent died or were severely poisoned. . . .

[An industry] propaganda effort did not quell the doubts about the safety of leaded gasoline. . . . It also became apparent that the companies were engaging in a cover-up of other deaths and illnesses among their workers in other plants. . . . Despite this, the [*New York*] *Times* was able to uncover the fact that there had been over 300 cases of lead poisoning among workers at [a] Deepwater [New Jersey] plant during the past two years. Workers at the DuPont facility, knowing something was amiss, had dubbed the plant "the House of the Butterflies" because so many of their colleagues had hallucinations of insects during their bouts of lead poisoning. . . .

## Surgeon General Convenes Conference

As a result of these continuing revelations·. . . , the Surgeon General of the Public Health Service contemplated calling a national conference to assess the tetraethyl lead situation. . . . [T]he Surgeon General announced at the end of April 1925 that he was calling together experts from business, labor, and public health to assess the tetraethyl lead situation.

The conference convened on May 20, 1925, in Washington, DC, with every major party represented. At the conference, the ideologies of the different participants were clearly and repeatedly laid out, thus providing an important forum by which we can evaluate the scientific, political, economic, and intellectual issues surrounding this controversy. In the words of one participant, the conference gathered together in one room "two diametrically opposed conceptions. The men engaged in industry, chemists, and engineers, take it as a matter of course that a little thing like industrial poisoning should not be allowed to stand in the way of a great industrial advance. On the other hand, the sanitary experts take it as a matter of course that the first consideration is the health of the people."

### *"Industrial Progress" Invoked*

The conference opened with statements from General Motors, DuPont, Standard Oil, and the Ethyl Corporation outlining the history of the development of leaded gasoline and the reasons why they believed its continued production was essential. Three themes emerged as central arguments by the companies. First, the manufacturers maintained that leaded gasoline was essential to the industrial progress of America. Second, they maintained that any innovation entails certain risks. Third, they stated that the major reason that deaths and illnesses occurred at their plants was that the men who worked with the materials were careless and did not follow instructions.

C. F. Kettering, of GM and Ethyl, and Robert Kehoe, scientific consultant to the industry, both stressed the importance of tetraethyl lead as a means of conserving motor fuel. But Frank Howard, representing the Ethyl Gasoline Corporation, provided the most complete rationale for the continued use of tetraethyl lead in gasoline. He noted that it was not possible to abstract the questions of public health from broader economic and political issues. "You have but one problem," he remarked rhetorically,

"Is this a public health hazard?" He answered that "unfortunately, our problem is not that simple." Rather he posited that automobiles and oil were central to the industrial progress of the nation, if not the world. "Our continued development of motor fuels is essential in our civilization," he proclaimed. Noting that at least a decade of research had gone into the effort to identify tetraethyl lead, he called its discovery an "apparent gift of God." By casting the issue in this way, Howard put the opposition on the defensive, making them appear to be reactionaries whose limited vision of the country's future could permanently retard progress and harm future generations. "What is our duty under the circumstances?" he asked. "Should we say, 'No, we will not use'" a material that is "a certain means of saving petroleum? Because some animals die and some do not die in some experiments, shall we give this thing up entirely?"

The stark portrayal of tetraethyl lead as a key to the industrial future of the nation led naturally into industry's second argument that any great advance required some sacrifice. Dr. H. C. Parmelee, editor of *Chemical and Metallurgical Engineering,* stated, "The research and development that produced tetraethyl lead were conceived in a free spirit of industrial progress looking toward the conservation of gasoline and increased efficiency of internal combustion motors." Parmelee believed that the companies did their best to safeguard the workers. In the end, he said "the casualties were negligible compared to human sacrifice in the development of many other industrial enterprises."

### Companies Say Workers at Fault

The final part of the industries' position was that workers, rather than the companies, were at fault for the tragedies at Bayway, Deepwater, and Dayton. Acknowledging that there were "certain dangers" inherent in the production of this essential industrial product, the Standard Oil Company asserted that "every precaution was taken" by the company to protect their workers. . . .

### A Public Health/Environmental Issue

Those who opposed the introduction of leaded gasoline disagreed with every fundamental position of industry representatives. First, opponents pointed out that what we would now denote as inorganic lead compounds were already known to be a slow, cumulative poison that should not be introduced into the general environment. Second, they believed because of industry's reckless disregard for workers' and the public's health the federal government had to assume responsibility for protecting the health of the nation. Third, they rejected the notion that the workers were the ones responsible for their own poisoning. Fourth, and most importantly, because they believed that the public's health should take precedence over the needs of industry, they argued that the burden of proof should be on the companies, to prove tetraethyl lead was *safe* rather than on opponents to prove that tetraethyl lead was dangerous.

Dr. Yandell Henderson, Yale physiologist, was the strongest and most authoritative critic of industry. He told the conference that lead was a serious public health menace that could be equated to the serious infectious diseases then affecting the nation's health. Unlike industry spokespeople who defined the problem as one of occupational health and maintained that individual vigilance on the part of workers could solve the problem, Henderson believed that leaded gasoline was a public health and environmental health issue that required federal action. He expressed horror at the thought that hundreds of thousands of pounds of lead would be deposited in the streets of every major city in America. His warning to the conference of the long-term dangers proved to be an accurate prediction: "conditions would grow worse so gradually and the development of lead poisoning will come on so insidiously . . . that leaded gasoline will be in nearly universal use and large numbers of cars will have been sold . . . before the public and the government awaken to the situation."

To meet such a public health menace, Henderson and other critics believed that it was essential for the federal government to take an active role in controlling leaded gasoline. . . .

Opponents were most concerned, however, about the industry propaganda that equated the use of lead with industrial progress, and the survival of our civilization itself. Reacting to the Ethyl Corporation representative's statement that tetraethyl lead was a "gift of God," Grace Durham of the Workers' Health Bureau said it "was not a gift of God when those 11 men were killed or those 149 were poisoned." She angrily questioned the priorities of "this age of speed and rush and efficiency and mechanics" and said that "the thing we are interested [in] in the long run is not mechanics or machinery, but men." . . . But it was Yandell Henderson who summarized the opponents' position and delineated the course for future policy makers. In a private letter to R. R. Sayers of the Bureau of Mines, he said, "In the past, the position taken by the authorities has been that nothing could be prohibited until it was proved to have killed a number of people. I trust that in the future, especially in a matter of this sort, the position will be that a substance like tetraethyl lead can not be introduced for general use until it is proved harmless."

For the vast majority of public health experts at the conference, the problem was how to reconcile the opposing views of advocates of industrial progress and those frightened by the potential for disaster. Although everyone hoped that science itself would provide an answer to this imponderable dilemma, the reality was that all evidence to this point was ambiguous. One major problem was that in the 1920s, no one had a model for explaining the apparently idiosyncratic occurrence of lead poisoning. Even the medical director of Reconstruction Hospital in New York, probably the only facility at that time devoted exclusively to the study and treatment of occupational disease and accidents, could not explain the strange manifestations of chronic tetraethyl lead poisoning. Of the 39 patients he treated after the Bayway disaster, he said, "some of these individuals gave no physical evidence and no symptoms or any evidence that could be found by a physical examination that would indicate that they were ill, but at the same time showed lead in the stools." He concluded that "perhaps a man may be poisoned from the tetraethyl lead without showing clinical evidence and that therefore, there may be a considerable number of individuals so poisoned who have not come under observation." The policy implications for him were that leaded gasoline "should be withheld from public consumption until it is conclusively shown that it is not poisonous."

Dr. Alice Hamilton, one of the country's foremost authorities on lead, agreed with those opposed to tetraethyl lead. At the conference she expressed her belief that the environmental health issues were far more important than the occupational health and safety issues, adding that she doubted that any effective measures could be implemented to protect the general public from the hazards of widespread use of leaded gasoline. "You may control conditions within a factory," she said, "but how are you going to control the whole country?" In an extended commentary after the conference on the issues that it raised, Hamilton stated, "I am not one of those who believe that the use of this leaded gasoline can ever be made safe. No lead industry has ever, even under the strictest control, lost all its dangers. Where there is lead some case of lead poisoning sooner or later develops, even under the strictest supervision."

*Further Tests, Studies Urged*

Most public health professionals did not agree with Henderson and Hamilton, however. Many took the position that it was unfair to ban this new gasoline additive until definitive proof existed that it was a real danger. In the face of industry arguments that oil supplies were limited and that there was an extraordinary need to conserve fuel by making combustion more efficient, most public health workers believed that there should be overwhelming evidence that leaded gasoline actually harmed people before it was banned. Dr. Henry F. Vaughan, president of the American Public Health Association, said that such evidence did not exist. "Certainly in a study of the statistics in our large cities there is nothing which would warrant a health commissioner in saying that you could not sell ethyl gasoline," he pointed out. Vaughan acknowledged that there should be further tests and studies of the problem but that "so far as the present situation is concerned, as a health administrator I feel that it is entirely negative." Emery Hayhurst also argued this point at the Surgeon General's Conference, maintaining that the widespread use of leaded gasoline for 27 months "should have sufficed to bring out some mishaps and poisonings, suspected to have been caused by tetraethyl lead." . . .

## Company Suspends Manufacture, Sales

*Blue Ribbon Committee to Investigate*

Despite the widespread ambivalence on the part of public health professionals and the opposition to any curbs on production on the part of industry spokespeople, the public suspicions aroused by the preceding year's events led to a significant victory for those who opposed the sale of leaded gasoline. At the end of the conference, the Ethyl Corporation announced that it was suspending the production and distribution of leaded gasoline until the scientific and public health issues involved in its manufacture could be resolved. The conference also called upon the Surgeon General to organize a blue ribbon committee of the nation's foremost public health scientists to conduct an investigation of leaded gasoline. Among those asked to participate were David Edsall of Harvard University, Julius Steiglitz of the University of Chicago, C. E. A. Winslow of Yale University and the American Public Health Association. For Alice Hamilton and other opponents of leaded gasoline, the conference appeared to be a major victory for it wrested from industry the power to decide on the future of an important industrial poison, and placed it in the hands of university scientists. "To anyone who had followed the course of industrial medicine for as much as ten years," Alice Hamilton remarked one month after the conference, "this conference marks a great progress from the days when we used to meet the underlings of the great munition makers (during World War I) and coax and plead with them to put in the precautionary measures. . . . This time it was possible to bring together in the office of the Surgeon General the foremost men in industrial medicine and public health and the men who are in real authority in industry and to have a blaze of publicity turned on their deliberations."

The initial euphoria over the apparent victory of "objective" science over political and economic self-interest was short lived. The blue ribbon committee, mandated to deliver an early decision, designed a short-term and, in retrospect, very limited, study of garage and filling station attendants and chauffeurs in Dayton and Cincinnati. The study consisted of four groups of workers, 252 people in all. Of these, 36 men were controls employed by the City of Dayton as chauffeurs of cars using gasoline without lead while 77 were chauffeurs using leaded gasoline over a period of two years. Also, 21 others were controls employed as garage workers or filling station attendants where unleaded gasoline was used and 57 were engaged in similar work where tetraethyl gas was used. As another means of comparison, 61 men were tested in two industrial plants known to have serious exposure to lead dust. As a result of their study, the committee concluded seven months after the conference that "in its opinion there are at present no good grounds for prohibiting the use of ethyl gasoline . . . provided that its distribution and use are controlled by proper regulations." They suggested that the Surgeon General formulate specific regulations with enforcement by the states. Although it appears that the committee rushed to judgment in only seven months, it must be pointed out that this group saw their study as only an interim report, to be followed by longer range follow-up studies in ensuing years. In their final report to the Surgeon General, the committee warned:

> It remains possible that if the use of leaded gasoline becomes widespread conditions may arise very different from those studied by us which would render its use more of a hazard than would appear to be the case from this investigation. Longer experience may show that even such slight storage of lead as was observed in these studies may lead eventually in susceptible individuals to recognizable or to chronic degenerative diseases of a less obvious character.

Recognizing that their short-term investigation was incapable of detecting such danger, the committee concluded that further study by the government was essential:

In view of such possibilities the committee feels that the investigation begun under their direction must not be allowed to lapse. . . . It should be possible to follow closely the outcome of a more extended use of this fuel and to determine whether or not it may constitute a menace to the health of the general public after prolonged use or other conditions not now foreseen. . . . The vast increase in the number of automobiles throughout the country makes the study of all such questions a matter of real importance from the standpoint of public health and the committee urges strongly that a suitable appropriation be requested from Congress for the continuance of these investigations under the supervision of the Surgeon General of the Public Health Service.

These suggestions were never carried out and subsequent studies of the use of tetraethyl lead were conducted by the Ethyl Corporation and scientists employed by them. In direct contradiction to the recommendations of the committee, Robert Kehoe who carried out the studies for Ethyl, wrote: "as it appeared from their investigation that there was no evidence of immediate danger to the public health, it was thought that these necessarily extensive studies should not be repeated at present, at public expense, but that they should be continued at the expense of the industry most concerned, subject, however, to the supervision of the Public Health Service." It should not be surprising that Kehoe concluded that his study "fails to show any evidence for the existence of such hazards."

*What Went Wrong?*

Today, looking back at the controversy of the 1920s, we may be tempted to look askance at public health professionals of the period who put their faith in the ability of scientific investigations to settle this thorny political and economic issue. After all, those like Alice Hamilton and Yandell Henderson who fought the introduction of lead into gasoline were the strongest advocates of governmentally sponsored scientific study to determine the safety or dangers of tetraethyl lead. What went wrong? Why is tetraethyl lead still a prime source of lead in the environment? Of course, there were those who had such an ideological commitment to industrial progress that they were willing to put their science aside to meet the demands of corporate greed. But, more importantly, we should look at those who considered themselves to be objective scientific investigators. Ultimately, it was impossible to separate their "science" from the demands of an economy and society that was being built around the automobile. How else, then, do we explain public health scientists' willingness to conduct a short-term study that could not resolve the long-term health issues. By agreeing to provide quick answers they guaranteed that this vital industry would not be disrupted. The symptoms of lead accumulation due to exhaust emissions would be unlike anything they had previously encountered in industrial populations. In the long run, those most affected would not be adults, but children, slowly accumulating lead. Their suffering speaks more to the interlocking relationships between science and society than to the absence of a link between lead and disease.

*Philip Shabecoff*

# A Fierce Green Fire (1993)

For many years, environmentalism was a disjointed, inchoate impulse; a revolution waiting for a manifesto; citizens' anger seeking a Bastille to storm. Was the cause love of nature or fear of pollution? Do we need to protect wildlife or is it human beings that are at risk? Were there any villains to attack? Was there any hope of salvation?

The answers came in a remarkable book by a remarkable woman. *Silent Spring* by Rachel Carson, excerpts of which were first published in *The New Yorker* in 1962, is now recognized as one of the truly important books of this century. More than any other, it changed the way Americans, and people around the world, looked at the reckless way we live on this planet. Focusing on a specific problem—the poisoning of the earth by chemical pesticides—*Silent Spring* was a broad examination of how carelessly applied science and technology were destroying nature and threatening life, including human life. Beautifully written and a best-seller, it sounded a deep chord which affected people emotionally and moved them to act. It may be the basic book of America's environmental revolution.

Born in 1907, Carson grew up in Pennsylvania, developed a deep love of the sea, and became a marine biologist. By all accounts a gentle, loving, somewhat reclusive but tough-minded woman, she was strongly influenced by the physician and humanitarian Albert Schweitzer's "reverence for life." The dedication of *Silent Spring* is: "To Albert Schweitzer, who said, 'Man has lost the capacity to foresee and to forestall. He will end up by destroying the earth.'" She worked for many years as a biologist for the Fish and Wildlife Service's experimental station in Patuxent, Maryland, before the success of *The Sea Around Us* and *The Edge of the Sea*, both best-sellers, enabled her to resign and devote full time to writing. Long alarmed by the dangers of DDT and other pesticides, she tried to sell an article to magazines on the subject but was turned down because the publishers feared loss of advertising from food and chemical companies. So she decided to write a book instead. *The New Yorker*, apparently not to be intimidated, condensed large portions of the book.

*Silent Spring* begins with two lines from John Keats's poem "La Belle Dame Sans Merci":

> *The sedge is withr'd from the lake,*
> *And no birds sing.*

Carson then goes on to describe "a town in the heart of America" surrounded by prosperous farms, fields of grain, green hillsides, trees and wildflowers, foxes and deer, pools filled with trout, and "countless birds." But then a "strange blight crept over the area," silencing the voices of the birds, causing the cattle to die and the chickens to lay eggs that would not hatch. Adults and children developed unexplained illnesses, and some of them died. The only clue was a white powder that had "fallen like snow upon the roofs and the lawns, the fields and streams."

That town did not exist, Carson explained, but all of the things she described had happened in towns around the country. "A grim spector has crept upon us almost unnoticed, and this imagined tragedy may easily become a stark reality we all shall know."

Most of the book is a careful exposition of the available scientific knowledge about the effects of DDT and other synthetic substances on the natural world. It shows how these chemicals kill far more than the species at which they are aimed. It demonstrates that the poisons remain in the environment for many years, contaminating the soil, rivers, lakes, coastal waters, and underground aquifers. It illustrates how the poisons pass through the food chain and become more concentrated the higher on the chain they get. It makes clear that these poisons carried in the chain eventually reach the men, women, and children who eat contaminated food or breathe contaminated air or drink contaminated water. It warns not only that humans are in danger of being poisoned by these substances but also that humanity is in grave danger of genetic damage from repeated exposure. "For the first time in the history of the world, every human being is now subjected to contact with dangerous chemicals from the moment of conception until death." These substances, moreover, were changing the very fabric of nature. "The most alarming of all man's assaults upon the environment is his contamination of air, earth, rivers and sea with dangerous and even lethal materials. This pollution is for the most part irrecoverable; the chain of evil it initiates not only in the world that must support life but in living tissues is for the most part irreversible. In this now universal contamination of the environment, chemicals are the sinister and little recognized partners of radiation in changing the very nature of the world—the very nature of its life."

Although the book is calm and reasoned in tone, many of its chapter titles make it clear that Carson consciously wrote a polemic intended to stir people to political action: "Elixirs of Death," "Needless Havoc," "And No Birds Sing," "Rivers of Death," "Indiscriminately from the Skies," "Beyond the Dreams of the Borgias," "The Human Price."

But *Silent Spring* ends on a hopeful, not a despairing note. There is an alternative to destroying nature with synthetic poisons—"The Other Road" Carson called it, a reference to Robert Frost's poem "The Road Not Taken." That road is a gradual turning away from pesticides and other life-killing synthetic substances. Alternatives such as biological controls on insects are available. She urges that people be informed of the danger so they may decide for themselves whether the risks are worth it. She calls for increased government action to monitor and regulate it. She urges that humans give up their arrogant efforts to control nature.

Carson did not do much of the research that showed the dangers of DDT or other synthetic substances. She was not even the first to cry the alarm—[Murray] Bookchin, the naturalist Edwin Way Teale, and a number of others had already sounded public warnings.

What Carson did in *Silent Spring,* however, was to present the scientific evidence in clear, poetic, and moving prose that demonstrated how the destruction of nature and the threat to human health from pollution were completely intertwined. She showed how all life, including human life, was affected by misguided technology. The book synthesized many of the concerns of the earlier conservationists and preservationists with the warnings of newer environmentalists who worried about pollution and public health. It made frighteningly clear that they were all skeins of a large web of environmental evil settling over the nation and the world. What killed trees and flowers, birds and animals, she demonstrated, could also sicken and kill human beings. She combined a transcendentalist's passion for nature and wildlife with the cool analytical mind of a trained scientist and the contained anger of a political activist. She touched an exposed wound.

By the late 1960s public awareness of the misuse of the land and its resources, of the toll that industrial pollution and dangerous new synthetic substances were taking on the air, the water, and human beings, reached a critical threshold. The fervor, activism, and ethical sensibilities of Bob Marshall, Aldo Leopold, David Brower, and other pioneer conservationists had driven home to many Americans the message that their land and resources were being badly abused. Lewis Mumford, Barry Commoner, René Dubos, and Murray Bookchin demonstrated how uncontrolled science and technology and unresponsive social organization were responsible for the degradation of the natural environment and represented a growing threat to humans themselves. Fairfield Osborn, Garrett Hardin, Paul Ehrlich, and the Club of Rome were among those who alerted the public to the danger that too many people were making excessive demands on air, water, food, and other resources needed to support life. Ralph Nader underscored the role of the corporation in polluting the environment and depleting resources, and William O. Douglas and David Sive were prominent among those who demonstrated that the law could be a weapon against environmental injustice.

Thanks to these and many other vigilant guardians of our ecological household, environmentalism in the United States had become a powder keg ready to explode. With *Silent Spring,* Rachel Carson lit the fuse.

# CHAPTER 6

# The Politics of Environmental Legislation

As explored earlier, there are powerful reasons, on economic, ethical and ecological grounds, for government intervention to protect the environment. Despite a broad consensus on the need for some form of collective action to protect the environment, there is sharp disagreement concerning what form that intervention should take. Decisions concerning regulatory policy are left to the political process. Legislators enact environmental protection laws in response to public concerns. These laws usually direct government agencies to issue regulations translating the laws into enforceable rules to affect the behavior of industries and individuals.

This chapter explores the political forces that have generated the complex web of environmental laws and regulations that prevails today. It examines the political choices that have been made when legislation is drafted, debated, and enacted. It also considers the factors that influence the implementation of environmental law and why there often is a significant gap between the promise and the product of environmental legislation.

The chapter begins with Robert Rabin's chronology of federal legislation enacted during the late 1960s and 1970s. Rabin describes this period as the "Public Interest era" because of the large volume of environmental and consumer protection legislation enacted by Congress. Rabin argues that the National Environmental Policy Act (NEPA) represented a sharp departure from the New Deal model of administrative reform by focusing on agency decision-making processes rather than rule-making procedures. He notes that Congress demonstrated considerable legislative maturity by incorporating action-forcing provisions into the Clean Air Act, imposing deadlines for agency action and authorizing citizen suits, because of distrust of agency implementation.

Donald Elliott, Bruce Ackerman, and John Millian explore the reasons for the sudden burst of environmental legislation during the late 1960s and early 1970s. They attribute the stringency of the first federal environmental statutes to the absence of groups who could serve as national brokers for environmental interests. Citing game theory's Prisoners' Dilemma, they maintain that the extreme popularity of environmental concerns during the early 1970s forced politicians into a "politicians' dilemma" in which they had to compete with one another to be the most strongly pro-environment. Without a national broker for environmental interests, who could agree to legislative compromises, this competition produced remarkably stringent laws, which industry was forced to accept to avoid a multiplicity of inconsistent state regulations.

Dan Farber explores alternative theories concerning the roots of this remarkable burst of federal environmental legislation. He rejects the notion that environmental legislation was largely the product of special interest deals spawned by rent-seeking behavior by industries and consumers. Instead, he theorizes that legislators occasionally experience what he calls "republican moments," when certain issues suddenly achieve high salience with the public—as occurred for the environment around the time of the initial Earth Day in 1970. Farber warns however, that bold legislation often is poorly implemented, producing largely symbolic results while allowing legislators to claim political credit without disrupting the status quo. He concludes that this pattern is not as extensive as others believe and explains why legislators are indeed concerned about implementation.

Reviewing what he calls the "environmental decades," the period from 1955 to 1985 that produced most of the laws we have today, historian Samuel Hays argues that the modern environmental movement differs markedly from the early-twentieth-century conservation movement exemplified by Gifford Pinchot's effort to develop physical resources more efficiently. He traces the roots of modern environmentalism to changes in public values and preferences that coincided with the massive social and economic transformation that followed World War II. Hays observes that a key factor in the early success of environmental organizations was their ability to provide legislators with technical data. Some of the first national environmental groups had been founded by scientists concerned about environmental trends, and most major organizations employed technical staff who supplied legislators with crucial information. Hays explains that environmental groups appreciated the importance of participating not only in the legislative process, but also in the administrative process agencies use to translate laws into regulations.

William Rodgers, Jr., examines some of the factors that have prevented the ambitious goals of the environmental laws from being achieved. Using an analogy from animal behavior (in which crows engage in deliberately deceptive behavior to convince owls not to attack them), Rodgers describes the various means by which politicians adopt tough-sounding environmental laws with subtle provisions that make them difficult to implement successfully. He provides a detailed catalogue of the various deceptive strategies legislators use to craft "consensus" legislation that ultimately proves to be far less than meets the eye.

*Robert L. Rabin*

# Federal Regulation in Historical Perspective (1986)

By 1970, the most dramatic environmental effects of unchecked industrialism had already received occasional attention. Beginning in the late 1950s, the hazards of atomic fallout became a matter of public concern. Rachel Carson's book *The Silent Spring*, an account of the ecological impact of pesticides, was a bestseller as early as 1962. Continuous smog alerts in Los Angeles became a subject of black humor by the late 1960s. The Santa Barbara oil spill in 1969 caused a widespread sense of revulsion against despoliation of the natural environment. The proposal to dam the Grand Canyon triggered a minipolitical movement in favor of protecting a cherished scenic wonder. Thus, at the tail end of the 1960s, it was simply a matter of creating a pattern and assigning meaning to these and other disparate episodes.

Moreover, when these discrete mishaps were viewed collectively, a more fundamental critique became apparent—a critique with clear implications for the administrative system. Rather than appearing as random catastrophes, the oil spills, smog alerts, and chemical hazards seemed to be the most visible manifestations of an inappropriately narrow conception of the role of public regulation. From an economist's perspective, these social costs came to be discussed in terms of externality analysis. From a political scientist's vantage point, the undesirable side-effects of industrialism were characterized as one consequence of pluralism. In fact, both critiques were on the mark because the regulatory system that had emerged from the New Deal was inadequate to the task of controlling the newly discovered dilemmas of the 1970s.

Two fundamental system-wide failures became apparent—corresponding to the dual aspects of the environmental problem. To begin with, pollution simply had never been taken seriously as a collective problem; its social cost had been treated as an externality borne for the most part by receptors as a class rather than assigned to polluters as a cost of doing business. The only weapons available to victims of pollu-

Robert L. Rabin, Federal Regulation in Historical Perspective, 38 Stan. L. Rev. 1189 (1986).

tion were an ineffectual common law remedy, the tort of private nuisance, and a collection of weak federal and state antipollution statutes.

Secondly, the growing conflict between industrial development and mass recreational use, on the one hand, and conservation of natural sites and species, on the other, had never been seriously confronted. The problem was not just one of externalities—the absence of an institutional framework for identifying and assigning liability for the residual costs of industrial and recreational activities—but, even more centrally, an attribute of the pluralist phenomenon. The existing regulatory institutions, whether one examined the Forest Service, the Federal Power Commission, or the Army Corps of Engineers, implemented their statutory mandates with a distinctive political bias. Almost invariably, such agencies viewed the world through the same prism as their regulatory clientele. These constituent groups, in turn, pressed for economic development projects rather than seeking to promote aesthetic and conservation values.

Thus, advocates of "the public interest," rendered suspicious of authority and skeptical of materialism by the events of the 1960s, joined the chorus of academic discontent in discerning an underlying pattern of institutional neglect beneath the surface of sporadic crises and catastrophes that made the newspaper headlines. There was a pervasive sense of grievance in the air and receptivity to change—and that was sufficient to launch a new wave of regulatory activity in Congress.

The forewarning that a new era was dawning came in 1966 when Congress passed the Auto Safety Act, a tribute in large part to the persistence of an obscure consumer activist, Ralph Nader. In his book *Unsafe at Any Speed,* Nader had shown the temerity to catalogue the auto industry's indifference to safety considerations. In doing so, he was publicly cast in the role of David battling Goliath by subsequent heavy-handed efforts of General Motors to discredit him. Once GM thrust Nader into the limelight, his findings had an impact reminiscent of the most visible Progressive era muckrakers.

Indeed, in many ways the consumerist impulses triggered by Nader's auto safety campaign built directly upon the foundations of Progressive era legislation. For example, the Wholesome Meat Act of 1967, passed in response to Nader's allegations of unsanitary conditions in meat processing plants, was designed to extend federal standards to the intrastate processors who were not covered by the 1906 meat inspection legislation. Similarly, the Magnuson-Moss Warranty and FTC Improvements Act of 1972 arose out of a crystallized perception of the structural deficiencies in the Federal Trade Commission Act. Further, the establishment of the Consumer Product Safety Commission a year later can be traced to the truncated consumer protection authority of the FTC.

Despite Nader's early consumerist influence, however, it was environmental concerns over health, safety, and conservation that dominated the Public Interest era. Within the short space of six years, Congress passed landmark legislation dealing with air and water pollution, occupational health and safety, hazardous wastes and toxic substances, and preservation of endangered sites and species. This legislative eruption affected virtually every sector of the economy. The regulatory system was studded with new acronyms, such as OSHA, EPA, and CEQ.

Two congressional enactments stand out among this outburst of activity as particularly dramatic departures in regulatory design. On the threshold of the new era, the National Environmental Policy Act (NEPA) was signed into law on January 1, 1970. Its text and legislative history suggest that NEPA may have been intended as a largely symbolic enactment, expressing the new mood of environmental concern, but without establishing any substantive bite. Title I of the Act reads more like an environmental Declaration of Fundamental Rights than a traditional regulatory statute. And the new agency established in NEPA, the Council on Environmental Quality, was given the relatively uncontroversial tasks of preparing an annual report on the state of the environment, assisting other agencies in implementing the statute, and monitoring environmental trends.

But in Section 102(2)(c), NEPA contained a provision which was to have a singular effect on regulatory decisionmaking—the requirement of an Environmental Impact Statement. . . .

The distinctiveness of this requirement can be fully appreciated only by taking account of the continuing shadow cast by the New Deal on the eve of the Public Interest era. . . . [T]he heated debate about the need for greater control over the discretion exercised by New Deal agencies had been temporarily resolved by the passage of the Administrative Procedure Act in 1946. . . .

. . . NEPA represented a wholly different strategy for controlling administrative discretion. Most importantly, the Act had a powerful substantive impetus that was absent from earlier plenary regulatory reform proposals. In essence, APA-type reform took the agency's "mission" as given, and aimed at creating a formal decisionmaking methodology which would be more conducive to careful deliberation, and to achieving "correct" outcomes. By contrast, NEPA directly challenged the premise that mission-oriented agencies were discharging their responsibilities with a proper regard to "the public interests," as long as they failed to give focused consideration to the impact of their decisions on the environment. NEPA anticipated an altered process of decision rather than simply better procedures for decision; the environmental impact statement was to be "action-forcing" in that every federal regulatory agency was to reassess its mandate in view of the environmental consequences of any major decision it might reach.

In addition to this highly significant substantive requirement, NEPA brought a different procedural perspective to regulatory reform. The environmental impact statement requirement constituted a departure from the classical approaches to controlling discretion just discussed. From the APA through the New Property, procedural reformers had turned to the adversary model of decisionmaking and proposed more extensive trial-type requirements for agencies. By contrast, NEPA was silent about hearings. In fact, Section 102(2)(c) is completely devoid of all the familiar trappings of procedural reform: There is no reference to the timing of an impact statement, the manner in which it should be prepared or the availability of judicial review.

The primary thrust of NEPA—which underscores its distinctive character—was its reliance upon an internal management technique that owed a greater debt to organization theory than to administrative law. Under the most optimistic scenario, the routinization of an impact statement requirement would necessitate specialized administrative personnel and the establishment of new channels of communication and information-flow within an agency. If these bureaucratic operating procedures were conscientiously pursued, a traditionally mission-oriented agency could exhibit a new sensitivity in defining its organizational goals.

NEPA did, in fact, have a tremendous impact on the administrative system, although not necessarily that which might have been anticipated. Within months of the Act's passage, a federal court had enjoined the Trans-Alaska pipeline on grounds of failure to prepare an impact statement. The message from that widely publicized case was clear: The agencies could not ignore the enactment of NEPA.

By 1975, the CEQ reported that in excess of a thousand impact statements had been filed annually over the preceding four years by federal agencies. And landmark cases like *Calvert Cliffs,* reading NEPA as a broad charter for requiring "individualized consideration and balancing of environmental factors," ensured that environmental litigants would have a potent weapon for attacking *pro forma* efforts at compliance with the requirement of an environmental impact statement. While it is difficult to generalize about the extent to which NEPA actually reordered the priorities of mission-oriented federal agencies, there can be no doubt that the prospect of close judicial scrutiny, and its attendant consequences of additional delay, information-gathering costs, and adverse publicity, had a dramatic impact on the way agencies approached their environmental responsibilities in the 1970s.

The second pathbreaking piece of environmental regulatory legislation was the Clean Air Amendments of 1970 (CAA). In many ways, the design of this landmark pollution control scheme is at the polar extreme from NEPA. Where NEPA is a broadly stated charter of environmental rights consisting of barely a page of text, the CAA is an extraordinarily technical document as lengthy as a decent-sized novel (although hardly as readable). Where NEPA was designed to influence the mandate of every federal agency, the CAA is addressed to a single specialized agency headed by a sole administrator. Where NEPA is directed exclusively at the federal agencies, the CAA allocates major implementation responsibilities to the states. And finally, where NEPA is designed to effectuate internal management reforms within the federal bureaucracy, the CAA relies upon traditional rulemaking and adjudication enforcement procedures—including private rights of action—and establishes various avenues for judicial review.

What unites the Clean Air Act with NEPA as a real innovation in regulatory design is congressional recourse to an action-forcing principle. The CAA, like NEPA, rejects the prevailing New Deal wisdom that agency experts could best bring their technical expertise to bear on problems of public policy if they were pointed in the right direction, whether allocation of air traffic routes, design of river rechannelization projects, or whatever, and told to regulate in "the public interest." NEPA challenged the received learning in a very explicit fashion. Its concern was that, without further direction, a water project administrator—to take one example—would be likely to approve the design of a project with single-minded reference to economic criteria. NEPA was meant to widen the administrator's horizons.

The CAA posed a very different challenge to the New Deal perspective. In setting stringent deadlines for administrative action, the CAA questioned the very will of the regulatory agencies to act. It warned that if air pollution controls were to be enforced by the New Deal strategy, 40 years of experience suggested that the regulators would delay, equivocate, and generally fail to establish in any precise way what "the public interest" required. Whereas NEPA's response was to rewrite the substantive mandate of the agencies, the CAA took the different tack of requiring that precise standards be established and explicit compliance timetables be met.

Rejecting the toothless provisions of earlier air pollution control legislation, the 1970 CAA established a series of tight deadlines for achieving the overriding objective of the Act: to control the emission of those pollutants which in the administrator's judgment had "an adverse effect on public health or welfare." To that end, the Act specified that the administrator was to propose ambient air quality standards, based exclusively on risk-related considerations, within 30 days of enactment and to set final standards within 90 days; the states, which were responsible for translating each air quality standard into emissions controls on stationary sources (industrial plants) within their air quality control regions, had another nine months to prepare state implementation plans; the administrator, in turn, was given four months in which to approve or disapprove the plans; and finally, the sources were allowed three years in which to attain the primary emissions standards applicable to them.

The strategy for new mobile sources (motor vehicles) was equally uncompromising: Using 1970 emissions as a baseline, the auto manufacturers were directed to achieve 90 percent reductions in carbon monoxide and hydrocarbon emissions by 1975, and to meet a similar level of reduction in oxides of nitrogen by 1976. The only leeway allowed was a possible one year, one-time-only extension, if the administrator found that certain infeasibility criteria were met.

Thus the CAA was a summons to action and a tribute to faith in technological innovation. The innovative character of the law, however, must not be overstated. Many of the central features of the Act were established regulatory strategies by 1970. For example, the Act creates a complex interplay of federal and state responsibility, assigning principal responsibility to the administrator for establishing ambient air quality standards and allocating major responsibility to the states for implementing the standards through emissions controls. But this federal-state cooperative strategy was not new; 40 years earlier Roosevelt had resorted to a similar approach in designing both the AFDC and unemployment compensation insurance schemes. And the post–New Deal era was marked by major grant-in-aid programs for highway construction, educational assistance, and public housing, among other large-scale spending schemes, in which funding and planning responsibilities were shared by federal and state regulatory officials.

In another widely noted feature of the Act, Congress ventured into the field of setting particularized standards. Consider, for example, the precision of the above-mentioned standards for new motor vehicles, in which the administrator was not simply instructed to "eliminate unreasonable hazards," but was required to reduce emissions 90 percent from a specified baseline for identified pollutants. . . .

A new congressional mood was evident—a willingness to go beyond the blank-check delegation of the past. Once again, however, this legislative venture is not without major precedents, such as the New Deal securities legislation and the Internal Revenue Code. Moreover, despite the significance that some commentators have attached to legislative precision as a means of controlling discretion, the Clean Air Act, read in its entirety, is not especially restrictive. The Act is replete with standards such as "best system of emission reduction," "reasonably available control technology," "lowest achievable emission rate," and "best available control technology." Such standards create only the illusion of precision. Administrative implementation of the Act confirms what common sense would suggest: "best system," "reasonably available technology," and so forth, are not self-defining terms. These standards serve as meaningful controls on discretion only if the courts are willing to exercise stringent judicial review.

Thus, the Act was not a *tour de force* of legislative innovation. Nonetheless, it was a significant departure in regulatory design to establish a tightly interlocking schedule of deadlines, timetables, and specific targeted air quality goals. Whatever room for discretionary choice exists in defining "lowest achievable emissions" or "best available technology," the notion of unquestioning deference to administrative expertise was dealt a sharp blow by the establishment of firm deadlines for compliance with specified air quality standards.

Many air quality regions remained in violation of the standards for stationary source pollutants throughout the 1970s, and automotive pollutants continued to be a seemingly intractable problem. Nevertheless, on virtually all fronts, there were significant reductions in levels of air pollution in the years following the passage of the Act. In addition, the law's technology-forcing strategy created numerous targets for litigation and a public forum for debate over appropriate pollution policy.

Putting aside the singular implementation strategies associated with NEPA and the CAA, certain generalizations can be made about the salient characteristics of Public Interest era regulatory reform from a historical perspective. At the time of enactment both NEPA and the CAA stirred up almost no controversy, despite the arguably draconian implications of each regulatory scheme. In both cases the most significant political compromises were negotiated in order to iron out differences between forces friendly to the legislation, rather than to pacify a hostile opposition.

For example, in the case of NEPA it was necessary for the two leading senatorial proponents of environmental reform, Senators Muskie and Jackson, to agree on questions such as whether the action-forcing impact statement mechanism was to encompass outside review by agencies other than the agency preparing the statement. Far more critically, the impact statement proviso, without which NEPA might have been an empty declaration of support for environmentalism, was only added on the advice of an outside consultant.

Similarly, in the case of the CAA, the major shift in emphasis was to strengthen the law, after its architect, Senator Muskie was stung by sharp criticism of his commitment to the cause of pollution control in a Nader report. Although there was an ineffectual eleventh-hour expression of industry protest, the CAA passed both houses of Congress with overwhelming majorities; in the case of NEPA, there was no discernible opposition.

Viewed in historical perspective, this phenomenon of virtual consensus support for landmark regulatory legislation turns out to be the norm rather than an aberration. From the enactment of the Interstate Commerce Act through the passage of New Deal legislation, major industrial groups were required to generate costly information, were circumscribed in access to markets, and were subjected to criminal enforcement schemes, with hardly a dissenting vote in Congress. Consequently, the smooth passage of the NEPA and the CAA should come as no surprise in itself.

In earlier times, however, the new regulatory scheme frequently produced apparent benefits to powerful regulated interests that helped to explain the relatively mild congressional opposition to proposals for substantial regulatory reform. On this score, the environmental laws of the 1970s, and the contemporaneous consumer protection legislation as well, require some further explanation. No one would seriously argue that lumber companies, highway builders, and electric power interests stood to gain from NEPA; or that steel, copper, and auto producers had any reason to stand up and cheer for the CAA. These statutes were not in the spirit of the Interstate Commerce Act and the National Industrial Recovery Act, which seemed to promise all things to all interest groups.

As James Q. Wilson has argued, much of the public interest regulation passed in the 1970s can be characterized politically as involving concentrated costs (on industry) and dispersed benefits (to "the public")—not a scenario that traditionally augured well for the enactment of regulatory legislation. But in the 1970s, big business was truly on the defensive as the public seemed responsive to a wide variety of concerns about the quality of life. An entire series of initiatives resulted—on auto safety, product design, air and water pollution control, scenic conservation, and occupational health and safety, to mention only the most significant—which manifested a distinct bias against economic growth. The political climate made it virtually impossible to oppose such programs in principle—and focused objections can always be pursued in the process of agency implementation.

A second striking feature of the Public Interest era legislation is that it was not the product of a social movement for reform, nor even the outcome of pluralistic, interest group politics. As Wilson noted, the passage of NEPA and the CAA might well be characterized as instances of "entrepreneurial politics"—situations in which astute politicians adopted anticipatory strategies, setting the agenda for regulatory action prior to clearly articulated interest group demands for change.

This phenomenon has been much more common that is generally recognized. Both New Deal and Great Society regulation represented efforts by political leaders to come to grips with broad-based social ills that had not been translated into focused constituency demands for reform. The distinctive aspect of Public Interest era regulation, however, was the extent to which exceedingly diffuse concerns about health, safety, and conservation were enacted into law with virtually no presidential initiative. By contrast, the New Deal regulatory agenda is strongly associated with Franklin D. Roosevelt, and the Great Society with Lyndon Johnson.

The occupant of the presidential office during the Public Interest era, Richard Nixon, was an uneasy participant from the outset in the movement for "quality of life" regulation. Although he created the EPA and unveiled an air pollution control bill of his own, Nixon's main constituency was quite clearly the business community. Throughout the period, Senator Muskie assumed the mantle of chief protector of the environment. And on the consumer protection side, Ralph Nader served as a one-man catalyst, prodding first one legislative subcommittee and then another to take action on a number of fronts.

A third aspect of the Public Interest era that warrants attention is the relatively limited ideological thrust of the reform measures that characterize the period. This assertion may seem at odds with the antigrowth theme evident throughout the era. Consider, however, that no substantial wealth redistribution impulse fueled the Public Interest reform efforts, and no discernible challenge was mounted against the autonomy of a market-based economy. Instead, the key legislation of the period suggested a return to the policing model of Progressivism. In the areas of pollution control, occupational safety, and consumer protection, the prevailing ideology anticipated the internalization of the previously unrecognized costs of industrial growth—a market-corrective strategy that posed no challenge to the premises of an exchange economy.

## E. Donald Elliott, Bruce A. Ackerman, and John C. Millian

# Toward a Theory of Statutory Evolution: The Federalization of Environmental Law (1985)

### Problem: Environmental Statutes of the 1960s and 1970s

An extraordinary outburst of lawmaking relating to pollution and the environment occurred at the national level during the 1960s and 1970s as a dozen major federal pollution control statutes were enacted. This network of national statutes—together with a much larger body of implementing regulations promulgated by the Environmental Protection Agency—now constitutes one of the most pervasive systems of national regulation known to American law. Today every discharge into the land, water or air—from the smallest smokestack to the largest landfill for the disposal of toxic chemicals—requires direct or indirect permission from the national government.

This comprehensive structure of environmental regulation by the federal government is a curious feature of American law for at least two reasons. First, it developed fairly suddenly, seemingly out of nowhere. For two centuries, the effects of industrial pollution on the natural environment had been generally free from regulation by government, except for sporadic nuisance actions under the common law and a few municipal ordinances to control smoke. Second, it is curious that the environmental law of the 1970s was made primarily at the national level, rather than by state or municipal governments which had traditionally had legislative authority over such mat-

E. Donald Elliott, Bruce A. Ackerman, and John C. Millian, Toward a Theory of Statutory Evolution: The Federalization of Environmental Law, 1 J. L. Econ. & Org. 313 (1985). Reprinted by permission of Oxford University Press.

ters. Any theory of the evolution of environmental laws must attempt to explain how and why this "orgy of statute-making" came about and why it occurred at the national level.

The environmental statutes of the 1960s and 1970s are distinctive not only for their number but also for their content. In a variety of ways, they represent a sharp break from the attitudes which preceded them. Consider the approach which the Clean Air Act takes toward economics and technology, for example. For hundreds of years, the common law held that no one had an absolute right to be free from the harmful effects of air pollution. Instead, the basic attitude of the law was one of accommodation and "reasonableness," balancing the harmful effects of air pollution on the one hand against the benefits of industrial activity and the availability and cost of abatement technology on the other (Restatement (Second) of Torts, §§826–28).

In the 1970 Clean Air Act, however, Congress stakes out a more extreme position. In setting mandatory national air quality standards, EPA is instructed to give no weight whatsoever to economic considerations (see *Lead Industries Assn.* v. *EPA*, 647 F.2d 1130, D.C.Cir. 1980, cert. denied, 101 S.Ct. 621, 1981). Nor is the technical infeasibility of pollution controls admissible as an excuse (*Union Electric Co.* v. *Environmental Protection Agency*, 427 U.S. 246, 1976). In essence, Congress declared that every American, including particularly sensitive groups such as asthmatics (S.Rep. No. 1196, 91st Cong., 2d Sess. 10, 1970), has a statutory right to be protected from "any known or anticipated adverse effects associated with air pollution" (Clean Air Act, §§109(b)(1) and (2), 84 Stat. 1679, 1970, 42 U.S.C. 7409(b)(1) and (2), 1980), *whatever* the cost.

In pointing to the extraordinary nature of the environmental statutes of the 1970s, we do not mean to suggest that there were no precursors. On the contrary, as will become apparent in what follows, we believe that statutes such as the Clean Air Act of 1970 were a natural outgrowth of a lawmaking process which began at least a decade earlier at the state level. Our point is only that the conditions which produced the environmental statutes of the 1970s are qualitatively different from those which accounted for the pattern of steady, incremental lawmaking during prior decades. As Krier and Ursin have observed, "The Clean Air Amendments of 1970 . . . [were] hardly . . . a tentative reaching out of the federal foot in a halting search for the route that offered least opposition. Rather, there was a dramatic plunge forward." . . .

## Collective Action and Prisoners' Dilemma

The model of legislative politics as a function of the organization of interest groups fails to account for the fact that strong environmental statutes were passed in the early 1970s without pressure from well-organized environmental advocacy groups at the federal level. It is difficult, moreover, to explain the rise of national environmental groups in terms of prevailing theories of voluntary organization. . . .

*Politicians' Dilemma*

The answer, or at least a more complete answer, can be discovered by considering the problems of environmental organizing and passing environmental legislation as analogous to the game of Prisoners' Dilemma.

Prisoners' Dilemma gets its name from a story about two prisoners who are separately interrogated about a crime. The two were the only witnesses, so if they both refuse to testify, the worst that can happen to them is a one-year conviction for illegal possession of firearms. However, a clever prosecutor approaches each prisoner and offers him a proposition: "If you confess and testify against your partner, he'll get life but you'll go free; the only hitch is that if you both confess, you'll both get a sentence of six years for armed robbery. I should tell you that I'm offering the same deal to your partner."

Assuming that the game is played only a single time, and assuming further that the prisoners are rational and motivated only by self-interest, they will both confess—and get six years in jail, rather than keep quiet and get off with only a year. The paradox, of course, is that by pursuing their individual self-interest, the prisoners behave in a way that is contrary to their shared collective interest in shorter sentences. If they could only organize their actions for their common benefit, they would both be better off.

In his recent book on collective action, Russell Hardin has shown that the problems of forming voluntary groups described by [Marcus] Olson are an application of Prisoners' Dilemma. In classic Prisoners' Dilemma, each prisoner confesses in an attempt to exploit his codefendant, and as a result they both end up worse off than they would have been if they had coordinated their actions for the collective benefit. Similarly, a citizen who wants clean air but refrains from joining an environmental group in the hope that she can free-ride on the efforts of others is also playing an exploitative strategy. She will be best off if she gets the benefits of clean air without paying her fair share of the costs for this collective good; her exploitative strategy will not work, however, if everyone plays the same strategy. When everyone, or nearly everyone, tries to free-ride, they all end up worse off than they would have been if they had been able to coordinate their actions to play a cooperative strategy. . . .

The hidden moral of the story of Prisoners' Dilemma is that forming a voluntary organization for collective benefit is not the only way to organize persons to engage in collective action; it is also possible to coordinate actions by altering the structure of incentives which motivate them. It is important to notice, moreover, that the prosecutor is not essential to the tale. She is merely a narrative device, a convenient personification of the institutional structure facing the prisoners. It is this institutional structure, not the prosecutor as a conscious actor, that defines the incentives facing the prisoners and explains their otherwise inexplicable actions.

This institutional perspective helps to explain the evolution of environmental law during the late 1960s and early 1970s. Not that the evolving institutional structure technically complied with all the conditions for the game of Prisoners' Dilemma—in contrast to the standard game, our story involves many relevant players, no single subset of which could have coordinated their strategies in a way that guaranteed them an optimal result. Nonetheless, like the prisoners, many of the key actors responded to institutional threats of terrible outcomes by rationally choosing strategies that were very far from first-best from their point of view. We shall, then, use the term *Politicians' Dilemma* to describe situations which are analogous to the game of Prisoners' Dilemma in that the structure of incentives facing the players creates a strong incentive for them to pursue a less than ideal outcome in order to avoid an even less desirable result. We believe that institutional structures which create the Politicians' Dilemma are a particularly important feature of our lawmaking system, since they provide one mechanism by which Kenneth Arrow's famous General Impossibility Theorem (1963) is resolved in practice, as groups are forced to abandon their true preferences to coalesce around compromise legislation.

### Politicians' Dilemma and Environmental Statutes

The first significant federal statutes regulating air pollution, the Motor Vehicle Pollution Control Act of 1965 (79 Stat. 992) and the Air Quality Act of 1967 (81 Stat. 485), were not passed because of the political power of environmentalists at the national level but because two well-organized industrial groups, the automobile industry and the soft coal industry, were threatened with a state of affairs even worse from their perspective than federal air pollution legislation—namely, inconsistent and progressively more stringent environmental laws at the state and local level. As a consequence of the structure of our federal lawmaking system, environmentalists were able to organize industry to do their bidding for them. Thus, the first federal legislation regulating air pollution was passed not because environmentalists solved their own organizational problems on the national level but because environmentalists exploited the organizational difficulties of their industrial adversaries at the state and local level.

The auto industry and the soft coal industry undoubtedly would have preferred no government regulation of air pollution rather than federal legislation. When faced with the threat of inconsistent and increasingly rigorous state laws, however, they resolved their Politicians' Dilemma by using their superior organizational capacities in Washington to preempt or control the environmentalists' legislative victories at the state level.

It does not matter to our argument whether environmentalists and industrialists were consciously pursuing the strategy we outline. Like the characters in the Prisoners' Dilemma, they may have been simply reacting rationally to the strategic implications of their situation. What we have found, in short, is empirical support for a paradox previously elaborated by theorists of federal systems. Rather than serving only as a mechanism for *decentralized* decisionmaking, federalism also creates strategic incentives for *national* lawmaking activities that would not have existed under simpler unitary constitutions. Thus, a political chain-reaction occurred in which organized industries used their resources at the federal level to offset the dangers posed by environmentalists' activities at the state level.

But pressure group analysis is never enough to explain the passage of a statute. The challenge, instead, is to show how rational legislators can make use of the changing political environment to further their own goals of re-election and political advancement. During the period of preemptive federalization this turns out to be a relative straightforward affair. Given the absence of significant federal legislation, the air pollution issue was ripe for political entrepreneurship by an ambitious legislator with presidential aspirations.

Our aspirant could point out that before *his* landmark legislation, the federal government had been doing little or nothing in the war against pollution. The fact that his initiative preempted or otherwise constrained even more stringent state legislation could be viewed (if it was perceived at all) as an unfortunate side-effect of the fact that pollution was a problem that required a coordinated national solution.

Moreover, the institutional structure of Congress provided one particular presidential aspirant with the organizational means to appropriate the political credit associated with a legislative breakthrough. By exercising his powers as chairman of the relevant Senate subcommittee, Edmund Muskie could claim credit for legislation at a time when other presidential aspirants had not yet invested in linking their names to a cleaner environment. Thus, our period of preemptive federalization reveals a second form of preemptive activity. Not only did the auto and coal industries seek to preempt activist state regulation, but Senator Muskie sought to associate his name so intimately with environmental protection that he would effectively preempt efforts by rival aspirants to claim credit for legislation on the issue.

The second phase of statutory creativity at the federal level we call Time Four, the period of aspirational lawmaking. It will modify both premises of the preceding structure. On the level of interest group organization, local environmental activists began to credibly threaten federal politicians with electoral retribution, although they were not yet organized as a coherent lobby in Washington. As a consequence, the organizational advantage shifted away from the hands of the Washington representatives of a few well-organized industrial interests.

At the same time, the effort by Senator Muskie to corner the credit-claiming market was placed in jeopardy by the entry of two rivals. Senator Henry Jackson, principal sponsor of the National Environmental Policy Act, and President Richard Nixon. It is this context of competitive credit-claiming that serves as the matrix generating the basic structure of environmental institutions of the present day: the National Environmental Policy Act of 1969, the Environmental Protection Agency, created in 1970, the Clean Air Act of 1970, and the Clean Water Act of 1972.

Competitive credit-claiming gives a double sense to our label of aspirational lawmaking: not only did environmental aspirations take on a new political significance as environmentalists organized at the local level, but, because there was not yet a coherent National Clean Air Coalition with whom a bargain could be struck, lawmaking was characterized by unrestrained competition among presidential aspirants for the credit to be gained from legislation assuring the public of a cleaner world. Thus, paradoxically, the failure of environmentalists to achieve full national organization during Time Four resulted in more stringent—not weaker—environmental laws.

*Daniel A. Farber*

# Politics and Procedure in Environmental Law (1992)

## The Sources of Environmental Legislation

*Special Interests and Environmental Law*

The simplest explanation for the passage of environmental laws is that they actually reflect the influence of special interests rather than the preferences of the general public. The special interest involved may be variously depicted as either a producer interest or a consumer interest.

*Environmental Statutes as Industry Rent-Seeking.* The producer theory is that environmental statutes are actually blinds for rent-seeking by the regulated industries themselves. Thus, as Jon Macey puts it, "environmental protection statutes, which appear to be classic public interest statutes designed to ensure the optimal production of a public good (i.e., a clean environment), often contain features consistent only with the protection of special interests." Taking advantage of the public desire for environmental protection, firms procure statutes that are actually designed to profit the purportedly regulated industries.

Environmental statutes clearly do impose heavy costs on firms. The special-interest story, then, involves differential costs between different segments of industry, which are thought to give the favored segments an advantage. There are two problems with this theory.

First, the broad scope of environmental legislation is at odds with the theory. The number of firms involved seems too high to be plausible. Environmental legislation such as the Clean Air Act involves virtually every industry. Even if only large firms

Daniel A. Farber, Politics and Procedure in Environmental Law, 8 J. L. Econ. & Org. 59 (1992). Reprinted by permission of Oxford University Press.

benefit, passage of the legislation would still require organizing the efforts of many politicians and of firms in multiple industries. Apart from the transaction costs involved in organizing a lobbying effort on this scale, such a widespread effort would create a high risk of public disclosure. There would be obvious rewards to any media firm that uncovered the industry conspiracy behind major pending legislation. Even if these organizational problems are not severe enough to make broad-scale legislation impossible, it clearly would be easier for the key firms in particular industries to organize than to organize a single economy-wide effort. (Note that there may be conflicts between industries, since efforts to increase rents for suppliers will usually disadvantage firms that purchase their products.) Hence, if firms were providing the primary impetus for environmental legislation, we would expect to find that most environmental regulation originated in industry-specific legislation. This pattern was characteristic of earlier economic regulation, but has not been typical of environmental laws.

Second, the idea that environmental legislation is essentially a sham, used to conceal only special-interest benefits to producer groups, is itself incompatible with positive political theory. Positive theory assumes that voters are economically rational. Such voters should have "rational expectations." But if the Olson theory is correct, and if voters have rational expectations, they cannot be deceived by the appearance of "public-interest" legislation. Knowing the Olson theory, rational voters would realize that the legislation must instead be intended to benefit some special interest at their expense. Hence, there would be no point to the deception; no one would ever believe that the purported public-interest motivation of the legislation was real.

The same problem attends a variant of the producer theory involving administrative delegations. Neil Komesar argues that widespread expressions of environmental enthusiasm by politicians do not translate into effective regulation because industry captures the implementation phase. This theory claims that producer groups cannot prevent the passage of legislation but can obtain a broad delegation of power to the agency, which they can thereafter capture.

This theory does fit common ideas about legislative motivation, according to which members of Congress prefer broad delegations so they can "pass the buck" and avoid taking responsibility for the consequences of legislation. If there is a conflict between important political groups, the last thing a legislator wants to do is to take sides, thereby making political enemies. If one group is better able than the other to monitor administrative action, the legislator can have the best of both worlds. The group with higher monitoring costs—here, the public—is pleased by the passage of apparently constructive legislation, but cannot monitor the ultimate administrative outcomes. The more observant group (industry) is mollified by the knowledge that the administrative action will actually work to its advantage. So everyone goes away happy.

Again, this theory depends on voter myopia. Voters who have rational expectations should know they have poorer monitoring abilities than industry. They should then predict that delegations will result in unfavorable administrative decisions. Hence, they should not be fooled by congressional delegations. Realistically, we cannot expect anything close to perfect rationality. But it is not implausible to expect that voters will realize that politicians may exploit their relative lack of information. Nor is it implausible to expect them to learn over time that they may be duped and to respond rationally to that knowledge. In short, the delegation and special-interest theories seem unsustainable as long-run equilibria.

This does not mean, of course, that industry groups play no role in shaping environmental legislation. To the extent that alternate regulatory methods can achieve similar environmental results, environmental groups may be relatively indifferent, so the final choice may be heavily influenced by industry lobbying. On occasion, environmental groups and industry also may form a coalition, to obtain legislation that for varying reasons is beneficial to both. Thus, domestic car producers may support safety standards that discriminate against foreign producers, or large textile or chemical firms may support environmental standards that discriminate against their smaller competitors. While the original "push" for this regulation may not have been to particularly hurt foreign or small competitors, that may have been the price that had to be paid to have the support of the affected industry. Moreover, industry opposition may often result in legislative compromises between economic and environmental goals. Industry may even promote environmental legislation on its own, as a way of heading off an environmental backlash. Thus, in various ways, industry may be an active participant in the passage of environmental legislation. Nevertheless, industry does not seem to provide the primary impetus for environmental legislation.

*Rent-Seeking by Consumers.* An alternative theory views environmental legislation as rent-seeking by "consumers" of environmental quality. In this view, environmental statutes are primarily designed to serve the interest of upper-middle class backpackers, who have an unusually high demand for environmental amenities.

One flaw in this theory is that some crucial environmental legislation passed before groups such as the Sierra Club had become politically formidable. For example, the National Environmental Protection Act and the Wilderness Act were passed in the 1960s, when the Sierra Club was a small California-based club of 35,000 members. Although it became an active litigant in the 1970s, not until 1980 did the Sierra Club engage in any political endorsements, and then on only a limited scale. Indeed, the Clean Air Act may have been strengthened as a result of the absence of any organized environmental lobby. Moreover, the financial resources available to environmental groups are much less than those of their industry opponents.

More fundamentally, this theory underestimates the prevalence of environmentalist attitudes. In 1989, 80 percent of the population agreed that "[p]rotecting the environment is so important that regulations and standards cannot be too high, and continuing environmental improvements must be made regardless of cost." It is doubtful that voters would really support environmental regulation "regardless of cost," but their willingness to endorse this statement does show that they place a high value on the environment. Other studies of public opinion characterize environmentalism as a "consensual" value in American society. Indeed, environmentalist attitudes are now well-nigh omnipresent in American society, as Mark Sagoff shows in an important recent paper; he quotes Richard Darman (currently head of the Office of Management and Budget) as offering a particularly vivid description of this situation:

> Increasingly, we are all environmentalists. The President is an environmentalist. Republicans and Democrats are environmentalist. Jane Fonda and the National Association of Manufacturers, Magic Johnson and Danny DeVito, Candice Bergen and "The Golden Girls," Bugs Bunny and the cast of "Cheers" are all environmentalist.

In particular, Sagoff points out environmentalist attitudes are now found in publications that cater to groups quite different from the backpacker stereotype, including farm magazines, car and truck magazines, and hunting and fishing journals. Thus, environmental legislation seems to have a base of public support much broader than "wine and cheese" nature lovers.

In either its producer or consumer form, the special-interest theory falls short as an explanation of environmental legislation. This is not to say, of course, that particular features of specific environmental statutes never reflect the influence of producer groups or elite groups of nature lovers; it would be surprising to find that these groups had zero political influence. Thus, environmental legislation will tend to represent a balance between industry and environmental interests. But taken as a whole, the existence of modern environmental legislation cannot be explained by the special-interest model. That model has a variety of weaknesses, and it is not surprising to find that it fails here. But its failure leaves a major puzzle. If environmental statutes do in significant part reflect a broad public demand, how does that demand get translated into legislation?

## Mass Politics and Political Entrepreneurs

*Public Opinion and Environmental Legislation.* Classical public-choice theory tends to cut any link between public opinion and legislation, giving center stage to special-interest groups, with more widely dispersed preferences having only a peripheral role. Indeed, public-choice theory has some well-known difficulties accounting for the fact that people vote at all. Given the small chance of any individual vote influencing the outcome, voting seems irrational as an instrumental activity. In short, we would expect to see very little public attention to or influence on legislation.

An alternative tradition of political thought, that of civic republicanism, is represented in a recent article by James Pope:

> Our history has from the outset been characterized by periodic outbursts of democratic participation and ideological politics. And if history is any indicator, the legal system's response to these "republican moments" may be far more important than its attitude toward interest group politics. The most important transformations in our political order . . . were brought on by republican moments.

As Pope defines these republican moments, their major features are (a) widespread public participation, taking the form of social movements and voluntary associations;

and (b) utilizing a moral discourse appealing to concepts of the common good. For present purposes, it is the first of these characteristics that is most significant.

Putting aside the normative aspects of this theory, it adds a significant temporal dimension to the analysis. The implication is that politics alternates between normal periods, in which public attention to an issue is weak, and extraordinary periods, in which the issue has high salience for the public. In those extraordinary periods when broad segments of the public are intensely involved with an issue, legislators find themselves in the spotlight, and their positions shift closer to those of the public at large. During republican moments, voters acquire information about legislative positions, but they also acquire information about the state of the world that may lead to a change in their own expressed preferences. These periods are likely to be attended by new legislative initiatives responding to this public demand, which is less likely than legislation passed in other periods to be responsive to the demands of conventional interest groups.

The original 1970 Earth Day looks very much like a "republican moment." An estimated 20 million Americans participated in a variety of public events that day. More than 2,000 colleges, 10,000 high schools and elementary schools, and 2,000 communities took part. Some 20 years later, the reverberations were still being felt, as millions of people took part in a celebration of the 20th anniversary of Earth Day. It is little wonder that environmental law has been used as a paradigm by republicans such as Sagoff.

The observation that environmental legislation has been driven by broad public opinion is not necessarily tied to republicanism or any normative political theory; it is ultimately an empirical assertion. Positive theory confirms that in periods of heightened public attention, legislative "shirking" will diminish, and legislative outcomes will be pushed in the direction preferred by the median voter.

This view of the popular origins of environmental legislation is confirmed by an important historical study. In their investigation of the passage of the 1970 Clean Air Act, [Elliott, Ackerman, and Millian] found that organized environmental groups did not play a major role, nor did the activities of traditional industry interest groups. Instead, the primary motivating force was public pressure for environmental protection.

The term "republican moment" is perhaps misleading, to the extent that it suggests that very short periods of high-pitched public interest alternate with periods of nearly total public apathy. Rather, there is a continuum. Earth Day of 1970 represented a peak, but there have been lesser peaks of public pressure sparked by events such as Love Canal or Three Mile Island. In between these peaks, public attention is lower, but not nonexistent.

*Legislative Motivation.* Popular enthusiasm cannot by itself produce federal legislation; the Constitution provides no mechanism for direct democracy. If popular enthusiasm is to be translated into legislation, then legislators have to be actively involved. What is their motivation?

The [Elliott, Ackerman, and Millian] study suggests that one powerful motivation is the desire to earn a public reputation by taking credit for major reform legislation. This incentive is especially strong in the Senate, where a significant number of members have presidential aspirations. For example, one driving force behind the Clean Air Act was Senator Muskie's desire to establish himself as "Mr. Environment." Once the legislative leadership defined the "environmentally sound" position, other legislators had a strong incentive to "get on board" or risk the wrath of an aroused public; the leadership proposal became the minimum measure of environmentally sound policy.

### Symbolic versus Substantive Legislation

*"Lash Yourself to the Mast" and "Strike When the Iron Is Cold."* The combination of republican moments and legislative credit-seeking provides a convincing explanation for the passage of environmental legislation. As the reference to republican "moments" itself suggests, however, waves of popular mobilization are usually intense but short. The rational strategy for legislators is, in the language of Roger Noll and James Krier, "to 'lash themselves to the mast' while waiting out the temporary siren calls for immediate overreaction"; the politicians then delegate to an agency on terms that will allow the "agency to 'strike when the iron is cold,' after the issue has lost its political salience." Thus, as Noll and Krier say, we would expect to find a temporal instability, in which apparently bold legislative measures result in little actual implementation.

This phenomenon is certainly not unknown in environmental law. In an exhaustive study, John Dwyer demonstrates how this story played out with section 112 of the Clean Air Act, which purported to ban all toxic air pollution but was never actually implemented in its original form. By enacting the law, legislators gained the benefits of symbolic endorsement for "health and the environment" and against "trading lives for dollars"; while Congress's failure to decide the hard policy issues actually made the provision essentially a dead letter.

If the only operative forces were popular mood and legislative credit taking, symbolic legislation would be ubiquitous. Yet, as pointed out earlier, it is hard to see how this situation could be sustained in the long run unless voters are not just ignorant or even irrational but also outright fools, incapable of learning even after sustained experience.

Environmental legislation often does have a strongly symbolic nature and is rarely implemented to the full extent promised by the statutory language. Perhaps the most notorious example was the promise of the 1972 Clean Water Act to eliminate all pollution by 1985. Yet, this is hardly the full story. Even section 112, the provision discussed by Dwyer, was extensively amended as part of the 1990 Clean Air Act. It now contains highly burdensome and complex requirements for hazardous air pollutants. Rather than being a dead letter, the new statute promises to cost industry billions of dollars.

The history of section 112 suggests some of the empirical problems with the simple symbolic-legislation (or "lash yourself to the mast") model. First, the demand for environmental laws is less fitful than the model suggests. Most environmental statutes are not one-shot efforts, which are thereafter forgotten; they are likely to be followed by further legislation. For example, the Clean Air Act was passed in 1970 and extensively amended in 1977 and 1990; the Clean Water Act was passed in 1972 with substantial amendments in 1977 and 1987.

Second, in general, environmental laws seem to have greater long-term efficacy than this model suggests. They produce years of regulatory effort, often prompted by active litigation. Participants in the legislative process are quite aware that only implementation, rather than mere passage of a law, produces environmental improvements.

Third, the programs contain far more substantive detail than can be easily accommodated by this model. While some of the legislation is symbolic, much of it seems to mean business. For instance, the 1990 amendments of the Clean Air Act demonstrate a serious commitment to implementation. Perhaps the most interesting provision is contained in the amendment to section 112. Cognizant of the possibility that Environmental Protection Agency (EPA) action may be hamstrung, the statute contains a burdensome default provision that promises highly stringent regulation unless EPA moves expeditiously. More generally, as [McCubbins, Noll, and Weingast] have explained, environmental statutes typically contain procedural mechanisms intended to preserve the original legislative deal. Usually, these mechanisms provide for hearing rights and judicial review at the behest of environmental groups, who can thereby keep the legislative effort from dissipating in the administrative process. In short, environmental law has much more durability and "bite" than seems plausible under the symbolic legislation model.

*Incentives for Nonsymbolic Legislation.* Why do legislatures enact real as opposed to symbolic legislation? Part of the motivation for environmental legislation may be ideological. For example, Earth Day was the brainchild of Senator Gaylord Nelson, who had previously demonstrated his environmental allegiance as governor of Wisconsin. Ideological legislators seek to screen legislation for substance as well as symbolism, since they care about policy outcomes.

This explanation assumes, of course, that legislators' ideology has some causal influence on their behavior. There is a wealth of empirical evidence supporting this proposition. There are also two strong theoretical explanations. Ideological behavior may represent "shirking" by legislators—that is, the use of their offices to serve their own goals rather than those of constituents or interest groups. There is at least some empirical support for this view of legislator ideology. An alternative view is that ideology serves constituents by decreasing monitoring costs. By voting for a legislator with a strong ideological commitment on issues of concern to them, constituents can be assured that the legislator will implement those interests. Hence, constituents need not invest so much in monitoring the actual performance of legislators.

Credit-seeking legislators also have good reason to seek effective legislation. Typically, they will not be able to establish their positions as leaders on particular issues overnight. Rather, only a series of legislative initiatives can convince the media of their leadership role. Because of this delay factor, however, information will become available on the implementation of the legislator's earlier proposals. If these earlier proposals were purely symbolic, the media will dismiss the legislator as a lightweight. To be an effective credit seeker, it is important to avoid the appearance of pure credit seeking—to show that one is not "all hat and no cattle" or "all sizzle and no steak." Yet it is difficult to develop an image as a substantive player without actually delivering some substance.

Political parties may also be a subsidiary source of regulatory durability. As Jon Macey argues, political parties provide a mechanism by which relatively diverse citizen interests are represented in the legislative process. The parties (as ongoing enterprises) have incentives like those of individual legislators to demonstrate ideological commitments on highly topical issues and to engage in credit-seeking behavior. These incentives are especially strong on issues like the environment, which are salient but nonconflictual among voters. Like individual legislators, parties also have some incentive to demonstrate that their commitment on particular issues is substantive rather than merely symbolic. Thus, party organizations may attempt to pressure individual legislators toward more substantive stands, although the extent of the pressure they can exert is unclear.

*Samuel P. Hays*

# Beauty, Health, and Permanence: Environmental Politics in the United States, 1955–1985 (1987)

Accounts of the rise of environmentalism frequently have emphasized its roots in the conservation movement of the early twentieth century. But environmental differed markedly from conservation affairs. The conservation movement was an effort on the part of leaders in science, technology, and government to bring about more efficient development of physical resources. The environmental movement, on the other hand, was far more widespread and popular, involving public values that stressed the quality of human experience and hence of the human environment. Conservation was an aspect of the history of production that stressed efficiency, whereas environment was a part of the history of consumption that stressed new aspects of the American standard of living.

Environmental objectives arose out of deep-seated changes in preferences and values associated with the massive social and economic transformation in the decades after 1945. Conservation had stirred technical and political leaders and then worked its way down from the top of the political order, but environmental concerns arose later from a broader base and worked their way from the middle levels of society outward, constantly to press upon a reluctant leadership. . . .

## The Politics of Legislation, Administration, and Litigation

*Legislative Politics*

Before the environmental decades citizen groups had engaged in political action in behalf of environmental values only sporadically. There was, for example, the unsuccessful attempt on the part of John Muir and the Sierra Club early in the twenti-

eth century to prevent the construction of Hetch Hetchy Dam and the successful defense of Echo Park from a similar proposal in the early 1950s. During the 1960s the
effort by the Sierra Club to prevent dam construction that would mar the Grand
Canyon constituted still another example of these political strategies. The major political tactic was a media campaign to arouse the public. Such efforts as these, occasional lobbying by groups organized on a regional or national basis, reaching the
public largely through the media, constituted the focus of this stage of citizen environmental politics.

In the 1960s lobbying became more frequent. Yet the resources of environmental
groups were small and their activities still limited. They did not serve as a continuous presence for decision makers; action was restricted to crises or specific cam-
paigns. In the late 1960s and early 1970s this changed. One could mark that change
when Washington-based national organizations began to issue regular publications
to their members to inform them of action and to enlist their aid. The National
Wildlife Federation published the first issue of its weekly *Conservation Report* in 1964;
this became the major news service about environmental legislative action in the nation's capital. By the end of the decade other organizations had established similar
services for their members; the *National News Report* of the Sierra Club began publication in 1968.

In late 1960s a leap forward took place in environmental legislative activities. Established organizations such as the Audubon Society, the National Wildlife Federation, the Sierra Club, and the Wilderness Society either initiated or expanded their
legislative capabilities. Often they were hampered because they were chartered as
charitable organizations so as to solicit funds from the general public as nonprofit,
nonpolitical organizations and hence make such contributions tax-deductible. During the 1960s, in the eyes of the Internal Revenue Service, the Sierra Club had gone
too far in its nationwide campaign against damming the Colorado River, and its nonprofit status was rescinded. The club thereby was freed to take a more vigorous political stance. It became known as more fully committed to political action than other
organizations and on that score drew much support from the general public.

New organizations with an active political program appeared in the late 1960s and
early 1970s. Environmental Action and Zero Population Growth came directly from
the campus ferment of the late 1960s, and the Environmental Policy Center was put
together by several national environmental organizations in order to lobby selected
subject areas. There were the new litigation organizations, the Environmental Defense Fund and the Natural Resources Defense Council; their nonprofit status prevented them from lobbying, but they were often invited by legislative committees to
testify on pending bills. Each of these sought to turn the less politically minded outdoor organizations of the past into an active political force and to add to them the
newer environmental interests. . . .

These organizations took part at almost every stage of the legislative process. They
participated in hearings on proposed legislation; this was a traditional part of legislative action and was fully open to citizen groups. An innovation that encouraged
greater external scrutiny from the public and provided a new opportunity for action

was a change in the way committees developed legislation in the initial markup sessions and the later revisions. Formerly such activities had been conducted behind closed doors, but now they were opened to the public. The National Wildlife Federation began to cover subcommittee proceedings in its *Conservation Report,* and environmental organizations began to attend these sessions, following them closely and seeking to influence the crucial committee votes.

Equally important were the informal contacts with the staffs of the committees and the legislators themselves, to whom environmental groups provided useful technical information. All this required effective communications with legislative assistants and elected representatives themselves. Environmentalists hoped to establish relationships with lawmakers, which lobbyists traditionally had cultivated, and to do a better job of it by serving as more reliable sources of information and assistance. . . .

The key factor in the success of environmental lobbyists in Washington was their ability with respect to information and communication in a society and politics increasingly based on technical information. Environmental organizations were able to carry out literature reviews of published studies that were of value to decision makers. They also kept abreast of research under way and made it available to legislators and their staffs. As legislative struggle hinged increasingly on the application of crucial information at strategic times, environmental activists in Washington quickly learned to cultivate these skills.

Most legislators, their assistants, and their committee staffs were limited in their information resources. They could rely on such congressionally based agencies as the Library of Congress, the General Accounting Office, and the Office of Technology Assessment, but much in the wider information world escaped their limited purview. As a result they often looked to private groups to supply such information. The private corporate world, with its enormous information resources, was the major source of such aid. Environmentalists hoped to compete effectively with their opposition on this score, and they were somewhat successful in this because many of the sources were readily available.

Environmentalists often brought together scientists and technical professionals with legislators. They established contacts with technical experts in a joint effort to probe environmental problems, and they sought to give that expertise some weight on the larger political scene. Robert Alvarez of the Environmental Policy Center, interested especially in radiation exposure to workers and the general public, kept in touch with scientists investigating such matters and kept legislative staffs informed; in a series of informal meetings and formal hearings in 1977 and 1978 he brought researchers, legislators, and their staffs together in Washington to share information and ideas. On a more formal level, the Environmental Study Group, founded in 1972 by members of the House and Senate to keep them abreast of environmental affairs, regularly sponsored similar meetings, often as a result of suggestions made by environmental organizations. . . .

Effective legislative politics also involved action at the grassroots. Members of Congress were responsive to the wishes of their constituents, and input from them usually was vital in determining how a legislator would vote. When environmental-ists approached a legislator, they were more successful if constituents had already created a receptive ear by sending in letters and telegrams on the subject. Washing-ton environmental lobbyists, therefore, sought to organize voters to contact their leg-islators so as to maximize the impact of their lobbying.

Some environmental organizations had an advantage in this respect because they had developed within their own structure local groups that served as a link with na-tional action. The Sierra Club and the Audubon Society had local units each with its own charter, officers, members, and activities. One of their main functions was to carry on outdoor activities such as hiking and birdwatching. Political education and action were now added to these activities. The Sierra Club had long maintained a dual program of outings and conservation, the latter referring to political action. The Audubon Society began to perfect such a program in the 1970s as its national politi-cal office in Washington sought to enlist additional member support for national leg-islation. Both the Sierra Club and the Audubon Society developed regional offices through which their national organizations hoped to stimulate political action. . . .

The environmental organizations on the Washington scene comprised a varied lot. There were those that had specific and limited interests, such as the Wilderness So-ciety, Zero Population Growth, and the Defenders of Wildlife, as well as those with far broader interests, such as Friends of the Earth and the Sierra Club. Some with more circumscribed concerns, such as the National Wildlife Federation and the Izaak Walton League, had branched into new fields related to their central focus. Others began with the general environmental interest and selected issues for specialization; two such organizations were the Environmental Policy Center and Environmental Action. These groups often set up specialized sections that became active in particu-lar policy fields, such as the American Rivers Conservation Council of the Environ-mental Policy Center. Finally there were the specialized older conservation groups such as the American Forestry Association and the Wildlife Management Institute.

The variety of environmental groups created a potential for considerable division of opinion. Yet a high degree of cooperative activity emerged. . . .

Environmental legislative strategists practiced much conventional political com-promise. They worked closely with members of Congress to secure what was possi-ble. Often they would retreat from one position to secure another. For example, in 1978 they backed off from earlier attempts to keep intact the 1973 Endangered Species Act when it was under attack in order to support a set of changes that would retain most of the law. Although the change weakened the law by shifting responsibility for critical conflict decisions from the Fish and Wildlife Service to a supervisory intera-gency body higher up the executive ladder, it did not turn sole ultimate authority over to the construction and development agencies.

One aspect of this strategy seemed to be control: If compromises were to be made with developmental influences, they should take place not at the beginning of the leg-islative process but at the final stage. One fought for clear-cut environmental objec-tives and avoided compromise at the start, and then tailored concessions to the demands of the given voting situation whether in committee or on the floor. The Washington-based environmental movement of the 1970s emphasized practical gains rather than affirmation of ideologies. The difficulty was in keeping a clear sense of direction for environmental objectives and the constant atmosphere of compromise inherent in the process of legislative give-and-take. . . .

Several trends are reflected in this review of environmental legislative politics. First, environmentalists adopted with some success many conventional strategies that had evolved over years of lobbying. Second, they developed an ability to work within the context of technical information, which had become a major medium of legislative action. Third, they participated in shaping a more open political system in which the details of action were better known and the scheduling of committee votes was open. And fourth, they organized action by the environmental public that led to a buildup of grass-roots support that constituted a permanent rather than an occasional presence. A transition had occurred from leadership groups based in Washington, deeply involved in legislative maneuvering, to a broader and sustained public political force. . . .

## Administrative Politics

Administrative politics was even more intense than legislative politics. For whereas the latter involved occasional input, the former involved day-to-day "watchdog" activities in relation to administrative agencies that were on the job continually and might make favorable or unfavorable environmental decisions at any time. Constant surveillance was required.

Administering a law was not merely a matter of executing the will of Congress, for in the law much was left to be decided. Frequently Congress did this intentionally because it was virtually impossible to draft wording that would translate policy into workable and detailed implementation. Hence the politics of specific choice began after a law was passed. What the agency decided could make as much difference both to the environmentalist and the developmentalist as did the legislation itself. Moreover, whereas passage of a law was only the first step to decision making, an administrative choice was more likely to be final, one from which escape was more difficult. The administrative arena was a series of moments of truth for the contending parties in which all realized the greater finality of decision.

The context of administrative choice was also more complex. Myriad specific aspects of administration, greater in range and number than in the legislation itself, were the subjects of choices that could go one way or another. Administrative issues were not difficult to comprehend, but the detail was extensive. Only those knowledgeable about that detail could successfully operate in the realm of administrative politics; a vast amount of information had to be kept in mind in order to make one's input relevant.

After a law was passed the various parties who had been active in the legislative debate transferred their interest to the agency. Each party hoped that the ensuing decisions could be shaped in accordance with its objectives. This was especially true of regulation that could lead to administrative choices that might diminish the force of implementation. The public seemed to believe that agencies merely carried out the laws Congress passed and that administrators should be thought of simply in terms of their honesty or capability in administration. But environmentalists soon learned that such was not the case. Administrators made new decisions of vast importance; the practical outcome of action would depend on the degree to which they could be persuaded that one decision was preferable to another.

Administrators did not act independently of the political forces around them. On the one hand, interest groups were constantly contacting them by telephone, by mail, or in person; on the other hand, administrators often sought the public's reaction to potential choices. Although they were relatively unconcerned about the political role of individuals on whom they might impinge, administrators were seriously concerned about those who represented organizations with the ability to act politically, acquire and apply technical information, arouse the public and the media, carry through litigation, and mobilize legislators or administrative superiors on their behalf. The political world that was most important to the administrator and that was most taken into account was one of groups with significant political resources and skills.

Environmentalists became influential in administrative politics by fashioning organizations with a continuing potential for effective action. A critical element was their contribution to the technical aspects of decisions. If environmentalists could convince a decision maker that important facts had been omitted or that detail was incorrect, there was a greater chance they would be heard. Environmental influence depended, then, on the degree to which generalized values and objectives of law could be translated into specific detail, which was the main language of administrative choice. By the mid-1980s half a dozen environmental organizations in the nation's capital scored high marks with administrative agencies for their effectiveness and reliability.

Public administration was heavily influenced by institutions with developmental objectives. Representatives of economic groups in agriculture, business, and labor were highly visible to administrators; equally visible were representatives of local, state, and national government with similar objectives. This is not to say that all these were in agreement when it came to agency choices—far from it. But it is to say that they represented a rather distinctive point of view in administrative politics different from newer environmental and ecological objectives. That developmental organizations outweighed environmental ones in number and strength could be observed repeatedly in the administrative process in comments on proposed rules and regulations, in hearings, and in written communications.

Administrative interpretation focused initially on the rules and regulations the agency drew up to translate the more general provisions of law into specific administrative actions. Rarely did the agency seek to expand its authority and power beyond the mandate of the law; more often it gave away some of that authority, which reduced the law's effectiveness. Developmental influences in rule making invariably worked in this direction, and on the other side environmentalists sought in their strategies to hold the line to make sure that rules and regulations carried out the full intent of the law. The stakes were high: If one did not achieve a general rule favorable to one's position, subsequent action would have to focus on specific cases, each requiring considerable time and effort and having more limited consequences. . . .

Over the years many governmental agencies had developed clientele relationships with those affected by their actions. The Corps of Engineers established close ties with private navigation lines on inland waters, the business firms that shipped goods on them, and the communities that wished to promote river navigation as a stimulus to local development or to protect themselves from flooding by means of upstream reservoirs. The Bureau of Land Management, the Forest Service, the National Park Service, and other agencies developed their particular clienteles. They did so because they knew that their actions could not be carried out in a vacuum, that most of those affected could appeal to Congress or the courts to restrain them and hence might well be headed off if the agency kept itself informed of the group's concerns.

Nor were agencies insulated from the general public. One of the major features in the evolution of administration, both public and private, had been to centralize management control so as to reduce, if not eliminate, potential claims for attention from the wider public. But after World War II citizen groups began to demand a role in making administrative decisions. This was not accepted by administrators with open arms, for they shared the management ideology that effective action depended on relative freedom from such influence. But given the general climate of interest in more citizen participation in government, they were forced to accept it. Hence the political world of the governmental agency came to be sharply different from the political world of corporate management.

Environmentalists worked hard to take part effectively in public administration so as to shape its choices. They sought to counter the heavy developmental weight in administrative politics and the similar predispositions among the professional and technical experts. The major focus was on agency procedures in decision making. The environmental-impact statement (EIS) provided a wedge for wider involvement in administrative choices. Agencies were required to include public review in this process; they were to submit a draft statement to the public for comment, permit ample notice of the availability of documents, provide them promptly without cost, allow sufficient time for review, and include in the final statement the text of comments received and the agency replies to specific points. . . .

Thus, two tendencies were at work in administrative environmental politics. On the one hand, there were those who sought to limit the arena of influence that affected decision, to confine the actors to a smaller circle of scientific, technical, and professional people who could establish the terms of debate and agree on the numbers. On the other hand, there were those who sought to define such decisions as political choices of consequence and to widen the arena of influence about them. Administrative agencies sought valiantly to deflect such input, giving ground often in the formalities of environmental-impact statements, studies, and planning but trying to present technical detail in such a way that the broader citizenry would have less influence than would the technical experts selected by administrators.

*William H. Rodgers, Jr.*

# The Lesson of the Owl and the Crows: The Role of Deception in the Evolution of the Environmental Statutes (1989)

Environmental lawyers are often fond of borrowing examples from natural history to illustrate propositions of law. There is more to this practice than habit, it seems to me, because the natural laws of evolution contain lessons in the results of competitive struggle that fit closely the experiences of legal gameplaying. . . .

. . . [N]ature gives examples of deliberately deceptive behavior: the title of my lecture is drawn from a tale of an owl and some crows who were reared in close proximity to one another. In order to discourage a steady and dangerous diet of silent swoops, any one of which could be fatal, the crows developed a strategy of wandering into easy range, "pretending" to be wholly unaware of the presence of the owl, only to sidestep the futile strikes with disdain and ease. By this stratagem, the crows "proved" to the satisfaction of the owl that crows could not be seized, under even the best of circumstances, and the unwanted attacks ceased altogether.

*Faking and Deception in the Development of the Environmental Statutes*

. . . [T]he process of enactment of the environmental statutes is a gameplaying phenomenon that is likely to yield legislation with both "consensus" and "betrayal" features. It is important to underscore the significance of deception, both in building the "consensus" necessary for enactment, and in accomplishing the "betrayal" often observed in the waning hours of enactment.

## Fakery: The Material of Consensus

*Process Entitlement, Hedges, and Bets.* It is no secret that process can consume substance, and the environmental laws offer many examples. Process is an excellent hiding place for lawmakers who wish to remain uncommitted to particular substantive outcomes. Students of the subject often are astounded by the profound indirection that grips the field of environmental law. Only occasionally does the law ask whether a particular course of conduct is compatible with environmental values. The question is more likely to be posed in process terms—expressed most prominently in the impact statement requirements.

*Ambiguity and Delegation.* Delegation of authority is another famous preference-hider that makes a regular appearance in the environmental statutes. To mention but one prominent example, the term "unreasonable risk" appears thirty-five times in the thirty-three pages of the Toxic Substances Control Act. There is great comfort for legislators who wish to hide in this thicket immune from the sharp scrutiny of predatory constituents.

*Dissembling and Manipulation.* Dissembling and manipulation are other devices found regularly in environmental statutes that allow legislators to remain noncommittal. "Dissembling should be taken to mean hoping to achieve A by voting for B and manipulation should be taken to mean a packing of the agenda to make dissembling possible." The phenomenon is described convincingly by Judge Abner Mikva who gives this account of the "careful nurturing" of a "difficult coalition" that included Morris ("Mo") Udall as he guided some strip mining legislation through the Congress:

> He [Udall] was the floor manager and a lot of us were sitting in the cloakroom when one of the Members from West Virginia, a mining state, got up and said, "Now will the gentleman from Arizona assure me that this bill protects state sovereignty and makes clear that the states continue to have an active and important role in how the strip mines are to be regulated." Udall said, "The gentleman from West Virginia is absolutely correct. The bill protects states' rights and state sovereignty and makes sure that the states continue to play an important role." A little later on in the debate one of the environmentalist Congressmen got up and said, "Now will the gentleman from Arizona assure me that this once and for all sets federal standards and makes it clear that there is a federal law that decides what kind of strip mining will be allowed?" And Udall said, "The gentleman is absolutely correct. The law once and for all will put the federal authorities in control." He then came into the cloakroom for a drink of water and we laughed and said, "Mo, they both can't be right." He said, "The gentleman is absolutely correct." The bill passed. Is it any wonder that the bill is not as clear and precise and specific as some of us might have wanted?

*Postponements.* Postponements, or "more study" provisions, are another useful prop for lawmakers who won't or can't decide. There are all kinds of reasons for putting off a decision until tomorrow, both benign and otherwise, so it is relatively easy for a lawmaker to justify a "more study" vote on principled grounds.

*Self-Nullifications.* Self-nullifications are legislative stand-offs "where command and countermand are stuffed into the same sorry package." A good example is the whistleblower protection provisions that are found in some of the environmental statutes. These provisions offer workers who give evidence of polluting behavior protection from employer retaliation, but the thirty-day statute of limitations withdraws a meaningful remedy in all but the unusual case. Nobody wins under this kind of legislation, of course, but nobody loses either, and that is why self-nullification in legislation is not at all uncommon.

*Teases or Aspirational Commands.* Teases or aspirational commands are additional techniques that allow lawmakers to be simultaneously "for" and "against" identifiable outcomes. Like the delegation tactic, commitment to a vague goal does not tie a lawmaker to any particular means of implementation. This is a dream political world without unsavory options and irascible victims. The hard choices must await initiatives by somebody else.

## Fakery: The Material of Betrayal

*Defections.* Defection is a term I've used to describe various end-of-the-game stratagems used to seize advantages at the expense of the unprepared and ill-equipped. An example is the legislative decision that allowed the Tellico Dam to go forward in the face of powerful environmental and economic objections:

> [T]he pork-barrel proponents, in forty-two seconds, in an empty House chamber, were able to slip a rider onto an appropriations bill, repealing all protective laws as they applied to Tellico and ordering the reservoir's completion. Despite a half-hearted veto threat by President Carter and a last-minute constitutionally-based lawsuit brought by the Cherokee Indians, the TVA [Tennessee Valley Authority] was ultimately able to finish the dam, close the gates, and flood the valley on November 28, 1979.

*Sleepers.* Sleepers, by definition, are legislative provisions with practical consequences far outstripping those anticipated by the formal legislative vision. It goes without saying that gameplayers who create or detect beneficial sleepers do not advertise the fact, since the strategy is to go for sizeable gains without paying any price in return. Obviously, pursuit of the sleeper strategy means that a law will look a great deal differently the day after enactment than it does the day before.

## Instability of the Legislative Product

Can we say anything useful about the fate of these environmental statutes that include a precarious mix of consensus and betrayal traits? First, let us define a statute as an act of the legislature that instructs persons and organizations to act in certain ways. The typical statute contains many instructions or norms within the legislative package, and these are subject to differing interpretations. This universe of plausible interpretations is taken to represent the population for purposes of analysis. Students of evolution emphasize that close attention must be paid to the sources of change within the population under study and to the selection mechanisms that yield differential survival rates.

After enactment, self-imposed constraints on the players are suddenly loosened. Players are free to urge interpretations heretofore undisclosed, or indeed unimagined. Sleepers, skewers [provisions that shift liabilities to nonparticipants], and defections are now in the open claiming unsuspecting victims. This frenzy of interpretation in the wake of enactment produces a long list of surprising readings and tactics. These include betrayals of sidebar agreements not recorded in the legislation, the invention of legislative history after-the-fact, and the attribution of meanings scorned by the negotiating principals. Legislative insiders routinely are offended by the extraordinary directions "their" legislation takes at the hands of outsiders, amateurs and skewees.

This strong centrifugal tendency toward different interpretations is reinforced by catalysts and accelerators that are part of the initial consensus product. The opportunistic decision-avoidance techniques necessary to secure a nonzero sum law feed these later changes; the postponements, such as the study or commission provisions, yield an empirical harvest that can be used to modify tentative legislative conclusions. Delegations are famous for returning to haunt those who took the easy way out. Other process deferrals rebound in similar fashion as experience proves them unworkable in fact. Variances and exemptions necessary for enactment look like ugly "gaps" from the fuller vantage point offered by time. Teases and half-laws are built-in invitations to complete the story. The victims of eleventh-hour defections are spoiling to settle the score, and may have good reason to believe they were done in by a bogus or unrepresentative law.

# CHAPTER 7

# Environmental Regulation: A Structural Overview

This chapter provides a basic overview of the structure of environmental law. It reviews both the common law and the environmental statutes that have come to dominate the field. It examines the principal regulatory approaches embodied in the environmental laws, as well as the institutions employed to protect the environment at both federal and state levels. The chapter also considers the relative competency of courts and administrative agencies to protect the public from exposure to environmental risks.

The chapter begins with an excerpt from a leading environmental law textbook, which summarizes the sources of environmental law in nontechnical terms. After examining the principal common law doctrines that serve as the roots of environmental law, it reviews the history of the major federal environmental statutes.

The Clean Air Act of 1970 was the first federal statute to establish a national regulatory program to protect against pollution. In an article written after the first decade of experience with the law, former EPA attorney William Pederson, Jr., argues that this legislation had serious flaws. He claims that the law was too cumbersome to administer and that it was poorly suited to address emerging pollution problems. Pederson's recommendation that these defects be alleviated by shifting to a national permit system like that required by the Clean Water Act now has been adopted in the 1990 Clean Air Act Amendments. In his influential article, Pederson explains the basic tasks that must be performed to regulate pollution successfully under a permit system. He also argues in favor of tradeable emissions allowances, another recommendation that was incorporated in the Clean Air Act's 1990 amendments.

The reading that follows provides a comprehensive review of the three principal approaches to federal-state relations embodied in the environmental laws. The approach of providing federal financial assistance to encourage states to adopt standards has now been largely abandoned in favor of a "cooperative federalism" approach. Under this model, federal law establishes minimum national standards; states either can qualify to implement them or leave implementation to the federal government. In a few cases the federal environmental laws preempt state standards, though more frequently they establish national minima, while leaving the states free to adopt stricter standards if they choose.

Much federal environmental regulation is premised on the notion that uniform national standards are necessary to prevent environmentally destructive competition among states to attract industry. This "race-to-the-bottom" premise is challenged by Richard Revesz in the reading that follows. Revesz argues that there is nothing inherently wrong with locational competition among states, for states are just as likely to compete to attract industry by offering *positive* environmental amenities. He maintains that efforts to prevent competition among states are doomed to failure in any event because states always can use nonenvironmental factors to compete for industry.

Peter Huber considers the legal institutions that are most capable of protecting the public from exposure to environmental risks. He harshly riticizes the courts' competency to make judgments concerning acceptable levels of public risk. Huber argues that the judiciary's precautionary approach tends to discriminate against new technologies, often leaving the public exposed to greater risks from existing sources. He recommends that public risk regulation be left to administrative agencies and scientific experts, and that government-licensed activities be insulated from tort liability.

Clay Gillette and James Krier dispute the notion that courts are systematically too precautionary in their approach to public risks. They argue that potential plaintiffs face substantial obstacles to recovery, particularly when public risks cause diffuse harm that becomes manifest only after a long latency period. Gillette and Krier observe that supposedly expert agencies have their own incentives to underregulate risks including powerful political and economic pressures that may preclude them from regulating risks adequately.

*Robert V. Percival, Alan S. Miller,*
*Christopher H. Schroeder, and*
*James P. Leape*

# Environmental Regulation: Law, Science, and Policy (1996)

## Sources of Environmental Law

What we call environmental law is a complex combination of common law, legislation, and international agreements. After centuries of wrestling with environmental conflicts, the common law has now been eclipsed by an explosion of environmental statutes. The public law that has come to dominate the field generally declares broad environmental goals while delegating to administrative agencies substantial responsibility for developing and implementing policy. Despite the ascendancy of public law, environmental law's common law roots remain important for several reasons. They articulate principles that have been highly influential in the development of public law, and they retain considerable vitality in their own right as common law actions make a resurgence in some areas today. Moreover, an appreciation of the inadequacies of the common law is crucial to understanding the rapid growth of public law and to evaluating its effectiveness in protecting the environment.

### Common Law Roots

Prior to the explosion of environmental legislation in the 1970s, the common law was the legal system's primary vehicle for responding to environmental disputes. For centuries common law courts had wrestled with what is perhaps the quintessential

From Robert V. Percival, Alan S. Miller, Christopher H. Schroeder, and James P. Leape, *Environmental Regulation: Law, Science, and Policy,* 2d ed. (Boston: Little, Brown, 1996).

question of environmental law: how to harmonize conflicts that inevitably occur when human activity interferes with the interests of others in the quality of their physical surroundings. The common law relied largely on nuisance law doctrines to resolve environmental controversies, although conduct that resulted in a physical invasion of property could be addressed as a trespass. Nuisance law is designed to protect against invasion of interests in the use and enjoyment of land, while trespass protects against invasions of interests in the exclusive possession of land. . . .

## The Public Law of Environmental Protection

*Environmental Statutes: A Historical Perspective.* The federal statutes that dominate the environmental law field today are the product of a remarkable burst of legislative activity that began in 1970, the year of the first Earth Day celebration. But it is useful to review the historical roots of this legislation, which extend further back in time. The history of U.S. environmental law can be divided into roughly six major phases [see Table 1]. Until the end of World War II, environmental law was largely a product of common law, as discussed above, with federal legislative efforts concentrated on the development, and later the conservation of public resources. We call this period the *Common Law and Conservation Era.*

In nineteenth-century America, regulatory legislation was left largely to state and local governments. State laws and local ordinances to protect public health and to require the abatement or segregation of public nuisances were common, although they were poorly coordinated and rarely enforced in the absence of a professional civil service. Like the early English antipollution laws, American smoke abatement ordinances did not clearly specify what level of emissions was proscribed.

Most federal legislation that affected the environment did so by promoting development of natural resources. The Homestead Act of 1862 and the Mining Act of 1872 unabashedly encouraged rapid development of public resources by authorizing private parties to lay claim to public land and the mineral resources it continued. Land grants to encourage railroad construction turned over up to 180 million acres of public lands to private developers. While the concerns of preservationists and conservationists helped spur establishment of the first national park in 1872, support also came from the railroads, which were seeking to promote tourism and to further the development

TABLE 1.   Six Stages in the History of U.S. Environmental Law

1. The Common Law and Conservation Era: Pre-1945
2. Federal Assistance for State Problems: 1945–1962
3. The Rise of the Modern Environmental Movement: 1962–1970
4. Erecting the Federal Regulatory Infrastructure: 1970–1980
5. Extending and Refining Regulatory Strategies: 1980–1990
6. Regulatory Recoil and the Return to Private Law Principles: 1991–Present

of western lands. The establishment of the national forest system in 1891 marked a turning point of sorts, for it withdrew forest lands from development under the Homestead Act.

During this period Congress did adopt some regulatory legislation, including the Rivers and Harbors Act of 1899 and the Pure Food and Drug Act of 1906. However, these statutes were not motivated primarily by concern over public health or environmental protection, but rather by a desire to promote the free flow of commerce. Congress banned discharges of refuse to navigable waters not out of concern for water quality, but rather to prevent obstructions to the free flow of commerce, which at that time was largely conducted on waterways. When it enacted the Pure Food and Drug Act in 1906 and the Federal Insecticide Act of 1910, Congress's primary concern was not to protect public health, but rather to prevent consumers from being defrauded by products that were not what they were advertised to be.

Congress was not entirely oblivious to public health concerns during this period. In an unusual case when a public health problem was particularly visible and obvious, Congress was capable of acting. For example, in 1838 Congress acted to impose safety regulations to prevent steamship boilers from exploding. Several decades later, when it was discovered that the use of white phosphorus in match manufacturing caused many workers to be inflicted with a horribly disfiguring disease called phossy-jaw, because it literally ate away that area of the face, Congress acted again. The Esch-Hughes Act of 1912 sought to eliminate the use of white phosphorous in match manufacturing to prevent this disease. Because Congress did not believe at the time that it had the constitutional authority to directly prohibit such an activity, it used the taxing system to make it prohibitively expensive to use white phosphorus in match manufacturing.

The period from 1945–1962 coincides with the second phase in the history of U.S. environmental law, the period of *Federal Assistance for State Problems*. Although federal law imposed few regulations on private industry that were animated by environmental concerns, after World War II the federal government became involved in encouraging the states to adopt pollution control measures of their own. The Water Quality Act of 1948 provided grants to states for water pollution control. In 1956, over President Eisenhower's veto, Congress provided funding for the construction of sewage treatment plants by municipalities. This funding was premised on the notion that cities otherwise would be reluctant to build sewage treatment plants that would primarily benefit downstream cities. While this became a major program of federal financial assistance, it did not create any system of federal regulation. Instead the federal government sought to encourage the states to regulate on their own.

The federal programs in the 1950s and 1960s were premised on the notion that environmental problems were the responsibility of state and local governments. The primary federal role was to assist with research and funding while letting the states decide how to control pollution. With expanding economic activity in the post–World War II era, the interstate character of pollution became increasingly apparent. The notion that pollutants do not respect state or even national boundaries was brought home by scientists' warning that the entire planet was being dangerously poisoned by radiation from nuclear tests in the atmosphere. The premise that the federal role in pollution control should be a non-regulatory one became increasingly tenuous. . . .

The third phase in the history of U.S. environmental law, the period from 1962–1970, coincides with the *Rise of the Modern Environmental Movement*. This is often traced from the publication of Rachel Carson's "Silent Spring," which alerted the public to the possibility that pesticides could be accumulating in the food chain in a way that could cause severe, long term environmental damage. In 1967 the Environmental Defense Fund was formed by a group of scientists who sought to have DDT banned. Another group, the Natural Resources Defense Council, was a product of efforts to force the Federal Power Commission to consider environmental concerns when licensing a pumped storage facility at Storm King Mountain. At the time, no federal agencies were given primary responsibility for responding to concerns about environmental protection. National environmental groups went to court to try to require government agencies to be more responsive to environmental concerns.

The growing popularity of outdoor recreation and concern over the environmental impact of public works produced landmark legislation during this period. In 1960, Congress adopted the Multiple-Use Sustained Yield Act, which directs federal agencies to manage the national forests to serve the multiple uses of "recreation, range, timber, watershed, and wildlife and fish purposes." Growing concern for the preservation of natural areas was reflected in the subsequent enactment of the Wilderness Act of 1964 and the Wild and Scenic Rivers Act in 1968. Other federal laws reflected public interest in protecting social and cultural values from the impact of public works programs. For example, §4(f) of the Department of Transportation Act of 1966 required that special effort be made to prevent federally funded construction projects from damaging parks, recreation areas, wildlife refuges and historic sites.

To the extent that federal law was regulatory in character prior to 1970, most of the targets of environmental regulation were government agencies rather than private industry. In legislation like the National Historic Preservation Act of 1966, Congress sought to ensure that government agencies respected social and cultural values when pursuing development projects. These laws laid the groundwork for the subsequent enactment of the landmark National Environmental Policy Act of 1969, which required federal agencies to take environmental concerns into account when taking any action with a significant impact on the environment. But the federal government did not enact regulatory legislation to control pollution during this period. That legislation came only after the formation of national environmental organizations.

During the fourth phase of the history of U.S. environmental law, the period from 1970–1980, an explosion of federal legislation erected the modern federal regulatory infrastructure. These statutes established the ground rules for environmental protection efforts by mandating that environmental impacts be considered explicitly by federal agencies, by prohibiting actions that jeopardize endangered species, and by requiring the establishment of the first comprehensive controls on air and water pollution, toxic substances, and hazardous waste. The explosion of environmental legislation in the 1970s was accompanied by a parallel opening up of the courts to judicial review of agency decisions that affected the environment. This gave concerned citizens sorely needed tools for challenging agency action and for ensuring that previously unresponsive agencies implemented the ambitious new legislative directives. . . .

Perhaps the final chapter in the *erection of the federal regulatory infrastructure* was the enactment in 1980 of the Comprehensive, Environmental Response, Compensation and Liability Act, known as CERCLA or the superfund law. This legislation went beyond the traditional command and control regulatory approach to controlling pollution and established a system of strict, joint and several liability for broad classes of parties associated with the release of hazardous substances. CERCLA creates powerful incentives for businesses to prevent releases of hazardous substances to avoid future liability.

From 1980–1990, the fifth phase in the history of environmental law, Congress *extended and refined the regulatory strategies* it had launched to protect the environment during the 1970s. As the initial environmental laws were reauthorized by Congress, they were broadened, strengthened, and made more specific. Comprehensive amendments to RCRA were adopted in 1984, to CERCLA and the Safe Drinking Water Act in 1986, to the Clean Water Act in 1987, and to the Clean Air Act in 1990.

Many of the amendments enacted during this period tried to force the federal environmental agencies to implement the environmental laws in a more expeditious fashion. Faced with an executive branch less sympathetic to environmental concerns, Congress imposed new deadlines for agencies to act and it established specific sanctions for agencies who failed to carry out the laws. "Hammer" provisions written into some laws specified regulations that would take effect automatically if an agency failed to adopt regulations of its own by a particular date. For example, the Hazardous and Solid Waste Amendments of 1984 said that all land disposal of hazardous waste would be banned by certain dates unless a specific determination was made that certain levels of treatment were sufficient to avoid future environmental problems. Sanctions for violating the environmental laws also were increased dramatically, with substantial criminal penalties imposed on those who intentionally violate the laws.

During this period there also was a move toward more innovative forms of regulation. The Emergency Planning and Community Right-to-Know Act [42 U.S.C. §§ 11001–11050], enacted in 1986, requires industries to report annually the volume of their releases of hundreds of toxic substances. The Act creates a national inventory of toxic releases that must be made accessible to the public, using information as a tool for mobilizing public pressure to reduce toxic emissions. The Clean Air Act Amendments of 1990 provide the first large-scale experiment with emissions trading approaches long advocated by economists as a more efficient means for reducing pollution. While mandating significant reductions in sulfur dioxide emissions, the law creates emissions allowances that may be bought and sold to ensure that the reductions are obtained in the cheapest manner possible.

210 PERCIVAL, MILLER, SCHROEDER, AND LEAPE

Early indications suggest that we may now have entered a sixth phase in the history of environmental law, which we call *Regulatory Recoil and the Return to Private Law Principles*. Beginning around 1991, the pendulum that swung so powerfully toward environmental protection during the 1970s and 1980s now appears to be moving in the other direction with a Congress and a judiciary decidedly more skeptical about environmental regulation. Even before the Republican sweep of the 1994 congressional elections, efforts to reauthorize some of the major federal environmental statutes had failed in both the 102d and 103d Congresses.

After the Republicans have taken control of both houses of Congress, the 104th Congress was decidedly less sympathetic toward environmental interests. It pursued an agenda that included sweeping cutbacks in the environmental laws. In March 1995 Congress enacted the Unfunded Mandates Reform Act, which makes it procedurally more difficult to apply new environmental regulations to entities of state and local governments unless federal funding for compliance is provided. Other legislative proposals including a regulatory moratorium, requirements that future regulations meet risk assessment and cost-benefit criteria, and legislation that would require compensation of landowners whose property values are adversely affected by regulation failed to win adoption after presidential vetoes were threatened.

Although the 104th Congress failed to repeal major provisions of the federal environmental laws, it used appropriations riders to prevent implementation and enforcement of various provisions of them. "[A]lthough repeals by implication are especially disfavored in the appropriations context," the Supreme Court has confirmed that "Congress nonetheless may amend substantive law in an appropriations statute, as long as it does so clearly." *Robertson* v. *Seattle Audubon Society* [503 U.S. 429, 440 (1992)]. In appropriations legislation that became law in 1995, Congress imposed a temporary freeze on the listing of new endangered species listings and required the U.S. Forest Service to increase timber harvests on federal lands.

In recent years, the federal judiciary also has become less sympathetic toward environmental concerns. In several recent cases, major environmental regulations have been voided by courts insisting that agencies provide greater and more specific evidentiary support for regulation. These decisions represent a move toward the kind of principles of individualized causation required in private law litigation, which the public law is designed to supplant by authorizing precautionary regulation. The judiciary also is making it more difficult for citizens to have access to the courts in environmental cases by tightening standing requirements.

*William F. Pederson, Jr.*

# Why the Clean Air Act Works Badly (1981)

Simplicity and consistency at the drafting level are basic tests for any statute. For title I of the Clean Air Act, however, these qualities derive a broader meaning from two particular aspects of the control scheme.

First, the Act does not exclusively call on either the federal government or the various state governments to achieve its ends. Instead, it yokes the two in an uneasy partnership in pursuit of a common goal. That, in turn, makes it all the more important that the decision-making procedures mandated by the Act be free from needless complexity.

Second, a fundamental purpose underlying the creation of the EPA was to provide a coordinated approach to pollution wherever it occurred. The ultimate goal was to base regulatory decisions on what best served a wide variety of environmental goals, and not simply on what would clean up the air or the water taken by themselves. The present statute contains little recognition that the EPA administers laws to control water pollution, solid waste pollution, ocean dumping of pollutants, and the safety of underground drinking water sources, or that each of these other types of pollution can affect or be affected by measures to control air pollution. . . .

The major theme of title I of the Act is the regulation of stationary sources through state implementation plans (SIPs) to achieve various air quality goals. Part A of the title provides the basic framework. It commands the EPA to issue air quality criteria for any widespread air pollutant that "may reasonably be anticipated to endanger public health or welfare." The EPA, on the basis of these criteria, must then set "national ambient air quality standards" (NAAQSs). . . .

The Act further requires each state to submit an implementation plan detailing how it will attain the NAAQSs promulgated by the EPA. The plans are intended to be comprehensive bundles of strategies and commands, containing all the requirements necessary to attain the NAAQSs in that state. The Act established this procedure in 1970, contemplating a reduction in air pollution to the level of primary NAAQSs by 1977 at the latest. In 1971, the EPA issued its most important air quality standards, and most states submitted implementation plans by 1972. 1977's arrival, however, revealed widespread failure to reach the clean-up level of the primary standards. . . .

. . . [SIPs are] specific to one of the six pollutants for which the EPA has developed NAAQSs. Any source of air pollution that emits more than one such air pollutant, then, will be bound by separate SIPs—separate regulatory systems—for each of those pollutants. . . . The statute contains no mechanism with which to coordinate the application of the different SIP requirements to a source, either with each other or with the separate requirements set through permits. . . .

. . .[A]ny change that a state wants to make in a SIP, no matter how routine, requires *both* state and EPA approval, and, generally, two rounds of public notice and comment. Both actors must turn the key before any new requirement is established. Most of the work on the EPA's side is handled by its ten regional offices. In these offices, the double-key system compels the EPA staff responsible for SIP revisions to spend a lot of time simply pushing paper. Any regulatory system as complicated as a SIP for an industrial state demands constant change. Requiring notice and comment and affirmative approval even for routine changes that the state has approved results in a substantial diversion of staff time to considering those changes. The costs in state and industry time of shepherding SIP revisions through the EPA must be equally substantial. . . .

Congress could greatly alleviate all of the problems discussed above by using permits issued to individual sources, not SIPs, as the major vehicles of regulation.

## Basing an Ambient Statute on Permits

Any regulatory system that relies upon individual permits faces two related requirements. First, some mechanisms must be created for establishing the specific control provisions contained in particular permits. Second, the terms of individual permits must be bound together into a common and unified regulatory scheme. Both of these needs arise with particular intensity in an environmental statute based primarily upon ambient, rather than technological, standards.

Under a technology-based scheme, permit issuance proceedings can be used to determine the appropriate technology for particular sources and require its installation there. Because questions about what technology is available at what cost may look similar and have similar answers from plant to plant within an industry, addressing each permit in a separate proceeding has definite costs. It requires duplication of effort to the extent that the sources involved are similar. If different standards result, the source subject to the stricter standard can argue that it has been treated unfairly. Even given these problems, however, the control scheme would work after a fashion.

Under an ambient approach, by contrast, it is not always possible to set requirements source by source in unrelated, individual proceedings. The questions that recur among permit proceedings in an ambient system are likely to be not just similar—

as with technology-based standards—but *the same.* The issuing agency must, for each permit proceeding, determine what the emission and pollution characteristics of a region are and what pattern of controls will bring the region to attainment, or prevent significant deterioration. Given this background, it follows that controlling sources to meet ambient requirements presents a problem that is "polycentric" in the classic sense. That is, the control requirements for source A may vary depending on the requirements set for sources B, C, D, and so forth. Thus, it is impossible to grant a permit to A without considering how to regulate the others.

One response to these problems could be simply to abandon the ambient approach. That, however, would also abandon much hope for efficient environmental regulation. The key task, therefore, is to find a way to address the problems that recur from permit to permit, or that link individual permit decisions together, under an ambient scheme. For both types of problems, the solution in principle is well established in administrative law. The control agency should issue rules, or set general principles, specifying how it will decide common or interlocking questions. Judges and professors have urged this course for more than a generation on established agencies that, like the Interstate Commerce Commission and the Federal Communications Commission, decide many related cases. There is no reason not to transpose it to the relatively new field of environmental law.

More concretely, a state or the EPA would issue a general rule that established the mechanisms needed to make ambient calculations for an area. The rule would specify the applicable air quality readings, the inventory of sources, the meteorological readings, and the model. These determinations would generally bind individual permit proceedings, though some departures might be allowed in particular cases. The agency would update the general rule as new knowledge developed, but the changes would have prospective effect only. Except in unusual cases, the agency would not reflect the rule changes in individual permits until they expired and were reissued at the end of their terms.

This approach would avoid duplication or inconsistency in the factual or analytical portions of individual proceedings. It would not, however, deal with the more difficult policy problem raised if any one of several sources could be controlled to attain a given ambient level, and the agency had to choose among these different control patterns. Two solutions to this problem are possible. First, and simplest, any conflicts could be directly addressed in a generic decision, either at the rulemaking stage if they surfaced there, or else in a permit proceeding to which all potentially affected sources were parties. This type of permit proceeding would be similar to a "comparative" hearing to award a TV or radio license or an airline route.

A comparative hearing approach, however, would seldom be the best solution. Comparative proceedings represent an effort to confront the complexities of a decision head on, without the preliminary use of simplifying assumptions. That effort has historically proved unwieldy and inefficient. These characteristics would probably persist even if adjudicatory hearings were not used. Furthermore, the nature of the problem of air pollution control neither allows nor demands the absolute precision that comparative hearings might appear to offer. Given the technical uncertainties that becloud the area, the actual ambient effect of any given emissions allocation is bound to be subject to a substantial margin of error. In addition, the potential harms caused by air pollution appear to vary smoothly rather than discontinuously with exposure levels. That in turn suggests that the costs of small mistakes in allocating emissions among sources would also be small.

All of these difficulties of a permits system based on comparative hearings could be alleviated by a second type of approach which would rely on broad rules of decision for allocating controls among several eligible sources. The most economically efficient variations of this approach would be to determine the total amount of emissions that could be tolerated, and then auction an equal number of emission "rights" off to the highest bidders. If that is not acceptable, a simple rule stating that no less (and, perhaps, no more) of the necessary reductions could be assigned to any one source would be sufficient. That rule would link together individual proceedings; more particularly, it would contain the most troublesome potential problem raised by issuing linked permits over time. The danger is that an agency might largely exempt from controls the first sources to receive permits by asserting that later sources would be tightly regulated, and then renege when the time arrived to issue those later permits. Although this test would be a rough one, any resulting inefficiencies could be reduced by allowing the sources to later trade the allowable emissions among themselves, as described earlier. The important point, no matter which of these variations is adopted, is that a framework of broad rules should be formulated to guide and link together individual permit proceedings.

## A Permit System and New Knowledge

Establishing a set of general rules to guide individual permit decisions would narrow the differences between a permit system and the present statute's structure. Certain rules—those that established the air quality baseline, the inventory, the model, and the permitting strategies—would mirror much of what SIPs now contain. Other general rules, as at present, might take the form of national regulations. Despite these similarities, the immediate mechanical virtues of a shift to permits would be preserved to the extent that permits alone contained federally enforceable regulatory provisions that actually bound individual sources, with general rules simply providing the backdrop.

More fundamentally, a statute that combined general rules for issuing permits with individual permits containing control requirements would handle new knowledge better than the present statute, both on a day-to-day level and in overall design. On the day-to-day level, the system's distinctive feature would be that the general rules for issuing permits could change at any time, while the individual permits themselves would seldom change before they expired and were reissued at the end of their terms.

The present Act provides no means of scheduling changes in a SIP, and forces any changes to take effect in time to meet the short statutory deadlines. The result has been a resistance to new knowledge because of the disruption and uncertainty that such knowledge generates. By providing a fixed period, during which permits would generally not change, and a predictable time at which they would be reexamined, a permit system would be "buffered" against the effects of new knowledge. That knowledge would enter the system only at definite times and in definite proceedings. Moreover, at the specified times for considering permit changes, the elimination of the double key would make them easier to accomplish.

These characteristics of a permit system reflect its more fundamental virtue: it corresponds more closely to our understanding of the kind of problem that air pollution is than does the existing system. The present SIP system is based on a short-term effort to achieve standards. It assumes that we know what is necessary, that what remains is to act, and that the need to act is urgent. This is the implicit message behind the directive that all SIPs be submitted at one time, that all necessary calculations and modelling be made then, that these calculations and modelling be speedily approved or disapproved, and speedily corrected where necessary, and that compliance follow promptly. It is also the implicit message behind the complete lack of any mechanism for handling change in an orderly manner.

This approach is, of course, not even intellectually appropriate where the air is already clean and regulation seeks to preserve its quality. Nor does it fit areas where efforts to attain standards have been successful, and keeping the air clean has become the issue. Even where the standards have not been met, the constant development of new knowledge casts considerable doubt on both the merits and workability of this system.

A permit approach would impose a different philosophy on the system. The universe of permits could be set to expire and be renewed at a relatively constant rate. Any necessary changes could be introduced into the regulatory system permit by permit over an entire renewal cycle, rather than being imposed simultaneously upon all sources, as is at least theoretically the case under the SIP system. As a necessary consequence, the artificial deadlines in the current law would be deemphasized in favor of a continual, gradual nudging of the regulatory system toward better results over time.

The permit-based approach, by allowing different permits with different expiration dates to contain somewhat different provisions, accepts and makes manageable the inability to do everything at once that is inherent in any complex regulatory scheme. It is the natural procedural vehicle by which to shift the Act from an emphasis on short-run acute effects to an effort of long-term maintenance and gradual improvement.

## Realizing the Full Benefits of a Market System

The Clean Air Act, as presently administered, imposes one substantial obstacle to broad reliance on a market system. For several important pollutants, the current regulatory approach relies heavily on detailed modelling and monitoring, not just of emissions in a region, but of the local impact of individual sources. The result can be to establish a fairly rigid system of source-specific emissions limitations, one that demands controls on a given source regardless of relative cost, because only controls on that source will be assured of removing measured or projected violations in a particular local area.

To the extent that the scientific and engineering design of the system itself thus precisely specifies the emission limits for each individual source, the efficiency benefits of reallocating those limits through the market become unattainable. Such a sacrifice of efficiency might be justified if detailed source-by-source modelling had unique advantages in preventing the harms that the Act seeks to control. Experience so far, however, seems to cast doubt on any such advantages.

Detailed modelling and monitoring of individual pollution sources has been difficult and expensive to apply in practice. The results obtained inevitably contain a substantial margin of uncertainty, and there is usually room for considerable doubt whether the health or welfare differences between two readings in roughly the same area are in fact significant. As a result, questions have been raised as to whether, even under the current control scheme, the statute may not unduly rely on modelling and monitoring.

The doubts about modelling multiply where measures to reduce the long-range impact of air pollution are at issue. Furthermore, many of the long-range effects of pollution are thought to result from the chemical transformation over time of pollutants in the atmosphere, thus introducing more complexity into modelling efforts. Finally, since both the causes and effects of long-range pollution cover wide regions and act on a large scale, detailed modelling of individual sources may always be of limited value in understanding or dealing with the problem.

These considerations suggest that an approach that looks more toward general reduction of pollutants that have long-range effects within a broad area is likely to be at least as effective as a system that relies on detailed assessment of individual sources. A regulation adopted under such an approach might state, for example, that "By the year 19__, sulfur oxides emissions in the X region shall not exceed Y million tons." This type of general ambient approach could be readily adapted to a market-based regulatory system. At the outset, the control agency under such a system would have to allocate the allowed regional emissions among sources. Subsequently, the system would have to provide some mechanism for transferring these "allowable emissions" among sources as sources expanded or closed down, or switched fuels, or improved their controls. The policy arguments for doing this through an "emission rights" approach under a permits system are even stronger than those for using such an approach under our current system. A scheme of general pollution reduction would almost certainly cover a far larger area and include more sources than current SIPs do. Increasing the number of sources covered would increase the potential for efficiency gains through a market approach by increasing the number of participants in the market.

At the same time, the switch to a policy concerned with total emissions, rather than site-specific impacts, would remove much of the need for detailed examination of individual transactions. The regulatory agency would only have to be satisfied that total emissions of all regulated sources would stay below the limits, and it would not focus on the exact impacts at each particular source. This limiting of the review standards would widen the class of permissible trades and would make it easier to determine in advance which trades qualified. That in turn would increase the potential for efficiency gains through trading while smoothing the mechanical workings of the statute.

*Robert V. Percival, Alan S. Miller,*
*Christopher H. Schroeder, and*
*James P. Leape*

# Environmental Regulation: Law, Science, and Policy (1996)

### Environmental Federalism: Three Models of Federal-State Relations

While the growth of environmental regulation largely has been driven by federal legislation, states continue to play an important role in the development and implementation of environmental policy. Even though the federal environmental laws often require states to meet minimum national standards, they generally do not preempt state law except in narrowly defined circumstances. State common law remains an important tool for seeking compensation for environmental damage. Some of the most innovative environmental protection measures are the product of state legislation, such as California's Proposition 65, New Jersey's Environmental Cleanup and Responsibility Act, and Michigan's Environmental Protection Act.

The federalization of environmental law was a product of concern that state and local authorities lacked the resources and political capability to control problems that were becoming national in scope. Congress has employed three general approaches for accomplishing its environmental protection objectives. The first approach is to provide federal financial assistance to encourage states to adopt environmental standards on their own. Conditioning the receipt of federal funds on state action to address environmental problems is a proper use of Congress's spending power that is consistent with the Tenth Amendment so long as the conditions "bear some rela-

From Robert V. Percival, Alan Miller, Christopher H. Schroeder, and James P. Leape, *Environmental Regulation: Law, Science, and Policy,* 2nd ed. (Boston: Little, Brown, 1996).

tionship to the purpose of the federal spending" [*New York* v. *U.S.*, 505 U.S. 144, 167 (1992)]. While this approach proved largely ineffective for controlling air and water pollution, it remains the principal federal approach to issues such as land use management where political opposition to federal regulation is particularly acute. Federal programs encourage state and local land use and solid waste management planning under the Coastal Zone Management Act, the Clean Water Act, and Subtitle D of the Resource Conservation and Recovery Act. The power of this approach as a tool for motivating states to act depends largely on the amount of federal financial assistance involved. As federal grant programs have declined, this approach has become a less significant vehicle for promoting state action.

The second model, which currently is the predominant approach to federal-state relations under the environmental statutes, can be called a "cooperative federalism" approach. Under this model, federal agencies establish national environmental standards and states may opt to assume responsibility for administering them or leave implementation to federal authorities. The Clean Air Act, the Clean Water Act, RCRA, and the Safe Drinking Water Act require EPA to establish minimum national standards, while authorizing delegation of authority to implement and administer the programs to states that demonstrate that they can meet minimum federal requirements. In states that choose not to seek program delegation, the programs are operated and enforced by federal authorities. The Supreme Court has stated that it is permissible for Congress to offer states a choice between regulating an activity "according to federal standards or having state law pre-empted by federal regulation," so long as Congress regulates activity that it has the authority to regulate under the Commerce Clause [*New York* v. *U.S.*, 505 U.S. 144, 167–168 (1992)].

Statutes that require the establishment of minimum federal standards are designed to prevent environmental standards from being undermined by competition among states to attract industry. Although this "race to the bottom" rationale for federal regulation has been criticized on theoretical grounds, see Revesz, Rehabilitating Interstate Competition: Rethinking the "Race-to-the-Bottom" Rationale for Federal Environmental Regulation [67 N.Y.U. L.Rev. 1210 (1992)], it is widely accepted that federal standards help prevent states from succumbing to local economic pressures. Uniform national standards have been criticized as inefficient or unrealistic in light of varying local conditions, see, e.g., Krier, On the Topology of Uniform Environmental Standards in a Federal System—And Why It Matters [54 Md. L. Rev. 1226 (1995)], though most laws employing the cooperative federalism approach actually allow states to vary the level of environmental protection they seek so long as they do not slip below the federal minimum. Surprisingly, several states have made the federal "floor" a "ceiling" by prohibiting state agencies from adopting standards more stringent than required by federal law. See Organ, Limitations on State Agency Authority to Adopt Environmental Standards More Stringent Than Federal Standards: Policy Considerations and Interpretive Problems [54 Md. L. Rev. 1373 (1995)].

There may be substantial economies of scale in having environmental standards established on a national scale while leaving their attainment to state authorities subject to federal oversight. When it enacted the Clean Water Act, Congress recognized the technical complexities of pollution control and it sought to overcome the "sporadic" and "ad hoc" nature of prior pollution control efforts [S. Rep. No. 92–414, p. 95 (1971), 2 Leg. Hist. 1511]. Also, as John Dwyer notes, the cooperative federalism approach is a practical necessity in many areas because the federal government needs "the substantial resources, expertise, information, and political support of state and local officials" to implement its programs sucessfully. Dwyer, The Practice of Federalism Under the Clean Air Act [54 Md. L. Rev. 1183 (1995)]. Dwyer also notes that cooperative federalism "paradoxically gives states greater opportunity and incentives to undertake policy experimentation" by stimulating states to develop their own bureaucracies to administer environmental programs.

Federal oversight of delegated state programs frequently has been a source of friction between federal and state officials. The federal government has had difficulty ensuring that state programs meet minimum federal standards, particularly during times of fiscal stringency. As federal financial assistance to state environmental programs has been reduced sharply, most states have failed to replace lost federal funds with funds of their own. Lester, A New Federalism? Environmental Policy in the States, in Vig & Kraft, eds., *Environmental Policy in the 1990s* 67 (1990). EPA has the authority to withdraw delegation of program authority to any state that is not meeting federal standards. However, this sanction is too blunt an instrument to be very effective and EPA has little incentive to add to its own responsibilities when it already is having difficulty finding funds to implement its own programs.

State environmental officials have formed their own organization, the Environmental Council of the States (ECOS), which is working to improve federal-state relations. EPA and the state environmental commissioners are working to develop better methods for evaluating state environmental programs to make federal oversight less paternalistic. ECOS is seeking to develop a set of environmental indicators that can replace EPA's current "bean counting" focus on the numbers of permits issued and enforcement actions undertaken.

A third approach to environmental federalism eschews state administration of federal standards in favor of federal control. Preemption of state law has been employed sparingly in the federal environmental laws. It usually is reserved for regulation of products that are distributed nationally where businesses favor nationally uniform regulation to avoid having to comply with balkanized regulatory standards. Examples include regulation of chemicals under the Toxic Substances Control Act (TSCA), pesticide registration under the Federal Insecticide, Fungicide, and Rodenticide Act (FIFRA), and provisions of the Clean Air Act governing vehicle emissions. Under these programs, federal regulation can preempt inconsistent state standards.

Out of respect for federalism concerns, courts have been reluctant to infer federal preemption in the absence of clearly expressed congressional intent to preempt. See, e.g., *Silkwood* v. *Kerr-McGee Corp.* [464 U.S. 238 (1984)] (holding that award of punitive damages under state law for exposure to nuclear material not preempted by the Atomic Energy Act); *Cippollone* v. *Liggett Group, Inc.* [112 S.Ct. 2608 (1992)] (Federal Cigarette Labeling and Advertising Act preempts only claims based on a failure to warn and the neutralization of federally mandated warnings but not claims based on express warranty, intentional fraud and misrepresentation or conspiracy); *Huron Portland Cement Co.* v. *Detroit* [352 U.S. 440 (1960)] (upholding municipality's smoke abatement ordinance as applied to ships on the Great Lakes against claims that it interfered with interstate commerce and that it was preempted by federal safety regulation of seagoing vessels); *Burbank* v. *Lockheed Air Terminal, Inc.* [411 U.S. 624 (1973)] (holding that the Noise Control Act and the Federal Aviation Act preempt a local noise abatement ordinance that effectively barred jet aircraft from taking off at night); *Pacific Gas & Electric* v. *California Energy Commission* [461 U.S. 190 (1983)] (upholding California state initiative that blocked the licensing of new nuclear powerplants in the state pending the development of a facility for disposal of high-level nuclear waste on ground that it is an economic measure rather than a safety regulation preempted by the Atomic Energy Act).

In cases where courts have found state regulations to be preempted, Congress can always act to remove the preemptive impact of federal regulation. For example, in 1986 the Supreme Court held that the Comprehensive Environmental Response, Compensation and Liability Act, the federal "superfund" legislation, preempted the use of state "superfunds" to fund the cleanup of hazardous substance releases covered by the federal legislation [*Exxon Corp.* v. *Hunt*, 475 U.S. 355 (1986)]. This holding was a narrow one because the Court indicated that states could use such funds to pay their required contributions to federal cleanups. Nevertheless, Congress promptly amended CERCLA in 1986 to clarify that states could require companies to contribute to state funds even if they were used for activities covered by the federal legislation. Even statutes with express preemption provisions, like FIFRA, which prohibits states from imposing labeling or packaging requirements different from those imposed by federal regulation, have not been interpreted to preempt other types of state or local regulation. In *Wisconsin Public Intervenor* v. *Mortier* [501 U.S. 597 (1991)] the Supreme Court unanimously held that FIFRA did not preempt municipal ordinances requiring that a permit be obtained before a pesticide is applied to certain private lands. . . .

As national regulation expands in scope, the range of potential conflicts between federal and state environmental regulation may increase. One response to this problem has been to adopt a kind of hybrid approach to preemption that establishes conditions that must be satisfied before state or local governments can adopt regulations that go beyond minimum federal standards. For example, the Clean Air Act amendments now authorize states to adopt stricter auto emission standards than the federal minimum, but only if those standards conform to the stricter standard that California has been allowed to adopt. The rationale behind this provision is that it will increase state flexibility to meet federal Clean Air standards while requiring vehicle manufacturers only to meet a standard that they already must comply with in the California market. This approach is designed to give states greater flexibility in tailoring standards to their environmental needs, while avoiding the creation of multiple standards that would be expensive for national manufacturers to meet.

Claims that federal environmental regulation has been too intrusive on state and local prerogatives have become a prominent part of the current political ferment over federalism. State and local officials have become increasingly upset about the cost of implementing federal requirements, such as regulations implementing the Safe Drinking Water Act, which limits contaminants in public water supply systems. Arguing that it is unfair for the federal government to impose "unfunded mandates," state and local officials lobbied Congress for legislation to restrict this practice. In an effort to defuse these concerns, President Clinton issued Executive Order 12875 [58 Fed. Reg. 58093], in October 1993. The executive order prohibits federal agencies from issuing regulations that impose unfunded mandates not required by statute unless the agency informs the Office of Management and Budget of its efforts to consult with state and local governments and its justification for the mandate. It also directs federal agencies to process applications for regulatory waivers from state and local governments within 120 days to the extent permitted by law.

In March 1995, Congress overwhelmingly approved legislation making it more difficult to impose federal mandates on state and local governments. The legislation, known as the Unfunded Mandate Reform Act of 1995 [Pub. L. No. 104-4, 109 Stat. 48 (1995)], requires that more detailed cost estimates be provided for federal mandates and it makes it easier for opponents of such provisions to defeat them in Congress. The law requires the Congressional Budget Office (CBO) to provide estimates of the future cost of legislative mandates if they may exceed $50 million annually for state or local governments or the private sector. Any member of Congress can raise a point of order demanding that mandates estimated to cost state or local governments more than $50 million annually be stricken from legislation unless federal funding is provided or the mandate is specifically approved by a majority vote. Mandates for which future federal funding is promised are to expire if the funding is not subsequently provided.

The legislation also imposes new requirements on agencies issuing regulations that impose federal mandates. The law requires federal agencies, prior to publishing a notice of proposed rulemaking, to prepare assessments of the anticipated costs and benefits of any mandate that may cost state or local governments or the private sector more than $100 million annually. It also prohibits federal agencies from issuing regulations containing federal mandates that do not employ the least costly method or that do not have the least burdensome effect on governments or the private sector unless the agency publishes an explanation of why the more costly or burdensome method was adopted. These provisions are subject to judicial review if the underlying agency action already is reviewable in court.

Federalism concerns also appear to be on the minds of the judiciary, as a sharply divided Supreme Court rethinks some of the constitutional foundations of our federal system. In April 1995 the Supreme Court for the first time in nearly 60 years overturned a federal law for exceeding Congress's authority under the Commerce Clause. In *U.S. v. Lopez* [115 S.Ct. 1624 (1995)], the Court held, by a bare 5–4 majority, that Congress does not have the authority under the Commerce Clause to prohibit the possession of firearms in the vicinity of schools. The Court stated that Congress has the authority to regulate three broad classes of activities under the Commerce Clause: (1) "the use of the channels of interstate commerce," (2) intrastate activities that threaten "the instrumentalities of interstate commerce, or persons or things in interstate commerce," and (3) "activities having a substantial relation to interstate commerce," the "proper test" of which is "whether the regulated activity 'substantially affects' interstate commerce" [id. at 1629–30].

While it is unclear to what extent *Lopez*'s "substantially affects" test will impose new restrictions on federal regulatory authority, Chief Justice Rehnquist's majority opinion suggests that Congress will have little problem regulating economic or commercial activity. He emphasized that the Gun-Free School Zones Act had "nothing to do with 'commerce' or any sort of economic enterprise, however broadly one might define those terms" [id. at 1630–31]. Citing with approval *Hodel v. Virginia Surface Mining & Reclamation Assn., Inc.* [452 U.S. 264 (1981)], which upheld federal regulation of intrastate coal mining under the Surface Mining Control and Reclamation Act, the Chief Justice stated that "[w]here economic activity substantially affects interstate commerce, legislation regulating that activity will be sustained" [115 S.Ct. at 1630]. Significantly, the Chief Justice did not question the validity of even *Wickard v. Filburn* [317 U.S. 111 (1942)], which he described as "the most far reaching example of Commerce Clause authority over intrastate activity," because it "involved economic activity in a way that the possession of a gun in a school zone does not" [115 S.Ct. at 1630]. In *Wickard* the Court upheld federal regulation of the production and consumption of home-grown wheat because of its cumulative impact on the price and market for wheat sold in interstate commerce. If *Wickard* remains good law, then *Lopez* apparently will not significantly restrict federal authority to regulate businesses or individuals when they engage in virtually any commercial activity.

The questions *Lopez* leaves open include how courts can distinguish between commercial and non-commercial activity and whether non-commercial activity can be regulated when it affects interstate commerce. Even actions that are not the product of commercial activity could cause environmental harm that itself substantially affects interstate commerce. The four dissenting justices in *Lopez* argued that it will be difficult, if not impossible, to find a principled means for distinguishing commercial from noncommercial conduct [id. at 1653], a difficulty the majority deemed a necessary price to pay to ensure that Congress's enumerated powers have "judicially enforceable outer limits" [115 S.Ct. at 1633]. In his concurrence, Justice Kennedy proposed to focus on "whether the exercise of national power seeks to intrude upon an area of traditional state concern." However, environmental law is replete with instances where matters traditionally viewed as state or local concerns became national concerns after state and local authorities failed to address them adequately.

The statute invalidated in *Lopez* contained "no jurisdictional element which would ensure, through case-by-case inquiry, that the firearm possession in question affects interstate commerce" [115 S.Ct. at 1631]. This would appear to distinguish *Lopez* from cases arising under the Clean Water Act, whose jurisdiction extends to "waters of the United States" [33 U.S.C. § 1362(7)], which have been defined by regulation to include waters whose use or misuse could affect interstate commerce. See *U.S. v. Riverside Bayview Homes, Inc.* [474 U.S. 121 (1985)]. However, the Court's "substantially affects" test could potentially restrict the breadth of federal jurisdiction depending upon what must be shown to demonstrate such an effect and how substantial it must be before activities can be regulated under the Act.

*Richard L. Revesz*

# Rehabilitating Interstate Competition: Rethinking the "Race-to-the-Bottom" Rationale for Federal Environmental Regulation (1992)

Perhaps the most widely accepted justification for environmental regulation at the federal level is that it prevents states from competing for industry by offering pollution control standards that are too lax. This competition is said to produce a "race to the bottom"—that is, a race from the desirable levels of environmental quality that states would pursue if they did not face competition for industry to the increasingly undesirable levels that they choose in the face of such competition.

Race-to-the-bottom arguments for federal environmental regulation became commonplace following two influential articles published by Professor Richard Stewart in 1977, and were explicitly cited by Congress as a central justification for the passage of important federal environmental statutes. More generally, the race to the bottom has been invoked as an overarching reason to vest regulation that imposes costs on mobile capital at the federal rather than the state level, and has been cited as one of the bases for the New Deal. . . .

Race-to-the-bottom advocates must clear an initial hurdle: for the competition among states to attract industry to be a race to the bottom, interstate competition must be socially undesirable. But interstate competition can be seen as competition among producers of a good—the right to locate within the jurisdiction. These producers compete to attract potential consumers of that good—firms interested in locating in the jurisdiction. Even though states might not have the legal authority to

Richard L. Revesz, Rehabilitating Interstate Competition: Rethinking the "Race-to-the-Bottom" Rationale for Federal Environmental Regulation, 67 N.Y.U. L. Rev. 1210, 1233–47 (1992).

prevent firms from locating within their borders, such firms must comply with the fiscal and regulatory regime of the state; the resulting costs to the firms can be analogized to the sale price of a traditional good.

If one believes that competition among sellers of widgets is socially desirable, why is competition among sellers of location rights socially undesirable? If federal regulation mandating a supra-competitive price for widgets is socially undesirable, why is federal regulation mandating a supra-competitive price for location rights socially desirable?

It is easy to identify possible distinctions between a state as seller of location rights and a firm as seller of widgets. These differences, however, provide scant support for race-to-the-bottom claims. In what follows, I briefly discuss each of the key differences between the state, as seller of location rights, and the market competitor, showing that none of the differences suggests that interstate competition in the environmental area will decrease welfare.

First, if individuals are mobile across jurisdictions, the costs that polluters impose on a state's residents will depend on who ends up being a resident of the state; the resulting supply curve is thus far more complex than that of a widget seller. The mobility of individuals, however, is not an element of race-to-the-bottom claims and should not be relevant to the plausibility of the claim that competition among states will decrease welfare.

Second, to the extent that the shareholders of a polluting firm reside in the jurisdiction, the state as seller of location rights would at least attempt to take their welfare interests into account in computing the price to charge. In contrast, the seller of widgets would be indifferent to the effect of the sale price on the welfare of the good's purchaser. If a firm's shareholders do not reside in the regulating jurisdiction, and if firms are immobile, a state could extract monopoly profits by setting suboptimally stringent standards; if firms are mobile, competition would eliminate this problem. The converse—that if shareholders reside in the jurisdiction, the environmental standards will be suboptimally lax—does not follow.

Third, states are not subject to the discipline of the market. If a producer of widgets sells at a price that does not cover its average costs, it will have to declare bankruptcy. A state, in contrast, will continue in existence even if it recklessly compromises the health of its residents. The difference merely establishes that a state might undervalue environmental benefits. But such undervaluation is possible even for an island jurisdiction and is not a consequence of the competition among states to attract firms.

Fourth, states do not sell "location rights" at a single-component price; they require that firms comply with a variety of regulatory standards and pay taxes. The resulting market is thus more complex than one involving the sale of a traditional good. For example, a jurisdiction that imposes a lax worker-safety standard but a stringent pollution standard will be desirable for a labor-intensive, non-polluting firm, whereas a jurisdiction with stringent worker-safety and lax pollution standards will be desirable for a capital intensive, polluting firm. It is far from clear, however, why this additional complexity in the market would make interstate competition destructive.

In sum, while the analogy between interstate competition for industrial activity and markets for traditional goods is not perfect, it raises serious questions about race-to-the-bottom claims. At the very least, it should place on race-to-the-bottom advocates the burden of identifying the relevant differences between the two markets and explaining why they turn otherwise desirable competition into a race to the bottom. . . .

. . . [T]he race-to-the-bottom hypothesis, though influential, lacks a sound theoretical basis. . . . [E]ven if there *were* such a race in the environmental arena, federal regulation would not necessarily be an appropriate response. The analysis centers on two important consequences of race-to-the-bottom arguments in favor of federal environmental regulation. First, if the premises underlying the race to the bottom hold, federal environmental regulation will have undesirable effects on other state regulatory or fiscal interests; the supposed benefits of federal environmental regulation should therefore be balanced against these undesirable effects. Second, logic compels the conclusion that arguments in favor of federal environmental regulation are a frontal challenge to federalism, because the problems that they seek to correct can be addressed only by exclusive federal regulatory and fiscal powers. Both these consequences, which have been unexplored in the literature, ought to cast even more doubt on the validity of race-to-the-bottom arguments for federal environmental regulation.

Race-to-the-bottom arguments appear to assume, at least implicitly, that jurisdictions compete over only one variable—in this case, environmental quality. So, jurisdictions that would choose to have stringent environmental quality standards in the absence of interstate competition adopt less stringent standards as a result of such competition, and, consequently, suffer a reduction in social welfare.

Consider, instead, the problem in a context in which states compete over two variables—for example, environmental protection and worker safety. Assume that, in the absence of federal regulation, State 1 chooses a low level of environmental protection and a high level of worker safety. State 2 does the opposite: it chooses a high level of environmental protection and a low level of worker safety protection. Both states are in a competitive equilibrium: industry is not migrating from one to the other.

Suppose that federal regulation then imposes on both states a high level of environmental protection. The federal scheme does not add to the costs imposed upon industry in State 2, but it does in State 1. Thus, the federal regulation will upset the competitive equilibrium, and unless State 1 responds, industry will migrate from State 1 to State 2. The logical response of State 1 is to adopt less stringent worker-safety standards. This response will mitigate the magnitude of the industrial migration that would otherwise occur.

Thus, federal environmental standards can have adverse effects on other state programs. Such secondary effects must be considered in evaluating the desirability of federal environmental regulation. Most importantly, the presence of such effects suggests that federal regulation will not be able to eliminate the negative effects of interstate competition. Recall that the central tenet of race-to-the-bottom claims is that competition will lead to the reduction of social welfare; the assertion that states enact suboptimally lax environmental standards is simply a consequence of this more basic problem. In the face of federal environmental regulation, however, states will continue to compete for industry by adjusting the incentive structure of other state programs. Federal regulation thus will not solve the prisoner's dilemma.

Consider an example in which State 1 and State 2, as island states, would impose high levels of both environmental protection and worker safety. When placed in a competitive situation, they respond in the different ways set forth above: State 1 chooses a low level of environmental protection and a high level of worker safety, whereas State 2 does the opposite. After the adoption of federal regulation, they both end up with high levels of environmental protection but low levels of worker safety; their social welfare has therefore been reduced by competition despite federal environmental regulation.

One might respond to these arguments by saying that worker safety should also be the subject of federal regulation. But states would then compete over minimum wage laws, fair labor standards, and so on. It is difficult to imagine a federal system in which all the regulatory requirements that impose costs on industry are mandated at the federal level.

Suppose, however, that this were the case. States impose burdens on industry not only through regulation but also through taxes, which fund a variety of state programs and functions. So, if all regulatory programs are federalized, states still will be able to compete through their fiscal powers. Consider, now, an example, in which State 1 and State 2, as island states, would impose both stringent regulatory standards and high corporate taxes. When placed in a competitive situation, State 1 chooses stringent regulatory standards and low corporate taxes, whereas State 2 does the opposite. If the federal government then requires stringent regulatory standards, State 2 will respond by lowering its taxes, and by, say, decreasing the size of its income maintenance programs. This reduction is a direct by-product of the federal regulatory scheme.

Thus, even if all regulatory functions are federalized, federal regulation will continue to have an adverse effect on other issues of state concern—in this example, social welfare programs. Moreover, such a scheme will not eliminate the reduction in social welfare that results from competition among the states.

The next logical step, of course, is to suggest preemption of state taxes, because otherwise the supposedly evil effects of interstate competition will persist. The race-to-the-bottom rationale for federal environmental regulation is, therefore, radically underinclusive. It seeks to solve a problem that can be addressed only by wholly eliminating state autonomy. The prisoner's dilemma will not be solved through federal environmental regulation alone, as the race-to-the-bottom argument posits. States will simply respond by competing over another variable. Thus, the only logical answer is to eliminate the possibility of any competition altogether. In essence, then, the race-to-the-bottom argument is an argument against federalism.

*Peter W. Huber*

# Safety and the Second Best: The Hazards of Public Risk Management in the Courts (1985)

Who should decide how much public risk is enough? Since some measure of public risk is not only inevitable but desirable, some institution must be directed to define the measure and specify its ingredients.

The battle over who should choose our public risks, of course, rages far above the head of the individual risk bearer. Public risk choices inherently require public control; they cannot be left to that most perfect of all risk managers, the private and autonomous individual, fully informed and freely selecting for herself the risks she will and will not choose to bear. Individual choice and public-risk management are mutually exclusive for two reasons that are worth delineating with some care at the outset.

First, individual consumers exposed to public risks may have insufficient information or incentive to enforce their individual risk rights. This is the traditional rationale for making risk choices through the collectivist vehicle of regulation. Perhaps no single consumer has a sufficient economic incentive to sue the polluter, even if every consumer starts with an entitlement not to be exposed to the smoke, and even if the smoke is being emitted in dangerous excess. Every consumer hopes that someone else will attend to the problem; every consumer, in other words, has an incentive to understate his own concern about the problem in the hope of "free-riding" on some other consumer's lawsuit against the risk creator. The result is that public risks may be created in excess; risk consumers can end up being exploited by risk creators.

Peter W. Huber, Safety and the Second Best: The Hazards of Public Risk Management in the Courts. This article originally appeared at 85 Colum. L. Rev. 277 (1985). Reprinted by permission.

The second difficulty in relying on individual action to manage public risks is an exact mirror image of the first. When it is in the collective interests of consumers to consent to a particular course of conduct that creates a public risk—the construction, for example, of a needed power plant, factory, prison, or hospital—the selfish individual is tempted to exact a very high price for her individual consent. Her incentive here is to *overstate* her aversion to the risk, in the hope that society will buy her off at a price commensurate with the large social benefit that the new facility may supply. The result of leaving risk choices to individual negotiation in this setting may be excess risk aversion; risk consumers end up, in effect, being exploited by other risk consumers.

Public control of public risks is therefore necessary, both to prevent the excess generation of public risk and to make possible the acceptance of as much public risk as is socially desirable. The government regulator, a single, central decisionmaker, acts as the consumers' collective "broker" in a particular risk market. The regulator—whoever it may be—must perform at least two tasks. One, of course, is to reject unfavorable investments in public risk. The regulator has the resources to proceed against creators of unacceptable public risks. Here we have the more familiar regulator, government, saying "no," placing limits on the risks individuals may create.

But the regulator's second function is to acquiesce in risk creation. To represent his principal effectively, a broker in a risk market, like a broker in any other setting, must be able to buy as well as to sell. A centralized risk-regulatory system must not only reject bad public risk choices but also supply the public's consent to good ones. This is most clearly illustrated in comprehensively regulated industries such as those producing electric power, drugs, pesticides, and many other products of modern technology. In these areas, risk creators start with no freedom to do anything at all until they receive express regulatory permission. The nay-saying regulatory role then effectively disappears; the regulator's task is to serve as a retail deregulator, giving case-by-case consent to new ventures that entail public risks.

The administrative agencies are, of course, the more familiar regulators, wielding authority over public risks of every variety. But the courts are also vigorous regulators, and it is their role that most concerns me here. The courts are pivotal actors in the prospective approval of new technological ventures. They possess considerable authority to review agency approvals of new sources of risk, whether the risk involves a new vaccine, power plant, pesticide, or food additive. And in areas not subject to comprehensive administrative regulation the courts can use injunctions to act as first-tier gatekeepers of the risk environment. The courts are also heavily engaged in the retrospective regulation of public risks. Damage actions sounding in nuisance, negligence, strict liability, and absolute liability are powerful instruments of regulation. Indeed, the legal community invented the "emission fee" for dealing with hazards such as pollution long before the economics had much to say about it. Every risk creator and every risk bearer knows that the damage action, and most particularly an action seeking punitive damages, is potent medicine for regulating public risks. . . .

## The Old-New Division

Judicial review of new technological ventures sharply (and altogether unapologetically) separates the risks of new technology from the old risks in our abundantly hazardous environment. We do not convene judicial panels to pass on the social acceptability of the automobile, or of burning coal to generate electricity. And judicial review certainly wastes no time with ancient natural hazards of pestilence, famine, drought, the cold of winter, and contagious or congenital disease. Searching judicial review of technology in practice means searching review of technological change. New technological risks, but not old ones, shoulder the considerable costs and delays of judicial review before they can be brought to market.

This phenomenon bears heavily against new sources of risk and thus encourages the retention of old ones. Courts rarely hand down an opinion overnight; courts drawing extensively on expert advice and adjudicating matters of vast social import tend to move with ponderous caution. Proponents of new risks thus face not only the staggering direct costs of extensive litigation but also the debilitating costs of delay. Old, already-established risks, on the other hand, bear none of these costs. The gap between the accelerated, premarket, regulatory costs imposed on new risks, and the postponed, postmarket costs borne by old ones, is often sufficient even under existing regulatory structures to freeze out ventures in new technologies. An intrusive second look by the courts accentuates the division even further.

The "go slow" judicial philosophy is not a choice between safety and risk. It is a choice in favor of old risks and against new ones. Though they may prefer to believe otherwise, the courts are incapable of saying only "no" to risk; the rejection of one risk is always the acceptance of another. To the extent that the courts are institutionally tilted against technological change, they are also, inevitably, tilted in favor of the established hazards of existing technology and the untamed natural world. Like it or not, when the courts choose to govern risks, they must choose among them. . . .

## The Public-Private Division

At first glance it might appear that the courts can do better when they address public risks retrospectively. Tort actions for damages invite judicial action only after the bodies have fallen. Perhaps it is easier to make sound risk choices at this stage. And perhaps not.

The favorite judicial targets for retrospective regulation are manmade risks created on a mass-production scale. Judicial risk deterrence obviously cannot be engaged when the risk creator is the Creator. Nor is it the cottage industry, the one-kitchen cannery, or the do-it-yourself home insulator who will be summoned to answer on the expansive "public law" theories of liability that some commentators would have us perfect. Mass exposure actions can be directed against the hazards of saccharin, but not against the hazards of pure sugar, against formaldehyde foam or asbestos insulation, but not against cold weather, against the polio vaccine, but not against the polio virus, against the manufacturer of the "alpha-drug" used to treat your cancer, but not against the untreated cancer itself or your basement apricot-pit distillery. Only mass-exposure defendants can practically be called to account for the risk—as distinguished from the harm—they create, and only in the mass-exposure context do the proportional liability rules and streamlined "public law" procedures make any sense.

Mass producers are not only the preferred defendants under evolving public-risk tort law, they are also held to especially stringent standards of liability. Indeed, the very concept of strict liability was invented in the context of mass-produced consumer products; discrete actors operate under the relatively lenient standard of negligence. . . . [O]nly mass producers can be required to pay accelerated compensation for risk created, and it is only mass producers [who] would be required to pay according to a proportional liability rule of causation. Retail producers of manmade risks will continue to be protected by the requirements of actual harm and preponderance-of-the-evidence proof of causation, if only to prevent everyone from suing everyone all the time. And Nature, a very large creator of risks, must, of course, remain entirely immune to liability. We have set in place, in other words, three different standards of liability to be applied against three different classes of risk producers that regularly sell in the same markets. The strictest standard applies to the wholesalers of manmade risks. The retailers benefit from a more lenient standard, and Nature enjoys the Creator's immunity.

The consequences are as one might expect. Liability rules that disfavor certain producers will either drive their risky products out of the market entirely, or inflate their prices so as to force at least marginal shifts in consumption toward less strictly regulated sources of hazard. Judicially created biases against public risks encourage, unsurprisingly enough, risk privatization. This is a risk preference that is most probably hazardous to the public's health. . . .

## In Search of Excess Public Risk

Lawyers and the courts are thus professionally and institutionally predisposed to make regressive risk choices. Can public risk selection in the courts be improved? . . . I doubt it. Distinguishing public risks that are part of the health problem from those that are part of the solution is a difficult, often speculative, and always time-consuming task, one that the courts are institutionally unsuited to carry out.

A prudent manager of public risks first identifies the risk baseline—the status quo in the risk environment—and then seeks to determine which products and services tend, overall, to improve conditions and which tend to make them worse. The search for suitable targets of attack in public risk regulation is a search for products and services that create what has been termed "excess risk." But excess risk remains a very elusive quantity when we search the diffuse, low-probability, and large-population statistics of public risks to distinguish risky activities that make life safer from risky activities that make it more dangerous. . . .

The difficulty in defining the appropriate boundary of the risk market in which substitutes are examined, and the extraordinary complexity inherent in making accurate risk comparisons once appropriate markets have been defined, are not reasons to abandon the process of risk comparison altogether. We have, in practical terms, no other choice. But they *are* compelling reasons to keep public risk regulation out of the courts. Courts and juries, confronted with narrowly focused problems, specific injuries, and the need for a simple, one-time solution, will invariably brush over the intricate technical and statistical questions that inhere in every meaningful evaluation of excess risk. A few injured plaintiffs make a far stronger impression than a thousand other users of the product bursting with health precisely because they used the Dalkon Shield and were thereby spared exposure to pregnancy or other hazardous substitute methods of contraception. Few risk amateurs have the Holmesian ear for the dogs that do *not* bark in the night. . . .

Even with risks that are very small compared with the background risk—as public risks almost always are—it will often be possible to extract from the statistics a specific element of risk increase. But it will always be impossible, using statistical tools at least, to extract any contribution to risk decrease. "Excess risk" *in total,* therefore, simply cannot be evaluated from raw, disease-specific, epidemiological statistics. These figures calculate only the "excess risk" of contracting a single, carefully selected disease—information that is of considerable interest for those who would take affirmative steps to protect against that disease, but is largely irrelevant to the policy planner who wishes to decide whether use of the risk-creating product should be encouraged or discouraged.

### The Safety of Wealth

The final analytical tool for evaluating excess risk in the aggregate is to examine the risk-reducing value of wealth.

Wealthier, it is well-established, is healthier. The wealthy eat better, enjoy better medical care, receive better education, live more safely, and therefore live longer. Wealth has a large and statistically significant impact on how much risk we bear. The producer of a valuable but risky product that adds to the wealth of the consumers who buy it therefore has a credible claim to a risk offset proportional to the consumer "surplus" generated when the product is sold.

Unfortunately, assessing this offset quantitatively requires an elaborate economic calculation of a kind not wholly free from speculative assumption. The producer of a public risk, making the case for the risk-reducing value of its product, must start by calculating the consumer surplus that sale of the product delivers—the difference between the actual price charged for the product and what consumers (including, of course, nonmarginal consumers) would be willing to pay for it. The needed information is readily obtainable from supply and demand curves for the product; unfortunately, supply and demand curves themselves are extremely difficult to ascertain. Next, the producer must link the increase in consumer wealth created by the product to the corresponding decrease in consumer risk. This requires a knowledge of the income elasticity of risk and the incomes of the product's consumers. Putting the figures together can, in principle, provide an estimate of the wealth-linked risk reductions attributable to use of the hazardous product or service. . . .

. . . To arrive at a true evaluation of excess risk the calculation evidently must examine alternative employment opportunities and assess how much surplus income, if any, is earned by employees willing to work in this particular setting. The general conclusions from a calculation like this are entirely accurate, but the fine details border on the fraudulent.

Once again, therefore, such calculations are unsuitable for courts engaged in the administration of corrective justice. An analysis in this vein is tolerable within a quasi-legislative body such as an administrative agency, though even there it must be performed informally and with healthy skepticism. But the regulatory agency can engage in ad hoc calculations of this type because its business is not the dispensation of corrective justice but the formulation of progressive social policy. Courts and juries, on the other hand, are almost certain to ignore the difficult half of the excess risk calculation, dismissing it as too speculative to be worth the effort. Nevertheless, if prudent risk management is the ultimate objective, we cannot conduct only one half of the risk calculation. . . .

## Deferring to the Experts

What, then, are the courts to do with individual or class actions that seek redress from risk or injury caused by an IUD, vaccine, herbicide, morning sickness drug, nuclear waste reprocessing facility, or the like? My general prescription is less, not more. The courts should defer to the experts.

Not experts summoned by the parties for the edification of the judiciary. The scientific community is large and heterogeneous, and a Ph.D. can be found to swear to almost any "expert" proposition, no matter how false or foolish. The expert public risk choices that *should* be respected are those made by a risk-regulatory agency concerned with the public risk in question.

This is not the current law. Judges, at present, generally feel quite free, when addressing risk problems, to ignore prior administrative determinations regarding which public risks represent progressive choices. The Restatement of Torts, for example, flatly declares that "compliance with a legislative enactment or an administrative regulation does not prevent a finding of negligence." And many risk-related administrative statutes, such as the Consumer Products Safety Act, firmly announce that compliance with safety rules is not to serve as a shield from tort liability. When the statute is silent or even the least bit ambiguous on the question of tort-remedy preemption, the courts will always presume that no preemption was intended.

This settled judicial refusal to defer to agency choices among public risks has spawned a never-ending cycle of truly perverse risk-regulatory decisions. . . . The FDA's experts may conclude after a careful examination of the substitutes that the IUD is a good bet as a comparatively safe contraceptive, or the NRC may conclude that a nuclear power plant is safer than the available alternatives. But a mass exposure lawyer and injured client can effectively overturn the expert judgments by finding what is almost too easy to find: a judge who is of the view that the courts have something useful to offer in these matters, and a sympathetic and well-meaning jury. The agency's blessing of the vaccine, or pesticide, or power plant, is usually no more than a prelude to a second tier of regulation in the courts.

The resulting you-say-yes but I-say-no pattern of public-risk decisionmaking is routinely explained by the courts—and often accepted by the agencies—on the ground that administrative risk regulation is intended to set only a safety "floor"—a threshold of performance, a minimum definition of "acceptable" safety. Agencies will point out that they rely mostly on data furnished by the regulatees themselves, and therefore cannot and should not be viewed as the final arbiters of how much safety is enough. It is, of course, politically comfortable for agencies to preserve the tort system as a safety valve. When bodies *do* fall the agency is grateful to see at least part of the victims' hostility directed at the regulatees.

This rationalization for judicial nondeference may make some sense when the administrative regulatory regime is casual or sporadic, as with consumer products. But it is wholly unpersuasive for comprehensively regulated industries. Vaccines, pesticides, aircraft, electric power plants and the like all entail potentially enormous mass-exposure hazards. Precisely because they can create public risk of this nature, these products and services are also subject to the most searching and complete state and federal safety regulation. Administrative agencies may find it politically convenient to disclaim final responsibility for the public risk choices that inhere in such licensing decisions. But the simple fact is that an agency cannot intelligently issue a license for such public-risk activities without comparing the licensee's risks to those of the competition and determining that the new offering represents some measure of progress, or, at worst, no measure of regression in the risk market in question.

Once that determination has been made by an expert licensing agency, the courts should respect it. Regulatory agencies are equipped to make the risk comparisons on which all progressive transformation of the risk environment must be based. The courts are simply not qualified to second-guess such decisions; when they choose to do so they routinely make regressive risk choices. Requiring—or at least strongly encouraging—the courts to respect the comparative risk choices made by competent, expert agencies would inject a first, small measure of rationality into a judicial regulatory system that currently runs quite wild. The Nuclear Regulatory Commission's licensing of a nuclear power plant or reprocessing facility *must* be viewed for what it is—considerably more, in other words, than a routine and irrelevant pleasantry, to be forgotten as soon as the first tort plaintiff enters the courthouse. . . .

The greatest vanity of the legal profession—a profession with more than a few vanities—is its conviction that there are no limits to the contributions lawyers can make to the public safety. The natural, self-aggrandizing instinct of altogether too many lawyers and judges is to stand up and do something—anything at all—when any aspect of life seems less than perfect. But the reality is that life has grown safer not because of the legal system but despite it. The technological community, far from ushering in an endless series of new terrors, can rightfully claim full credit for the extraordinarily safe society it has built. Pesticides and vaccines save lives, although they also create some risks of their own. It is undoubtedly futile to curse the darkness of starvation and disease. But it is insane to snuff out with legal paper those who would light the candle of a cure.

The path to a safer existence lies in fewer, not more legal constraints on those whose genius allows for the replacement of old and grave risks with less grave new ones—scientists, engineers, the mass-manufacturers of drugs, pesticides, and consumer products, the suppliers of water, food, energy, and transportation. Public risk investments still hold out the promise of large, risk-reducing returns. Hotspur was right. It is out of the nettle, danger, that we pluck the flower, safety.

# Clayton P. Gillette and James E. Krier

---

# Risk, Courts, and Agencies (1990)

Some [have called] for a reduction of the judicial role in risk assessment and management, and for more reliance on administrative agencies. Agencies, they argue, have more expertise, are more objective and rational, can be more attentive to the net effects of technological advance. Courts, they conclude, should defer to them.

This is the set of views that we call into question here. . . . [C]omparative analysis of courts and agencies . . . leads us to conclude that ambitious proposals to increase the scope of agency authority at the expense of judicial scrutiny are remarkably premature. We stop short of saying that the present institutional arrangements are, however imperfect, the best we can hope for given current understanding. We insist, though, that those critics who would alter existing arrangements through sweeping delegations to experts and bureaucrats have utterly failed to carry a reasonable burden of proof. A careful comparative assessment simply raises too many doubts about the wisdom of wholesale abdication to technocratic rule. . . .

Public risks . . . are commonly latent in their manifestations, diffuse in their impacts, and of low probability. Moreover, as their name suggests, they share the characteristics of collective goods (or, here, collective bads). They tend to be nonrival: their adverse effects may have simultaneous consequences for a multitude of victims. Given the nature of modern technologies, these nonrival effects will commonly be dispersed over large geographic areas, so that victims—potential plaintiffs—are themselves broadly distributed. And as is always the case with collective goods and bads, public risks tend to be nonexclusive. This means that the benefits of abatement (should it occur) necessarily extend to all victims, and cannot be withheld on a piecemeal basis. . . .

In short, public risk litigation is structurally biased against victim access. Victims who might wish to seek redress in the courts confront significant obstacles that di-

Clayton P. Gillette and James E. Krier, Risk, Courts, and Agencies, 138 Univ. Pa. L. Rev. 1027 (1990).

minish the incentive to sue. Prosecution may well not be worthwhile from any individual victim's self-interested perspective, even if it would be socially desirable. . . .

. . .[T]he argument on behalf of agency expertise fails to provide a satisfying systemic account. Suppose, for example, that courts *do* end up biased against public risk. Might agencies tend to be biased in the opposite direction? Barriers to access could, after all, result in agency bias if they limit the ability of potential public risk victims—but not public risk producers—to influence agency thinking. Similarly, agencies might process risk decisions in a biased way. Or suppose that courts *are* incapable of dealing with risk in a highly competent fashion. Might administrative agencies and the experts they employ be something less than competent themselves? . . .

Whether, and how much, bias is likely to result from asymmetric access to the administrative process depends considerably on the nature of any particular item on the regulatory agenda. In the case of public risk generally, though, the problem appears to be a substantial one, as should be obvious from our discussion of how the typical characteristics of public risk—impacts that are latent, diffuse, widely dispersed, or low probability, and nonexclusive—limit the ability of potential and actual public risk victims to gain access to the courts. Our point here is that they can also frustrate the efforts of victims to mobilize for the purpose of influencing agency decisions about risk. Whatever the objective of the mobilization effort (it might be to prepare and provide a good research product for agency consideration, or to present a convincing brief for the victim point of view, or to gather a crowd to attend public hearings, or to organize an effective lobby), considerable amounts of time, effort and money will be required. These resources will also, however, be hard to find. The diffuseness of public risks, coupled with the fact that materialization of any physical injury will usually be remote in time (latent) and in probability, reduces incentives to contribute much to the common cause. So does the nonexclusive nature of favorable agency action. Efforts to overcome some of these obstacles by appealing directly to potential group members for support confront the same obstacles. The appeals themselves require a force of personnel sufficiently large and energetic to address victims who will usually be dispersed over broad geographic areas. Hence the problem of mobilization remains.

Look now at the other side of the story, and consider the ability of public risk producers to muster effective interest groups. Their organizational burdens will generally be lighter for any number of well-known reasons: there are fewer potential group members; each member will usually know the identity of most others; each member is likely to have a relatively large, concentrated, and immediate stake in agency decisions, as compared to public risk victims; each has greater assets (wealth, information, personnel, facilities, and so forth) to tap than any one or several (or even many) victims; commonly all or many of the members will already be organized, say through a trade association. Taken together, these considerations facilitate effective communication, provide opportunities to monitor individual contributions and chastise noncontributors, increase the likelihood that the private benefits of group action will exceed private costs, and forestall freeriding behavior. In short, the costs of organizing collective efforts will generally be lower for the producers than for the victims of public risk, and this in turn means producers will generally enjoy a considerable comparative advantage in mobilizing interest groups and exercising influence, whether by benign or sinister means. . . .

## A Summary

. . . [T]he public risk debate proceeds along two lines, one concerning attitudes (should public risk be feared, or should it be favored?) and the other institutions (should courts be much involved with public risk regulation, or should they defer to agencies?). These lines are necessarily tangled together, but we tried to follow each separately, beginning with institutions. On the question whether judicial rule deters public risk unduly, we concluded that given what we know now, the interplay of access and process bias makes it very hard to say. On the matter of judicial competence, we said an informed judgment turns on the alternatives—in this case administrative rule—because courts might be limited but then agencies might be too. So we turned to agencies and considered some reasons, again having to do with access and process bias, why they might end up regulating public risk too little, and then considered how this might cut, on balance, in the context of a larger regulatory system that includes courts and agencies alike. Again, it's hard to say, but we are inclined to the view that without substantial judicial intervention there would probably be too much public risk. At the least, critics of the courts (and champions of the agencies) simply have not carried their case. We went on to consider the question of expert administrative competence, and found little reason to alter this conclusion.

Much of our inquiry has, of course, been speculative, but it is worth noting that the chain of argument can afford weak links. For example, interest group capture is not essential to our critique of agencies, because body counting could bias uncaptured agencies, as could problems of competence and the limitations of expert rationality. Each of these influences is probably powerful by itself. That they might work in tandem only adds to our concerns.

The purpose of our examination of agencies and experts was not, however, to show that they are plainly inferior to courts; the point, rather, was to question the premises from which the argument for deference to expertise proceeds and to show how proponents of the argument have failed to carry their burden that agency rule would be superior. The case for administrative superiority rests in large part on selective idealization, but the lesson to be drawn from capture, body counting, and bounded rationality is that administrators, like judges, are prisoners of their own environment and victims of their own human limitations. Agencies and courts alike proceed episodically, the one pushed on by interest groups, the other by litigants. Agencies and courts alike bring particular perceptions to questions of risk. Agencies and courts alike cope with uncertainty in a fashion far from perfect.

Even supposing agencies could be much better than they are at what they do, we have suggested how they might nevertheless be good at the wrong thing, resulting in more public risk than the public, for its own sound reasons, wants. This recalls the debate about attitudes and the question of what risk means. Until that question is resolved, much of the ongoing debate about how to control public risk is emphatically off the point. No one can talk sensibly about whether judicial control yields too little public risk, or administrative control too much, without knowing how risk itself is to be conceived. One conception might suggest one set of reforms, and the other another. If, for example, risk is to be measured by body counts, then agencies seem to have an advantage. But if risk means what the public would have it mean, then agencies look to be remarkably limited and courts much less so. The courts are, after all, criticized in part precisely because they accommodate the public's attitudes. A purported liability of judges and juries—that they are not experts—turns out to be an asset.

# CHAPTER 8

# Alternative Approaches to Regulation

This chapter considers the various approaches to regulation employed by the environmental laws. It begins with an article by Bruce Ackerman and Richard Stewart, who are sharply critical of environmental regulation's emphasis on technology-based, command-and-control standards. Ackerman and Stewart argue that such standards are notoriously inefficient because they fail to take into account variations among plants and industries in the costs of reducing pollution, as well as geographic variations in the effects of pollution. They maintain that technology-based controls disadvantage new industries and retard technological innovation. Ackerman and Stewart recommend that regulatory policy shift toward a more flexible system that varies levels of control depending on anticipated control costs and levels of harm caused by pollutants. They favor economic incentive approaches to regulation, such as marketable emissions allowances.

Howard Latin rejects the arguments of Ackerman and Stewart, maintaining that they single-mindedly pursue efficiency to the exclusion of other important goals. He argues that uniform standards have numerous advantages over more flexible approaches once one considers the fact that regulatory policy must be made in the face of pervasive uncertainty, high decision-making costs, and strategic behavior by regulated industries. According to Latin, more flexible approaches would reduce the effectiveness of environmental regulation and would in many cases not be feasible to implement.

Economists argue that more efficient regulatory approaches will make more resources available to society as a whole. However, Sidney Shapiro and Thomas McGarity point out that the victims of pollution will not necessarily get larger pieces of the supposedly larger social pie that cost-benefit approaches to regulation are assumed to create. Defending technology-based occupational health and safety standards on normative grounds, they argue that, because the benefits of the larger pie are likely to be diffusely distributed to consumers and shareholders at the expense of workers, cost-benefit approaches to regulation are simply unfair because they sacrifice lives to provide economic benefit to others. Shapiro and McGarity emphasize that the technology-based approach "has been an enormous success in the real world," and they claim that technology-based regulation has not been nearly as inefficient as its critics have asserted.

Carol Rose suggests that the choice of the most efficient resource management strategy may turn on the level of pressure on the commons. She notes that, until resource use creates congestion or exceeds the carrying capacity of the commons, a do-nothing strategy is most efficient. Once congestion occurs, zoning approaches that limit access to the commons have the least net administrative cost. However, as the level of resource use increases, it becomes more efficient to use regulations that limit the technology that can be used to exploit the commons. Finally, at very high levels of resource use, an economic incentive approach that creates property rights in the commons may have the lowest management costs. If Professor Rose's theory is accurate, then the winner of the debate between Ackerman/Stewart and Latin depends on how great the pressure to use the commons has become.

Shortly before it was abolished by Congress, the Office of Technology Assessment (OTA) conducted a comprehensive review of approaches to environmental regulation. In their ensuing report, *Environmental Policy Tools: A User's Guide,* OTA found that no single regulatory approach was superior in all circumstances. The report concluded that each approach has its advantages and disadvantages and that the best mix of regulatory strategies depends on the specific problem to be addressed and the relative weights given different criteria for evaluating such strategies. Thus, the proper approach to regulation depends on the goals and values that animate specific environmental policies, as explained in the report's discussion of the factors that should influence the choice of regulatory strategies. The report also makes recommendations for encouraging regulatory innovation.

The chapter concludes with an excerpt from the report of the President's Council on Sustainable Development, a group composed of a broad cross-section of representatives from industry, environmental groups, and the public sector. The report finds that environmental regulation has produced dramatic successes during the last quarter-century. However, it concludes that a new framework for regulation should be developed that incorporates a broader range of environmental protection strategies. The council recommends that regulators pursue approaches that provide enhanced flexibility coupled with strong compliance assurance mechanisms and that market forces be used more extensively by reforming tax and spending policies to promote environmental results. It finds that policy makers should simultaneously pursue making the existing regulatory system more efficient while developing an alternative management scheme that employs more innovative approaches.

The readings in this chapter reveal that we already know a great deal about what policies work best to protect the environment. The more difficult question is whether society has the political will to employ them.

*Bruce A. Ackerman and*
*Richard B. Stewart*

# Reforming Environmental Law: The Democratic Case for Market Incentives (1988)

## The Existing System

The existing system of pollution regulation is primarily based on a best available control technology (BAT) strategy. If an industrial process generates some non-trivial risk, the responsible plant or industry must install whatever technology is available to reduce or eliminate the risk, so long as the costs of doing so will not shut down the relevant plant or industry. BAT requirements are largely determined through centralized uniform federal regulation. Under the Clean Water Act's BAT strategy, EPA adopts nationally uniform effluent limitations for some 500 different industries. A similar BAT strategy is used in the Clean Air Act for new industrial sources of air pollution, new automobile and industrial sources of toxic air pollutants. BAT strategies are also widely used in many fields of environmental regulation other than air and water pollution.

BAT was embraced by Congress and administrators in the early 1970s in order to impose immediate, readily-enforceable, federal controls on a relatively few, widespread pollutants, while avoiding widespread industrial shutdowns. Subsequent experience and analysis has demonstrated:

1. Uniform BAT requirements waste many billions of dollars annually by ignoring variations among plants and industries in the costs of reducing pollution and by ignoring geographic variations in pollution effects. A more cost-effective strategy

Bruce A. Ackerman and Richard B. Stewart, Reforming Environmental Law: The Democratic Case for Market Incentives, 13 Colum. J. Envt'l L. 171 (1988).

of risk reduction could free up enormous resources for additional pollution reduction or other purposes.

2.  BAT controls, and the litigation which they provoke, impose disproportionate penalties on new products and processes. A BAT strategy typically imposes far more stringent controls on new sources because there is no risk of shutdown. Also, new plants and products must run the gauntlet of lengthy regulatory and legal proceedings to win approval; the resulting uncertainty and delay discourage new investment. By contrast, existing products and processes can use the legal process to postpone or water down compliance requirements. Also, BAT strategies impose disproportionate burdens on more productive and profitable industries because they can "afford" more stringent controls. This "soak the rich" approach penalizes growth and international competitiveness.

3.  BAT controls can ensure the diffusion of established control technologies. But they do not provide strong incentives for the development of new, environmentally superior strategies and may actually discourage their development. Such innovations are essential if we are to maintain economic growth in the long run without simultaneously increasing pollution and other forms of environmental degradation.

4.  BAT involves centralized, uniform determination of complex scientific, engineering and economic issues involving the feasibility of controls on hundreds of thousands of pollution sources. Such determinations impose massive information gathering burdens on administrators and provide a fertile ground for litigation, producing reams of technical data, complex adversary rulemaking proceedings and protracted judicial review. Given the high cost of regulatory compliance and the potential gains from litigation brought to defeat or delay regulatory requirements, it is often more cost effective for industry to invest in litigation rather than compliance.

5.  A BAT strategy is inconsistent with intelligent priority setting. Simply regulating to the hilt whatever pollutants or problems happen to get on the regulatory agenda may preclude an agency from dealing adequately with other more serious problems that come to scientific attention later. The BAT strategy also tends to reinforce regulatory inertia. Foreseeing that "all or nothing" regulation of a given substance under BAT will involve very large administrative and compliance costs, and recognizing that resources are limited, agencies will seek to limit the number of substances on the agenda for regulatory action. . . .

## Reform Is Realistic

A BAT system has an implicit environmental goal: achievement of the environmental quality level that would result if all sources installed BAT controls on their discharges. The usual means for implementing this goal are centralized, uniform regulations that command specific amounts of cleanup from specific polluters. When a polluter receives an air or water permit under existing law, the piece of paper does not content itself, in the manner of Polonius, with the vague advice that he "use the best available technology." Instead, the permit tries to be as quantitatively precise as possible, telling each discharger how much of each of the regulated pollutants he may discharge.

Reformers propose to build upon, and do not abandon, this basic permit system. Indeed, they have only two, albeit far-reaching, objections to the existing permit mechanism. First, existing permits are free. This is bad because it gives the polluter no incentive to reduce his wastes below the permitted amount. Second, permits are not transferable. This is bad because polluter A is obliged to cut back his own wastes even if it is cheaper for him to pay his neighbor B to undertake the extra cleanup instead.

The basic reform would respond to these deficiencies by allowing polluters to buy and sell each other's permits—thereby creating a powerful financial incentive for those who can clean up most cheaply to sell their permits to those whose treatment costs are highest. This reform will, at one stroke, cure many of the basic defects with existing command-and-control regulation. A system of tradeable rights will tend to bring about a least-cost allocation of control burdens, saving billions of dollars annually. It will eliminate the disproportionate burdens that BAT imposes on new industries and more productive industries by treating all sources of the same pollutant on the same basis. It will provide positive economic rewards for the development by those regulated of environmentally superior products and processes. It will . . . reduce the incentives for litigation and simplify the issues in controversy.

But would allowing the sale of permits lead to a bureaucratic nightmare? Before proceeding to the new administrative burdens marketability will generate, it is wise to pause to consider marketability's great administrative advantages.

First, it would immediately eliminate most of the information processing tasks that are presently overwhelming the federal and state bureaucracies. No longer would the EPA be required endlessly to hold hearings to determine the best available control technologies in each major industry of the United States, and defend its determinations before the courts; nor would federal and state officials be required to spend vast amounts of time and energy to adapt these changing national guidelines to suit the particular conditions of every important pollution source in the United States. Instead of giving the job of economic and technological assessment to bureaucrats, the marketable rights mechanism would put this information-processing burden precisely where it belongs: upon business managers and engineers who are in the best position to figure out how to cut back on their plant's pollution costs. If the managers operating plant A think they can clean up a pollutant more cheaply than those in charge of plant B, they should be expected to sell some of their pollution rights to B at a mutually advantageous price; cleanup will tend to occur at least cost without the need for constant bureaucratic decisions about the best available technology. While the reformed system may impose new regulatory tasks, it removes the greatest roadblock to administrative efficiency: it allows inevitably ill-informed bureaucrats to avoid technological and economic decisions best made by the people operating the plants.

Second, marketable permits would open up enormous financial resources for effective and informed regulation. While polluters would have the right to trade their permits among themselves during the $n$ years when they are valid, they would be obliged to buy new ones when their permits expired at an auction held by the EPA in each watershed and air quality control region. These auctions would raise substantial sums of money for the government on a continuing basis. While no study has yet attempted to make global estimates for the United States as a whole, existing work suggests that auction revenues could well equal the amount polluters would spend in cost-minimizing control activities. Even if revenues turned out to be a third of this amount, the government would still be collecting more than $6-$10 billion a year. Moreover, it seems reasonable to suppose that Congress would allow the EPA (and associated state agencies) to retain a share of these revenues. Since the current EPA operating budget is $1.3 billion, using even a fraction of the auction fund to improve regulatory analysis, research and monitoring would allow a great leap forward in the sophistication of the regulatory effort. Given its revenue-raising potential, environmental reform is hardly a politically unrealistic pipe dream. To the contrary, it is only a matter of time before the enormous federal deficit forces Congress and the President to consider the fiscal advantages of an auction scheme.

Third, the auction system would help correct one of the worst weaknesses of the present system: the egregious failure of the EPA and associated state agencies to enforce the laws on the books in a timely and effective way. Part of the problem stems from the ability of existing polluters to delay regulatory implementation by using legal proceedings to challenge the economic and engineering bases of BAT regulations and permit conditions. But agencies also invest so little on monitoring that they must rely on polluters for the bulk of their data on discharges. Since polluters are predictably reluctant to report their own violations, EPA systematically generates a Panglossian view of regulatory reality. For example, a General Accounting Office investigation of 921 major air polluters officially deemed in compliance revealed 200, or twenty-two percent, to be violating their permits; in one region, fifty-two percent were out of compliance. Even when illegal polluters are identified, they are not effectively sanctioned. For example, the EPA's Inspector General in 1984 found that it was a common practice for water pollution officials to respond to violations by issuing administrative orders which effectively legitimize excess discharges. Thus, while the system may, after protracted litigation, eventually "work" to force the slow installation of expensive control machinery, there is no reason to think this machinery is being run well when it is eventually installed. Although there are many reasons for this appalling weakness in enforcement, one stands out above all others: the present system does not put the pressure on agency policymakers to make the large investments in monitoring and personnel that are required to make the tedious and unending work of credible enforcement a bureaucratic reality.

The auction system would change existing compliance incentives dramatically. It would reduce the opportunity and incentive of polluters to use the legal system for delay and obstruction by finessing the complex BAT issues, and it would limit dispute to the question whether a source's discharges exceeded its permits. It would also eliminate the possibility of using the legal system to postpone implementation of regulatory requirements by requiring the polluter that lost its legal challenge to pay for the permits it would have been obliged to buy during the entire intervening period of noncompliance (plus interest).

The marketable permit system would also provide much stronger incentives for effective monitoring and enforcement. If polluters did not expect rigorous enforcement for the term of their permits, this fact would show up at the auction in dramatically lower bids: Why pay a lot for the right to pollute legally when one can pollute illegally without serious risk of detection? Under a marketable permit approach, this problem would be at the center of bureaucratic attention. For if, as we envisage, the size of the budget available to the EPA and state agencies would depend on total auction revenues, the bureaucracy's failure to invest adequately in enforcement would soon show up in a potentially dramatic drop in auction income available in the next budgetary period. This is not a prospect that EPA administrators will take lightly. Monitoring and enforcement will become agency priorities of the first importance. Moreover, permit holders may themselves support strong enforcement in order to ensure that cheating by others does not depreciate the value of the permit holders' investments.

A system of marketable permits, then, not only promises to save Americans billions of dollars a year, to reward innovative improvements in existing cleanup techniques and to eliminate the BAT system's penalty on new, productive investment. It also offers formidable administrative advantages. It relieves agencies of the enormous information-processing burdens that overwhelm them under the BAT system; it greatly reduces litigation and delay; it offers a rich source of budgetary revenue in a period of general budgetary stringency; and it forces agencies to give new importance to the critical business of enforcing the law in a way that America's polluters will take seriously. But, of course, there is no such thing as a free lunch in bureaucracy-land. Against these formidable advantages, the new system will generate new tasks. Are these new functions more or less onerous than the command-and-control operations that have been reformed away?

Begin by isolating four distinct bureaucratic functions required by the new system. First, the agency must estimate how much pollution is presently permitted by law in each watershed and each air quality region. Second, it must run a system of fair and efficient auctions in which polluters can regularly buy rights for limited terms. Third, it must run an efficient title registry in each region that will allow buyers and sellers to transfer rights in a legally effective way. Fourth, it must consistently penalize polluters who discharge more than their permitted amounts.

And that's that. So far as the fourth bureaucratic task is concerned, we have already given reasons to believe that the EPA would enforce the law far more effectively under the new regime than it does at present. So far as the first three management functions are concerned, we think that they are, in the aggregate, far *less* demanding than those they displace under the BAT system. Taking the three functions in reverse order, we assume that everybody agrees that a system of title registration is within the range of bureaucratic possibility. In contrast, the second task—running fair and efficient auctions—is a complicated affair, and it is easy to imagine such a system run incompetently or corruptly. Nonetheless, other agencies seem to have done similar jobs in satisfactory fashions: If the Department of Interior can auction off oil and gas leases competently, we see no reason the EPA could not do the same for pollution rights. Finally, there remains the task of estimating the total allowable wasteload permitted under existing law in each watershed and air control region. If the BAT system functioned properly, these numbers would be easy to obtain. EPA's regional administrators would simply have to add up the allowed amounts appearing in the permits that are in their filing cabinets. We have no illusions, however, about present realities: So much bureaucratic time and energy has been diverted into the counterproductive factfinding tasks generated by the BAT system, and so little attention has been paid to actual discharges, that even the data needed for these simple arithmetic operations may well be incomplete and inadequate. Nonetheless, total permitted emissions in a region can be approximated in order to get a system of permits and auctions started. Surely this start-up effort would be less complex that the unending inquiries into available technologies required by existing law.

## Toward Democratic Dialogue

So far we have been approaching reform in the much-maligned mode of the social engineer—offering to build you a better mousetrap, as it were, than the Rube Goldberg model now in operation. While we do not join in the fashionable disdain for such matters of "instrumental rationality," there is obviously more to political life than building efficient bureaucratic machines. The ultimate political questions involve ends, not means: How important is a healthy environment anyway? It isn't enough to say "very," since environmental quality is a very expensive good, which must compete with other precious public values—education, welfare, social security, etc. Somehow or other tough choices must be made: When should we stop pouring money into a clean environment to make room for a first-rate educational system or .... How much is enough?

Our basic problem with the BAT system is that it discourages a serious political encounter with such questions. BAT focuses Congressional debate, as well as administrative and judicial proceedings, upon arcane technological questions which rapidly exhaust the time and energy that most politicians let alone the larger public, are willing to spend on environmental matters. In contrast, the marketable permit system will allow the policymaking debate to take a far more intelligible shape. Rather than debating the difference between the "best available control technology" and "lowest achievable emission rate," citizens may focus upon a different question when the environmental acts come up for revision: During the next $n$ years, should we instruct the EPA gradually to decrease (or increase) the number of pollution rights by $x$ percent? Environmentalists will, of course, argue for big reductions; others, who are more impressed with the costs of control, for smaller reductions or even selective increases. But at least the Congressional debate would be encouraged to focus upon the fundamental question: Speaking broadly, do the American people believe existing environmental objectives to be too ambitious (in which case Congress should increase the number of rights) or do we think that we should further cut back on pollution (by cutting back on the number of rights)?

*Howard A. Latin*

# Ideal Versus Real Regulatory Efficiency: Implementation of Uniform Standards and "Fine-Tuning" Regulatory Reforms (1985)

Many environmental, public health, and safety statutes place primary emphasis on the implementation of uniform regulatory standards. In return for benefits that are often difficult to assess, "command-and-control" standards promulgated under such statutes as the Clean Air Act (CAA), Occupational Safety and Health Act (OSH Act), and Federal Water Pollution Control Act (FWPCA) impose billions of dollars in annual compliance costs on society and also entail significant indirect costs including decreases in productivity, technological innovation, and market competition. As these costs have become increasingly evident, prominent legal scholars such as Bruce Ackerman, Steven Breyer, and Richard Stewart have concluded that command-and-control regulation is inefficient and should be replaced by more flexible strategies. Their principal criticisms may be summarized as follows: Uniform standards do not reflect the opportunity costs of environmental protection, they disregard the individual circumstances of diverse conflicts, they do not achieve environmental protection on a "lowest-cost" basis, and they fail to provide adequate incentives for improved performance.

In response to these alleged deficiencies in the present system, advocates of "regulatory reform" argue that environmental controls should be tailored to particularized ecological and economic circumstances, regulatory benefits weighed against the costs of environmental protection, and increased reliance placed on economic incentive mechanisms, such as taxes on environmentally destructive activities or transferable pollution rights. Professor Stewart, for example, recently advocated "a more individualized or 'fine-tuning' approach to regulation." Critics of command-and-control standards differ on suggested "fine-tuning" prescriptions, but there is widespread agreement that some alternative must be preferable to the current regulatory system.

This article contends that the academic literature on "regulatory reform" reflects an excessive preoccupation with theoretical efficiency, while it places inadequate emphasis on actual decisionmaking costs and implementation constraints. Any system for environmental regulation must function despite the presence of pervasive uncertainty, high decisionmaking costs, and manipulative strategic behavior resulting from conflicting private and public interests. Under these conditions, the indisputable fact that uniform standards are inefficient does not prove that any other approach would necessarily perform better. In a "second-best" world, the critical issue is not which regulatory system aspires to ideal "efficiency" but which is most likely to prove effective.

In recognition of severe implementation constraints on environmental regulation, this article identifies numerous advantages of uniform standards in comparison with more particularized and flexible regulatory strategies. These advantages include decreased information collection and evaluation costs, greater consistency and predictability of results, greater accessibility of decisions to public scrutiny and participation, increased likelihood that regulations will withstand judicial review, reduced opportunities for manipulative behavior by agencies in response to political or bureaucratic pressures, reduced opportunities for obstructive behavior by regulated parties, and decreased likelihood of social dislocation and "forum shopping" resulting from competitive disadvantages between geographical regions or between firms in regulated industries. A realistic implementation analysis indicates that "fine-tuning" would prove infeasible in many important environmental contexts; indeed, the effectiveness of environmental regulation could often be improved by reducing even the degree of "fine-tuning" that is currently attempted. . . .

## The Limits of Technocratic Rationality

Regulatory critics often portray environmental conflicts as technical problems that can be "solved" in an "efficient" manner if decisionmakers are insulated from political pressures and are forced to consider all relevant circumstances. This assumption is clearly reflected, for example, in Bruce Ackerman's studies of environmental regulation. In *The Uncertain Search for Environmental Quality*, Professor Ackerman criticized the scientific underpinnings of the uniform water quality standards adopted in the Delaware River Basin. The regulations were partly based on a pioneering Public Health Service study of effluent levels and ecological effects in the four-state region. Despite years of effort at substantial expense, the scientific analysis incorporated many unrealistic simplifying assumptions. In conjunction with each technical criticism, Ackerman stressed the need for more complex and comprehensive scientific evaluations: In order to determine the benefits of alternative levels of pollution control, the agency should have assessed the aggregate impacts of all pollutants, of all significant ecological interdependencies, and of dynamic changes in natural conditions and pollutant discharge rates. Ackerman ridiculed the decision to implement uniform standards throughout the Delaware basin on the grounds that stringent controls would produce few if any tangible benefits in heavily polluted stretches of the river. He argued that society, rather than wasting multimillion dollar expenditures in the pursuit of illusory improvements, should adopt a cost-benefit balancing approach tailored to local circumstances and should impose strict pollution control only in smaller environmental enclaves with high-quality conditions. . . .

The central theme in *The Uncertain Search* and *Clean Coal/Dirty Air* is the same: Decisionmakers should consider all environmental conditions, all economic circumstances, and all possible control strategies in order to devise "efficient" regulatory systems. As an ideal, this degree of analytical sophistication is surely desirable. But regulators can seldom approach it in practice. In both critiques Ackerman emphasized environmental complexity and uncertainty to attack the basis for the promulgated regulations, but he never acknowledged that those constraints, together with budgetary and time restrictions, severely limit the ability of agencies to develop technocratic solutions for environmental problems. In *The Uncertain Search,* Ackerman did not attempt to demonstrate that existing scientific knowledge was sufficient for protection of his proposed environmental enclaves. He also failed to consider the cumulative decisionmaking costs and extended time requirements associated with comprehensive scientific analyses of many "high-quality" regions possessing dissimilar characteristics. Instead, Ackerman presented his preferred strategy, reliance on marketable pollution rights, in an idealized manner without any discussion of the environmental complexities he emphasized in his criticisms of the Delaware River study.

In *Clean Coal/Dirty Air,* Ackerman again presented his proposed alternatives in an idealized form without a balanced consideration of the legal, political, and implementation constraints that would prevent their introduction or degrade their performance. In contradiction to his dismissive characterization of "mindless" EPA decisionmaking, another discussion of the rulemaking proceeding noted that: "The NSPS process included the most extensive national impacts analysis EPA has performed for a new standard." When the Court of Appeals for the District of Columbia Circuit approved the NSPS in all respects, the decision emphasized the breadth and detail of the agency's analysis. Although the Court identified some analytical imperfections, Judge Wald described the NSPS as reasonable in light of several factors: the "terrible complexity" of the issues; the "extraordinarily technical and often confusing" evidence and "obfuscation" introduced by parties representing "conflicting interests"; the large areas of scientific, technological, and economic uncertainty; the EPA's responsibility to reach an accommodation among the partly incompatible goals of the CAA; the congressional insistence on "speedy decisionmaking"; and the need for "finality" in administrative rulemaking. Ackerman and other proponents of technocratic decisionmaking consistently underestimate these constraints in their attempts to identify "efficient" regulatory solutions. When inherently complex and controversial environmental problems are considered, the development of even moderately effective control strategies can never be a simple undertaking.

. . . Agencies have strong incentives to promulgate technically and politically defensible standards, or none at all. If officials do not believe they can answer the "right
questions" with a sufficient degree of reliability to insulate themselves from criticism,
insisting that they must nonetheless do so will not lead to "efficient" regulation. This
demand will instead produce very little regulation. Moreover, the delay created by
legal requirements that agencies must "answer" complex and uncertain questions
would frequently entail serious irreversible consequences: People's exposure to toxic
substances would continue during the interim, as would depletion of natural resources and threats to endangered species. Effective environmental protection may
require agencies to treat some scientifically and economically relevant, but currently
unresolvable, issues as legally irrelevant; that is precisely what command-and-control standards frequently do.

Ackerman's call for additional research . . . illustrates a common technocratic assumption that expanded research efforts will produce dispositive information. Many
important environmental uncertainties, however, stem from inadequate scientific understanding rather than merely from inadequate data. Breakthroughs in scientific
knowledge are unpredictable and cannot be guaranteed by increased research budgets.
Our nation almost certainly has underinvested in ecological and technological research
in comparison with expenditures on environmental regulation. Yet the central question
is whether the problematical value of additional research justifies delaying regulation
until "enough" knowledge is available. The resolution of this issue requires a political,
not technocratic, judgment. Congress recognized the existence of pervasive scientific
uncertainty when it enacted the principal regulatory statutes, and nonetheless chose to
emphasize the need for prompt injury prevention over the need for an optimal balance
between regulatory benefits and costs. Before it can be argued that "fine-tuning" regulation is more "efficient," critics of uniform standards must demonstrate that particularized knowledge can feasibly be obtained. Very often, it cannot. . . .

In a recent critique of command-and-control standards, Richard Stewart correctly
observed that environmental, health, and safety regulation has retarded social and
market innovation. Although he conceded that regulation has not been the major
cause of a "lag" in productivity, Professor Stewart advocated restructuring environmental protection programs to promote greater innovation. He noted, for example,
that the relatively short "lead times" and frequent revisions of current standards produce a "moving target" effect that impedes development of the "stable market" necessary for creation of innovative technologies. He contended that the "moving target" problem could be remedied if Congress and government agencies would establish
regulatory standards further in advance, allowing industry greater time to achieve
compliance. Stewart criticized the imposition of stricter controls on new sources of
environmental degradation than on existing sources. . . .

Throughout this critique, Stewart treated the goal of increasing innovation as if it
should take precedence over all incompatible objectives. His proposal for longer lead

times and less frequent revisions of standards would delay the diffusion of available control methods and would prevent agencies from responding promptly to new environmental and technological knowledge. Stewart recognized these social costs, but his article implies that the benefits of creating a "stable market" generally outweigh the disadvantages. Yet he never provided a quantitative or qualitative argument to support that conclusion. Stewart similarly acknowledged that his proposal for negotiated rulemaking would increase the ability of affected parties to impede regulation through obstructive behavior in the negotiations process, but he failed to emphasize their strong *motivation* to do so. With regard to his recommendation for increased reliance on economic incentive mechanisms, he observed that:

> Different regulatory tools or strategies will allocate the burden of uncertainty and change in different ways. For example, under a command-and-control system, unexpectedly high control costs will be borne by the industry unless the stringency of regulations is relaxed. Under a fee system, these costs will result in lower levels of control unless fees are increased. In the first case, the risk of unexpectedly high control costs is imposed on firms; in the second, it is imposed on the environment and those exposed to pollution, health, and safety risks.

Stewart has stressed in other essays that uncertainty and change are pervasive aspects of environmental decisionmaking. Yet he never explained in this critique why the asserted ability of economic incentive mechanisms to promote innovation should outweigh the propensity of those strategies to decrease environmental protection under conditions of uncertainty. Moreover, to the extent that market incentive programs can be adjusted flexibly in response to changing knowledge and social priorities, they would produce the same "moving target" effect Stewart criticized in conjunction with command-and-control regulation. . . .

## Motivations of Actors in the Regulatory Process

Academic commentaries often assume that participants in the regulatory process want to reach "efficient" decisions and would cooperate to do so if political pressures and decisionmaking constraints were eliminated. In reality, strategic behavior to further conflicting objectives is the norm rather than the exception in environmental controversies: Regulated industries attempt to minimize compliance costs, environmentalists may seek to protect ecological features and public health at any cost, and agency bureaucrats often try to expand discretion and budgets while defusing public criticism. Uniform regulatory standards have been developed in adversarial rulemaking proceedings and appellate cases dominated by the tenacious pursuit of private interests. No realistic appraisal of competing control strategies can simply assume a benign, cooperative regulatory climate, but that is what proponents of "fine-tuning" often have done. . . .

The central theme here is that a meaningful comparison of regulatory approaches must include: (1) a realistic appraisal of the motives of industry and environmental advocates, and (2) a realistic prediction of how those parties would act in different decisionmaking systems. It is equally necessary to consider how agency officials will behave under competing regulatory approaches. If, for example, a negotiated rule-making process is instituted, as Stewart proposed, an agency's effectiveness would be measured by its ability to achieve cooperation among participating interest groups. Even if the agency retains authority to impose standards on the parties when no consensus is reached, that circumstance would be regarded as a "failure" of the negotiation process and of its institutional sponsor. The appearance of agency partiality would frustrate any regulatory system based on voluntary agreements. Thus, administrators are likely to conclude that it would be improper or impolitic for them to advocate specific regulatory initiatives. Yet Congress clearly wanted regulatory agencies to be "partial" in developing affirmative solutions for pressing environmental problems, rather than merely to serve as neutral arbiters among those interest groups that happen to participate.

Stewart acknowledged that: " 'Fine-tuning' would not only involve additional decision costs. It also would allow regulated firms more opportunities to obstruct and delay by insisting on hearings or more formal procedures to consider the particular circumstances of each product or process." A regulatory approach that requires an agency to consider *everything* would encourage parties to submit *anything* that might further their ends, either directly or indirectly through additional delay. Given the decisionmaking and budgetary constraints under which agencies function and the personal incentives of agency officials, the wealth of information and conjecture that could be introduced in particularized regulatory proceedings would often retard effective regulation. This result would occur even if reviewing courts did not, as they now do, compel agencies to respond in detail to party submissions. Nevertheless, Stewart, Ackerman, and most other regulatory critics advocate "fine-tuning" approaches because of the theoretical efficiencies they promise.

## Idealized Institutional Reforms

Critics of environmental standards often contend that regulatory efficiency would be greatly improved if decisionmaking responsibilities were shifted to another institution. Ackerman, for example, portrayed Congress as the worst of many incompetents in the NSPS process. He claimed that "Congress's well-intentioned effort . . . has driven EPA to an extraordinary decision that will cost the public tens of billions of dollars to achieve environmental goals that could be reached more cheaply, more quickly, and more surely by other means." He then argued that Congress should define basic policy premises but should not specify the means required to realize those legislative goals. In place of congressional meddling, Ackerman advocated the "New Deal ideal" of "an independent and expert administrative agency creatively regulating a complex social problem in the public interest." He asserted that "it is the expert agency, unencumbered by abstract legalisms, that promises to craft a policy responsive to the complexities of environmental relationships."

This hypothetical "New Deal agency" bears little resemblance to any actual agency created in the New Deal era or any other. Even if such a *deus ex machina* were accepted for the sake of argument, Ackerman provided no explanation of why independent agency expertise would ensure "efficient" regulation. He instead conceded that agency decisionmakers at best could only produce "high-visibility guesswork" because "we do not now know enough about how sulfates of different kinds and quantities harm us." In view of "large gaps in our knowledge," practical restrictions on agency budgets, and the existence of incompatible social objectives, there is no reason to believe that elimination of congressional "interference" would lead to optimal regulatory decisions.

## Conclusion

It would be relatively easy to improve environmental regulation if the major inefficiencies stemmed from stupidity, venality, and agency capture by extremist factions—we could simply appoint more intelligent and courageous administrators. But this characterization is simplistic. Many critical problems result from inherent limitations on environmental decision making and from conflicts between the legitimate but incompatible interests of diverse parties. Idealized regulatory theories provide no assurance that "efficient" approaches will prove effective under these intractable implementation constraints. Most "fine-tuning" strategies require marginal harm-based determination of precisely the type that agencies have been unable to make in a scientifically and legally defensible fashion. "Fine-tuning" would require assessments of particularized circumstances, and would therefore usually increase decision-making costs, delays, inconsistencies, bureaucratic discretion, and opportunites for manipulative behavior by regulated parties.

In many environmental protection contexts, society's real choice may be to rely either on crude regulation or on no regulation. Insistence upon "fine-tuning" in these cases may be not only intellectually misguided but politically naive. Although "fine-tuning" conceivably may be practicable and desirable in some regulatory settings, proponents of "regulatory reform" have not identified those specific contexts and have never demonstrated that "fine-tuning" would *generally* increase, rather than decrease, society's ability to achieve environmental and health protection in a reasonably effective manner.

*Sidney A. Shapiro and*
*Thomas O. McGarity*

# Not So Paradoxical: The Rationale for Technology-Based Regulation (1991)

## The Normative Basis for Technology-based Regulation

The choice of any regulatory approach can be debated on normative and instrumental grounds. In this section, we argue that normative considerations make technology-based approaches preferable to cost-benefit approaches. In the following section, we address the instrumental concerns involved in determining the relative effectiveness of . . . proposed reforms and technology-based approaches.

Economists defend the use of cost-benefit standards in formulating social policy on risk reduction by arguing that, in some cases, it is less expensive for society when employers pay compensation for illnesses rather than spending money to prevent them. This argument, however, ignores the ethical distinction between preventing death and compensating the victim's family after death occurs. As the Supreme Court's *Cotton Dust* reading of the OSHA Act's legislative history indicates, Congress apparently had this in mind when it rejected cost-benefit analysis for OSHA health standards. In addition, placing the entire burden of less stringent cost-benefit-based standards on workers is inequitable. Even if milder standards would ultimately make more resources available to society, there is no reason why workers should not be fully compensated for the losses they sustain that could have been prevented under more stringent standards. In other words, the resources saved by a switch to less stringent standards should go to the injured workers, rather than to the employers or their customers. Yet few economists advocate redistributing the efficiency gains of cost-benefit approaches to workers.

Indeed, economic analysts respond that the distributional consequences of their prescriptions are beyond their bailiwick. For example, [Professor John] Mendeloff recognizes that the winners of a policy prescription do not necessarily have to pay the losers for their losses under his cost-benefit approach:

> Those who die because society rejects inefficient lifesaving programs will not be around to benefit from the bigger pie. Does this fact require condemnation of any policy that stops short of a maximum effort to prevent deaths? No. It is inevitable that public policy will create losers who are beyond the reach of compensation. But this fact should spur thinking about who the losers are and how we feel about their plight.

Surviving family members of workers whose deaths could have been prevented at a cost somewhat greater than the economist's optimal expenditure will take no comfort in the assurance that the loss of their loved one will stimulate scholars to think more about how society should feel about their plight.

When the distributional consequences of a cost-benefit regulatory world are considered, it becomes obvious that cost-benefit approaches undercompensate workers in two ways. First, cost-benefit analysts underestimate the value of a life. Second, compensation systems pay workers less than the full value of their lives, as defined by economists. Indeed, some workers are not compensated at all. Although public policy may inevitably create some losers beyond the reach of compensation, the cost-benefit approach creates too many uncompensated losers when compared with technology-based approaches.

In a world where workers are seldom fully compensated for occupational illness, the merit of a technology-based approach is that it reduces the need for victims to resort to the compensation system to a much larger degree than does the cost-benefit approach. Under the cost-benefit approach, significant financial burdens fall on those who are least able to sustain them, i.e., workers and their families. In comparison, the additional costs imposed by technology-based standards are passed on to consumers or absorbed by stockholders. The individual impact of these costs on any one consumer or stockholder is insignificant compared to the burden imposed on uncompensated or undercompensated workers and their families, who are forced to absorb the entire cost of their illnesses. Protecting workers with technology-based standards may be more costly to society than compensating them after-the-fact. But in the absence of a realistic mechanism to ensure adequate compensation, fairness demands that workers be protected from incurring the costs of illness where possible.

Mendeloff and other economic critics have difficulty believing that Congress really rejected the use of cost-benefit analysis. Because no rational consumer would pay $25 in a private market for something that is worth only $20, the economist assumes that voters also intend for their representatives to reject policies whose costs exceed their "economic" benefits.

However, the economist fails to understand that public, social decisions provide citizens with an opportunity to give certain things a higher valuation than they would otherwise choose to give them in their private activities or in their capacity as individuals. In public forums, individuals are often willing to vote for outcomes that economic analysis would characterize as inefficient because these outcomes can confirm and serve important noneconomic values. As consumers, we may dislike paying more for manufactured products because of the costs of protecting workers, but as citizens we can rationally vote for these types of costly and (by the economist's "willingness to pay" measure) irrational goals. We vote in favor of such costly goals because they permit us to reaffirm our ideal that preventable occupational diseases are not merely inefficient—they are *wrong*. . . .

. . . Technology-based regulation is concededly imperfect. It spawns messy legislative and judicial struggles, is subject to industry and agency manipulation, and often appears irrational when measured by comprehensive analytical rationality standards. But this "academic failure" has been an enormous success in the real world.

In addition to the proven effectiveness of the technology-based approaches, technological requirements reflect a considered *normative* choice about the proper balance between lives and monetary costs. Acknowledging that society cannot vest workers with an unqualified right to an absolutely safe workplace, one may rationally assert that workers do have a right to insist that employers "do the best they can" to protect human health. In other words, society might justifiably decide to reduce risky behavior beyond the point indicated by a cost-benefit test. Indeed, society may choose to limit its protection of workers only at the point where the protection would cause industry substantial economic dislocation. . . .

. . . Although we agree that a judicious use of market-oriented implementation techniques might well improve the current system, we believe that Professor [Cass] Sunstein's enthusiasm [for them] is misplaced. More importantly, in his attacks on the technology-based approach to regulation, Sunstein often mixes normative arguments about regulatory goals with instrumental arguments about reaching those goals. For example, Sunstein does not clearly recognize that incentive-based tools may be used to reach the normative goal of installing the best available technology. Instead, Sunstein appears to view BAT and market-based approaches as mutually exclusive. In the process, Sunstein overstates both the ease of implementing [economic incentive approaches] and the difficulty of implementing technology-based commands.

Specifically, in discussing market-based incentives, Sunstein asserts that "[i]f the ultimate goal is to reduce pollution sharply, then we should simply issue few permits." He also assumes that risks from toxic substances could easily be reduced by simply assessing high taxes on, for examples, toxic waste disposal and automobile emissions. These optimistic assessments may underestimate the difficulties inherent in estimating risks and benefits. In addition, the incentive-based approach adds new uncertainties to the prediction of the number of permits and level of taxes necessary to achieve a given level of risk reduction, on top of the already existing uncertainties about how various levels of exposure to toxic substances affect humans and the environment. Unless agencies are prepared to tolerate potentially high exposures and/or devastating short-term economic consequences during the time it takes for the system to reach "steady state," proceedings examining the level of tax or the issuable number of permits are likely to be highly contentious. Moreover, because industry will likely resist any change to the status quo, especially if it requires immediate outlays, implementation of any market-based program is likely to be slow.

Sunstein cites the history of environmental legislation in support of his conclusion that an incentive-based approach could be implemented more easily than could the BAT approaches. In particular, he compares the productive results under the Clean Air Act (CAA) and the Clean Water Act (CWA) with the government's less effective attempts to regulate toxic substances. Ironically, the CAA and CWA both adopted technology-based approaches to a large extent. Moreover, when Congress recognized that the overwhelming uncertainties and analytical quagmires concerning risk assessment were bogging down the toxic substance programs, Congress first amended both statutes specifically to allow the EPA to implement technology-based approaches. Later, Congress moved to establish more stringent standards in cases where BAT failed to adequately protect the public health. Thus, Congress recognized, as Sunstein does not, that "the practical consequence of making particularized risk estimates legally relevant . . . is to emasculate the regulation of carcinogens under prevailing conditions of scientific certainty."

The recent amendments to the CAA that permit states to use emissions trading and pollution taxes do not refute this point. Congress has already established the permissible levels of exposure for conventional pollutants in the CAA itself. Thus, financial incentives do not affect the decision of what ambient air quality standards are appropriate. Consequently, we do not oppose the added flexibility that the 1990 amendments give states to reach the predetermined goals.

However, Congress has been slow to apply this lesson across the board. In fact, one of the reasons that OSHA has regulated so few toxic substances is that it is required to make individual risk assessments for each substance regulated. In the *Benzene* case, the Supreme Court read the risk assessment requirement into OSHA's legislative mandate although . . . little in the text or history of the Act supports this interpretation. We have elsewhere proposed that Congress should give OSHA a choice between adopting less stringent BAT regulations and more stringent regulations based on individual risk determinations. We are confident that this relatively modest change would speed up the decisionmaking process, just as the changes to the Clean Air Act and Clean Water Act did.

In addition to providing a speedier approach to regulation, BAT strategies, when compared to market-based approaches, stack up well on other instrumental grounds. A comparison of Sunstein's four indictments of BAT with the probable implementation difficulties of a market-based approach indicates that BAT is not nearly as oafish as Sunstein suggests, and that market-based approaches are not nearly as neat.

First, Sunstein argues that because BAT strategies ignore the enormous differences among plants in industries and among geographical areas, these strategies are "wildly inefficient." According to Sunstein, emissions trading programs perform more efficiently because they allow firms with high abatement costs to buy additional permits to pollute from firms with low abatement costs. However, BAT systems do not operate in the blind manner that Sunstein indicates. No agency ignores the types of geographical and intra-industry differences Sunstein cites. Rather, agencies utilize a system of variances to account for these differences. Emissions trading may be less expensive to administer than the relatively cumbersome system of variances, and the variance process can be abused to allow unjustified departures from the national standards. However, characterizing the BAT approach as "wildly" inefficient is an inaccurate overstatement of BAT's performance in practice.

Moreover, Sunstein fails to discuss the administrative costs associated with the reforms that he proposes. For example, because we do not know exactly how much abatement a pollution or injury tax would cause, the tax would likely have to be adjusted several times to meet the abatement goals. Aside from the problem of whether Congress (or any legislature) would be willing to alter the tax after it has been initially set, the costs associated with these changes must be factored into any comparison of BAT and market-related incentives.

Second, Sunstein argues that BAT strategies are "extremely expensive to enforce, imposing extraordinary monitoring burdens" on EPA and OSHA. But this is not reality. BAT strategies are less expensive to enforce because inspectors are only required to determine whether a firm has installed the required technology and continues to operate it properly. By comparison, emissions trading and pollution taxes require inspectors to monitor constantly the amount of pollution that a plant emits. In many cases, monitoring all the possible discharge points for air and water pollution will be far more expensive and difficult than identifying whether a firm is using a required technology. In the air pollution context, the incentive-based approach would create an incentive to abuse the system by hiding emissions in all but the very simplest plants.

Third, Sunstein contends that because BAT strategies impose stricter regulatory requirements on new plants and industries than old ones, they penalize new products and thereby perpetuate old, dirty technology. In contrast, pollution taxes and marketable permits would, according to Sunstein, induce firms to invest in new technologies. To the extent the system is adequately policed to ensure that firms do not avoid paying the taxes in the first place, or cheat by emitting in excess of their permits, we agree with this assessment. However, the current income tax system, with its monument to the ingenuity of tax avoidance, does not inspire optimism on this point.

Finally, Sunstein objects to using regulation to pursue redistributive objectives, because it is less efficient in obtaining these objectives than more direct redistribution techniques. Thus, if society prefers to shift the costs of occupational disease from workers to their employers, Sunstein would advocate revamping workers compensation rather than using BAT strategies to accomplish this goal. Although we have already expressed normative objections to choosing compensation over prevention, we also believe that compensation is unlikely to be increased to the point where it fully compensates workers for their injuries and illnesses. . . .

Even with its problems, technology-based regulation compares favorably with market-related incentives from a strictly instrumental perspective. We therefore consider a more incremental path to occupational safety and health reform more likely. Congress might be persuaded to authorize OSHA to use BAT, while at the same time allow OSHA to regulate more stringently if necessary to reduce or eliminate significant workplace risks. Unlike drastic workers compensation reform, this step would protect workers before they are injured, and reduce the number of illnesses for which employees would never be fully compensated because of difficulties in establishing cause-effect relationships between workplace exposures and individual diseases.

*Carol M. Rose*

# Rethinking Environmental Controls: Management Strategies for Common Resources (1991)

## Four Strategies of Commons Management

What are the ways we can usefully categorize commons management strategies? Some writers focus on who the "strategists" are, and they divide strategies into "private" and "public," according to whether controls are imposed by insiders (private) or by outside authorities (public or governmental). This may be a useful division; the identity of the controlling body as "private" or "governmental" may identify some issues, particularly the "rent-seeking" and public choice problems that are thought to distort public bodies' decisionmaking process. Nevertheless, private and governmental managers often use techniques that are quite similar in content—as has been shown in the classic case of the fisheries. The public/private divide, taken alone, misses the substantive content of these various techniques or strategies, whereas the focus of this Article is precisely on those substantive characteristics of management, regardless of whether the managers themselves are public or private.

What, then, are the substantive types of commons management techniques? One economist, Stephen Cheung, has made a very useful list, and indeed he listed his strategies more or less in ascending order of the difficulty and expense of administration.

(1) *Do-Nothing*. First, of course, even before we get to Cheung's strategies, we could adopt the very easiest strategy and do nothing—that is, we could leave our fishing ground an open-access commons. This no-control option, which I rather boringly call DO-NOTHING, is a kind of baseline over against which we can measure the effectiveness of other strategies.

(2) *Keepout.* Second (and now we are taking up Cheung's list), we could exclude newcomers, a strategy to which I will refer to as KEEPOUT: Once we get to a congestion point, where we feel the pinch of overcrowding and resource depletion, we keep out everybody else. Our "insider" fishers, on this model, would continue to fish in any way they chose, but they would cut off the access of newcomers. This would mean, of course, that although the fish levels might be preserved, they would only be accessible to the insiders—outsiders wouldn't get any.

(3) *Rightway.* Third, we could regulate the way in which the resource is used or taken, effectively prescribing the methods by which users may take the resource; I refer to this strategy as RIGHTWAY. In our fishing area, for example, we could limit fishing to fly-casting and not allow trawling or the giant fishnets that have been in the news lately as destroyers of ocean wildlife. Under this RIGHTWAY scheme, fishing would be open to all who want to fish, but only if they fish in a certain way—a way, we hope, that limits the overall number of fish they are likely to catch.

(4) *Property.* Finally, we could manage the fish by giving individualized property rights to them, a strategy that I term PROP. For example, a PROP regime could set a limit on the total allowable take of fish, and then auction off fishing rights to those who wanted to purchase such rights. In a sophisticated version, the fishers could trade these rights among themselves. Alternatively, we could try to figure out a per-fish or per-pound price that would discourage fishing above an acceptable level, and then require each fisher to pay a bounty on each unit taken.

There are of course equivalents to all these strategies in our past, present, and hypothetical future environmental law. Take air pollution control (to which I will return in more detail later): Strategy One, DO-NOTHING, is represented by the "anything goes" attitude to air pollution that we used to find—especially in undeveloped areas. Strategy Two, KEEPOUT, corresponds to a kind of crude land-use control, in which new facilities are halted; new shopping centers, for example, have sometimes been disallowed on the ground that they may increase air pollution from the auto traffic that they attract.

Strategy Three, RIGHTWAY, is widely reflected in our law. The prohibitions on "unreasonable use" in classic nuisance law, although rather malleable, effectively restrain the manner of using air; these prohibitions disallow practices that deviate from the customary and normal. In a much more complex fashion, the modern "command and control" environmental measures have also prescribed the manner in which air may be used, but in a highly specific fashion. These measures have demanded that would-be polluters use the air only in the "right way"; that is, they may emit pollutants into the air, but only through the use of specific control equipment (the "best available technology") such as scrubbers to contain the emissions from coal burning exhaust stacks or catalytic converters on automobiles.

Finally, Strategy Four, PROP, through which resource rights are turned into individual entitlements, is a technique that has been much discussed lately, both in academic literature and in legislative proposals for purchasable and tradeable pollution rights. Indeed, Congress has now incorporated this strategy into the controls on acid rain.

These various strategies are not necessarily mutually exclusive—and indeed they are often combined. For example, KEEPOUT is often combined with either RIGHT-WAY or PROP. In the customary pattern, newcomers are excluded altogether (KEEP-OUT), while the "insider" oldtimers only use the resource in a well-established customary manner (RIGHTWAY), or according to customary limits on total use (PROP). Such practices are common, for example, among established shellfishers and users of commonly owned grazing areas. A somewhat different combination of the KEEP-OUT and RIGHTWAY strategies appears in some modern air pollution controls: Pre-existing polluters have been treated as if they had a common KEEPOUT entitlement to foul the air more or less as they had in the past, whereas the "kept-out" new polluters have been required to install highly technical RIGHTWAY pollution control devices.

Cheung's article catalogued these generic strategies but did not specify how to choose among them, although he suggested that in principle a choice should be possible. The way to make that choice is to consider costs—to select the strategy that limits use at the lowest cost. This determination, however, is context dependent.

## Management Costs and Rent Dissipation

Cheung and others have made explicit one important insight about managing resources: It costs something to manage resources. Thus generally speaking, even if we can find a MAXLEVEL of resource use that we think most appropriate, we need to recognize that holding use to that level will not be done for free. We still need to find the strategy that holds use at the appropriate level, *at the lowest total cost*.

What are the cost components of these various strategies? Any answer, of course, will grossly oversimplify, but one has to start somewhere, and so I propose the following three components:

(1) *Administrative or system costs.* These comprise the system-wide costs of running a management strategy, including both organizational and policing costs.

(2) *User costs.* These are the costs of extra equipment, such as scrubbers or catalytic converters, that individual resource-users must acquire to satisfy the requirements of any given management strategy. Because many of these costs are technological, I will sometimes call them "technology costs."

(3) *Overuse or failure costs.* This cost category accounts for breakdowns and slippages, and it comprises the continuing "externalities" under a given strategy—the continuing conflicts and damage caused by resource depletion that escapes the control system. These costs reflect the point that no management strategy is perfect; because of management failure, we may still wind up somewhere beyond our acceptable MAXLEVEL—that is, beyond the point at which we feel it is healthy, safe, or comfortable to permit continuing resource depletion.

Now, when we choose one or another control strategy, the combination of administrative costs, user-technology costs, and overuse/failure costs will vary according to what the literature of common resources often refers to as "pressure." "Pressure" on a resource occurs when more people try more intensely to use the resource.

Why does a resource come under pressure? One way to explain this is through the economic concept of "rents." It is often said that there are rents to be gained in natural resource exploitation, this means that a given resource may yield revenues and pleasures above the cost of taking the resource. "Rent" is the name given to such excess values. These rents are of course desirable to have, and when rent-yielding resources are up for grabs, they tend to attract people who try to grab them. When a resource's rents are low, people may more or less ignore the resource; under those circumstances, the few users of the resource may enjoy whatever little-known or idiosyncratic "rent" they derive without competition or congestion from other seekers. In the fishing example, this is the stage in which there is little pressure on a fishing ground—only a few fanatical fishers bother to buy the equipment and brave the cold to catch the elusive trout.

But if more people value the resource (for example, if trout-eating or trout-fishing becomes a fad) or perhaps if the resource becomes cheaper to exploit (for example, if new nets or boats are invented), the difference between the resource's value and the cost of exploitation may widen. That difference, of course, is the resource's rent, and as it becomes larger, more people will undertake greater efforts to exploit the resource. In our fishing example, increasing rents translate into increasing pressure on the fishing area, which becomes crowded with rent-seeking competitors for fish.

The problem is that if more and more people try harder and harder to catch fish, so much effort may be poured into fishing that the fish are threatened with depletion, and the cost of catching them will rise while the return declines. Thus unless something restrains the fishers, their competition for the fish (or other renewable resources) dissipates the very rents that attracted them in the first place—rents that might have been preserved by exploiting the resource at a more appropriate level. It is for this reason—to hold down resource exploitation and prevent rent dissipation—that we institute management regimes for resources. . . .

## Comparing the Costs of Management Strategies: Which Is Best?

It should now be clear that our goal should be to choose the least-cost management strategy, that is, the one with the lowest mix of rent dissipating factors. What follows is a . . . graphic [Figure 8-1] that illustrate[s] the cost mixes of different management strategies under different levels of pressure on a resource. [It] represents the idea that larger rents themselves indirectly bring about higher management costs, because at higher rent or pressure levels, more institutional effort is required to restrain overuse. More technically, then, the graph[] depict[s] the relationships between rents and rent dissipation; . . . the horizontal line represents pressure on the resource (technically, rents from the resource), whereas the vertical line represents the total costs of the given

FIGURE 8-1.

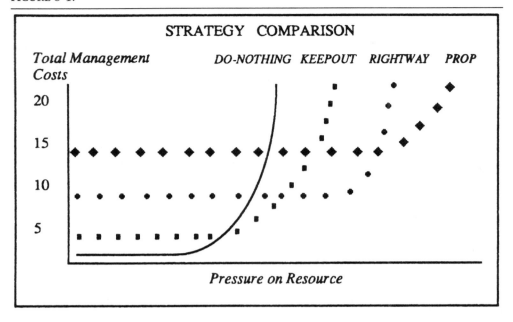

control strategy, (dissipation of rents under that strategy), due to its mix of system costs, user costs, and failure/overuse costs.

I begin with Strategy One, DO-NOTHING: In essence, the costs of DO-NOTHING simply replicate the congestion cost curve. As people want a resource more, they work harder and harder to get it. In the absence of any constraints, their increased efforts translate directly into an increased total exploitation; but, of course, exploitation depletes the resource, and as this happens, individual exploiters may wind up with less and less, as their increasing efforts cause ever-greater difficulties to one another. Thus, their ever-more-strenuous efforts to gain the resource's rents dissipate those very rents. The chief costs of the DO-NOTHING strategy, then, fall into the category of overuse or failure costs. When the resource is depleted substantially, the discomfort, conflict, and diminished return entailed by overuse may be substantial. Because of these overuse costs, as Scott Gordon laconically observed, fishermen are not wealthy.

But sometimes the DO-NOTHING strategy might be most appropriate. When demand for the underlying resource is slight, DO-NOTHING is especially cheap: There are no administrative costs for organization and policing; no user technology is specifically dedicated to control; and because no one is trying very hard to get the resource, overuse or depletion costs are still low, if they are felt at all. But once again, if values rise, and more and more people attempt to get the resource, overuse costs rise—perhaps even dramatically—and they may overwhelm any savings that can be made by dispensing with administrative and technical controls. Aside from fishing, a familiar example might be a pleasant, open-access, town beach that is "discovered" by outsiders, where the resulting overcrowding leads the townspeople to reconsider open-access and to think of more active strategies for limiting access.

One strategy that the townsfolk (and the fisherfolk) are very likely to think of is the second strategy, KEEPOUT, which abandons the open access of DO-NOTHING, and instead excludes outsiders or new uses.

. . . [W]hen we introduce KEEPOUT, administrative or system costs are obviously higher than DO-NOTHING; someone may have to do a good deal of organizational work to get the control system introduced, especially if many people see an advantage in the older system of open access. The system also requires a monitoring effort: The insiders may have to police the pond, or hire police to keep interlopers off, and they may need boats and weapons. And, like any new system, this one may not work very well at the outset, so the failure/overuse costs may remain fairly high. Finally, there are morale costs, especially at the beginning: Some may grumble that we really don't need all this control activity, because there are still plenty of fish, and keeping out new fisherfolk just looks stingy and ungenerous.

But if pressure on the fishery continues to rise, and more and more people try to take the fish, then the system may seem worth the effort (at least to the beneficiary insiders)—that is, its total costs may look lower than a "do-nothing" solution. Once the system is in place, we don't have to do much more organizing work, or buy a whole new fleet of police boats. Besides, the system may work better with experience, and it may really reduce total take from the fishery, no matter how hard outsiders try to break the system. Morale issues may improve too, once the homefolks grow accustomed to the system; once they think it is doing them some good, they may be quite willing to enforce it. The increasing outsider disgruntlement may offset this gain, however.

Indeed, supposing we continue to move further out on the horizontal line of pressure, outsider poachers and interlopers may overrun the KEEPOUT control system. Insiders may have to hire more and more cops and boats, perhaps with less and less effect; thus policing costs rise, as do the failure costs of conflict and depletion.

One way to deal with this problem is to permit the outsiders to enter, but to control the means by which all fishers can take the resource—that is, to move to Strategy Three, RIGHTWAY, that controls the way the resource is used.

With this strategy, we move to something akin to nuisance law, or to some kindred control regime that specifies how people are allowed to use resources. One of the surreptitious attractions of RIGHTWAY, in fact, is that it may not be so far from KEEPOUT, in that established resource users are apt already to have the prescribed boats or rods or whatever. But RIGHTWAY does have additional system costs that are likely to be higher than the costs of simply banning outsiders. Now we have to think about which fishing devices (such as nets and traps) we need to outlaw and which devices (such as fly-fishing equipment) will be permitted. Our everyday policing costs are going to be somewhat higher too, because our cops have to do more than just check on some simple sign of "insider" status, such as an I.D. card. Instead they have to look for something more complicated—i.e., whether we are pole fishing or secretly floating a few nets, as well. Just as important, there are additional user costs for the individual fishers: With RIGHTWAY, the fishers must buy poles instead of the perhaps more cost-effective nets, and they must spend a lot more time to land an equal number of fish. On the morale point, RIGHTWAY controls might cause initial resentment because they look like a lot of silly and costly formalities.

On the other hand, this strategy may be more effective for controlling total uses, even under higher levels of pressure on the fishing grounds. RIGHTWAY strategies make individual fishing efforts less productive, because our fishers could have caught more with nets than with poles. Although this means that some effort is wasted, this is arguably an advantage of sorts: Greater effort now does not deplete the fish as much, and fishers impose fewer externalities on one other. And indeed, RIGHTWAY might look more attractive when there is more fishing pressure; fishers get used to the restraints and think them valuable in preventing depletion—and as a greater percentage of fishers invest in the requisite fishing equipment, it is easier for the police to catch nonconforming cheaters.

But down the line, this control strategy faces rising total costs. For one thing, RIGHTWAY requirements may squander fishers' efforts to an uncomfortable degree, and this may induce cheating, especially if more fishers arrive who don't know or care about the existing rules. In addition, RIGHTWAY controls do not explicitly attend to the total take of fish, as long as each fisher is using a pole and rod; thus RIGHTWAY restraints on nets may do little to preserve the fish if the lake is chockfull of pole-and-line fishers who fish day and night. In the end, overuse costs may start to rise, and the previously flat or slowly-rising cost curve may take a steeper turn upward. In view of this problem, we could shift to a different version of RIGHTWAY, such as permitting only flycasting, but there are costs involved in such a strategy: First, there would be a fresh round of organizing costs; second, there might be new efficiency losses in what amounts to the requirement that everyone use higher-effort equipment; third, there would be lost technical expenditures that existing fisherfolk already put into conventional pole-and-lines; and finally, because of all of the above, there could be an increased resentment and unwillingness to follow new regulations.

Rather than upping the ante on RIGHTWAY, then, we might instead turn to Strategy Four, PROP, in which we figure out how large a total fish-take is acceptable and auction off the rights as individualized entitlements.

A PROP strategy actually may be quite cheap for resources that are easily subdivided and individualized without external effects. But for fish, or for other environmental resources, the perceived expenses of a PROP strategy may be the highest of all. Initial organizational costs include some explicit decision about an acceptable cap on the fish harvest, and this may cause considerable conflict, because it is hard to agree on the correct MAXLEVEL—different fishers are likely to have different views on the total take that should be allowed, and if nonfishers get into the discussion, they will add yet more views. Then we have to figure out and define exactly what the "property right" will consist of—numbers of fish or units of catch weight. When defining that "property right," we also have to look for a unit that is relatively easy to monitor, which illustrates yet another expense: Even in the fishing context, where rights definitions seem considerably more straight-forward than in other environmental resources, monitoring and policing of those rights make up an important cost factor. Our cops cannot now check just on the fishing equipment, as they could in a RIGHTWAY regime; they have to poke around in the bilge to measure the units of fish taken, to make sure that the proper payment has been made for all units.

An especially divisive issue in a PROP strategy is the initial allocation of those fishing rights: Shall we have an auction, or a giveaway to existing fishers, or some other allocation scheme? Although the answer to this question may not influence efficiency if the rights are well-defined, it matters a great deal to those who want to fish; old-timers are likely to want the rights allocated to themselves, whereas newcomers might prefer an auction or lottery. Because of the distributional issues in this decision, it is likely to be hotly contested—indeed, these distributional issues about initial entitlements, taken together with the difficulties of striking a bargain, may prevent a PROP system from getting started at all. Over and above all these problems, some fishers may resist the very idea that there should be upper bounds on fishing at all, or that anyone should have to pay for fishing. This sentiment is likely to be especially strong when we are still hovering near the congestion point, where fish seem to be relatively plentiful.

Despite all these costs, the PROP strategy may look better as the pressure on fishing resources grows higher: People may grow more accustomed to the idea that undiminished fishing has costs and should be paid for. Counteracting this increased tolerance to PROP is the fact that, as fish become increasingly valuable, fishers will have to be charged more and more for the right to fish, because undercharging might lead to overfishing. One way to make charges more palatable might be to use the payments for a re-stocking fund or for some other conservation measures. In addition, even though fishing rights may cost more and more, one advantage of the PROP strategy is that it does not bind individual fisherfolk to any particular fishing technology. They can decide for themselves what equipment to use, and the system gives them an incentive to find the cheapest and most effective way to extract the fish—or to get whatever other pleasures that fishing brings them. And that is, of course, the basic idea behind the introduction of an individualized property scheme of resource use: At some level of pressure on the fishery, a full-fledged property regime is the cheapest management strategy.

Many of us who teach property law think that all these control strategies represent different kinds of property regimes, but conventional usage only calls the individualized right a property right. Be that as it may, [the previous Figure] represents how the various control strategies look when one puts them all on the same chart. If this admittedly stylized version of the various management strategies bears any relation to reality, it is pretty clear that the "best" control strategy depends on something else: It depends on how far we have travelled along the horizontal line of resource pressure. The[] sketched-in figure[] [is] "made up," of course, but historically, we have actually observed something like this progression from one strategy to the next as our common resources have come under increasing pressure.

*Office of Technology Assessment*

# Environmental Policy Tools: A User's Guide (1995)

## Moving to a More Risk-Based Approach

Over the last 25 years, Congress has followed two broad types of strategies for environmental regulation: 1) *risk-based strategies* and 2) *technology-based strategies.* In a risk-based strategy, the target that individual or groups of sources must meet is based on modeled or measured environmental quality. For example, stationary sources of air pollutants such as sulfur dioxide may not emit that pollutant in quantities that would violate air quality standards in the vicinity of the facility. Under a technology-based strategy, the targets that sources must meet are based on technological capability or potential to lower pollution, rather than a directly specified level of environmental quality. Under this type of strategy, the level of environmental protection is indirectly specified by the stringency of the abatement requirement. For example, sewage treatment plants are required to remove a percentage of the pollutants entering the facility.

Congress has sometimes preferred one, and at other times the other, but has most often attempted to solve environmental problems through a combination of these two approaches to environmental protection. At first, under the Clean Air Act of 1970, Congress preferred a risk-based approach (with the notable exception of technology-based regulations for new pollution sources). The difficulties of actually implementing risk-based parts of the Act seemed to push Congress toward the other approach by the time of the Clean Water Act of 1972. Both strategies have advantages and disadvantages and, although certain types of problems might be better suited to one approach, the choice of approach depends to a great extent on the values of the decisionmaker.

Both types of strategies, of course, have environmental protection as their goal. The

From U.S. Congress, Office of Technology Assessment, *Environmental Policy Tools: A User's Guide*, OTA-ENV-634 (Washington, D.C.: U.S. Government Printing Office, September 1995).

two differ most sharply in the means to achieve their goals and in the way the goals are translated into specific targets. To implement risk-based strategies, regulators need a fairly well-developed understanding of the science of pollutant transport, fate, and effect. Under technology-based strategies, regulators must have good knowledge of pollution prevention and control.

Those who favor a risk-based approach may regard technology-based strategies as the equivalent of "ready, fire, aim." Those who favor technology-based approaches often consider the other as the equivalent of "ready, aim, aim, aim . . ." There are elements of truth to both views.

Typically, the uncertainty surrounding the risks posed by pollutants is far greater than the uncertainty surrounding the potential for abatement. A high degree of uncertainty can lead to EPA's inability to implement congressional goals; at best, it will certainly slow the agency down. EPA's slow pace in issuing standards for hazardous air pollutants under the 1970 Clean Air Act is a prime example. Before the 1990 Amendments, when the Act was significantly changed, EPA had listed eight substances as hazardous air pollutants and promulgated emission standards for seven of these. Section 112 followed a harm-based strategy, requiring EPA to establish emission standards at a level that provides "an ample margin of safety to protect the public health." In the 1990 Amendments, Congress added a technology-based strategy to the harm-based approach of this section, requiring EPA to issue emission standards for 189 pollutants. These emission standards, to be set by EPA, are to achieve the maximum degree of emissions reduction deemed possible by EPA.

As shown in [TABLE 8-1], some of the policy instruments covered in this study follow a risk-based approach, some are primarily technology-based, while others can be based on either approach. For those instruments with fixed targets that apply to single sources or products—the most common tools in use today—the choice of strategy guides one to particular instruments. If the analytical capability to support a risk-based approach exists, either harm-based emission standards or product bans and limitations are possible. A technology-based strategy can be implemented through either design standards or technology specifications.

[The table] also includes multisource instruments and two of the instruments that do not have fixed targets. Note that most of these instruments can be used following either a risk-based or technology-based approach. For example, for both integrated permitting and tradeable emissions, all that is required is a fixed emissions target. The target can be set based on the level of risk posed by the emissions or simply on the technical potential for, and often the cost of, control. In the case of emissions trading to control acid rain, the congressional specification of allowable nationwide emissions seems to be based on a combination of the two strategies.

Pollution charges high enough to alter behavior have most often been discussed by economists in the context of a harm-based approach, that is, set at a level appropriate to damages that result from remaining emissions, but the charge can easily be technology based as well. For example, Sweden has set emission fees on nitrogen oxide emissions from electric utilities based on the expected cost of a particular tech-

TABLE 8.1 Instruments Used for Risk-based
Strategies and Technology-based Strategies

| | **Instrument** | |
| --- | --- | --- |
| | Risk-based strategy (based on acceptable risk) | Technology-based strategy (based on technical potential) |
| **Tools *with* fixed targets—single-source:** | | |
| Product bans and limitations | often | occasionally |
| Technology specifications | rarely | often |
| Design standards | rarely | often |
| Harm-based standards | often | rarely |
| **Tools *with* fixed targets—multisource:** | | |
| Integrated permitting | occasionally | often |
| Tradeable emissions | often | often |
| Challenge regulations | occasionally | often |
| **Tools *without* fixed targets:** | | |
| Pollution charges | occasionally | often |
| Liability | often | occasionally |

Instrument often follows strategy
Instrument occasionally follows strategy
Instrument rarely follows strategy

SOURCE: Office of Technology Assessment, 1995.

nology (selective catalytic reduction) considered to be the best available technology at the time the fee was set.

For many problems, regardless of whether Congress prefers a risk-based strategy or a technology-based strategy, if ignorance of the risks posed by pollutants is too great, the option to use risk-based approaches is pragmatically foreclosed. Increasing research offers no guarantee of providing answers with the degree of rigor that Congress might desire. But reducing ignorance about the health and ecological risks posed by pollutants may at least create the opportunity to pursue harm-based regulatory strategies.

Thus Congress might consider several actions for improving the ability to use harm-based strategies. First, Congress could increase funding for research on risk assessment methods development. The estimated $75 million per year spent on methods development ($65 million for health risks and $10 million for ecological risks) clearly has not provided a firm foundation for EPA decisionmaking. For example, a user fee of one cent per pound on the pollutants reported released or disposed of to the environment by facilities required to report emissions under the [Toxics Release Inventory], could be used to support research to help understand the environmental implications of the emissions reported. This would increase by 50 percent the funds available for risk-related methods research.

Second, when either establishing or amending an environmental protection program that follows a risk-based strategy, Congress could provide funds to be used specifically for the research needs to support that program. New risk-based regulations are likely to require considerable investments in research to improve capabilities for exposure assessment, for effects assessment, or both, in order for new initiatives to succeed.

Finally, Congress could direct EPA to use its existing authority under the Toxic Substances Control Act (TSCA) to require the sources of pollution to finance the chemical-specific data needed for use in risk assessments. EPA is currently planning to use this authority to request new information from sources of hazardous air pollutants (HAPS). EPA may soon issue a Federal Register proposal announcing its intent to require test data for about 20 of the 189 HAPS listed in the CAA, saving the agency an estimated $30 million to $40 million in testing costs.

## Becoming More Results Oriented

Regardless of which policy instrument or combination of instruments is chosen, when Congress, EPA, or state regulatory agencies specify end results rather than the means for achieving the results, sources will have greater flexibility to achieve the targets in ways that are most cost effective or otherwise beneficial to them. Several of the policy instruments are inherently results oriented or performance based. Harm-based standards and tradeable emissions, which are expressed in terms of allowable emissions, are examples.

Other instruments can be expressed as either end results or as the means of achieving those results. Design standards are probably the best example of these. Under the Clean Water Act, Congress requires EPA to issue design standards as effluent limits or concentrations, that is, has mandated that they be performance based. This is not always the case, however, and some design standards end up looking more like technology specifications to sources. Sometimes this happens at the federal level; more often, it occurs as the permit is issued, typically at the state level.

The absence of accurate, reasonably simple, and affordable monitoring technology is one of the primary reasons that performance-based regulations are sometimes rejected. Moreover, this is often a reason that multisource instruments are avoided in favor of single-source approaches. From the opposite perspective, improved monitoring capabilities have been used to promote flexibility and increase assurance.

The more advanced the monitoring technology—relatively inexpensive, automated, reliable, and capable of frequent sampling—the easier it is to use policy tools that depend heavily on end results. When monitoring capabilities are poor, regulators are often hesitant to move from source-by-source instruments such as design standards to multisource approaches such as tradeable emissions and integrated permitting. Design standards at least offer some options for using surrogate measures for assuring compliance without the necessity of directly monitoring pollutants. For example, concern over the adequacy of methods to quantify volatile organic compound (voc) emissions has been a stumbling block to establishing marketable emission program for controlling urban ozone.

When monitoring technology is well developed, the likelihood of public and regulatory acceptance of alternative approaches, such as trading or fees, increases. An innovative program in Minnesota allows a tape manufacturer, 3M, more regulatory flexibility in exchange for substantial overall reductions in voc emissions and the development of a continuous emissions monitoring system for vocs.

To encourage the development and use of better monitoring technology, Congress could take several actions. First, it could increase funding to EPA for research on new emissions monitoring technologies. Research and development funding by EPA for new emissions monitoring methods is currently quite modest. Funding has averaged about $90 million per year over the last three fiscal years. About half of the research is for methods applicable for multiple media; of the single-media research, most is for air pollution monitoring.

Alternatively, Congress could encourage the use of preferred technologies by establishing economic incentives based on the characteristics of the methods chosen. For example, Congress could instruct EPA to develop discount factors similar to an approach adopted by Massachusetts, which rewards facilities for the use of better emission quantification techniques but still allows current methods. Massachusetts has designed an air pollution emissions trading program that uses a multiplier to adjust the emission reduction credits available for trading. Massachusetts leaves the type of monitoring up to each source but discounts emission reductions quantified through less accurate methods. Sources receive full credit for reductions that come from irreversible process changes, between 80 and 95 percent credit for reductions monitored using continuous emissions monitors, and so on to as low as 50 percent for reductions that are estimated rather than monitored. Thus there is a considerable economic incentive to use the more accurate methods.

## Learning More about the Strengths and Weaknesses of Less-Often Used Tools

Even when decisionmakers decide on the criteria they wish to emphasize, knowing which instruments will be most effective is often difficult. Lack of experience using many of the tools and, consequently, the poor base of information about their performance are major stumbling blocks.

. . . [W]e have the most extensive experience with implementing single-source, fixed-target tools such as harm-based standards, design standards, and product bans or limitations. Information reporting, subsidies, and technical assistance are being used more frequently now in environmental protection programs than in the past, and we have some experience using these tools in related policy areas, such as agriculture and energy. For others—tradeable emissions, pollution charges, integrated permitting, and challenge regulation—we have even fewer experiences or evaluations of experiences on which to base decisions about appropriate uses.

In the United States, for example, use of pollution charges has been limited almost exclusively to volume-based fees for residential solid waste disposal. Other OECD countries have used pollution charges more widely to reduce emissions and, somewhat less often, for landfilled and incinerated wastes. However, these countries have only recently begun to experiment with setting the charges at a level high enough to ratchet emissions downward. In addition, OECD was able to find little systematic evaluation of these programs. Thus, as in the United States, little evidence exists for drawing conclusions about the problems for which pollution charges might be most effectively used and the type of institutional problems to be expected during implementation.

Yet interest in learning more about how these instruments actually work in practice, rather than in theory, is clearly growing. State and local governments, as well as EPA, have been incorporating less familiar policy tools to construct innovative approaches to meeting environmental goals. Industry trade associations, individual companies, and some environmental groups have joined in these efforts to find new approaches that are effective in achieving many of the criteria while making progress toward goals. To date, however, many more of these new approaches have been proposed than implemented, and many more implemented than evaluated.

Most evaluations of these instruments are done analytically or ex ante—that is, before the instruments are selected and implemented—to try to anticipate or predict likely outcomes. Post facto evaluations, based on sound methodological approaches, are almost never completed. Even when an evaluation is completed for a new approach, drawing clear lessons from the experiences of one or two facilities that could then be transferred with confidence to other facilities, companies, industries, regions, or problems is difficult.

If Congress wants information about instruments that have seldom been used in environmental programs, better information about instruments that are used widely, or better diffusion of the little information already available, two approaches might be considered.

First, Congress could encourage experimentation with some of the less well-known tools to learn more about their effectiveness in specific situations before advocating their widespread use. For example, Congress could establish a limited number of state or regional experiments using instruments or combinations of instruments with which the United States has little experience (e.g., challenge regulation, integrated permitting, and pollution charges). These experiments might involve many facilities (e.g., associated by an industry or a watershed) to increase the likelihood of identifying lessons about opportunities and problems across multiple facilities. This limited experimentation could improve the confidence policymakers have in using tools selectively to respond to state and local differences or particular problem characteristics.

Note that EPA is beginning to experiment with alternative regulatory strategies as part of the larger Clinton Administration effort to "reinvent government" In Project XL, EPA is trying to determine how to allow firms that are environmentally "good actors" to replace existing regulatory requirements with more flexible alternatives—assuming they achieve better results than expected under existing law. In the Common Sense Initiative, EPA is experimenting with sector-wide industry agreements as a "complement to, or as a replacement for" traditional single-source regulations. These and other regulatory experiments are still in their early stages and Congress may wish to follow them closely.

Congress may also want to consider actions to establish or strengthen evaluations of implementation experiences with both unfamiliar and commonly used policy tools and to disseminate the results. To ensure that these evaluations build our knowledge base about the effectiveness of tools, they could be required to track the implementation and results of both experimental and existing programs. This knowledge could then be shared with the public and others in government and industry to improve the choices that are made in the future. Good ideas don't speak for themselves. Thus, Congress might want to consider asking EPA to strengthen its role in facilitating the transfer of information about how these instruments actually work in various settings.

# President's Council on Sustainable Development

# Sustainable America: A New Consensus—Building a New Framework for a New Century (1996)

The U.S. system of environmental management, built largely since 1970, has dramatically improved the country's ability to protect public health and the natural environment. The air and water are cleaner, exposure to toxic wastes is lower, erosion of prime cropland has been reduced, and some wildlife species are back from the brink of extinction. Much still remains to be done, however, to continue these gains and address new environmental threats.

For the last 25 years, government has relied on command-and-control regulation as its primary tool for environmental management. In looking to the future, society needs to adopt a wider range of strategic environmental protection approaches that embrace the essential components of sustainable development: economic prosperity, environment health, and social equity and well-being. The relationships among these components are clear. Sustained economic growth is dependent on a clean and healthy environment. Further, the ability of the economy to grow, create jobs, and increase overall well-being can suffer if environmental protection strategies deliver low results at a high cost. Resources for other economic and social needs will be diverted if strategies to achieve environmental goals are not designed to achieve results in the most cost-effective way. We, as a

From The President's Council on Sustainable Development, *Sustainable America: A New Consensus for Prosperity, Opportunity, and a Healthy Environment for the Future* (Washington, D.C.: U.S. Government Printing Office, 1996).

Council, have concluded that this will require the nation to develop a new framework for a new century.

There are a number of tools, approaches, and strategies that, if carefully tailored to different challenges, could result in more environmental protection, less economic cost, and—in some cases—greater opportunity for the poor and disadvantaged. It should be clear that market mechanisms are not the right solution for every problem, any more than technology-based standards are the right answer in all cases. The nation should create a new framework for integrating economic and environmental goals that lets all stakeholders take advantage of these opportunities and ensures that tools are applied to the right problem, in the right way, at the right time.

The experience of the last 25 years has yielded the following lessons, which would be wise to heed in developing a new framework to achieve the objectives of sustainable development:

- Economic, environmental, and social problems cannot be addressed in isolation. Economic prosperity, environmental quality, and social equity need to be pursued simultaneously.
- Science-based national standards that protect human health and the environment are the foundation of any effective system of environmental protection.
- The adversarial nature of the current system precludes solutions that become possible when potential adversaries cooperate and collaborate.
- Technology-based regulation can sometimes encourage technological innovation, but it can also stifle it; pollution prevention is better than pollution control.
- Enhanced flexibility for achieving environmental goals, coupled with strong compliance assurance mechanisms—including enforcement—can spur private sector innovation that will enhance environmental protection at a substantially lower cost both to individual firms and to society as a whole.
- Science, economics, and societal values should be considered in making decisions. Quality information is essential to sound decisionmaking.
- Many state governments have developed significant environmental management capacity. Indeed, many of the most creative and lasting solutions arise from collaborations involving federal, state, local, and tribal governments in places problems exist—from urban communities to watersheds.

Learning to use new approaches to achieve interrelated goals simultaneously will be an evolutionary process. It needs to build on the strengths and overcome the limitations of current economic and regulatory systems and recognize the interrelationships between economic and environmental policies. This will require pursuing change concurrently on two paths: making the existing regulatory system more efficient and more effective, and developing an alternative system of environmental management that uses innovative approaches. Besides improving the cost-effectiveness of the current system, the Council believes that the nation needs to develop policy tools that meet the following broad criteria:

- *Provide Greater Regulatory Flexibility with Accountability.* The regulatory system must give companies and communities greater operating flexibility, enabling them to reduce their costs significantly in exchange for achieving superior environmental performance. While allowing flexibility, the system must also require accountability to ensure that public health and the environment are protected.
- *Extend Product Responsibility.* A voluntary system of extended product responsibility can be adopted in which designers, producers, suppliers, users, and disposers accept responsibility for environmental effects through all phases of a product's life.
- *Make Greater Use of Market Forces.* Sustainable development objectives must harness market forces through policy tools, such as emissions trading deposit/refund systems and tax and subsidy reform. This approach can substantially influence the behavior of firms, governments, and individuals.
- *Use Intergovernmental Partnerships.* Federal, state and tribal governments need to work together in partnership with local communities to develop place-based strategies that integrate economic development, environmental quality, and social policymaking with broad public involvement.
- *Encourage Environmental Technologies.* The economic and environmental management systems need to create an environment that encourages innovation and the development and use of technologies that will create jobs while reducing risks to human health and harm to the environment. . . .

## Developing a More Cost-effective Environmental Management System Based on Performance, Flexibility, and Accountability

In the past, government has relied mainly on regulatory approaches to managing environmental problems. Under this system, federal and state governments have set health-based standards, issued permits for discharges, and monitored and enforced standards set under each environmental statute. In some cases, regulations implementing these standards prescribe specific technologies to control pollution.

Over the years, the value and limits of this regulatory approach have become clear. There is no doubt that some regulations have encouraged innovation and compliance with environmental laws, resulting in substantial improvements in the protection of public health and the environment. But at other times, regulation has imposed unnecessary—and sometimes costly—administrative and technological burdens and discouraged technological innovations that can reduce costs while achieving environmental benefits beyond those realized by compliance. Moreover, it has frequently focused attention on cleanup and control remedies rather than on product or process redesign to prevent pollution.

Such concerns have contributed to a growing consensus that the existing regulatory system may be greatly improved by moving toward performance-based policies that encourage pollution prevention. Regulations that specify performance standards based on strong protection of health and the environment—but without mandating the means of compliance—give companies and communities flexibility to find the most cost-effective way to achieve environmental goals. In return for this flexibility, companies can pursue technological innovation that will result in superior environmental protection at far lower costs. But this flexibility must be coupled with accountability and enforcement to ensure that public health and the environment are safeguarded.

Just as the manufacturing sector has adopted a goal of zero defects, the nation can aspire to the ideal of a zero-waste society through more efficient use and recycling of natural resources in the economy and more efficient use of public and private financial resources in the regulatory system. The nation should pursue two paths in reforming environmental regulation. The first is to improve the efficiency and effectiveness of the current environmental management system. The second is to develop and test innovative approaches and create a new alternative environmental management system that achieves more protection at a lower cost. To help achieve this, the administrator of the U.S. Environmental Protection Agency (EPA), working in partnership with other federal agencies and other stakeholders, should have the authority to make decisions that will achieve environmental goals efficiently and effectively.

Although moving away from a one-size-fits-all approach will reduce costs to the private sector, creating an optional system could increase administrative and policy burdens on federal agencies, at least in the short term. Like clothing, custom-tailored environmental management may cost the public sector more to deliver than the off-the-rack variety. The new alternative system is designed to reduce aggregate costs to society, but it will require both industry and government to use new skills and resources, especially at the beginning. Negotiating facility-by-facility agreements is labor-intensive compared to administering permit compliance checklists. Developing facility-specific performance measures to ensure business accountability for negotiated goals is more expensive than enforcing uniform standards. Convening stakeholder workshops to reach agreeable environmental goals requires additional travel and staff time. The system would also require a farsighted investment posture on the part of businesses seeking to break out of prescribed solutions to create their own. Nonetheless, the improved environmental protection system is designed to reduce total costs to the private and public sectors over time and will improve the nation's overall economic performance.

Partnerships and collaborative decisionmaking must be encouraged and must involve all levels of government, businesses, nongovernmental organizations, community groups, and the public at large. Initiatives are needed to verify that increased operational flexibility on a facilitywide basis can produce environmental performance superior to the current system while greatly reducing costs. To help ensure accountability, demonstrations also are needed to increase public involvement and access to information. The new system should facilitate voluntary initiatives that encourage businesses and consumers to assume responsibility for their actions. At the same time, the regulatory system must continue to provide a safety net of public health and environmental protection by guaranteeing compliance with basic standards.

Movement toward a performance-based system will be aided by public-private partnerships promoting the research, development, and application of cost-effective technologies and practices. Continued, long-term investment in technology will help ensure U.S. competitiveness and leadership in global technology markets. New manufacturing technologies and processes can lower material and energy use while reducing or eliminating waste streams. Focusing efforts to develop cleaner and more efficient products for domestic and overseas markets will help base U.S. economic growth on the concept of better—rather than just more—products and processes.

## Greater Use of Market Forces

In the American economic system, the marketplace plays a central role in guiding what people produce, how they produce it, and what they consume. The choices and decisions made by millions of consumers and firms determine prices for the wide range of goods and services that constitute the national economy. The marketplace's power to produce desired goods and services at the lowest cost possible is driven by the price signals that result from this decentralized decision process.

Despite the nation's commitment to a free market economic system, governmental policy substantially influences the workings of the marketplace. For example, tax levels on different products and activities lower or raise their market prices and artificially encourage or discourage their use. Some government subsidy programs encourage activities that result in economic inefficiency as well as destructive use of resources. At other times, government tax and spending subsidy programs may be essential if the short-term rewards of the marketplace do not coincide with the long-term goals of the nation. To ignore the importance of economic policy is to miss opportunities to encourage economic, environmental, and equity goals.

To improve environmental performance, the design of environmental and natural resource programs should take advantage of the positive role the marketplace can play once environmental goals and market signals are aligned. Current policies generally do not use the power of the marketplace, and at present, some environmental costs in the product chain may be shifted to society at large, rather than be fully reflected in the product price. The cost of air, soil, and water pollution associated with materials and energy used in production as well as the expense to local communities for product disposal are two examples of costs not typically included in a product price. But if these types of costs are reflected in the price of a product, the marketplace sends an important signal. All other things being equal, consumers generally will purchase the lower priced product, creating an important incentive for a company to reconsider how it makes a product. Increasing the use of market forces can create opportunities to achieve natural resource and environmental goals in the most cost-effective way possible by encouraging the innovation that flows from a competitive economic system.

# Part III

## The Regulatory Process in a Participatory Democracy

*Environmental protection policy is the product of fierce battles between conflicting interests—large and small businesses, grassroots citizen organizations, national environmental groups, industry trade associations, scientists and public health authorities, state and local officials, and others. This part of the book explores how these groups have helped shape environmental policy and the arenas in which they operate. It examines the process by which agencies translate laws into regulations and the forces that influence how the laws are implemented. It concludes by exploring whether regulatory priorities should be set in response to the public's concerns or on the basis of comparative risk assessments by experts.*

*Chapter 9 begins with Edward Abbey's fictional account of "monkeywrenching" by a band of environmentalists committed to taking direct action to disrupt projects despoiling desert wilderness in the American Southwest. It then recounts the true story of how a group of scientists, horrified by their discoveries about the effects of DDT on bird life, launched a campaign to get the pesticide banned—thereby giving birth to one of the nation's most influential environmental organizations. The chapter also includes Joe Sax's description of how citizen groups used the courts to make agencies respond to environmental concerns and Chris Stone's famous proposal to grant legal standing to natural objects.*

*The environmental laws generally direct administrative agencies, such as EPA and the U.S. Department of the Interior, to issue regulations restricting polluting activities and managing natural resource use. The process by which regulations are developed and implemented is examined in Chapter 10. The chapter explores why the ambitious promises articulated in the laws often get lost during the implementation process. It examines why some laws have been implemented more successfully than others and the political and social factors that explain why agency performance has so frequently been disappointing.*

*Risk assessment recently has become an important part of the regulatory policy process. To help decide how stringently to regulate products or activities, agencies frequently perform risk assessments—a systematic process to characterize the nature and magnitude of risks posed by a regulatory target. More recently, proposals to use comparative risk assessments to set agency priorities have gained support. These proposals are controversial because assessments of relative risk by "experts" are systematically different from those made by the general public, raising concerns about diminishing the public's influence on the policy process. These concerns are explored in Chapter 11.*

# CHAPTER 9

---

# Who Speaks for the Environment?

Citizen involvement has been a distinctive feature of environmental law in the United States during the last three decades. Beginning in the late 1960s, an unprecedented outpouring of public concern for the environment spurred Congress to enact a flood of environmental legislation. These laws established the basic regulatory infrastructure that remains in place today. This chapter considers the role of citizen groups in the environmental policy process. It examines how these organizations sought to require government agencies to pay attention to environmental concerns and how they helped open up the courts to the beneficiaries of environmental regulation. The chapter examines how individuals can make a difference—influencing policy through lobbying, litigation, and other action.

The chapter begins with an excerpt from Edward Abbey's *The Monkey Wrench Gang*, a fictional account of a colorful band of misfits united only by their concern over despoilation of the American Southwest. Among the group's members are Seldom Seen Smith, described by Abbey as "Jack Mormon, polygamist and river runner and wilderness guide extraordinaire"; Doc Sarvis, a "not so respectable Albuquerque physician by day; respectable billboard pyromaniac by night"; Bonnie Abbzug, an "exile from the canyons of the Bronx" who "now runs amok in the labyrinthine canyons of the Southwest"; and George Washington Hayduke, an ex-Green Beret, ex-Viet Cong medic who believes that "[s]omething is wrong with his beloved desert and he intends to find out who's responsible." The members of this group try to throw a monkeywrench into the gears of development by pouring sand in the gas tanks of heavy equipment, pulling up surveyors' stakes, and destroying billboards. In the excerpt below they talk about blowing up the Glen Canyon Dam.

Abbey's passion for nature was stoked during fifteen years working in the national parks of the American Southwest, the primary subject of his magnificent writings. He was the author of nine novels and several nonfiction works, including *Desert Solitaire:*

*A Season in the Wilderness.* Abbey described his writings as "simple narrative accounts of travel and adventure, with philosophical commentary added here and there to give the prose a high-toned surface gleam." In his final work of nonfiction, *Beyond the Wall,* Abbey expressed his dismay at the seemingly inexorable forces destroying the environment. He concluded that: "What we need now are heroes. And heroines. About a million of them. One brave deed is worth a thousand books. Sentiment without action is the ruin of the soul."

While Abbey's "monkeywrench gang" is fictional, Thomas Dunlap tells the true story of how a determined group of scientists employed a different form of direct action—*legal* action—to change the world. Concerned about the effects of DDT on bird life, they formed an environmental group, hired lawyers, and went to court to stop its use. Despite the absence of legislation or judicial precedents, the group forged ahead, crafting new legal theories to fight the use of pesticides that bioaccumulate in the food chain. Dunlap describes the uphill battle they initially faced attacking chemicals that had visible benefits and powerful industry defenders, out of concern over environmental effects that "appeared much later, were not obviously the result of pesticide use, and were not of immediate economic interest to anyone." He recounts the legal skirmishes the Environmental Defense Fund had to fight in order to obtain a forum to put pesticide use on trial and ultimately to convince environmental officials to ban DDT and other pesticides. Dunlap's account shows how lawsuits can have effects far beyond their immediate legal impact by bringing problems to public attention and informing public opinion on issues of environmental health.

The importance of opening up the courts to citizen groups is emphasized by Joe Sax in his influential 1970 book, *Defending the Environment.* Sax describes why the New Deal model of the expert administrative agency proved inadequate to protect the public interest in the face of intense political and economic pressure from regulated industries. Sax makes a powerful case for using the courts to counter forces that had largely excluded citizen groups from the administrative process. He argues that litigation is a vital means of citizen access to governmental decision-making processes.

Sax notes that environmental quality is threatened because the public has not been permitted to assert its rights in the maintenance of clean air, clean water, or preservation of public resources. He recommends that courts adopt a "public trust" doctrine that would allow private parties to assert such rights in court, giving the courts the authority to stop development projects that would unnecessarily damage the environment. Sax argues that the judiciary should broaden its focus beyond ensuring procedural regularity by agencies, to become the protector of the public trust, resolving environmental policy disputes on a case-by-case basis. Sax's proposal was influential in the enactment of Michigan's Environmental Protection Act, which authorizes courts to develop a common law of environmental protection along the lines he proposed.

Like Sax, Christopher Stone decries the public's inability to assert legal rights on behalf of natural resources held in common. A portion of his famous 1972 article arguing that "trees should have standing" is reproduced in this chapter. After noting that the history of law has witnessed the extension of rights to broader and broader classes, including inanimate rightsholders, such as corporate entities, Stone argues that a logical next step would be to extend legal rights to natural objects in the environment. According to Stone, this would mean allowing actions to be brought on behalf of such objects, requiring courts to take injury to them into account in granting relief and ensuring that such relief run to their benefit. Stone explains that this could be accomplished by allowing courts to appoint guardians who could bring legal actions on behalf of the environment, much as is done to protect incompetent persons under the law.

Stone's idea received wide attention, most prominently in a dissent by Justice William O. Douglas in a Supreme Court decision on environmental standing. While the courts have not adopted Stone's idea, standing rules have been liberalized to the point that environmental organizations now routinely have access to the courts upon showing that their members' aesthetic or other interests are directly threatened by the action they seek to challenge. Despite recent efforts by courts to tighten requirements for standing, current doctrines of standing, coupled with citizen suit provisions inserted into most of the federal environmental laws, have given citizens powerful tools for influencing environmental policy and ensuring that the laws are implemented and enforced.

*Edward Abbey*

# The Monkey Wrench Gang (1975)

### The Wooden Shoe Conspiracy

The passengers, dry and refurbished, came straggling in one at a time, the doctor first. He placed his tin cup on the bar, installed one miniature iceberg and poured himself a double shot from his bottle of Wild Turkey.

"It is a beauteous evening, calm and free," he announced.

"That's true," Smith said.

"The holy time is quiet as a nun."

"You said a mouthful, Doctor."

"Call me Doc."

"Okay, Doc."

"Cheers."

"Same to you, Doc."

There was some further discussion of the ambience. Then of other matters. The girl came up, Abbzug, wearing long pants and a shaggy sweater. She had shed the big hat but even in twilight still wore the sunglasses. She gave a touch of tone to Marble Gorge.

Meanwhile the doctor was saying, "The reason there are so many people on the river these days is because there are too many people everywhere else."

Bonnie shivered, slipping into the crook of his left arm. "Why don't we build a fire?" she said.

"The wilderness once offered men a plausible way of life," the doctor said. "Now it functions as a psychiatric refuge. Soon there will be no wilderness." He sipped at his bourbon and ice. "Soon there will be no place to go. Then the madness becomes universal." Another thought. "And the universe goes mad."

"We will," Smith said to Abbzug. "After supper."

"Call me Bonnie."

"Miss Bonnie."

"Miz Bonnie," she corrected him.

"Jesus fucking Christ," muttered Hayduke nearby, overhearing, and he snapped the cap from another can of Coors.

Abbzug cast a cold eye on Hayduke's face, or what could be seen of it behind the black bangs and the bushy beard. An oaf, she thought. All hairiness is bestial, Arthur Schopenhauer thought. Hayduke caught her look, scowled. She turned back to the others.

"We are caught," continued the good doctor, "in the iron treads of a technological juggernaut. A mindless machine. With a breeder reactor for a heart."

"You said a mouthful, Doc," says Seldom Seen Smith. He started on the steaks, laying them tenderly on the grill, above the glowing coals.

"A planetary industrialism"—the doctor ranted on—"growing like a cancer. Growth for the sake of growth. Power for the sake of power. I think I'll have another bit of ice here." (*Clank!*) "Have a touch of this, Captain Smith, it'll gladden your heart, gild your liver and flower like a rose down in the compost of your bowels."

"Don't mind if I do, Doc." But Smith wanted to know how a machine could "grow." Doc explained; it wasn't easy.

Smith's two repeaters from San Diego emerged from the bushes, smiling; they had unrolled his sleeping bag between their own. One young woman carried a bottle. Something about a river trip always seems to promote the consumption of potable drugs. Except for Abbzug, who sucked from time to time on a little hand-rolled Zig-Zag cigarette pinched between her fastidious fingers. There was the smell of some kind of burning hemp in the air around her head. (Give a girl enough rope and she'll smoke it.) The odor reminded Hayduke of dark days and darker nights. Muttering, he set the table, buffet-style, with the salad, the sourdough bread, corn on the cob, a stack of paper plates. Smith turned the steaks. Doc explained the world. . . .

All eyes turned toward the fire as the darkness of the canyon gathered around them. Little blue and green flames licked and lapped at the river wood—sculptured chunks of yellow pine from the high country a hundred miles away, juniper, pinyon pine, cottonwood, well-polished sticks of redbud, hackberry and ash. Following the sparks upward they saw the stars turning on in staggered sequence—emeralds, sapphires, rubies, diamonds and opals scattered about the sky in a puzzling, random distribution. Far beyond those galloping galaxies, or perhaps all too present to be seen, lurked God. The gaseous vertebrate.

Supper finished, Smith brought out his musical instruments and played for the assembled company. He played his harmonica—what the vulgar call a "mouth organ"—his Jew's harp, or what the B'nai B'rith calls a "mouth harp," and his kazoo, which last, however, added little to anyone's musical enrichment.

Smith and the doctor passed around the firewater. Abbzug, who did not as a rule drink booze, opened her medicine pouch, removed a Tampax tube, took out some weed and rolled a second little brown cigarette twisted shut at one end. She lit up and passed it around, but no one cared to smoke with her except a reluctant Hayduke and his memories.

"The pot revolution is over?" she said.

"All over," Doc said. "Marijuana was never more than an active placebo anyway."

"What nonsense."

"An oral pacifier for colicky adolescents."

"What utter rubbish."

The conversation lagged. The two young women from San Diego (a suburb of Tijuana) sang a song called "Dead Skunk in the Middle of the Road."

The entertainment palled. Fatigue like gravitation pulled at limbs and eyelids. As they had come so they departed, first Abbzug, then the two women from San Diego. The ladies first. Not because they were the weaker sex—they were not—but simply because they had more sense. Men on an outing feel obliged to say up drinking to the vile and bilious end, jabbering, mumbling and maundering through the blear, to end up finally on hands and knees, puking on innocent sand, befouling God's sweet earth. The manly tradition.

The three men hunched closer to the shrinking fire. The cold night crawled up their backs. They passed Smith's bottle round and around. Then Doc's bottle. Smith, Hayduke, Sarvis. The captain, the bum and the leech. Three wizards on a dead limb. A crafty intimacy crept upon them.

"You know, gentlemen," the doctor said. "You know what I think we ought to do. . . ."

Hayduke had been complaining about the new power lines he'd seen the day before on the desert. Smith had been moaning about the dam again, that dam which had plugged up Glen Canyon, the heart of his river, the river of his heart.

"You know what we ought to do," the doctor said. "We ought to blow that dam to shitaree." (A bit of Hayduke's foul tongue had loosened his own.)

"How?" said Hayduke.

"That ain't legal," Smith said.

"You prayed for an earthquake, you said."

"Yeah, but there ain't no law agin that."

"You were praying with malicious intent."

"That's true. I pray that way all the time."

"Bent on mischief and the destruction of government property."

"That's right, Doc."

"That's a felony."

"It ain't just a misdemeanor?"

"It's a felony."

"How?" said Hayduke.

"How what?"

"How do we blow up the dam?"

"Which dam?"

"Any dam."

"Now you're talking," Smith said. "But Glen Canyon Dam first. I claim that one first."

"I don't know," the doctor said. "You're the demolitions expert."

"I can take out a bridge for you," Hayduke said, "if you get me enough dynamite. But I don't know about Glen Canyon Dam. We'd need an atom bomb for that one."

"I been thinking about that dam for a long time," Smith said. "And I got a plan. We get three jumbo-size houseboats and some dolphins—"

"Hold it!" Doc said, holding up a big paw. A moment of silence. He looked around, into the darkness beyond the firelight. "Who knows what ears those shadows have."

They looked. The flames of their little campfire cast a hesitant illumination upon the bush, the boat half grounded on the sandy beach, the rocks and pebbles, the pulse of the river. The women, all asleep, could not be seen.

"There ain't nobody here but us bombers," Smith said.

"Who can be sure? The State may have its sensors anywhere."

"Naw," Hayduke said. "They're not bugging the canyons. Not yet anyhow. But who says we have to start with dams? There's plenty of other work to do."

"Good work," the doctor said. "Good, wholesome, constructive work."

"I hate that dam," Smith said. "That dam flooded the most beautiful canyon in the world."

"We know," Hayduke said. "We feel the same way you do. But let's think about easier things first. I'd like to knock down some of them power lines they're stringing across the desert. And those new tin bridges up by Hite. And the goddamned road-building they're doing all over the canyon country. We could put in a good year just taking the fucking goddamned bulldozers apart."

"Hear, hear," the doctor said. "And don't forget the billboards. And the strip mines. And the pipelines. And the new railroad from Black Mesa to Page. And the coal-burning power plants. And the copper smelters. And the uranium mines. And the nuclear power plants. And the computer centers. And the land and cattle companies. And the wildlife poisoners. And the people who throw beer cans along the highways."

"I throw beer cans along the fucking highways," Hayduke said. "Why the fuck shouldn't I throw fucking beer cans along the fucking highways?"

"Now, now. Don't be so defensive."

"Hell," Smith said, "I do it too. Any road I wasn't consulted about that I don't like, I litter. It's my religion."

"Right," Hayduke said. "Litter the shit out of them."

"Well now," the doctor said. "I hadn't thought about that. Stockpile the stuff along the highways. Throw it out the window. Well . . . why not?"

"Doc," said Hayduke, "it's liberation."

The night. The stars. The river. Dr. Sarvis told his comrades about a great Englishman named Ned. Ned Ludd. They called him a lunatic but he saw the enemy clearly. Saw what was coming and acted directly. And about the wooden shoes, *les sabots*. The spanner in the works. Monkey business. The rebellion of the meek. Little old ladies in oaken clogs.

"Do we know what we're doing and why?"

"No."

"Do we care?"

"We'll work it all out as we go along. Let our practice form our doctrine, thus assuring precise theoretical coherence."

The river in its measureless sublimity rolled softly by, whispering of time. Which heals, they say, all. But does it? The stars looked kindly down. A lie. A wind in the willows suggested sleep. And nightmares. Smith pushed more drift pine into the fire, and a scorpion, dormant in a crack deep in the wood, was horribly awakened, too late. No one noticed the mute agony. Deep in the solemn canyon, under the fiery stars, peace reigned generally.

"We need a guide," the doctor said.

"I know the country," Smith said.

"We need a professional killer,"

"That's me," Hayduke said. "Murder's my specialty."

"Every man has his weakness." Pause. "Mine," added Doc, "is Baskin-Robbins girls."

"Hold on here," Smith said, "I ain't going along with that kind of talk."

"Not people, Captain," the doctor said. "We're talking about bulldozers. Power shovels. Draglines. Earthmovers."

"Machines," said Hayduke.

A pause in the planning, again.

"Are you certain this canyon is not bugged?" the doctor asked. "I have the feeling that others are listening in to every word we say."

"I know that feeling," Hayduke said, "but that's not what I'm thinking about right now. I'm thinking—"

"What are you thinking about?"

"I'm thinking: Why the fuck should we trust *each other*? I never even met you two guys before today."

Silence. The three men stared into the fire. The oversize surgeon. The elongated riverman. The brute from the Green Berets. A sigh. They looked at each other. And one thought: What the hell. And one thought: They look honest to me. And one thought: Men are not the enemy. Nor women either. Nor little children.

Not in sequence but in unison, as one, they smiled. At each other. The bottle made its penultimate round.

"What the hell," Smith said, "we're only talkin'."

*Thomas R. Dunlap*

# DDT: Scientists, Citizens, and Public Policy (1981)

By the late 1950s some scientists and citizens had become concerned about the deaths of birds from concentrated sprays used against the insect vector of Dutch elm disease, but most Americans ignored DDT until 1962, when Rachel Carson's *Silent Spring* appeared. The book touched off a heated debate, for Carson, dissenting from the common view that DDT and similar compounds were harmless, vigorously attacked both the chemicals and the experts who recommended them.... Although there was no immediate change in pesticide policy, *Silent Spring* permanently changed the climate in which the policy would be made. Pesticides were now a public issue and, through the 1960s at least, public concern over the environment would continue to increase....

Despite the growing case and the increasing efforts of the conservationists, there was no change in pesticide policy, and there seemed to be no redistribution of power—agricultural interests still had the only effective voice on the issue. To a certain extent, this apparent stability was an illusion, for as the events of 1968–1972 made clear, public opinion was slowly but surely shifting to the environmentalists' side. The defenders of persistent pesticides, though, had real advantages in bringing their case to the public and in affecting policy. The industry was quite willing to defend DDT, and the USDA, through its extension agents, had the ear of most of the farmers in the country. To go against the "massive promotional efforts of the industry and the propaganda of the Department of Agriculture" was, Audubon president Buchheister said in 1962, like "whistling into the teeth of a tornado."

A significant advantage, particularly apparent in the early 1960s (though the industry relied on it through the last rounds of the fight), was the appearance of famous scientists with outstanding records. Wayland J. Hayes was the most prominent of these figures, but as late as 1972 others could be found to defend DDT. Norman Bor-laug, a Nobel Prize winner, appeared to testify for DDT at the Environmental Protection Agency (EPA) hearings. More important in terms of policy was the industry's support in Congress. In the 1930s the FDA had contended with [Congressman] Clarence Cannon [a champion of agricultural interests] to get funds for studies of lead and arsenic residues; in the 1960s the foes of DDT had a similar battle with Jamie Whitten, a Congressman from Mississippi who held a key position on the House Agriculture Appropriations Subcommittee. Whitten vigorously defended the use of DDT—even writing a book, *That We May Live,* attacking *Silent Spring*—and he used his influence to slow or halt action unfavorable to its continued use. When the regulation of pesticides was transferred to the new Environmental Protection Agency in December 1970, Whitten retained his power; two months later the House gave his sub-committee control over environmental protection and consumer affairs.

The industry also profited from the confusion of public debate, the lack of a clear-cut division of interests, a stark contrast between good and evil. Pesticides had im-mediate visible, in some cases dramatic, benefits. Their drawbacks, on the other hand, generally appeared much later, were not obviously the result of pesticide use, and were not of immediate economic interest to anyone. Persistent pesticides, in short, had a natural constituency to whom they were very important; they had no enemies with a similar interest in suppressing them. Pesticides profited, too, from the general acceptance of science and technology; the public, at least into the early 1960s, was not inclined to question closely the miracles of modern science.

The industry's advantages left the environmentalists completely frustrated. Their case was growing, as scientists added new evidence, but their arguments seemed to carry no weight with the public, and the government seemed a closed corporation, deaf to their pleas and pressures. The only way out was to find some forum in which the defenders of DDT could not use their advantages of excellent public relations, im-pressive scientific figures, and powerful political support. The new way was found by a new organization, the Environmental Defense Fund (EDF), formed in 1967 to pre-serve the environment through legal action backed by scientific testimony. The for-mation of the EDF, with its tactics of confrontation and litigation, marked another change in the opposition to DDT. The early protests against the misuse of the chemi-cal had shifted to opposition to its use, on the grounds that, once placed in the envi-ronment, it spread. Now the tactics shifted from public education (or propaganda) and lobbying to a direct legal challenge. The EDF was going outside the earlier arena, moving the contest out of the agencies, Congress, and the newspapers (though it was to use all these in some form) to the courts.

The EDF, now a national environmental group with offices in New York, Washing-ton, Berkeley, and Denver, and with a budget of a million dollars a year, started with a small group of people on Long Island determined to do something about the local use of DDT. The original members were Victor J. Yannacone, Jr., a lawyer, and his wife Carol; Charles F. Wurster, Jr., a marine biologist at the State University of New York at Stony Brook; George M. Woodwell, an ecologist working at Brookhaven National Laboratory; Anthony S. Taromina of the New York Department of Environmental Conservation; Robert E. Smolker, another Stony Brook biologist; Dennis Puleston, head of Brookhaven's Information Division; Robert Burnap, conservationist, publicity man, and fund-raiser; Arthur Cooley, a high school biology teacher, and (the only member off Long Island) H. Lewis Batts, a Michigan scientist. It grew out of the interest, concerns, and observations of the members. Wurster, Taromina, and Woodwell were professionally and personally concerned with the environment. Cooley and Taromina had helped form the Brookhaven Town Natural Resources Committee in late 1965 to preserve the natural resources and wild areas around Brookhaven. Wurster had, at about the same time, done a study of the effect of Dutch elm disease sprays on robin populations in Hanover, New Hampshire. Woodwell had seen the spruce budworm spraying problem in Maine and New Brunswick and had, somewhat warily, corresponded with Rachel Carson about his observations. Yannacone had become involved with the Brookhaven Town National Resources Committee and with local fishermen in attempts to stop the degradation of the Great South Bay—first by the pollution from . . . duck farms, then through dredging operations. A common thread was a life-long concern with nature. Indeed, one member wrote "it was a joke that to be hired by EDF in the early days you had to be a bird-watcher." By the time they formed the EDF, the members were experienced in environmental education and scarred by several battles.

It was not the scientists, though, who started the legal action; it was Carol Yannacone, and she did not do it out of a scientific concern with the environment but because she thought DDT was ruining Yaphank Lake, where she had grown up. During the 1960s, she had become increasingly disturbed about the fish kills there; in 1966 she had learned that the kills were due to DDT and that the Suffolk County Mosquito Control Commission was planning to dump in another 60,000 gallons of DDT solution to kill the mosquito larvae. She decided that something had to be done and persuaded her husband Victor to take the case. In April he filed a suit on behalf of Carol Yannacone and "all others entitled to the full use and enjoyment" of the lake, asking for an injunction forbidding the use of DDT by the county mosquito control commission. It was around this case *Yannacone* v. *Dennison,* that the group that formed the EDF came together, and it was here that they tried out their approach: environmental quality through legal action. The Brookhaven Town National Resources Committee joined the action, with Cooley, Woodwell, and Puleston working to prepare the scientific case. Wurster read about it in the newspapers and joined, eventually becoming the organization's scientific advisor and head of the DDT project.

*Yannacone* v. *Dennison* came to trial in November, and the presentation showed the preparation and tactics that were to mark the EDF's approach: an assertion of the rights of each citizen to a clean environment, an argument that the use of persistent pesticides, because of their properties, was destructive of that environment, and a reliance on careful, detailed, scientific testimony to prove its point. Speaking for the group, Yannacone asserted that the suit was not one for personal damages, nor was it to abate a nuisance; the entire population of Suffolk County had an interest in a clean, undegraded environment, and they were there to defend that right. The scientific testimony centered on the properties that made DDT dangerous when applied to the environment and on the evidence of that damage. Yannacone used cross-examination to show that the mosquito commission was not well acquainted with that evidence. DDT, the group's scientists argued, was not necessary for mosquito control and its use was dangerous to other forms of life. Using DDT in the lake, Wurster argued, was like using atomic bombs against street crime in New York City. Finally, the scientists reinforced their point with a technical appendix to Yannacone's legal brief—copies of the scientific papers that buttressed their position.

This case, like many of the EDF's, was a partial victory. The group convinced the judge that DDT was harmful—he maintained a temporary injunction against the mosquito commission for a year—but he refused to ban its use. Only the legislature, he concluded, had the power to take such action. Legally, the environmentalists had lost. In fact they had won. The commission, by now used to alternatives to DDT and fearful of more suits, continued to use other means of control. Yannacone and the scientists had managed to obtain what conservationists had struggled for for some years, a ban on a use of DDT. They had also discovered a new weapon against DDT: an alliance of legal tactics with scientific information in a forum outside the government agencies or Congress—a practical way to influence policy.

Everyone was enthusiastic and wanted to continue the partnership, taking on DDT in other places. There were two problems: setting up an organization and finding money to support the cases. The first was easily solved, though it took some time and discussion. In the spring of 1967 Woodwell sent around a scheme for an organization to be called the Institute for Ecological Jurisprudence; Wurster outlined plans for Conserve America; and Robert Burnap came up with something called the Environmental Defense Fund. Eventually, Yannacone recalled, they pooled ideas, taking Burnap's name and something from everyone's structure. Yannacone, the lawyer, was to be legal counsel, Woodwell, head of the scientists' advisory committee, and Dennis Puleston, head of the board of trustees. The rest of the group were the other members of the board and constituted EDF's total membership until April 1970, when it opened membership to the public.

Money was harder to find, although there was considerable support for the new organization among conservationists. The Audubon Society had, with some reluctance, supported the mosquito case, finding funds for court transcripts, but it was still not ready to engage in direct legal action. In September 1967 Yannacone made a speech at the society's annual meeting in Atlantic City, calling for legal action to preserve the environment. The system of adversary litigation, he said, was the best method of redressing public wrongs, and he called on Audubon to support such action. H. Lewis Batts, another member of the group, presented a resolution endorsing this plan at the members' meeting. It was "approved enthusiastically." The executive committee, though, hesitated, and the EDF was incorporated without a formal commitment from the Audubon Society. On 8 October the group had an organizational meeting, and shortly afterward Yannacone filed formal incorporation papers.

The formation of the EDF was, in part, a response to the frustrations of the founders, but it was also sparked by a sense of urgency. By 1967 they were convinced that action must be taken soon if irreparable damage to various ecosystems and to several species of birds was to be avoided. The threat could not be met simply by setting aside certain areas of the world—DDT spread beyond the places where it was applied. As a result, the EDF abandoned the genteel tradition of conservation. Yannacone's motto was "Sue the Bastards!" and, although the other trustees did not endorse the words, they agreed with the sentiment. To Lorrie Otto, Wurster wrote, "May I *strongly* recommend that you take legal action against whatever agency plans to do the spraying. File suit to prevent it." Public education, he wrote in another letter, was "too slow and ineffective. . . . EDF represents an attempt to do things another way; it is for those who have lost patience. . . . When it comes to changing an established order of society, then I shall have to get action more rapidly than can usually be achieved through conventional routes."

The EDF's neglect of lobbying and public education and its enthusiasm for confrontations with regulatory agencies distinguished it from other organizations. Its aims also set it apart; the EDF wanted to do more than simply protect wildlife. Woodwell said that EDF existed to "define human rights through research, education, and litigation." There was not enough scientific information to enable man to manage the earth's ecosystems in a stable and sustained fashion, and it was "the purpose of the Environmental Defense Fund, Inc., to provide a direct means of bringing science to bear on environmental issues." The other members agreed, though there was, at least in retrospect, some division over the exact nature of EDF's mission. Yannacone recalled that the organization was designed as a temporary group to build a body of case law to establish citizens' rights to a clean environment and to educate the public through legal action. Wurster, in 1975, stressed much more the need to get results. He was much less concerned with public education and legal precedents, he said, than with getting action.

The EDF began on shaky ground. Appealing as the idea of a citizen's right to a clean environment was, it was not well established in law, as Yannacone freely admitted. "We were," he said, "practicing a form of legal guerilla warfare. . . . There was no standing, there was no jurisdiction, there were no courses of action. . . ." This did not particularly bother him, for he viewed the law as an instrument of social change, a way of resolving differences without appeal to force. "[I]f there is a social need that must be filled, and something must be done for the People, with a capital P, there must be a legal way to do it." It was the lawyer's job to find it, and if he could not find it, to "invent it."

Yannacone was an excellent choice for the unorthodox task of bringing suit against a chemical on behalf of a hitherto undefined citizens' right to a clean environment. Besides his legal skill and dedication to the law as a means of settling issues, he had personal qualities that made him extremely valuable—aggressiveness, flamboyance, a quick mind, and the ability to grasp the essential points of an argument and shape them into a legal brief or an attack on an opponent. Scientists briefing him or being questioned by him were surprised at the speed with which he absorbed material and arguments. He was neither daunted by the odds nor particularly bothered by the lack of precedents in this area. From his work with civil rights cases, he was accustomed to building a case rather than appealing to already established rules. Even his colorful courtroom manner was an advantage. The environmentalists needed, particularly in their first cases, to get public attention, both as a means of making their case outside the courtroom and of bringing in money, and Yannacone was always good copy for any reporter.

The lack of a firm legal position did not stop the EDF from taking immediate action. One of the directors, H. Lewis Batts, was from Michigan, had done research on DDT and dieldrin, and wanted to challenge the pesticide programs in his state. He pledged $10,000. Ralph MacMullan, head of the Michigan Department of Natural Resources, also urged the EDF to come. It did, filing two suits. One challenged a cooperative state-federal insect control program—the Michigan and U.S. Departments of Agriculture planned to spray two and a half tons of dieldrin over part of Berrian County, Michigan, to exterminate an "infestation" of Japanese beetles. The other asked for an injunction against nine towns in western Michigan that were using DDT for Dutch elm disease control. Five days after celebrating its incorporation, amid mutual promises not "to rush into anything," the EDF had its hands full.

It won a series of partial victories. On 24 October 1967, when the dieldrin case came up, Judge Fox promptly threw the EDF out of the Michigan Court of Appeals "high, wide and handsome," ruling that under the Eleventh Amendment to the U.S. Constitution the organization had no standing. That afternoon, Yannacone got an emergency temporary injunction and went to the Michigan Supreme Court. It also denied the EDF relief, but the legal maneuvers delayed the program past the best spraying time, and it was put off for a year. The EDF was more successful against the Dutch elm disease control program. None of the towns contested the suit; all stipulated that they would not use DDT. EDF promptly filed another suit, naming fifty-six towns in the state using DDT. Within a year they all agreed to stop using it. Still, the EDF had not attained one of its objectives, the chance to present its full case in open court. It wanted to try DDT before the bar and before the court of public opinion.

In October 1968, the EDF returned to the Dieldrin action, bringing suit in United States District Court for the Eastern District of Wisconsin. This was environmental law with a vengeance. To establish jurisdiction EDF had to show that the state of Wisconsin had a vital interest in a "regional ecosystem," Lake Michigan, and that the use of dieldrin in Berrian County, Michigan, would cause damage to that ecosystem. The court record shows just why the environmentalists found litigation a useful, but not a perfect or easily applied, remedy.

Michigan vigorously supported the use of persistent pesticides. In 1967 the governor had forbidden the employees of the Department of Natural Resources, including MacMullan, to testify for the EDF, and in 1968 the assistant attorney general, representing the state department of agriculture, disputed the EDF's standing, the court's jurisdiction, and the charge. The case, he contended, was the same one that had been thrown out of the Michigan courts, and it could not be brought in Wisconsin. The action did not arise in Wisconsin, nor did the plaintiffs live there. Their charge was also defective; the EDF lacked an essential party to the suit—the Secretary of the USDA. The attorney general also claimed that the action was causing serious economic damage.

As long as the nurserymen of Michigan had to contend with the Japanese beetle, their business was hampered by federal quarantine regulations.

Yannacone replied that there was concurrent jurisdiction. Both states had an interest in the lake, which would suffer "permanent and irreparable damage" from the proposed sprays. As for the damage to nurserymen, this was "nonsense." New York nurserymen had managed to carry on their business for years under these regulations. His basic argument, though, was that the EDF did not get a fair trial in Michigan. It had had only one day to present its evidence, and this had caused a severe contraction of the scientific testimony. The justice of a "day in court," he said, was not met by a literal day. The plaintiffs needed a chance to present all the evidence.

The judge did not, at least, throw the EDF out; he allowed it to proceed with the case. It opened with a strong attack on the wisdom and necessity of the dieldrin program. Yannacone put B. Dale Ball, director of the Michigan Department of Agriculture, on the stand and asked him about the criteria his department used to define an infestation. It was planning to treat 4,800 acres because it had found a few beetles in traps. How many beetles made an "infestation"? One? Ball was extremely evasive on this point, and Yannacone finally moved to strike his testimony on the grounds that Ball did not understand the concept. Even if there was an infestation, he went on, was eradication the best means of coping with it? The department had already eradicated the beetle from the area around Battle Creek several times. Since there were recurrent infestations, was it worth the cost and the damage to wildlife? What evidence was there that the beetle would cause any loss to Michigan's agriculture?

The EDF then presented witnesses to show that the program would cause damage to the ecosystem of the lake. Ralph MacMullan, director of the Michigan Department of Natural Resources, said that the proposed sprays would be dangerous to wildlife of the area; dieldrin was "one of the larger, more important [pollution] problems" threatening the state. It was persistent, mobile, and broadly toxic. He strongly supported the EDF's original argument; Lake Michigan was, he said, a regional ecosystem, and any dieldrin that entered the lake was of concern to both states. Three more witnesses testified on specific parts of the argument. Howard D. Johnson, assistant professor of fisheries and wildlife at Michigan State University, said that the lake was already polluted. DDT residues in Lake Michigan fish were two to five times those in Lake Superior specimens, and there were measurable dieldrin residues in the former. Charles T. Black, a biologist, testified that if dieldrin were applied to the Berrian County lakeshore, as the Department of Agriculture planned to do, it would move into the atmosphere and the lake, causing damage to the ecosystem. Finally Wurster gave evidence of the toxicity of dieldrin and DDT to various phyla and on the properties that made these substances so dangerous to the ecosystem—broad biological activity, mobility, chemical stability, and bioconcentration through food chains.

In the end, though, the EDF got little more than it had received in Michigan. The judge rejected their arguments, cut their presentation short, and allowed the spraying to proceed. The environmentalists turned again to DDT and Dutch elm disease control, the subject that had brought them to Wisconsin, and here they found their forum against persistent pesticides. The new case was the result of the efforts of local conservationists to halt the use of DDT. In the wake of *Silent Spring*, a group of Wisconsin conservationists, organized into the Citizens' Natural Resources Association of Wisconsin, Inc., (CNRA) had actively complained against persistent pesticides, holding seminars to educate the public and testifying against the use of DDT for Dutch elm disease. The group had some success; a few towns in the state stopped using DDT, but progress was not rapid. In August 1968, Lorrie Otto found a notice in the local paper: The Wisconsin Department of Agriculture had again recommended DDT for Dutch elm disease control, and the towns around here, and Bayside as well, were planning to use it. She called Joseph Hickey, who agreed that the only thing left was a suit. A week later, when they attended a National Nature Conservancy meeting on Long Island, she and Hickey went to see Wurster, with whom she had been corresponding for over a year.

The meeting was useful to both parties. Hickey and Otto needed legal help if they were to fight the sprays; the EDF needed a good case if it was to survive. What made Otto's case so attractive was the information she had been collecting on DDT use in Milwaukee County. Wurster promised that the EDF would come to Wisconsin and represent the CNRA in a lawsuit against DDT use. He asked Otto to find a lawyer to introduce Yannacone at the bar, to start a campaign to raise at least $15,000, and to tell reporters the story. The EDF wanted, and needed, a lot of publicity. The CNRA subsequently filed a complaint with the Wisconsin Department of Natural Resources (DNR), which was responsible for oversight of these programs, naming as defendants the city of Milwaukee and Buckley Tree Service, which it alleged had a contract with the city to spray the elms. Maurice Van Susteren, chief hearing examiner for the department, assigned himself to the case and set the hearing for 18 October.

The hearing, held a week after the dieldrin case, was a fiasco. It began with a two and a half hour off-the-record discussion that effectively closed the case. The city and Buckley agreed not to use DDT and showed that there was no contract between them. (They further agreed not to take any action against the plaintiffs—specifically a countersuit.) Yannacone then asked for a three-day adjournment to prepare an amended complaint, and a six-day hearing in which to present the full case; Buckley of Buckley Tree Service had agreed to act as the defendant in the action. Van Susteren, though, said that this was impossible. The hearing schedule was full for the next two months, and the complaint was, with the stipulations of Buckley and Milwaukee, moot.

It seemed that all the environmentalists' efforts had been wasted, and some of them, including Lorrie Otto, began to cry. Van Susteren remarked to the clerk that these people were crazy. They had won, what did they have to be unhappy about? What, he asked Yannacone, was the matter? The lawyer explained that their goal was not so much to ban DDT in any particular place as to find a public forum and an impartial arbiter before whom to present their scientific evidence and get a judgment. Van Susteren pointed out that if that was the case, they had chosen the wrong legal route. Wisconsin law provided a declaratory ruling procedure that was much more suitable. Any Wisconsin citizen could ask a government department for a ruling on the applicability of a particular set of facts to any rule enforced by the department. The concerned agency would then hold a public hearing in which each side in the dispute would present its case, subject to rules of evidence and cross-examination. CNRA members, for example, could ask the Department of Natural Resources if DDT was a water pollutant under the Wisconsin water-quality standards. The department would then hold a hearing in which the EDF could attempt to show that DDT did, in fact, contaminate the waters of the state and injure the human or animal life of the area.

This was ideal. A hearing on the declaratory ruling, designed to allow the clarification of administrative rules and procedures without a justiciable matter, would allow the EDF to concentrate on its scientific case, rather than any particular use of the insecticide. It could sue DDT. It lost no time doing so. On 28 October Frederick L. Ott, on behalf of the CNRA, asked the Department of Natural Resources for a declaratory ruling: was or was not DDT a water pollutant? Van Susteren assigned himself to the action and arranged for a ten-day hearing, to begin 2 December in Madison. The EDF had its case.

*Joseph L. Sax*

# Defending the Environment: A Strategy for Citizen Action (1971)

We are a peculiar people. Though committed to the idea of democracy, as private citizens we have withdrawn from the governmental process and sent in our place a surrogate to implement the public interest. This substitute—the administrative agency—stands between the people and those whose daily business is the devouring of natural environments for private gain.

The administrative agency is neither sinister nor superfluous; indeed, it is an essential institution to regulate the myriad daily activities which require that standards be set, permits granted, and routine rules enforced. But it has become more than merely a useful supplement to private initiatives and participation in the governmental process. It has supplanted the citizen as a participant to such an extent that its panoply of legal strictures actually forbid members of the public from participating even in the complacent process whereby the regulators and the regulated work out the destiny of our air, water, and land resources. The citizen who seeks to intervene in an administrative proceeding or to bring a complaint before the judiciary is shunted aside as a busybody or crank, and a whole arsenal of legal weapons are wheeled out against him. The implementation of the public interest, he is told, must be left "to those who know best." . . .

. . . [T]he bureaucratic perspective tends to intensify the problem of the so-called "nibbling phenomenon," the process in which large resource values are gradually eroded, case by case, as one development after another is allowed. The danger is that in each little dispute—when the pressure is on—the balance of judgment will move ever so slightly to resolve doubts in favor of those with a big economic stake in development and with powerful allies.

It is so easy for an administrator to adopt the position that this is the last intrusion

From Joseph L. Sax, *Defending the Environment: A Strategy for Citizen Action* (New York: Alfred A. Knopf, 1971). Reprinted with the permission of Joseph L. Sax.

to be permitted, that no bad precedent is being set, and that the line will be drawn at the next case. After all, taken singly, no decision . . . is likely to appear arbitrary; environmental problems, such as estuarine protection, arise preeminently in urbanizing areas where demand for development is high and where—almost by definition—the specific land at issue has long since lost its ecologic virginity. Yet the same influences which [lead to a] decision that no objections should be interposed . . . are equally likely to apply when the next application—now in the comfortably vague future—is brought forward for decision. And will it not then also seem quite rational to approve that very small incursion, with the same reservations about its successor? There is no sharp, scientific line of demarcation; areas are only more or less pristine, and each case in a developing area is likely to be just slightly different than the one before it.

Thus, all the political and economic pressures which serve to tip the scale in favor of a specific project, though producing a seemingly rational result when considered in isolation, may serve cumulatively to produce exactly the opposite of the overall policy that the administrators want to achieve, that they are mandated to achieve by law and policy statements, and that they may think they are achieving. The greatest problems are often the outcome of the smallest-scale decisions precisely because the ultimate, aggregate impacts of those decisions are so difficult to see and the pressures so difficult to cope with from the perspective of the insider. It is much easier to tell a developer that he cannot dam up the Grand Canyon than to tell each real estate investor, one by one over time, that he cannot fill an acre or two of marshy "waste" land.

In these ways the administrative process tends to produce not the voice of the people, but the voice of the bureaucrat—the administrative perspective posing as the public interest. Simply put, the fact is that the citizen does not need a bureaucratic middleman to identify, prosecute, and vindicate his interest in environmental quality. He is perfectly capable of fighting his own battles—if only he is given the tools with which to do the job. And . . . battles are best fought out between those who have direct stakes in the outcome.

. . . [T]he courtroom is an eminently suitable forum for the voicing of citizen concerns over the maintenance of environmental quality. The real virtues of environmental litigation have little to do with the common conception of niggling lawyers battling over the intricacies of some ambiguous words in an obscure statute. Rather, the availability of a judicial forum is a measure of the willingness of government to subject itself to challenge on the merits of decisions made by public officials; to accept the possibility that the ordinary citizen may have useful ideas to contribute to the effectuation of the public interest; and to submit to them if—in the rigorous process of fact gathering—those ideas are shown to have substantial merit. *Litigation is thus a means of access for the ordinary citizen to the process of governmental decisionmaking.* It is in many circumstances the only tool for genuine citizen participation in the operative process of government.

. . . The citizen who comes to court in environmental cases has traditionally been told that he is in the wrong place—that he should take his complaints to the legislature. A careful examination of these cases will show, however, that the citizen often comes to court precisely in order to *preserve* his opportunity to put his case before the public. It is not the citizen plaintiff in such cases, but his opponent, who is likely to be undermining the opportunity for open and genuine public debate on uncertain or unresolved issues of public policy. Thus we . . . see highway departments paving over valuable parklands because some statute gives them authority to "improve" the lands of the state; a federal agency prepared to sell public lands for timber-harvesting before the Congress has had a chance to examine the relative merits of logging as against demands for wilderness maintenance; and developers about to bulldoze priceless fossil beds at the very moment the legislature is debating their maintenance as a national monument. It is in settings such as these that one begins to understand the demand for judicially declared moratoria, or orders for legislative reconsideration, as part of the effort to assure that democracy is made to work in practice as well as in school book theory.

The elaborate structure of administrative middlemen we have interposed between the citizen and his interest in environmental quality has had another pernicious effect. It has dulled our sensitivity to the claim that citizens, as members of the public, have rights. The citizen who comes to an administrative agency comes essentially as a supplicant, requesting that somehow the public interest be interpreted to protect the environmental values from which he benefits. The citizen who comes to court has quite a different status—he stands as a claimant of rights to which he is entitled.

The changed status of the proceeding draws attention to an essential element in environmental disputes. Environmental quality is threatened so often because we have not put any price on it or marketed it as we do ordinary objects of private property. Clean air and water, public beaches, and open space, for example, are treated as essentially free goods, and for that reason it is little wonder that they have been used extravagantly.

They are treated as free in large part because no one has been entitled to assert a right in the maintenance of those values; no member of the public has been permitted to claim a legal right to the maintenance of clean air or water in the sense that the owner of a specific tract of land may demand the protection of the values inherent in that tract. In short, we have neglected to develop a sense of public-rights consciousness parallel to our concepts of private-rights consciousness. As a result our public values are degraded with abandon.

This is no merely legalistic or technical distinction. It reflects fundamentally upon our ability to protect public resources (which is simply another way of talking about the environment), and it goes far to explain why environmental values have been so substantially impaired. To devise a theory of public rights and a means of enforcing them is thus an essential step toward protecting environmental values.

. . . [L]itigation promotes environmental values by putting a price on them. That price is not always reckoned in dollars, to be sure. A public shoreline or park, for example, may be insulated from developmental pressures unless and until the public—through direct legislative assent—is satisfied that this trade is worth making, just as a private owner must be satisfied with a trade for his property. Similarly, courts may hold that environmentally disruptive construction must be enjoined until conditions are fulfilled that will assure protection of the values threatened.

The price exacted for environmental modifications is usually some form of genuine public assent, which may be effectuated through the remedy of the judicially de-clared moratorium, or remand to legislative action, mentioned above. The enforce-ment of public rights, at the behest of members of the public, is thus the application of dem-ocratic theory to the allocation of natural resources. . . .

It should be clear from these observations that the problems of environmental qual-ity management go far deeper than conventional efforts to patch up the present ad-ministrative process. In an important sense, they require a repudiation of our tradi-tional reliance on professional bureaucrats. For a society which is ready to recognize public rights can no more leave the destiny of those rights in the hands of bureau-crats than it would leave the enforcement of an individual's property rights to some bureaucrat to vindicate when, and if, he determines them to be consistent with the public interest.

Thus far neither our courts nor our legislatures have significantly faced up to the implications of public rights. They continue to be fixated on the administrative process as *the* mechanism for identifying and enforcing the public interest. The pub-lic remains an outsider, to be tolerated as a recipient of notices and participant at for-mal hearings, but not as central player. Elaborate schemes are devised for studies by agencies and for coordination among them, but the administrative agency continues to be viewed as the key instrument of decision-making. Even the most sympathetic courts today recoil at the prospect of questioning an agency's discretion or its sup-posed expertise about the public interests. The public itself is thought to possess *no* expertise about the public interest.

The consequence of all this, as we shall see, is an incredible tangle of agencies with noble-sounding mandates and small budgets; court decisions which, in their reluc-tance to question administrative discretion, send cases back for interminable "further studies" or with directions for correcting various little procedural blunders they have made; and proceedings that go on for years—and even decades. And when it is all over, we have, as at the beginning, a decision reflecting the agency's response to its political necessities—its insider perspective about the public interest.

Our need is not for more or fancier procedures before the same old agencies—it is for a shift in the center of gravity of decision-making. The recognition of public rights can, to a striking degree, effect that shift. . . . [O]ne important means for doing that job [is] using the courtroom as a tool to enhance the leverage of individual citizens and citizen groups.

Nothing in this book is meant to suggest the substitution of judicial action for leg-islative policy-making. Indeed, if there is a single theme in this book, it is that citizen litigation is designed to promote and protect the authority of legislatures to make public policy and to make it more responsive to the interests of their constituents than is presently the case.

Neither is anything here meant to advocate the abolition of administrative agencies. They have their place; it is only hoped that the techniques suggested here will help them also to know their place. They are the servants of the citizenry. Their planning and regulatory functions are needed elements of good governments, but those tasks must never be insulated from scrutiny demanded by those for whose benefit they are performed.

Today the management of environmental controversies is in disarray. Administrative agencies have been gravely deficient, and public confidence in them is eroded to an extreme degree. Citizens have reached out to the legislatures for help. New statutes are abundant, but their rhetoric far exceeds their effect. Unable thus far to perceive the fundamental issues raised by the environmental mess, legislators continue to pile more and more burdensome procedures upon agencies whose problems are far deeper than procedural failings. New councils, task forces, and commissions proliferate, but they seem little more than a revival of old institutional mistakes with new names.

In desperation citizens have turned to the courts. Judges have begun to lower the technical barriers to citizen suits, but they do not know where to go from that point. They fear that they will be asked to become scientists and technicians—to have to decide the relative merits of various pesticides or how a pipeline should be built across arctic tundra. The consequence is delay, confusion, and general bewilderment.

This situation must not be permitted to endure. . . .

There is no good reason why we should hesitate to adopt a theory of public rights to environmental quality, enforceable at law, nor is there any reason to think we cannot adjudicate the reasonable accommodations needed to protect against unnecessary threats to the environment. If the courts viewed the public interest in the Alaskan environment or the Hudson River as they do private property, they could go straight to the merits of the claims which citizens want to make. The same questions asked in private cases apply to public complaints: Is the activity necessary? Is there enough information to support the allegations that it can be carried on without undue harm to the environment? Are there better alternatives, or is there a reason to delay until we know more or have done better experimental work?

The reason we have not moved in this direction thus far is that we have not treated environmental resources as property entitled to be maintained and protected for the benefit of its owners, the public, subject to infringement only when it can be demonstrated that some other need is paramount and is being carried on with the minimum possible harm. Rather, we have treated those resources as the domain of no one, as wild fruits to be plucked at will by the first hungry claimant. We have designated a zero price for them, and we are reaping the inevitable consequence in the form of extravagant and largely unrestrained use.

What will happen if we begin to treat these resources as rights which citizens are entitled to maintain at law? Does this mean that no development can ever go forward, that we will be condemned to remain at a standstill without another tree cut, another stream dammed, or another road built? Of course the answer is a resounding no. Just as a landowner or first homebuilder in a neighborhood may not enjoin all subsequent homebuilding just because it would impair his unrestricted view of the scenery out of his livingroom window, the public, as a holder of rights, has no absolute claim against developments which will affect that right. The public right to public resources, like private rights, must be subject to the reasonable demands of other users, whether they be factories, power companies, or residential developers.

Thus a public right to clean air will not necessarily be a right to maintain the air as fresh as it is on the top of the highest mountain. Rather, it will be a right to maintain it as clean as it ought to be to protect health and comfort when considered against the demands for spillover use of the air by other enterprises—and with due consideration of the need for such uses, the alternatives available to the enterprisers, existing and potential technology, and the possibility of other less harmful locations. Those are the issues at stake in environmental disputes to which courts must now begin to turn their attention.

Of course, no one can identify in advance the precise resolution of any given potential controversy. This is one of the reasons it is necessary to provide for the process of elucidating litigation, and this is why litigation must go forward in the fashion of the common law—meeting individual cases on their particular merits, rather than in the restrictive style of conventional judicial review of administrative action.

It should be reiterated here that insofar as legislatures are satisfied that they know what balance ought to be struck in any given problem area—whether it be the proximity of airports to cities, the amount of mercury that can be dumped in a stream, or the availability of marshland for filling and development—they ought to embody those standards, with the greatest precision possible, in statutes, and thus minimize the need for common-law litigation. Until and unless that process covers the entire spectrum of environmental problems, however, there will remain a need for public action in the courtroom.

*Christopher D. Stone*

# Should Trees Have Standing?— Toward Legal Rights for Natural Objects (1972)

## Introduction: The Unthinkable

In *Descent of Man*, Darwin observes that the history of man's moral development has been a continual extension in the objects of his "social instincts and sympathies." Originally each man had regard only for himself and those of a very narrow circle about him; later, he came to regard more and more "not only the welfare, but the happiness of all his fellowmen"; then "his sympathies became more tender and widely diffused, extending to men of all races, to the imbecile, maimed, and other useless members of society, and finally to the lower animals. . . ."

The history of the law suggests a parallel development. Perhaps there never was a pure Hobbesian state of nature, in which no "rights" existed except in the vacant sense of each man's "right to self-defense." But it is not unlikely that so far as the earliest "families" (including extended kinship groups and clans) were concerned, everyone outside the family was suspect, alien, rightless. And even within the family, persons we presently regard as the natural holders of at least some rights had none. Take, for example, children. We know something of the early rights-status of children from the widespread practice of infanticide—especially of the deformed and female. (Senicide, as among the North American Indians, was the corresponding rightlessness of the aged). Maine tells us that as late as the Patria Potestas of the Romans, the father had *jus vitae necisque*—the power of life and death—over his children. A fortiori, Maine writes, he had power of "uncontrolled corporal chastisement; he can modify their personal condition at pleasure; he can give a wife to his son; he

Christopher D. Stone, Should Trees Have Standing?—Toward Legal Rights for Natural Objects, 45 S. Cal. L. Rev. 450 (1972), reprinted with the permission of the Southern California Law Review.

can give his daughter in marriage; he can divorce his children of either sex; he can transfer them to another family by adoption; and he can sell them." The child was less than a person: an object, a thing.

The legal rights of children have long since been recognized in principle, and are still expanding in practice. Witness, just within recent time, *In re Gault,* guaranteeing basic constitutional protections to juvenile defendants, and the Voting Rights Act of 1970. We have been making persons of children although they were not, in law, always so. And we have done the same, albeit imperfectly some would say, with prisoners, aliens, women (especially of the married variety), the insane, Blacks, foetuses, and Indians.

Nor is it only matter in human form that has come to be recognized as the possessor of rights. The world of the lawyer is peopled with inanimate right-holders: trusts, corporations, joint ventures, municipalities, Subchapter R partnerships, and nation-states, to mention just a few. Ships, still referred to by courts in the feminine gender, have long had an independent jural life, often with striking consequences. We have become so accustomed to the idea of a corporation having "its" own rights, and being a "person" and "citizen" for so many statutory and constitutional purposes, that we forget how jarring the notion was to early jurists. . . .

The fact is, that each time there is a movement to confer rights onto some new "entity," the proposal is bound to sound odd or frightening or laughable. This is partly because until the rightless thing receives its rights, we cannot see it as anything but a *thing* for the use of "us"—those who are holding rights at the time. . . . Such is the way the slave South looked upon the Black. There is something of a seamless web involved: there will be resistance to giving the thing "rights" until it can be seen and valued for itself; yet, it is hard to see it and value it for itself until we can bring ourselves to give it "rights"—which is almost inevitably going to sound inconceivable to a large group of people.

The reason for this little discourse on the unthinkable, the reader must know by now, if only from the title of the paper. I am quite seriously proposing that we give legal rights to forests, oceans, rivers and other so-called "natural objects" in the environment—indeed, to the natural environment as a whole.

As strange as such a notion may sound, it is neither fanciful nor devoid of operational content. In fact, I do not think it would be a misdescription of recent developments in the law to say that we are already on the verge of assigning some such rights, although we have not faced up to what we are doing in those particular terms. We should do so now, and begin to explore the implications such a notion would hold.

## Toward Rights for the Environment

Now, to say that the natural environment should have rights is not to say anything as silly as that no one should be allowed to cut down a tree. We say human beings have rights, but—at least as of the time of this writing—they can be executed. Corporations have rights, but they cannot plead the fifth amendment; *In re Gault* gave 15-year-olds certain rights in juvenile proceedings, but it did not give them the right to vote. Thus, to say that the environment should have rights is not to say that it should have every right we can imagine, or even the same body of rights as human beings have. Nor is it to say that everything in the environment should have the same rights as every other thing in the environment.

What the granting of rights does involve has two sides to it. The first involves what might be called the legal-operational aspects; the second, the psychic and socio-psychic aspects. . . .

## The Legal-Operational Aspects

### *What It Means to Be a Holder of Legal Rights*

There is, so far as I know, no generally accepted standard for how one ought to use the term "legal rights." Let me indicate how I shall be using it in this piece.

First and most obviously, if the term is to have any content at all, an entity cannot be said to hold a legal right unless and until *some public authoritative body* is prepared to give *some amount of review* to actions that are colorably inconsistent with that "right." For example, if a student can be expelled from a university and cannot get any public official, even a judge or administrative agent at the lowest level, either (i) to require the university to justify its actions (if only to the extent of filling out an affidavit alleging that the expulsion "was not wholly arbitrary and capricious") or (ii) to compel the university to accord the student some procedural safeguards (a hearing, right to counsel, right to have notice of charges), then the minimum requirements for saying that the student has a legal right to his education do not exist.

But for a thing to be *a holder of legal rights*, something more is needed than that some authoritative body will review the actions and processes of those who threaten it. As I shall use the term, "holder of legal rights," each of three additional criteria must be satisfied. All three, one will observe, go towards making a thing *count* jurally—to have a legally recognized worth and dignity in its own right, and not merely to serve as a means to benefit "us" (whoever the contemporary group of rights-holders may be). They are, first, that the thing can institute legal actions *at its behest;* second, that in determining the granting of legal relief, the court must take *injury to it* into account; and third, that relief must run to the *benefit of it.* . . .

### *The Rightlessness of Natural Objects at Common Law*

Consider, for example, the common law's posture toward the pollution of a stream. True, courts have always been able, in some circumstances, to issue orders that will stop the pollution—just as the legal system . . . is so structured as incidentally to discourage beating slaves and being reckless around pregnant women. But the stream itself is fundamentally rightless, with implications that deserve careful reconsideration.

The first sense in which the stream is not a rights-holder has to do with standing. The stream itself has none. So far as the common law is concerned, there is in general no way to challenge the polluter's actions save at the behest of a lower riparian— another human being—able to show an invasion of *his* rights. This conception of the riparian as the holder of the right to bring suit has more than theoretical interest. The lower riparians may simply not care about the pollution. They themselves may be polluting, and not wish to stir up legal waters. They may be economically dependent on their polluting neighbor. And, of course, when they discount the value of winning by the costs of bringing suit and the chances of success, the action may not seem worth undertaking. . . .

This second sense in which the common law denies "rights" to natural objects has to do with the way in which the merits are decided in those cases in which someone is competent and willing to establish standing. At its more primitive levels, the system protected the "rights" of the property owning human with minimal weighing of any values: *"Cujus est solum, ejus est usque ad coelum et ad infernos."*[1] Today we have come more and more to make balances—but only such as will adjust the economic best interests of identifiable humans. For example, continuing with the case of streams, there are commentators who speak of a "general rule" that "a riparian owner is legally entitled to have the stream flow by his land with its quality unimpaired" and observe that "an upper owner has, prima facie, no right to pollute the water." Such a doctrine, if strictly invoked, would protect the stream absolutely whenever a suit was brought; but obviously, to look around us, the law does not work that way. Almost everywhere there are doctrinal qualifications on riparian "rights' to an unpolluted stream. Although these rules vary from jurisdiction to jurisdiction, and upon whether one is suing for an equitable injunction or for damages, what they all have in common is some sort of balancing. Whether under language of "reasonable use," "reasonable methods of use," "balance of convenience" or "the public interest doctrine," what the courts are balancing, with varying degrees of directness, are the economic hardships on the upper riparian (or dependent community) of abating the pollution vis-a-vis the economic hardships of continued pollution on the lower riparians. What does not weigh in the balance is the damage to the stream, its fish and turtles and "lower" life. So long as the natural environment itself is rightless, these are not matters for judicial cognizance. Thus, we find the highest court of Pennsyl-

---

[1]To whomsoever the soil belongs, he owns also to the sky and to the depths. See W. Blackstone, 2 Commentaries 18.

At early common law, the owner of land could use all that was found under his land "at his free will and pleasure" without regard to any "inconvenience to his neighbour." *Acton v. Blundell*, 12 Meeson & Welsburg 324, 354, 152 Eng. Rep. 1223, 1235 (1843). "He [the landowner] may waste or despoil the land as he pleases . . ." R. Megarry & H. Wade, The Law of Real Property 70 (3d ed. 1966). See R. Powell, 5 The Law of Real Property ¶725 (1971).

vania refusing to stop a coal company from discharging polluted mine water into a tributary of the Lackawana River because a plaintiff's "grievance is for a mere personal inconvenience; and . . . mere private personal inconvenience . . . must yield to the necessities of a great public industry, which although in the hands of a private corporation, subserves a great public interest." The stream itself is lost sight of in "a quantitative compromise between *two* conflicting interests."

The third way in which the common law makes natural objects rightless has to do with who is regarded as the beneficiary of a favorable judgment. Here, too, it makes a considerable difference that it is not the natural object that counts in its own right. To illustrate this point, let me begin by observing that it makes perfectly good sense to speak of, and ascertain, the legal damage to a natural object, if only in the sense of "making it whole" with respect to the most obvious factors. The costs of making a forest whole, for example, would include the costs of reseeding, repairing watersheds, restocking wildlife—the sorts of costs the Forest Service undergoes after a fire. Making a polluted stream whole would include the costs of restocking with fish, water-fowl, and other animal and vegetable life, dredging, washing out impurities, establishing natural and/or artificial aerating agents, and so forth. Now, what is important to note is that, under our present system, even if a plaintiff riparian wins a water pollution suit for damages, no money goes to the benefit of the stream itself to repair *its* damages. This omission has the further effect that, at most, the law confronts a polluter with what it takes to make the plaintiff riparians whole; this may be far less than the damages to the stream, but not so much as to force the polluter to desist. For example, it is easy to imagine a polluter whose activities damage a stream to the extent of $10,000 annually, although the aggregate damage to all the riparian plaintiffs who come into the suit is only $3000. If $3000 is less than the cost to the polluter of shutting down, or making the requisite technological changes, he might prefer to pay off the damages (i.e., the legally cognizable damages) and continue to pollute the stream. Similarly, even if the jurisdiction issues an injunction at the plaintiffs' behest (rather than to order payment of damages), there is nothing to stop the plaintiffs from "selling out" the stream, i.e., agreeing to dissolve or not enforce the injunction at some price (in the example above, somewhere between plaintiffs' damages—$3000—and defendant's next best economic alternative). Indeed, I take it this is exactly what Learned Hand had in mind in an opinion in which, after issuing an anti-pollution injunction, he suggests that the defendant "make its peace with the plaintiff as best it can." What is meant is a peace between them, and not amongst them and the river.

. . . None of the natural objects, whether held in common or situated on private land, has any of the three criteria of a rights-holder. They have no standing in their own right; their unique damages do not count in determining outcome; and they are not the beneficiaries of awards. In such fashion, these objects have traditionally been regarded by the common law, and even by all but the most recent legislation, as objects for man to conquer and master and use—in such a way as the law once looked upon "man's" relationships to African Negroes. Even where special measures have been taken to conserve them, as by seasons on game and limits on timber cutting, the dominant motive has been to conserve them *for us*—for the greatest good of the greatest number of human beings. Conservationists, so far as I am aware, are generally reluctant to maintain otherwise. As the name implies, they want to conserve and guarantee *our* consumption and *our* enjoyment to these other living things. In their own right, natural objects have counted for little, in law as in popular movements.

As I mentioned at the outset, however, the rightlessness of the natural environment can and should change; it already shows some signs of doing so.

## Toward Having Standing in Its Own Right

It is not inevitable, nor is it wise, that natural objects should have no rights to seek redress in their own behalf. It is no answer to say that streams and forests cannot have standing because streams and forests cannot speak. Corporations cannot speak either; nor can states, estates, infants, incompetents, municipalities or universities. Lawyers speak for them, as they customarily do for the ordinary citizen with legal problems. One ought, I think, to handle the legal problems of natural objects as one does the problems of legal incompetents—human beings who have become vegetable. If a human being shows signs of becoming senile and has affairs that he is de jure incompetent to manage, those concerned with his well being make such a showing to the court, and someone is designated by the court with the authority to manage the incompetent's affairs. The guardian (or "conservator" or "committee"—the terminology varies) then represents the incompetent in his legal affairs. Courts make similar appointments when a corporation has become "incompetent"—they appoint a trustee in bankruptcy or reorganization to oversee its affairs and speak for it in court when that becomes necessary.

On a parity of reasoning, we should have a system in which, when a friend of a natural object perceives it to be endangered, he can apply to a court for the creation of a guardianship. Perhaps we already have the machinery to do so. California law, for example, defines an incompetent as "any person, whether insane or not, who by reason of old age, disease, weakness of mind, or other cause, is unable, unassisted, properly to manage and take care of himself or his property, and by reason thereof is likely to be deceived or imposed upon by artful or designing persons." Of course, to urge a court that an endangered river is "a person" under this provision will call for lawyers as bold and imaginative as those who convinced the Supreme Court that a railroad corporation was a "person" under the fourteenth amendment, a constitutional provision theretofore generally thought of as designed to secure the rights of freedmen. . . .

The guardianship approach, however, is apt to raise two objections, neither of which seems to me to have much force. The first is that a committee or guardian could not judge the needs of the river or forest in its charge; indeed, the very concept of "needs," it might be said, could be used here only in the most metaphorical way. The second objection is that such a system would not be much different from what we now have: is not the Department of Interior already such a guardian for public lands, and do not most states have legislation empowering their attorneys general to seek relief—in a sort of *parens patriae* way—for such injuries as a guardian might concern himself with?

As for the first objection, natural objects can communicate their wants (needs) to us, and in ways that are not terribly ambiguous. I am sure I can judge with more certainty and meaningfulness whether and when my lawn wants (needs) water, than the Attorney General can judge whether and when the United States wants (needs) to take an appeal from an adverse judgment by a lower court. The lawn tells me that it wants water by a certain dryness of the blades and soil—immediately obvious to the touch—the appearance of bald spots, yellowing, and a lack of springiness after being walked on; how does "the United States" communicate to the Attorney General? For similar reasons, the guardian-attorney for a smog-endangered stand of pines could venture with more confidence that his client wants the smog stopped, than the directors of a corporation can assert that "the corporation" wants dividends declared. We make decisions on behalf of, and in the purported interests of, others every day; these "others" are often creatures whose wants are far less verifiable, and even far more metaphysical in conception, than the wants of rivers, trees, and land.

As for the second objection, one can indeed find evidence that the Department of Interior was conceived as a sort of guardian of the public lands. But there are two points to keep in mind. First, insofar as the Department already is an adequate guardian it is only with respect to the federal public lands as per Article IV, Section 3 of the Constitution. Its guardianship includes neither local public lands nor private lands. Second, to judge from the environmentalist literature and from the cases environmental action groups have been bringing, the Department is itself one of the bogeys of the environmental movement. (One thinks of the uneasy peace between the Indians and the Bureau of Indian Affairs.) Whether the various charges be right or wrong, one cannot help but observe that the Department has been charged with several institutional goals (never an easy burden), and is currently looked to for action by quite a variety of interest groups, only one of which is the environmentalists. In this context, a guardian outside the institution becomes especially valuable. Besides, what a person wants, fully to secure his rights, is the ability to retain independent counsel even when, and perhaps especially when, the government is acting "for him" in a beneficent way. I have no reason to doubt, for example, that the Social Security System is being managed "for me"; but I would not want to abdicate my right to challenge its actions as they affect me, should the need arise. I would not ask more trust of national forests, vis-a-vis the Department of Interior. The same considerations apply in the instance of local agencies, such as regional water pollution boards, whose members' expertise in pollution matters is often all too credible.

# CHAPTER 10

# The Regulatory Process

The environmental laws are not self-implementing. After both houses of Congress have approved legislation and the president has signed it into law, the regulatory process has only just begun. The environmental laws generally require administrative agencies to translate statutory directives into specific rules. Before these rules can be adopted, agencies must study the nature of the problems they seek to rectify and the characteristics of the regulatory targets to which rules will be applied. This chapter examines the factors that influence how effectively the environmental laws are implemented. Many early regulatory directives were aspirational in nature, requiring regulated industries to do their best to reduce pollution or to develop new pollution control technology. James Henderson and Richard Pearson explain that such laws were of limited effectiveness when industry did not share the values that animated the law's aspirational command. Using the analogy of a monarch who commands a poet to do his best to write a poem that will please him, without specifying the monarch's preferences, they argue that such aspirational commands are unrealistically vague. Yet many of the environmental laws have given agencies and industries vague commands precisely because Congress was unable to determine specifically what to do about a problem. Henderson and Pearson argue that this difficulty can be overcome only by lawmakers' acquiring greater expertise to enable them to write more specific statutes, or by regulated industries' becoming more sympathetic to environmental concerns—both of which are now beginning to occur.

Surveying several decades of experience with environmental law, William Rodgers identifies what he considers to be the seven most successful environmental statutes. Rodgers uses these "seven statutory wonders" to explore the factors that affect how well laws are implemented and their success in achieving legislative goals. The laws he identifies are generally statutes with unusually bold or innovative provisions. Rodgers explains that these laws were enacted when the forces that usually water down legislation were temporarily absent or because the provisions were "sleepers" that did not incite opposition to force weakening amendments.

Even bold laws often produce disappointing results when their implementation is left to overburdened administrative agencies. Howard Latin identifies what he calls eight "laws" of administrative behavior that help explain why environmental statutes are often so poorly implemented by the agencies responsible for them. Latin argues that the gap between the text of the laws and their implementation "has grown so wide that most regulatory practices cannot be understood by studying the applicable legislation." The problem cannot be solved simply by passing more detailed laws, Latin concludes. Instead legislators and agency officials must design ways to overcome the bureaucratic incentives that work against implementation of regulatory statutes.

*James A. Henderson, Jr., and*
*Richard N. Pearson*

# Implementing Federal Environmental Policies: The Limits of Aspirational Commands (1978)

There is an understandable tendency, whenever reliance is placed upon legal institutions for solutions to complex and pressing social problems, to pay relatively scant attention to the inherent limits upon the effectiveness of law. This tendency has been particularly evident when the need for solutions is perceived to be urgent, as it currently is in the field of environmental regulation. This Article examines the limits of a regulatory technique frequently relied upon by federal lawmakers in recent years: attempts to compel industries and organizations to cooperate in good faith—to "aspire" in implementing federal environmental policies. Frequently these attempts occur in the context of forcing addressees to develop pollution control technology. . . .

## Aspirational Commands and the Legal System

From the very beginnings of our jurisprudence, common-law judges recognized that only essentially nonaspirational patterns of conduct may effectively be compelled by threats of legal sanctions. Thus, criminal law had traditionally consisted almost entirely of commands which are negative, specific and nonaspirational. Tort law, although vaguer in some respects, is also predominantly negative and nonaspirational. Courts have generally refused to rely upon affirmative, aspirational commands even

James A. Henderson, Jr., and Richard N. Pearson, Implementing Federal Environmental Policies: The Limits of Aspirational Commands. This article originally appeared at 78 Colum. L. Rev. 1429 (1978). Reprinted by permission.

when they are confronted with specific contexts in which such commands might have appeared to be especially desirable—where, for example, a helpless person could be rescued by the active intervention of another. This same reluctance is reflected in the traditional refusal of courts to order specific performance of personal service contracts, and in the concern in administrative law with constraining, rather than compelling, the exercise of administrative discretion. It is no less clearly reflected in the restraint with which federal lawmakers in the American system have approached the delicate task of attempting to direct the conduct of the states. . . .

## The Difficulty of Enforcing Aspirational Commands

It is important to distinguish the difficulties inherent in the enforcement of aspirational commands from the problems involved in the enforcement of law generally. Even nonaspirational commands will be difficult to enforce if the resources devoted to law enforcement are inadequate to the task, or if there is a general disrespect for the source of the law. Aspirational commands present problems of a different order, however. These difficulties stem from the divergence of values between addressor and addressee, a condition which is likely to occur when a lawmaker relies upon threats of sanctions. Thus, when the addressee of an aspirational command is indifferent to, or hostile toward, the values and objectives reflected in an assigned task, aspiration of the sort desired by the addressor will typically be absent. Instead of seeking to maximize the accomplishment of the addressor's values, such an addressee may be expected to respond by either secretly resolving not to aspire in the performance of the task, masking his unwillingness with feigned sincerity, or by honestly misperceiving the addressor's objectives, which typically will only be vaguely described in an aspirational command, and consequently aspiring to perform in a manner which is only marginally useful to the addressor. Indeed, these responses have been characteristic of the experience in civil rights cases.

It must be emphasized that the addressor's problems are not ameliorated by threats of sanctions. The addressor cannot determine, with sufficient accuracy to support a consistent application of sanctions, whether the addressee has secretly refused to aspire. Furthermore, he cannot reduce the risk of the addressee's misinterpretation of his intent because generally he must keep his instructions vague if he is to leave the addressee free to aspire. Of course, both risks could be reduced by telling the addressee specifically what to do. If the addressor could have been specific, however, there would have been no need to rely upon an aspirational command. Thus, there are two basic and unavoidable problems with employing sanction-backed aspirational commands. There are, first, the problem of nonverifiability, inhering in the addressor's inability to determine whether the addressee has actually aspired in performing an assigned task; and second, the problem of vagueness, inhering in the characteristic openendedness of aspirational commands. . . .

The problems that arise in connection with the unavoidable vagueness of aspirational commands tend to be more subtle than the problems associated with nonverifiability. A hypothetical example for purposes of clarification will be useful. Assume that a powerful but artistically inept monarch commands a poet to do his best, under threat of sanction, to write a poem that will please the monarch. Of course, such a command would present the poet with an opportunity to dissemble. However, unless the monarch's and the poet's aesthetic tastes coincide (which would be unlikely given the monarch's reliance upon a threat of sanction), the command would place even an honest poet in a quandary about what to do. Should the poem be long? Short? Lyric? Tragic? Presumably, basic parameters covering these elements could be established. But even if the monarch were to narrow the poet's choices by a general description of his preferences, the remaining possibilities would be practically limitless. Assuming a time limit has been imposed, and given the difficult task of determining the mix of aesthetic values peculiar to the monarch with any degree of precision, eventually the poet would be compelled to sit down and write with only minimal guidance from the mandate. Bearing in mind that the poet is not required to please the monarch, but only to try his best to please him, the poet should be safe from sanction. But given the inherent vagueness of the command, the monarch would run a substantial risk of being disappointed with the results, even assuming a skillful poet, aspiring to please the monarch, and satisfied in his own mind with the work product.

The core of the problem threatening the efficacy of the aspirational command in this example resides in a mismatching of skills and values. The poet possesses the skills, but lacks the "proper" (*i.e.*, the monarch's) aesthetic values. By contrast, the monarch possesses the proper values, but lacks poetic skills. In effect, the monarch is attempting to commandeer the poet's skills and bend them to his own aesthetic value structure. Because the monarch can only communicate his aesthetic preferences in vague terms, however, the end result is very likely to be poetry which, aside from the fact that it may fit some clumsy, monarch-imposed parameters of being long and tragic, or short and lyric, does not accurately reflect the monarch's aesthetic values. A dilemma is thus presented: the monarch lacks the skills to be sufficiently specific in his task description, and the poet lacks the ability to substitute the monarch's values for his own. Moreover, assuming a monarch with an appetite for poetry in a kingdom in which poets do not share the monarch's tastes, the dilemma is largely unavoidable. The same factors which necessitate the monarch's commanding the poet to aspire to write poetry also prevent him from telling the poet specifically what to do. . . .

## Aspirational Commands and Regulatory Agencies

The foregoing analysis of the limits of aspirational commands is supported by the existence of a phenomenon much commented upon by observers of American administrative law—the capture of regulatory agencies by those persons and organizations that the agencies are supposed to regulate. A major function of administrative agencies is to translate vague and aspirational mandates of the legislature into specific, nonaspirational rules of conduct for those to be regulated. In technically complex matters, which are often the subject of administrative regulation, agencies often lack the expertise necessary to promulgate regulations that are specific and nonaspirational. In these circumstances, the agencies must rely upon those possessing the expertise—in most instances, the same firms which are to be regulated—for substantial assistance in the rulemaking process. And because the firms will not, and to a large extent cannot, effectively separate their technical expertise from their values, the regulations which emerge from such a process tend to reflect the values of the firms rather than any independent, congressionally imposed values. In this respect, the agencies are in very much the same position as was the monarch who attempts to capture the poet's skills without accepting the poet's aesthetic values. In the end, both the monarch and the regulatory agencies are themselves captured by their dependence upon the expertise of those whom they seek to regulate. Even agencies established by Congress for the express purpose of asserting regulatory independence are unavoidably exposed to this risk of capture.

The typical vagueness of mandates from Congress to federal agencies presents problems not only for agencies, but also for Congress and the federal executive (hereafter the Congress/Executive) in regulating the behavior of the agencies. The fact that agencies often respond affirmatively, even enthusiastically, to their mandates is due in substantial measure to a coincidence in the values of the agencies and of the Congress/Executive. Because the Congress/Executive are responsible for establishing, staffing, and maintaining the federal administrative agencies, they will often aspire in directions compatible with expressions of congressional and executive intent. Viewed in this way, the agencies are not being compelled to aspire, but rather are being allowed to do so. Thus, the paramount concern of federal administrative law has been directed not at stimulating agency action in pursuit of congressionally established objectives, but rather at correcting instances of agency overzealousness by confining exercises of administrative discretion within the bounds established by Congress. Consistent with the foregoing analysis, however, where the values of an agency are perceived to diverge from those of the Congress/Executive, efforts by the latter to assert meaningful control over agency values have generally been met with considerable resistance.

## Possible Alternatives?

### Establishing Specific Objectives

The addressor might be able to remove the requirement of aspiration from the command by first estimating the range of performance reasonably to be expected from an addressee, and then insisting that a specifically described, readily verifiable performance objective within the upper reaches of that range be achieved. In theory, such an approach would remove both impediments to the effectiveness of aspirational commands. As long as the addressor is able to describe the objectives to be achieved with adequate specificity, and as long as those objectives are within the upper ranges of the addressee's capabilities, sanction-backed performance objectives should succeed in compelling aspiration. Indeed, this alternative approach has been suggested as one solution to the difficulties encountered in attempting to enforce the affirmative action obligations imposed by federal law.

The obvious limitation of this technique lies in the inability of the addressor to assess the addressee's performance potential accurately. If the declared objectives are set too low, best efforts will not be stimulated; if set too high, sanctions will be imposed upon addressees who tried their best. Of course, if the addressor's purpose is to achieve the stipulated objective irrespective of whether or not the addressee aspires in the performance of the task, the risk of setting objectives too low will not be presented. But the risk of setting objectives too high will remain in spite of the addressor's indifference to whether or not the addressee aspires. The threat to the viability of a system of governance by declared rules, presented by the possibility of routinely demanding the impossible, places severe constraints upon the addressor's ability to set ambitious objectives. Thus, substantial problems will be encountered whenever the addressor's objectives fall in the upper range of the addressee's capabilities.

## Conclusion

. . . [T]here are no easy solutions available to federal lawmakers seeking to regulate decisions and activities significantly affecting the environment. Like the monarch who wanted to capture the skills but not the values of the poet, federal lawmakers are confronted in this context with an institutionalized, potentially threatening separation of skills and values. Business firms and state governments possess both the technical skills to develop solutions and the logistical capabilities to carry them out. Often, however, they are trapped in destructive patterns of short-run competition which preclude them from giving adequate consideration to environmental values. In contrast, federal lawmakers are in a position to establish their proper values, but frequently lack the technical skills and logistical capabilities to implement them without substantial cooperation from the firms and the states. The foregoing analysis suggests that this separation may not successfully be bridged by aspirational commands aimed at commandeering the institutional adressees' skills and bending them to the federal lawmakers' values. It follows that if the harmful consequences of this separation of skills and values are to be reduced, the separation itself must somehow be reduced: either the federal lawmakers must acquire sufficient expertise to be able, either directly or indirectly, to tell the institutional addressees more specifically what to do, or the institutional addressees must be restructured to reflect the lawmakers' values more closely.

*William H. Rodgers, Jr.*

# The Seven Statutory Wonders of U.S. Environmental Law: Origins and Morphology (1994)

## Introduction

Students from around the world often ask my opinion on the most influential or effective of the United States environmental laws. I offer an opinion based on two criteria: What laws have contributed most to protection of the natural world and what laws have been most emulated? The second criterion is obviously an indicator of output, not of direct consequence. However, a linkage between the spread of strong laws and degree of environmental protection is assumed. In theory, of course, the questions of "how much protection" and "how many laws" can be answered empirically. But this story is available only in the sketchiest of terms, so opinions will have to suffice.

Here are the nominees for the seven great U.S. environmental laws:

(1) section 409 of the Food Additives Amendment of 1958, known popularly as the Delaney Amendment, which states in part that no food additive "shall be deemed to be safe if it is found to induce cancer when ingested by man or animal";

(2) section 2 of the Land and Water Conservation Fund Act of 1965, which established a special fund from certain federal revenues—including receipts from oil and gas leasing on the Outer Continental Shelf—that can be used for the acquisition of parks and conservation lands;

(3) section 2 of the Wilderness Act of 1964 which established the National Wilderness Preservation System and defines wilderness "as an area where the earth and its community of life are untrammeled by man, where man himself is a visitor who does not remain";

William H. Rodgers, Jr., The Seven Statutory Wonders of U.S. Environmental Law: Origins and Morphology, 27 Loyola of L.A. L. Rev. 1009 (1994).

(4) section 102 of the National Environmental Policy Act of 1969 (NEPA), which requires that environmental impact statements accompany all actions by federal agencies that may have a significant effect on the human environment;

(5) section 301 of the Federal Water Pollution Control Act Amendments of 1972 (Clean Water Act or CWA), which makes unlawful the discharge of any pollutant by any person;

(6) section 7 of the Endangered Species Act of 1973 (ESA), which states that no federal agency shall take action "likely to jeopardize" the continued existence of a protected species or result in the "destruction or adverse modification" of its habitat; and

(7) section 107 of the Comprehensive Environmental Response, Compensation, and Liability Act of 1980 (CERCLA), which imposes strict and joint and several liability on any person whose disposal of hazardous substances causes the owner of the affected property to incur response costs.

The measures of influence of these extraordinary enactments can be underscored in various ways. And now for my choices, in descending order of significance:

My first-place vote goes to the Land and Water Conservation Fund Act, which, since its inception, has resulted in expenditures of $6.8 billion to maintain, purchase, and acquire parklands, changing the face of urban and rural America for the better.

A close second is the Wilderness Act, which has given rise to a tenfold expansion in protected acreage since 1964—now close to 100 million acres—and coincidentally offers the opportunity to secure advances in the protection of North American biodiversity.

In third place is the Delaney Amendment, which is much more than a low-level, pollutants-in-food law. This statute should be best remembered for bringing down DDT and putting in motion a worldwide social revolution against the serious problem of pesticide pollution. In an irony that may yet be too conspicuous to escape the notice of Congress, the cancer studies that helped ban DDT twenty-five years ago have been supplemented dramatically by recent findings implicating the chemical as an indicator of human breast cancer.

In fourth place is section 7 of the ESA, which is the most protective of all domestic environmental laws and admired throughout the world. Much of section 7's influence is measured in hope and not results. But the U.S. courts have embraced this protective law, which has accounted for no small number of impressive victories for the creatures of the North American continent.

In fifth place is section 102 of NEPA, which has been replicated in rapid fashion throughout the United States and around the world. NEPA is the most frequently copied and most frequently cited of all U.S. domestic environmental laws. It also must be credited with significant gains in environmental quality on many fronts, although there is some disagreement at the margins of this proposition.

My sixth-place finisher is section 301 of the Clean Water Act, which deserves a lion's share of the credit for the significant gains in the quality of U.S. surface waters in the last quarter century.

In seventh place is section 107 of CERCLA. In thirteen short years, this statute has thoroughly revolutionized commercial property management and exchange in the United States. More than any other single enactment, section 107 has brought environmental law into the blue-ribbon law firms of every major city. In no small way, this statute has transformed the practice of environmental law from fringe novelty to mainstream reality.

Another perspective on the influence of this wondrous seven is to ask whether anybody has noticed. Turned around in this fashion, one is hard put to identify seven more controversial landmarks on the contemporary legal and political landscape. Land acquisitions and wilderness set-asides are under attack by the "wise-use" and other landowner movements. The Delaney "paradox" has tied Congress in knots for the last decade. Section 7 and other features of the ESA are under perpetual reconsideration, with the spotted owl adding new fuel to these flames. Congress has nibbled away at NEPA with sufficient frequency so as to give rise to a separate literature on the subject. Section 301 of the CWA has been exposed as the epitome of a "command and control" statute, a pejorative of no small moment among legal academics who claim to know something about environmental law. As of this writing, the legislative reauthorization process of section 107 of CERCLA is underway and Congress is receiving a barrage of new information about transaction costs, gross unfairness, and the legal springs and traps that haunt this unpopular law.

Most remarkable about this process, though, is that many believe that these seven extraordinary laws have become virtually repeal-proof. According to this view, the details can change; screens, clouds, and shrouds can appear; decelerators and modifiers can emerge; but the central features of these seven statutes will remain unchanged as a kind of functional constitutional law. Whether or not this estimate is accurate, the suggestion encourages a closer look at the common features of these seven impressive laws. What are the ingredients of a great environmental law?

## Common Features of the Seven Statutory Wonders

Undoubtedly, a host of different theories of congressional behavior, political timing, constituency service, and what-not might be unfurled to explain the striking trajectory of a successful law. This Essay focuses on (1) strong leadership; (2) an inspirational and even radical message; (3) growth and sleeper potential; (4) research implantation; and (5) attentive monitoring.

### Strong Leadership

One conspicuous feature of the super seven is that these laws were advanced by strong leaders—respected and powerful members of Congress, savvy staffers, influential outsiders—sometimes all three. Entrepreneurial skills, sheer passion, and force of will figured in the outcome. The Delaney Amendment was the product of a crusty

New York City congressman who was moved to help a friend who was worried about the long-range effects of the post–World War II pesticides. The name most closely associated with the Land and Water Conservation Fund Act is Stewart Udall, the highly respected Secretary of Interior in the Kennedy Administration, and a card-carrying environmentalist. Although the Wilderness Act was a long time in incubation and boasts a list of sponsors that grows as memories fade, it was written by non-lawyer and nonmember of Congress, Howard Zahniser of the Wilderness Society, which might account for the superior quality of the prose. . . .

The first message, then is that great laws are the product of great deeds. The process of enactment is chaotic and unpredictable, to be sure, but opportunity is not waiting on every corner. A close analogy, perhaps, is the process of extraordinary scientific discovery, which is filled with enough accidents to be called "serendipity," but comes only to those who created the opportunities and are in a position to seize them.

## The Inspirational and Radical Message

A second conspicuous and surprising feature of these laws is that they lack the compromised and ambiguous form normally associated with an act of Congress. This bold portrait may be part mirage because trade-offs may be buried elsewhere in what is always a complex legislative picture. Or it may be partly attributed to the entrepreneurial verve that brings these laws into being. But something more seems to be involved. In the first place, these laws successfully make connection with what can best be described as a widely shared human sense of justice and fair dealing. The genius of Delaney is that it hit upon a theme—who would put cancer in our food?—with a universal appeal that continues to stymie the most clever of legislative second guessers. The Land and Water Conservation Fund Act was moved by images of children of many colors coming together in public playgrounds. Recreational opportunities for the poor and underprivileged were a prominent theme of this Act, which became the first and most successful step in what has recently become known as the "environmental justice movement."

The Wilderness Act succeeded in tapping the psychological and emotional roots—some would say religious feelings—that tie humans to the pristine physical environments that are part of our distant evolutionary history. NEPA exploited the popular cautionary principle by identifying government as the culprit at a time when technological blunder and agency boosterism had become empirically unmistakable. Section 7 of the ESA appeals to similar sentiments, not to mention the emotional attachment to other living creatures that is shared by many members of the species of *Homo sapiens*. Again, who could stand up and argue for the entitlement of public officials to kill, maim, or cripple the few members of a species close to the brink of extinction? The Clean Water Act, too, has an inspirational core that challenges the very morality of dumping pollutants into the community water supply. CERCLA expresses the same sort of contempt for polluters and their legally derived refinements of fault that stand in the way of retaliation. The ruling proposition is that the "polluters pay," and behind this proposition is the sentiment that they should pay. After all, they made the earth uninhabitable, we did not. Polluters are perfectly appropriate lightning rods for the moralistic aggression sent their way.

The more interesting part of the story, though, is that the moralism of these laws is unbounded. Protections are relentless, paybacks unforgiving, qualifiers swept away. On this level, these seven great laws are radical, extremist, and absolutist. *No* cancer-causing substances in the food? Even to the tune of parts per trillion? Natural carcinogens in infinitesimal amounts? And is the march to parkland so irresistible that the park becomes the paradigm and the people the spectators? Does the wilderness really care if a few hammers and nails put in a functional appearance? NEPA extends to *all* federal actions with significant effects. The ESA can stop the project *without* regard to cost. The Clean Water Act says *no* discharge of any pollutants, and it backs this up with the no-discharge goal of subsection 101(a)(1), which simply says that the discharge of pollutants into navigable waters shall be eliminated by 1985. The hypothetical reach of CERCLA liability is often illustrated by the fable of the high school chemistry teacher who makes the mistake of sending a small amount of laboratory waste to the Hanford nuclear reservation for treatment: This individual is jointly and severally liable for the entire fifty billion dollars or so that will be needed to clean up the Hanford facilities.

Some writers have dwelt on the difference between *goals* statutes built upon aspirations and *rules* statutes that are meant to happen. My aim, however, is not to discuss whether the rules on the ground will catch up to the goals on the books. Rather, it is to show that statement and overstatement, rules and goals, duty and aspiration are all part of the same successful package. These are daredevil laws and are much admired for it; audacity is an integral part of the successful package. People can subscribe to the visionary missions of wholesome food, pristine wilderness, and clean water. Nobody takes to the streets in support of marginal cost.

### Growth and "Sleeper" Potential

A strong leader sometimes can sell generalities with the details to follow. For this reason, many of these great laws did not confront opposition at the moment of enactment. Several of them, moreover, were enacted as "sleepers" in the sense that the full reach and application of the legislative hand were not imagined at the moment of enactment. Like weeds in a field, these great laws suddenly appeared without the usual residue of legislative reflection, give and take, trading and compromise.

That great law is in large measure inadvertent law is a proposition that many might doubt, so let me reinforce the conclusion with a few examples. The conventional account of the expansion in the influence of Delaney is that extraordinary technological developments in our ability to detect chemicals in food since 1958 have rendered obsolete the "zero tolerance" standard that the amendment represents. Thus, according to this view, a law that in 1958 meant to exclude a few offending chemicals from the food supply now threatens our agricultural way of life because of wholly unanticipated technological change. Similar tales of evolutionary change, legislative surprise, and unexpected application attend the other great laws. NEPA, enacted without expectation of lawsuit, has produced thousands of lawsuits. The ESA slipped through for the benefit of a few warm and cuddly mammals, and now section 7 is being unfurled in the interests of plants, mice, and insects. CERCLA emerged at the eleventh hour with limited ambitions, and has become a legal monster. Section 301 of the Clean Water Act was itself not a sleeper; however, the principle it embraced was a reincarnation of the 1899 Refuse Act, which has a "no discharge" ultimatum that is one of the great sleepers of our time.

Obviously, these great laws do not remain "sleepers" for long. Their influence quickly becomes conspicuous and impressive. But the key to success in law, as in other evolutionary systems, is in getting started. The contributions of the leader and the sleeper features help these great laws get started. Their inspirational character assures maintenance and nourishment by enthusiastic constituencies. Other support for these laws is found in their scientific anchorage, discussed in the following section.

*Research Implantation*

While causes and effects are obscure, another feature of the seven great laws is their ability to attract and hold scientific constituencies and to generate scientific questions. This result may be an accidental artifact of the breadth and reach of these laws, a fallout consequence of their spectacular influence, or a necessary ingredient built into the legal structure that contributes to the credibility of the endeavor. All of these laws have a scientific component, and some of them have contributed in no small way to advancing the particular sciences with which they are associated. For example, the entire Clean Water Act has generated a host of questions on subjects such as chemistry, biology, hydrology, and land morphology. The ESA is closely associated with a variety of new work in population and conservation biology, CERCLA with a number of sciences related to groundwater, and the Delaney Amendment with the toxicology, epidemiology, and other sciences brought to bear in the real world of risk assessment. Interestingly, the Wilderness Act came into being with a specific research component, and who would be surprised? The whole idea of setting lands apart in protective status suggests the notion of a "natural" baseline, which has obvious implications for scientific comparisons with properties that might be treated differently. NEPA, of course, is definite in its embrace of the science of ecology, and the central idea of predictive impact statements cries out for follow-up research to validate or contradict the predictions.

It is hard to tell what to make of the scientific connections found in the great environmental laws. Here is one possibility: All of these laws assert bold propositions about humans, nature, and the physical environment—for example, carcinogenic toxics should be excluded from the food supply, pollutants should be banned from the water, and the habitat of endangered species should be absolutely protected. If one puts aside the normative content, what remains are striking scientific hypotheses: Introducing animal carcinogens to human food will produce human cancers; discharging pollutants into water will result in dead fish; endangered species can survive only if their habitats are protected. In an indirect way, the Dingells, Muskies, and Delaneys of the world advance propositions about how nature works that are as challenging as those advanced by Einstein, Hubble, or Turing. Needless to say, scientists will respond to the challenge.

### Attentive Monitoring

With the exception of the Land and Water Conservation Fund Act, and perhaps the Wilderness Act, all of the great laws are prohibitive, and sweepingly so. This means that there will be compliance problems. How well do these great laws exploit various mechanisms of social control—such as self-monitoring, neighbor monitoring, formal legal sanctions, and market influences—that are identified in the literature? Reasonably well, which leads us to another secret to the success of a great law.

At first glance there appears to be nothing unusual or especially effective about how these laws exploit traditional legal sanctions or market influences. Indeed, these two staples of environmental law enforcement are largely missing from the pages of the great laws. Occasionally, one can find a prosecution for discharging without a permit, the dumping of hazardous waste, or the taking of endangered species. But the numbers are hardly impressive, and it is difficult to believe that one-step-ahead-of-the-prosecutor fears figure, in any meaningful way, in the record of compliance with the great seven laws. Similarly, economic incentives are not prominent on this scene in a practical sense, not to mention the problem that many of these absolutist prohibitions forbid behavior that is expected and encouraged by the underlying economic theory. The "reasonable person" of economic theory does not withhold all discharges into the water, avoid negligible insults in food, or throw away a dam to save a tiny fish. It is also difficult to embrace any scenarios of maniacal enforcement, business reputation, and so on, that encourage reliable compliance as a matter of sound economic choice. . . .

Some progress might be made on the compliance front by recognizing that the inspirational messages of the seven great laws advance the cause of self-monitoring as manifested by the pangs of conscience, accumulated remorse, or even the fears of supernatural retribution. The inspirational tones of Delaney, the Endangered Species Act, and the Clean Water Act obviously can reach observers and sympathizers, but they can also be heard by would-be offenders. The business world is not filled exclusively with people who resist the killing of endangered species or the polluting of food with carcinogens only if benefits are likely to exceed costs.

With this said, the triumph of these laws is that they successfully exploit what I describe as "attentive monitoring." This includes personal activities such as face-to-face observation, emotions such as shame and pride, and group sanctions such as ostracism and citizen lawsuits. Structural legal changes often facilitate this attentive monitoring. The business of federal land acquisition is furthered obviously by an identifiable source of funds, but it is also assisted by a personalized, hands-on lawmaking in the Congress that makes each transaction very much a small-numbers game. Wilderness set-asides create constituency managers and users that are highly motivated and keenly attentive to abusive practices. Both NEPA and the ESA have elaborate consultative arrangements where the proposals of the agencies are displayed to friend and foe alike, criticized and refashioned, and bound up in commitments of various sorts—with varying degrees of credibility—among the principals. Compliance in the early stages is high because everyone is watching. Eventually, compliance breaks down as time, space, and personnel changes displace attentive monitoring with formal monitoring. Section 301 of the Clean Water Act long was backed by a highly effective citizen-suit mechanism that only in recent years has been dismantled by Supreme Court decisions. The genius of section 107 of CERCLA is that it exploits the model of nuisance law by strengthening the legal hand of the owner whose property is polluted; this is the epitome of face-to-face, neighbor-to-neighbor enforcement. Delaney lacks an effective day-to-day system of attentive monitoring, which might help explain its general reputation for being widely violated.

The important point is that great laws cannot stand indefinitely on the reputation of the leader, the inspiration of the message, or the interest of the scientific community. Somehow, the zeal that brought these laws into being must be sustained at the level of monitoring and enforcement.

## Conclusion

The secrets of the seven great environmental laws are simple enough: All that is needed is a messianic leader with a stirring message containing seeds of growth in a sustainable environment. In practice, legal oases of this sort are few and far between.

*Howard A. Latin*

# Regulatory Failure, Administrative Incentives, and the New Clean Air Act (1991)

. . . Congress has enacted dozens of ambitious environmental protection programs in the past quarter-century, but regulatory implementation has seldom conformed to legislative expectation and rarely if ever achieved the desired degree of protection. Indeed, the gap between the text and implementation of environmental laws has grown so wide that most regulatory practices cannot be understood by studying the applicable legislation. The central lesson of this history is that good implementation, not good legislative intentions, is the key to effective environmental protection. . . .

. . . [C]omplexity and scientific uncertainty, diverse private and public interests, and sharply conflicting values are inescapable attributes of environmental policy making. Given the difficulty of the ecological, biological, economic, and political issues that regulators must confront, no environmental protection program does nor could function in an ideally efficient manner. After reviewing past attempts to implement pollution control programs, I [previously have reached] two thematic conclusions:

1) The most "efficient" regulatory strategies in theory will frequently be the least effective in practice because they (a) require more information, resources, and administrative effort, (b) raise issues beyond the state of scientific knowledge, and (c) allow greater opportunities for obstructive behavior by affected interest groups.

2) Implementation constraints that degraded the performance of command-and-control regulatory approaches, such as high decision making costs, scientific uncertainty, and strategic behavior, would also impair the effectiveness of proposed regulatory reforms including fine-tuning and economic incentive programs. No regulatory

Howard A. Latin, Regulatory Failure, Administrative Incentives, and the New Clean Air Act, 21 Envt'l L. 1647 (1991).

critique can be complete or sensible unless it carefully assesses how its recommendations may misfire under realistic implementation conditions.

This Article again emphasizes the critical importance of implementation, but it develops a different thesis: *There are inherent limits to legislative control of regulatory behavior, and effective implementation consequently requires more careful attention to the institutional incentives of agencies and to the professional and personal incentives of regulators than Congress has recognized.*

Regulatory failure is a complex phenomenon with many causes and manifestations. In contrast to the prevailing administrative law focus on imperfect legislation and judicial review, I believe the seeds of regulatory failure are most often grounded in the intrinsic characteristics of regulatory processes. Society asks regulators to do impossible things; we ask them to do difficult things under impossible time and resource constraints; we ask them to behave decisively, selflessly, heroically in ways that are incompatible with normal modes of human behavior. We may be disappointed when regulation falls short of legislative ideals, but we should not be surprised—for regulatory agencies remain imperfect human institutions and administrators are human beings no better or worse than most. Vast theoretical literatures have developed on regulatory reform and interpretation of regulatory statutes, while systemic limitations on legislative control of administrative behavior have received much less attention. . . .

. . . Congress cannot command agencies or administrators to disregard diverse political, economic, and professional factors that affect the implementation burdens and popularity of regulatory programs. Legislators must instead learn to create agency and bureaucratic incentives that may indirectly encourage desired regulatory behavior. High-level administrators similarly cannot compel bureaucrats to ignore various professional and personal considerations. Agency managers must therefore also learn to develop incentive systems that will induce better regulatory performance. I do not contend that attention to administrative incentives can solve all regulatory problems, but I believe Congress will continue to repeat past mistakes until it recognizes that the discrepancy between environmental goals and implementation cannot be remedied simply by drafting more and more detailed statutes. A realistic assessment of implementation constraints and related incentives is essential if legislators are to revitalize existing environmental protection programs and develop effective new ones.

## Eight "Laws" of Administrative Behavior

The gap between environmental laws and implementation can be explained partly by budget and personnel constraints, shifts in American economic circumstances, and the Reagan Administration's overt hostility to government regulation. If these were the main causes of ineffective environmental control programs, regulation could be improved simply by allocating more resources to "better" bureaucrats. I believe, however, that inaction and inefficient action were predictable results of the difficult implementation problems confronting all environmental regulators. Yet, most environmental statutes devoted little attention to how agencies and their staff would function under severe implementation constraints.

For heuristic purposes, I have chosen to describe agency and bureaucratic responses to implementation constraints in terms of several "laws" of administrative behavior. These are not laws in a Newtonian sense; they describe customary modes of regulatory behavior, and occasional counter-examples would not invalidate them. If agencies *usually* obey these laws regardless of the content of particular organic statutes, a better understanding of administrative incentives and the limits of legislative control is necessary for the development of effective environmental protection programs.

### A. In Conflicts Between Political Considerations and Technocratic Requirements, Politics Usually Prevails

In a seminal article published nearly two decades ago, Louis Jaffe contended that agencies cannot function absent widespread political support, regardless of how much authority the regulatory statutes appear to provide.[1] Experience with many environmental programs confirms Professor Jaffe's generalization, or at least shows that administrators themselves believe it. Environmental regulation is an expensive and controversial enterprise that may impact on innumerable activities. It cannot be surprising, then, that agencies often respond to political and social circumstances not enumerated, and sometimes clearly excluded, in the applicable legislation. . . .

### B. Agencies Avoid Making Regulatory Decisions That Would Create Severe Social or Economic Dislocation

. . . Legislative attempts to confine the scope of administrative discretion cannot prevent agencies from considering the political and economic consequences of their decisions because regulators must be concerned about possible erosion of public support for their agencies and their regulatory missions. Most environmental statutes were passed by overwhelming majorities in Congress, but that record in no way ensures continued congressional support if agency decisions disproportionately affect particular states or regions. Social dislocation and competitive disadvantages from environmental regulation will invariably provoke intense opposition that from an agency's perspective may lead to many undesirable consequences. Administrators will therefore avoid these kinds of politically controversial choices if Congress fails to provide unambiguous and unqualified directions. EPA correctly noted the absence of any legislative consensus on acid rain issues in the 1980s, and no existing statutory authority could make the Agency intrude where Congress feared to tread.

---

[1]Jaffe, The Illusion of the Ideal Administration, 86 Harv. L. Rev. 1183, 1198 (1973).

## C. Agencies Avoid Resolving Disputed Issues Unless They Can Render Scientifically Credible Judgments

. . . Some commentators contend that Congress must force agencies to address the "right" environmental issues, even if resolution of those issues requires "innumerable guesses." This assumes that when Congress says "guess," agencies invariably will guess. Past regulatory experience suggests the opposite, that agencies usually refuse to make speculative judgments. The legislative histories of many environmental statutes indicate that Congress was aware of serious information gaps and yet mandated imposition of protective controls despite the uncertainty. EPA officials nonetheless proved unable or unwilling to develop the necessary scientific findings. With regard to toxic controls under the CAA and CWA, groundwater contamination, pesticide residues, and acid rain precursors, for example, EPA had ample statutory authority for regulation but would not resolve the difficult technical and policy issues posed by these problems.

If one examines administrative behavior realistically, there are numerous reasons why regulators would resist any statutory prescription to "guess." EPA and other agencies must function in a setting where every factual finding, scientific inference, and policy choice is vigorously contested by affected parties. Agency judgments must also survive intensive judicial review in which regulators normally bear the burden of proving regulatory decisions are rational and supported by substantial evidence. If agencies concede they have had to guess, their decisions may become fair game for interest-group and media ridicule; yet, a realistic administrator would not expect much legislative support if the wolves begin howling. Environmental protection programs often entail high regulatory costs that agencies may be reluctant to impose on the basis of speculation, but that is precisely the effect of regulation under uncertainty. Finally, but not least important, officials responsible for complex technical decisions will often try to protect their image of professional competence by complying with norms of the disciplines in which they are trained. Good scientists are often unwilling to guess about indeterminate issues, even if good regulators should not be. . . .

## D. Agencies Will Not Meet Statutory Deadlines If Budget Appropriations, Personnel, Information, or Other Resources Are Inadequate

This "law" of administrative behavior is in part a corollary of the preceding one. No matter how precise and emphatic the deadlines prescribed in environmental statutes may be, agencies will not meet target dates unless they can support regulatory determinations with credible scientific, economic, or political rationales. When agencies lack adequate information, personnel, budget allocations, or other essential resources, inaction and further "study" will generally be more attractive bureaucratic options than imposing expensive control requirements on the basis of superficial analyses—analyses that are likely to be the subject of extensive criticism by affected interest groups and politicians. . . .

## E. Regulators Are Influenced by Disciplinary Norms That May Conflict with Statutory Mandates

In an insightful 1972 essay that deserves to be more widely read, Ned Bayley described several reasons for the reluctance of regulators in the 1960s to respond to problems raised by Rachel Carson's *Silent Spring* and growing political concern about the environmental effects of pesticide usage.[2] Bayley noted that the U.S. Department of Agriculture's (USDA) pesticide division, which he directed, was placed within the agency's research office and was dominated by a scientific viewpoint. This scientific orientation led USDA bureaucrats to emphasize the weakness of some of Carson's evidence, to dismiss harmful effects not proven with reasonable scientific certainty, to request more funding for long-term pesticide research than for regulation, to adopt the extended timeframe typical of scientific research, and to underestimate the political clout of the nascent environmental movement. Bayley concluded: "Although scientific data are essential to decisionmaking on pesticide regulations, I believe (as a scientist who has had to modify his thinking drastically as an administrator) that having a regulatory function operate under a science-dominated administration is a mistake." . . .

## F. Bureaucrats Are Conditioned by Criticism or Other Forms of Negative Feedback

I have found little evidence that EPA and other agencies are "captured" by regulated interests as a result of bribes or career opportunities for bureaucrats who adopt pro-industry policies. More subtle influences, however, often do condition the behavior of administrators in favor of regulated interests. Agency officials, like most human beings, prefer to avoid criticism and controversy whenever possible. Industry representatives appear regularly in agency proceedings and can usually afford to offer detailed comments and criticisms on possible agency decisions, while environmental groups intervene on an intermittent basis and the unorganized public seldom participates at all. This routine asymmetry will increase agency responsiveness to industry criticisms. No matter how sincere and public-spirited officials are when appointed, a process of negative feedback will produce shifts toward the positions espoused by regulated parties. Given cognitive dissonance, agency personnel may fail to recognize when they have made undesirable accommodations to lessen criticism of their decisions. . . .

## G. Agency Behavior Is Partly Conditioned by Manipulative Tactics of Regulated Parties

Industry often has large economic interests at stake and may be willing to expend commensurate efforts in agency proceedings to weaken or delay prospective environmental controls. Agencies are, moreover, required by administrative law and judicial review to consider in detail most industry evidence and arguments. When agencies find the mandated consideration creates a severe drain on their resources or

[2]See Bayley, Memoirs of a Fox, 2 Envt'l Aff. 332 (1972–1973).

otherwise prevents them from making timely progress, they may reach a "compromise" position that industry accepts precisely because it is relatively lenient. Manipulative behavior by affected interests is the regulatory norm rather than the exception. Mashaw and Harfst characterized actions of the automobile manufacturers in NHTSA proceedings as an "all court press" that successfully defeated proposed safety regulations. Strategic behavior by industry and environmental groups is just as prevalent in EPA regulatory proceedings. Indeed, Professor Rodgers recently suggested that commentators should ordinarily adopt a "game theory" view of environmental regulation, replete with "manipulation," "fakery," "dissembling," and "betrayal." . . .

## H. Administrators of Multiple-Purpose Statutes Usually "Simplify" the Decisional Process to Emphasize Only One or Two Statutory Goals

This eighth "law" of administrative behavior reflects many considerations previously discussed—scientific, professional, budgetary, and political. . . . There are numerous reasons why regulatory agencies prefer to emphasize a limited set of goals even when the applicable statute mandates balancing of many competing considerations. An agency's staff may have expertise in some areas and not in others required by environmental protection missions. Any requirement to examine and balance a multitude of criteria will increase budget and time demands, and may detract from an agency's ability to perform the functions it has traditionally managed. The more objectives an agency must consider, the more certain it becomes that regulators will be subjected to constant criticism and lobbying activities by diverse affected parties. Organized groups representing some statutory objectives will normally be able to maintain closer contact with agency staff and provide more effective criticism than adherents of competing interests who may interact with regulators on only an intermittent basis. Organized interest groups may also attain more political leverage on specific issues through their ability to generate campaign funds for politicians at all levels of government. Agency officials who live among the constituents most directly affected by the economic impacts of regulatory decisions, such as ranchers or lumberjacks, may come to share the values and priorities of people with whom they have daily contact. Local officials may be especially sensitive to the social and economic dislocation resulting from environmental protection policies in areas dependent upon resource exploitation industries for jobs and taxes.

Aside from these various external influences, agencies may choose to focus on only a few statutory goals in response to pressures exerted by their own regulatory culture. Organizations require criteria on which to evaluate their performance and that of their staff, but some objectives are more amenable than others to the development of clear and consistent performance standards. For example, while the Forest Service can easily determine how many thousand board-feet of timber are yielded by each national forest every year and can make rough estimates of recreational use based on annual camping permits and vehicle entries, there is no comparable "objective" way for the Service to assess the value of wilderness preservation and watershed protection activities. If the performance of policemen is partly measured in terms of arrests made or tickets issued, it should not be surprising when agencies try to measure performance in a similarly quantitative manner: number of permits negotiated by EPA or state officials (the effectiveness of pollution controls incorporated in each permit is not as easily determinable); revenues obtained by the Forest Service and Bureau of Land Management from timber and grazing programs (long-term ecological harm from these programs cannot be easily measured); barrels of oil or kilowatt-hours of expanded energy production (harmful effects of these resource exploitation programs cannot be as readily determined and may fall outside the jurisdiction of the energy agency). . . .

Environmentalists often complain that regulatory agencies have been "captured" by the industries or activities they are supposed to control. To the extent this perception is accurate, the factors identified [here] are more important causes of the "capture" phenomenon than is the venality of some administrative officials. I believe the characterization of bureaucratic "rent-seeking" in many law and economics critiques of regulation is abstract and sterile to the point of irrelevance. Anyone who has extensive contacts with regulators will find the great majority are sincere, intelligent people who take pride in their vision of the public interest. Yet, problems invariably arise in defining the public interest under incompatible regulatory goals and in maintaining administrators' commitments to the public interest as they are beaten down by the never-ending exigencies of regulatory life. Congress can seldom eliminate the external and internal pressures described here by adding another statutory goal or by directing agencies to reassign the priorities of competing and partly conflicting goals.

I considered including two more "laws" of administrative behavior: *Short-term "crises" come to dominate most regulatory processes, while problems that require long-range commitments of agency resources are underemphasized;* and *The "squeaky wheel" gets the regulatory grease.* However, these tendencies for the most part appear to be consequences of previously identified behavioral factors, including budgetary and personnel constraints, agency concern for political support, and bureaucratic aversion to criticism. Other commentators might produce a different set of behavioral "laws" and could doubtless cite many other agency decisions to illustrate my list of generalized rules. The number and arrangement of "laws" is not important—the central point is that congressional control of agency behavior is limited in many intractable ways, and legislators must therefore learn to create administrative incentives that will indirectly promote regulatory activities or attitudes they cannot simply mandate. Legislators and other policy makers cannot simply identify the social goals, priorities, and procedures they want implemented. They must also devote close attention to the kinds of questions that regulatory agencies are expected to resolve and to professional and personal motivations that influence the behavior of agency officials.

# CHAPTER 11

---

# Risk Assessment and Regulatory Priorities

How should society decide basic questions of health and safety, such as what risks to regulate and how safe is "safe"? Should regulators answer these questions by responding to public concerns, or should we entrust experts to determine what is good for us? This chapter explores these issues which involve questions concerning the role science should play in the regulatory processs. It considers whether regulatory policy would be improved by placing greater reliance on risk assessment and less emphasis on responding to what the public believes to be the most pressing environmental concerns. The readings in the chapter review some of the criticisms of quantitative risk assessment and the policy implications of using risk assessment to set regulatory priorities. The chapter examines some of the difficulties involved in educating the public about risks and the implications for participatory democracy of giving scientists a larger role in establishing regulatory priorities.

Risk assessment is a systematic process used to identify and characterize the nature and significance of risks from particular substances, pollutants, or activities. It involves three initial steps: hazard identification (does a substance cause cancer or other adverse effects?), dose-response assessment (how potent a carcinogen is it?), and exposure assessment (how many humans are exposed to the substance, for how long, and at what levels?). The final step in the risk assessment process is to use the information obtained through the first three steps to characterize the significance of the risk (how many people will get cancer from exposure to the substance, or what is the likelihood that any particular exposed individual will get cancer?).

The use of risk assessment in regulatory policy making has been controversial. As a result of a Supreme Court decision in 1980 that directed OSHA to determine that risks were significant prior to regulating workplace toxins,[1] agencies began performing risk assessments more frequently. During his second term as EPA administrator, William Ruckelshaus was an enthusiastic proponent of using risk assessment to help the agency decide whether or not to regulate, and how stringently to regulate, toxic substances. He recognized the enormous uncertainties involved in risk assessment and the dangers of giving supposed experts the responsibility for making major public health decisions. In the reading below, Ruckelshaus addresses the difficulty of building public confidence in risk assessment when the public's assessment of risk is systematically different from that of the "experts." He stresses the importance of improving communication and public debate over risk management policy, describing an experiment in public education which he tried when the EPA was considering how stringently to regulate arsenic emissions from an old copper smelter in Tacoma, Washington.

Environmentalist David Doniger decries Ruckelshaus's approach as a campaign to require the public to accept more risk. Doniger argues that it is immoral to trade off lives for economic benefit and that such an approach would be inconsistent with the health-based standard for regulating toxic air pollutants under Section 112 of the Clean Air Act. Section 112 requires the EPA to provide an "ample margin of safety" to protect the public against exposure to hazardous air pollutants. Because the EPA had regulated only a handful of substances in twenty years of experience with this provision, it was amended in 1990 to require the initial application of a maximum-achievable-control-technology approach to nearly two hundred hazardous air pollutants. Citing the enormous uncertainties and data gaps that confront most risk assessment exercises, environmentalists initially were critical of placing greater reliance on risk assessment in decision making. More recently, representatives of regulated industries have questioned whether risk assessments are too conservative and systematically overstate environmental risks because of precautionary assumptions they employ.

The EPA has become an enthusiastic proponent of using risk assessment to help set regulatory priorities. In two comparative risk assessment studies, *Unfinished Business* and *Reducing Risk,* the EPA determined that its regulatory priorities are much more in line with the general public's ranking of environmental concerns than with the opinions of experts. Agency officials argue that they should be given more flexibility to reorder regulatory priorities to reflect the experts' assessments.

Richard Stewart was a proponent of comparative risk assessment even before the EPA studies were undertaken. He discusses the roles that courts and administrative agencies should play to respond to the "portfolio of risks" society faces. Stewart argues that many regulatory statutes rest on the false premise that it is possible to distinguish between "safe" and "unsafe" levels of exposure to toxins when in fact no clear safe thresholds exist. While cautioning that courts are not free to ignore the laws as written, he suggests that they at least can help expose some of the erroneous assumptions on which the laws are based. Stewart recommends that administrators and the courts be creative in their interpretation and implementation of the laws to

---

[1] *Industrial Union Department, AFL-CIO v. American Petroleum Institute,* 448 U.S. 607 (1980).

incorporate a "risk portfolio" approach. Under this approach, an agency could justify less than full-fledged regulation of a particular risk by demonstrating that it instead was focusing on other, more serious problems.

Professor Donald Hornstein criticizes the use of comparative risk assessment as a primary decision tool for regulators. Hornstein argues that basing regulatory decisions on comparative risk assessments may actually undermine environmental protection policy rather than making it more rational. He notes that the simple, expected value analysis that risk assessments produce fails to consider important subjective factors such as individual risk aversion, and it ignores differences in the benefits produced by different risks, as well as the distribution of risks. Hornstein argues that an important attribute of environmental law is that "it must be able to reflect and define our values, not simply count how many of us will suffer." By focusing primarily on one attribute of risk—aggregate effects on population—comparative risk assessment disserves decision making, according to Hornstein, "by masking rather than revealing the full dimensions of public health risks." If comparative risk assessment is used to shift priorities away from risks of greatest concern to the public, Hornstein argues, its decisions will be "despised as antidemocratic," undermining its legitimacy as a policy tool. He also claims that reliance on comparative risk assessment will make it more difficult to pursue holistic policies that address the underlying causes of environmental problems because it will focus attention on discrete treatment of what often are arbitrarily-defined categories of risks.

# William D. Ruckelshaus

# Risk in a Free Society (1984)

When I began my current, and second, tenure as Administrator of the Environmental Protection Agency (EPA), my first goal was the restoration of public confidence in the Agency, and it was impressed upon me that straightening out the way we handled health risk was central to achieving it. Needless to say, EPA's primary mission is the reduction of risk, whether to public health or the environment. Some in America were afraid. They were afraid that toxic chemicals in the environment were affecting their health, and more important, they suspected that the facts about the risks from such chemicals were not being accurately reported to them, that policy considerations were being inappropriately used in such reports, so as to make the risks seem less than they were and excuse the Agency from taking action. Even worse, some people thought that the processes we had established to protect public health were being abused for crass political gain.

Whether this was true or not is almost beside the point; a substantial number of people believed it. Now in a society such as ours, where the people ultimately decide policy—what they want done about a particular situation—the fair exposition of policy choices is the job of public agencies. The public agency is the repository of the facts; you can't operate a democratic society, particularly a complex technological one, unless you have such a repository. Above all, the factual guardian must be trusted; a failure of trust courts chaos. Chaos, in turn, creates its own thirst for order, which craving in its more extreme forms threatens the very foundation of democratic freedom. So in a democracy a public agency that is not trusted, especially where the protection of public health is concerned, might as well close its doors.

I described a possible solution to this problem last June in a speech to the National Academy of Sciences. The Academy had stated in a recent report that federal agencies had often confused the assessment of risk with the management of risk. Risk assessment is the use of a base of scientific research to define the probability of some harm

William D. Ruckelshaus, Risk in a Free Society, 14 Envt'l L. Rep. 10190 (1984). Reprinted with permission.

RISK IN A FREE SOCIETY   339

coming to an individual or a population as a result of exposure to a substance or situation. Risk management, in contrast, is the public process of deciding what to do where risk has been determined to exist. It includes integrating risk assessment with considerations of engineering feasibility and figuring out how to exercise our imperative to reduce risk in the light of social, economic, and political factors.

The report proposed that these two functions be formally separated with regulatory agencies. I said that this appeared to be a workable idea and that we would try to make it happen at EPA. This notion was attractive because the statutes administered by many federal regulatory agencies typically force some action when scientific inquiry establishes the presence of a risk, as, for example, when a substance present in the environment, or the workplace, or the food chain, is found to cause cancer in animals. The statutes may require the agency to act according to some protective formula: to establish "margins of safety" or "prevent significant risk" or "eliminate the risk."

When the action so forced has dire economic or social consequences, the person who must make the decision may be sorely tempted to ask for a "reinterpretation" of the data. We should remember that risk assessment data can be like a captured spy: if you torture it long enough, it will tell you anything you want to know. So it is good public policy to so structure an agency that such temptation is avoided.

But we have found that separating the assessment of risk from its management is rather more difficult to accomplish in practice. In the first place, values, which are supposed to be safely sequestered in risk management, also appear as important influences on the outcome of risk assessments. For example, let us suppose that a chemical in common use is tested on laboratory animals with the object of determining whether it can cause cancer. At the end of the test a proportion of the animals that have been exposed to the substance show evidence of tumor formation.

Now the problems begin. First, in tests like these, the doses given are extremely high, often close to the level the animal can tolerate for a lifetime without dying from toxic non-cancer effects. Environmental exposures are typically much lower, so in order to determine what the risk of cancer is at such lower exposures—that is, to determine the curve that relates a certain dose to a certain response—we must extrapolate down from the high-dose laboratory data. There are a number of statistical models for doing this, all of which fit the data, and all of which are open to debate. We simply do not *know* what the shape of the dose-response curve is at low doses, in the sense that we know, let us say, what the orbit of a satellite will be when we shoot it off. . . .

Historically at EPA it has been thought prudent to make what have been called conservative assumptions; that is, in a situation of unavoidable uncertainty, *our* values lead us to couch our conclusions in terms of a plausible upper bound. As a result, when we generate a number that expresses the potency of some substance in causing disease, we can state that it is unlikely that the risk projected is any greater.

This conservative approach is fine when the risks projected are vanishingly small; it is always nice to learn that some chemical is *not* a national crisis. But when the risks estimated through such assessments are substantial, so that some action may be in the offing, the stacking of conservative assumptions one on top of another becomes a problem for the policymaker. If I am going to propose controls that may have serious economic and social effects, I need to have some idea how much confidence to place in the estimates of risk that prompted those controls. I need to know how likely *real* damage is to occur in the uncontrolled and partially controlled and fully controlled cases. Only then can I apply the balancing judgments that are the essence of my job. This, of course, tends to insert the policymaker back into the guts of risk assessment, which we had concluded is less than wise.

This is a real quandary. I now believe that the main road out of it lies through a marked improvement in the way we communicate the realities of risk analysis to the public. The goal is public understanding. We will only retain the administrative flexibility we need to effectively protect the public health and welfare if the public believes we are trying to act in the public interest. There is an argument, in contradiction, that the best way to protection lies in increased legislative specificity, in closely directing the Agency as to what to control and how much to control it. If we fail to command public confidence, this argument will prevail, and in my opinion it would be a bad thing if it did. You cannot squeeze the complexity inherent in managing environmental risks between the pages of a statute book.

How then do we encourage confidence? Generally speaking there are two ways to do it. First, we could assign guardianship of the Agency's integrity—its risk assessment task—to a group of disinterested experts who are above reproach in the public eye. This is the quasi-judicial, blue-ribbon panel approach, which has a strong tradition in our society. If we have a complex issue, we don't have to think about it very much, just give it to the experts, who deliberate and provide the answer, which most will accept because of the inherent prestige of the panel.

The discomfort associated with imagining, in 1984, a conclave of Big Brothers to watch over us only strengthens my conviction that such panels cannot serve the general purpose of restoring and maintaining confidence. It turns out that the experts do not agree, so instead of an unimpeachable and disinterested consensus you get dissenting advocacy. Once again, experts have values too.

Alternatively, we could all become a lot smarter about risk. The Agency could put much more effort into explaining what it is doing and what it does, and does not, know. Here I do not mean "public involvement" in the usual and formal sense. This is embodied in administrative law and has always been part of our ordinary procedure in promulgating rules. Nor do I mean a mere public relations campaign to popularize agency decisions. Public relations smoothes over; I think we need to dig up. We have to expose the assumptions that go into risk assessments. We have to admit our uncertainties and confront the public with the complex nature of decisions about risk.

Living in a technological society is like riding a bucking bronco. I do not believe we can afford to get off, and I doubt that someone will magically appear who can lead it about on a leash. The question is: how do we become better bronco busters? I think a great part of the answer is to bring about a major improvement in the quality of public debate on environmental risk.

This will not be easy. Risk assessment is a probabilistic calculation, but people do not respond to risks "as they should" if such calculations were the sole criterion of rationality. Most people are not comfortable with mathematical probability as a guide to living and the risk assessment lingo we throw at them does not increase their comfort. Tell someone that their risk of cancer from a 70-year exposure to a carcinogen at ambient levels ranges between $10^{-5}$ and $10^{-7}$, and they are likely to come back at you with, "Yes, but will I get cancer if I drink the water?" Also, attitudes toward risk are subjective and highly colored by personal experience and other factors not fully captured by risk assessments.

We have research that points out that people tend to overestimate the probability of unfamiliar, catastrophic and well-publicized events and underestimate the probability of unspectacular or familiar events that claim one victim at a time. Many people are afraid to fly commercial airlines, but practically nobody is afraid of driving in cars, a victory of subjectivity over actuarial statistics.

In general, response to risks is most negative when the degree of risk is unknown and the consequences are particularly dreaded. Expert assessment does not seem to help here. People will fight like fury to keep a hazardous waste facility out of their neighborhood, despite expert assurances that it is safe, while people living under high dams located on earthquake faults pay scant attention to expert warnings.

Other hazard characteristics influence public perceptions of risk. For example, the voluntary or involuntary nature of the risk is important. People will accept far greater risks from driving an automobile than they will from breathing the emissions that come out of its tail pipe; the former is voluntary, the latter, involuntary. People also take into consideration whether the risk is distributed generally throughout the population or affects only a small identifiable group. Public response to the discovery of a toxicant that may result in 200 additional cancers nationwide is liable to be quite different from public response to the same number of cases in one county with a population of say, 3,000.

The way risks and options are presented also influences perceptions. You might be worried if you heard that occupational exposure at your job doubled your risk of some serious disease; you might be less worried if you heard that it had increased from one-in-a-million to two-in-a-million. Surveys using physicians as subjects found that their preferences for treatment options were expressed in terms of lives saved rather than in terms of deaths occurring, even though the two forms of expression that were compared were mathematically identical. Finally, research has shown that beliefs about risk are slow to change, and show extraordinary persistence in the face of contrary evidence.

Many people interested in environmental protection, having observed this mess, conclude that considerations of risk lead to nothing useful. After all, if the numbers are no good and the whole issue is so confusing, why not just eliminate all exposure to toxics to the extent that technology allows? The problem with such thinking is that, even setting aside what I have just said about the necessity for improving the national debate on the subject, risk estimates are the only way we have of directing the attention of risk management agencies toward significant problems.

There are thousands of substances in the environment that show toxicity in animals; we cannot work on all of them at once, even with an EPA 10 times its current size. More important, technology does not make the bad stuff "go away"; in most cases it just changes its form and location. We have to start keeping track of the flow of toxics through the environment, to what happens *after* they are "controlled." Risk management is the only way I know to do this.

In confused situations one must try to be guided by basic principles. One of my basic principles is reflected in a quotation from Thomas Jefferson: "If we think [the people] not enlightened enough to exercise their control with a wholesome direction, the remedy is not to take it from them, but to inform their discretion." Easy for *him* to say. As we have seen, informing discretion about risk has itself a high risk of failure.

However we do have some recent experience that supports the belief that better information inclines people to act more sensibly. In Tacoma, Washington, we have a situation where a copper smelter employing about 600 people is emitting substantial amounts of arsenic, which is a human carcinogen. We found that the best available technology did not reduce the risk of cancer to levels the public might find acceptable. In fact, it looked as if reducing to acceptable levels of risk might only be possible if the plant closed. I felt very strongly that the people in Tacoma whose lives were affected by my decision ought to have a deeper understanding of the case than they could get from the usual public hearing process.

Accordingly, we organized an extraordinary campaign of public education in Tacoma. Besides the required public hearing, we provided immense quantities of information to all communications media, arranged meetings between community leaders and senior EPA officials, including myself, and held three workshops at which we laid out our view of the facts. I think most people appreciated this opportunity, and we certainly raised the level of discussion about risk. So unusual was this kind of event that some inferred that I was abdicating my responsibility for this decision, or that somehow the Tacoma people were going to vote on whether they wanted jobs or health. After some initial confusion on this score we made it clear that it was entirely my decision, and that while I wanted to hear, I was not committed to heed.

Although I suppose some would have been happier continuing in their fond belief that we could provide absolute safety with absolute certainty, and were disturbed by these proceedings, in all I would call it a qualified success. Those who participated came away with a better understanding of the anatomy of environmental decisions, and local groups were able to come up with options that increased protection while allowing the plant to remain open, options that are well worth considering as we put together our final decision.

What are the lessons of Tacoma? Shortly after we began the workshops, people started sporting buttons that said, "BOTH," meaning they were for both jobs and health. I took this as a good sign, that people were attending to the balance between economic realities and environmental protection. "Both" is a good idea, and in most cases we can have it, if we are smart. Another lesson is that we must improve the way we present risk calculations to the public. There was too much tendency to translate risks of cancer into cases, with no regard for qualifying assumptions and uncertainties. Cancer threats make great headlines and the inclination to infer certainty where none exists is very powerful. We must take seriously our obligation to generate lucid and unambiguous statements about risk. Finally, Tacoma shows that we have to prepare ourselves for other Tacomas. Environmental stress falls unevenly across the land and we have a special responsibility to people in communities that suffer more than their share. We are prepared to make the extra effort in such communities, as we did in Tacoma.

We must also improve debate on the national level. This may prove more difficult, as Washington is a most contentious place. Also, at the national level things tend to polarize perhaps more than they should, given how much we know about environmental health questions. Typically, where we obtain evidence of an environmental threat, opinion divides between those who want to eliminate the risk as quickly as possible, with little concern about cost, and those who deny the threat exists. Fights between these groups can go on for a long time, during which the object of the battle, the pollutant, remains in the environment. . . .

. . . Let me now propose some principles for more reasonable discussions about risk.

First, we must insist on risk calculations being expressed as distributions of estimates and not as magic numbers that can be manipulated without regard to what they really mean. We must try to display more realistic estimates of risk to show a range of probabilities. To help do this we need new tools for quantifying and ordering sources of uncertainty and for putting them in perspective.

Second, we must expose to public scrutiny the assumptions that underlie our analysis and management of risk. If we have made a series of conservative assumptions within the risk assessment, so that it represents an upper bound estimate of risk, we should try to communicate this and explain why we did it. Although public health protection is our primary value, any particular action to control a pollutant may have effects on other values, such as community stability, employment, natural resources, or the integrity of the ecosystem. We have to get away from the idea that we do quantitative analysis to find the "right" decision, which we will then be obliged to make if we want to call ourselves rational beings. But we are not clockwork mandarins. The point of such analysis is, in fact, the orderly exposition of the values we hold, and the reasoning that travels from some set of values and measurements to a decision.

Third, we must demonstrate that reduction of risk is our main concern and that we are not driven by narrow cost-benefit considerations. Of course cost is a factor, because we are obliged to be efficient with our resources and those of society in general. Where we decline to control some risk at present, we should do so only because there are better targets; we are really balancing risk against risk, aiming to get at the greatest first.

Finally, we should understand the limits of quantification; there are some cherished values that will resist being squeezed into a benefits column, but are no less real because of it. Walter Lippman once pointed out that in a democracy "the people" as in "We the People," refers not only to the working majority that actually makes current decisions, and not only to the whole living population, but to those who came before us, who provided our traditions and our physical patrimony as a nation, and to those who will come after us, and inherit. Many of the major decisions we make on environmental affairs touch on this broader sense of public responsibility.

I suppose that the ultimate goal of this effort is to get the American people to understand the difference between a safe world and a zero-risk world with respect to environmental pollutants. We have to define what safe means in light of our increasing ability to detect minute quantities of substances in the environment and to associate carcinogenesis with an enormous variety of substances in common use. According to Bruce Ames, the biochemist and cancer expert, the human diet is loaded with toxics of all kinds, including many carcinogens, mutagens and teratogens. Among them are such foodstuffs as black pepper, mushrooms, celery, parsnips, peanut butter, figs, parsley, potatoes, rhubarb, coffee, tea, fats, browned meat, and alfalfa sprouts. The list goes on; my point is that it would be hard to find a diet that would support life and at the same time impose no risk on the consumer.

So what is safe? Are we all safe at this instant? Most of us would agree that we are, although we are subjected to calculable risks of various sorts of catastrophes that can happen to people listening to lectures in buildings. We might be able to reduce some of them by additional effort, but in general we consider that we have (to coin a phrase) an "adequate margin of safety" sitting in a structure that is, for example, protected against lightning bolts but exposed to meteorites.

I think we can get people to start making those judgments of safety about the arcane products of modern technology. I do not think we are ever going to get agreement about values; a continuing debate about values is the essence of a democratic policy. But I think we must do better in showing how different values lead rationally to different policy outcomes. And we can only do that if we are able to build up a reservoir of trust, if people believe that we have presented fairly what facts we have, that we have exposed our values to their view, and that we have respected their values, whether or not such values can be incorporated finally in our decisions. We have, I hope, begun to build that sort of trust at EPA.

*David Doniger*

# The Gospel of Risk Management: Should We Be Converted? (1984)

William Ruckelshaus is on a crusade to persuade the American public to fundamentally change its ideals about public health and the environment. We should, he says, "accept" risk. We should lower our expectations of the Environmental Protection Agency (EPA). We should not dare to hope for more than "reasonable" protection from carcinogens and other hazards.

There are grave moral and practical consequences to what EPA Administrator Ruckelshaus advocates. Some of these consequences show up plainly in the regulation of hazardous pollutants. EPA has proposed standards for benzene, arsenic, and radionuclides, for example, which many feel fall far short of what is required. Let me highlight four of the generic issues the EPA hazardous pollutant proposals have raised.

## The Ethical Basis for "Risk Management"

When the Administrator urges the American people to accept a philosophy of deliberately trading off lives and health against the economic costs of pollution controls ("risk management"), he is both disregarding the requirements of the Clean Air Act and swimming against the strong tide of public opinion. Section 112 of the Clean Air Act embodies the public's adherence to a fundamental goal that no one should be required to sacrifice his or her life or health on account of air pollution. The testimony and written comments of so many individuals living near the ASARCO smelter in Tacoma, Washington, and elsewhere around the country show that when lives and health are on the line, the general public will not accept a philosophy which abandons that goal and legitimizes such trade-offs. This philosophical and moral rejection

David Doniger, The Gospel of Risk Management: Should We Be Converted? 14 Env'l L. Rep. 10222 (1984). Reprinted with permission.

of the Administrator's policy is not going to change, for such trade-offs are deeply repugnant to most people.

The strength of public feeling on this issue is nothing new. It dates from the 1970 enactment of the Clean Air Act and before. The Administrator's argument is also nothing new. "Risk management" appears to be nothing more than a new name for cost-benefit analysis. No matter what the name it is given, the public consistently rejects it.

The force of this conviction is something that EPA must accept and respond to. EPA has to find a way to administer §112 of the Clean Air Act in a way that respects, rather than offends, this fundamental conviction of the nation's citizens. This means that EPA must embrace, rather than abandon, the health goal of §112.

## The Increase in Danger Deemed "Acceptable"

My second point concerns the historical contrast of these proposals with earlier standards. Taking the Agency's quantitative risk assessments at face value, the benzene, arsenic, and radionuclide proposals indicate EPA's apparent willingness to leave individuals exposed to far higher risks of cancer than were tolerated in past hazardous air pollutant decisions. We are not just referring to the risk assessment for the Tacoma smelter. The quantitative risk estimates for the most exposed persons near some of the other facilities, and near numerous sources that EPA has proposed not to regulate at all, are substantially higher than those implied by hazardous air pollutant standards EPA has set before. They are within a range, I submit, that strikes most people as shocking. This public reaction is partly no more than a corollary of the public's rejection of deliberately making trade-offs between lives and economic costs. But it also reflects a public concern of a comparative nature: now EPA is prepared to supply even less protection from cancer-causing chemicals than it did just a few years ago.

## Fairness for Those Trapped in "Islands of Risk"

My third point has to do with equity. The arsenic proposals do not address the fairness of leaving people trapped in what have been termed "islands of risk." For the people of Tacoma, who are clearly exposed to the highest concentrations of arsenic, the Administrator has deliberately framed the issue as a trade-off between allowing continued high risks of cancer or closing a plant—a grim either-or proposition. The Administrator has failed even to ask a fundamental question of fairness: Doesn't the government, representing the rest of the American people fortunate enough to live in what we think are safer places, owe some form of relief to those who are trapped in the islands of risk? When the dioxin-contaminated town of Times Beach, Missouri, was judged unsafe to inhabit, EPA used Superfund monies to purchase the residents' homes, relieving them of the awful choice between their health or their homes. While the Superfund itself is not available for use regarding air emissions from ASARCO-Tacoma, doesn't the issue of fairness still need to be addressed?

There are feasible options. Such aid could take a variety of forms: low-interest loans to ASARCO for further pollution control investments, or adjustment assistance for displaced employees and for the city, to mention just two. Rather than encourage Tacomans to choose between their health or the smelter, the Administrator could have taken a leadership role to explore such assistance. He still can.

It is no answer to say that such assistance is not provided for by the current terms of §112; the Administrator has not been bashful in suggesting other legislative changes to that provision.

## The Dubious Rationality of "Risk Assessment"

My fourth point is a technical one. The current techniques for estimating the size of cancer risks are not up to the task to which the Administrator has assigned them. They are too uncertain and fragile to be a rational basis for the "risk management" decisions the Administrator wishes to make. Neither knowledge about how chemicals cause cancer once we are exposed, nor techniques for estimating the extent of exposure, are advanced enough to be the primary basis for deciding what substances to regulate and to what degree. The Agency does not have support even for its contention that its estimates are confidently conservative; a variety of factors not taken into account can lead to significant underestimates of risk.

In the arsenic proposals, risk estimates have been put forward as justification for not requiring use of known and practical emissions control technology. In the recent benzene decisions the Administrator has made even heavier use of risk assessments to justify exempting whole categories of sources because of allegedly "small" risks.

Under a precautionary statute that directs EPA to play it safe rather than sorry, quantitative risk assessments are sometimes useful in indicating that a proposed control plan is clearly inadequate. They may also be used to illustrate gross inequities between the protection afforded one group of people versus another, as discussed above. But EPA's use of its current techniques to justify not applying available controls cannot be supported either as a rational application of the statutory criteria or as a sensible public health policy judgment.

Risk assessments are terribly uncertain. Administrator Ruckelshaus would admit that you wouldn't try to send a man into orbit on the strength of these equations. As he wrote in these pages, "We simply do not know what shape of the dose-response curve is at low doses, in the sense that we know, let us say, what the orbit of a satellite will be when we shoot it off." These numbers are no more reliable for protecting public health.

So should we be converted? I think not. Will we be? As far as I can see, the public is not coming around to Mr. Ruckelshaus's point of view.

*Richard B. Stewart*

# The Role of the Courts in Risk Management (1986)

## An Ideal Risk Management System

Our institutions, legal and otherwise, ought to be judged by their fitness for making and carrying out wise social choices. In the area of environmental risk management, such choices should, ideally, respond to the following five principles:

1. Subject to resource constraints, institutions should encourage timely and accurate risk and risk reduction assessment. We confront a portfolio of risks to human health and natural systems, generated by industrial processes, products, and their residuals. The risks vary in magnitude according to the potency of the risk mechanism, the severity and extent of exposure, the size of exposed populations, and other factors. The function of risk assessment is to measure the relative as well as absolute magnitudes of the risks contained in the portfolio.

The risks also vary according to the extent to which they can be reduced by a given commitment to societal resources. The extent of reduction depends upon the availability and efficacy of technology for reducing the generation of risks or for avoiding their adverse consequences; it also depends upon opportunity costs. The function of reduction assessment is to determine the magnitude of the resources needed to produce a given reduction in risk.

2. The overall goal of risk management should be the progressive reduction of the risk in the existing portfolio.

Inevitably, there will be disagreement as to how ambitious our ultimate goal should be and how quickly we should attempt to achieve it. Most who have considered the matter would agree that, while zero risk is generally neither feasible nor desirable, our risk reduction goal should be more ambitious than that which would be

Richard B. Stewart, The Role of the Courts in Risk Management, 16 Envt'l L. Rep. 10208 (1986). Reprinted with permission.

dictated by any contemporaneous cost-benefit calculation. While the decision as to how far and how fast to reduce is ultimately a political judgment, in an affluent society we should be able to move steadily towards an overall reduction of risk.

Of course, risks differ qualitatively, and cannot be quantified or summed up in any mechanical way. For example, human health risks differ according to whether they are assumed voluntarily, according to the magnitude of individual (as opposed to aggregate) risk, according to whether they are life-threatening, and so forth.

The definition of risk portfolio objectives involves decisions concerning the overall risk reduction goals, the rate of such reduction, and the allocation of priorities among different qualitative types of risk. Institutions should promote informed public and governmental consideration and selection of risk portfolio objectives.

3. Institutions should manage risk to achieve risk portfolio reduction objectives in the most cost-effective manner. To reduce waste and to secure greater and faster progress in achieving risk portfolio objectives, priority should be given to those risks that will yield large reductions in risk at relatively low economic and administrative cost. The priorities should be adjusted to take into account the qualitative differences in risks that have been recognized in risk portfolio objectives. Priority risks should not necessarily be controlled to the maximum extent economically and technologically feasible, as this might involve a waste of scarce resources that could be used better elsewhere. The extent of control should be guided by consideration of cost-effectiveness.

4. Institutions should facilitate an appropriate portfolio turnover strategy. The overriding goal of risk reduction implies that the creation of new risks should be prohibited or minimized. This objective, however, should be pursued on a net-balance basis. The creation of a new risk by a new product or process may be acceptable, because it displaces an existing product or process that generates a substantially greater risk. A strategy of minimizing new risks, viewed in isolation from existing risks, may discourage new investment and a turnover of the portfolio that might substantially decrease net risk.

5. A risk portfolio strategy must deal with the question of compensation. Under prevailing tort law, those creating environmental risks ("defendants") are presumptively liable to those injured by reason of exposure to the risk ("plaintiffs") for the injury suffered. Liability theoretically serves the following purposes: deterrence; risk-spreading; and vindication of the right not to suffer harm as a result of involuntary exposure to risk.

The presumption favoring compensation, however, may be overcome where: 1) the transaction costs of providing defendant-plaintiff compensation are high; 2) alternative incentive systems are available; 3) the gains from risk-spreading are low or alternative means exist to achieve risk-spreading; 4) the risk is voluntarily assumed or could be avoided more readily and cheaply by the plaintiff; 5) insurance against risk can be more cheaply or appropriately provided by plaintiff's or government; or 6) provision of defendant-plaintiff compensation results in serious adverse side-effects (*e.g.*, overdeterrence). Institutions should respond to these considerations in deciding how and when to provide compensation.

Of course, our world is far from ideal. Information and transaction costs make it difficult for the government to acquire and analyze data, determine social objectives, and achieve the coordinated management necessary to carry out this ideal program. In addition, the need to maintain citizen confidence in government may require that a low-priority but highly-publicized risk be controlled before a more serious but less publicized risk. It seems appropriate, nonetheless, to inquire how far our institutions—including our legal institutions—can encourage and enable us to choose and achieve risk portfolio objectives that accord with the principles sketched above.

## Institutional Implications of the Portfolio Approach: The Need for Administrative Management

The basic institutional implication of a portfolio approach to risk management is clear: primary responsibility for managing risk must be given to administrative agencies.

The portfolio approach to risk management requires consistency and coordination in decisionmaking to achieve risk reduction in a rational and cost-effective manner and to ensure that similarly situated, competing generators of risk are treated equally. Administrative agencies (in contrast to both courts and legislatures) are centralized and specialized. Accordingly, they can achieve a greater degree of consistency and coordination and are better suited to serve as the frontline mechanism for regulating risk.

The reasons leading to this conclusion are essentially the same as those which led to the creation of administrative commissions to regulate railroad rates in the nineteenth century. Effective regulation was then needed to ensure that the overall revenues generated by hundreds of different rates were sufficient to cover the carriers' costs without providing monopoly profits, and that similarly situated, competing carriers and shippers were treated equally. Since a decentralized judicial system of case-by-case adjudication could not offer the consistency and coordination necessary for effective regulation, administrative agencies were established to accomplish these goals.

In addition to centralization, administrative management of portfolio risk offers advantages of specialization: it allows for economies of scale in handling similar cases, use of informal, nonforensic fact-finding and decisionmaking procedures, and cultivation of expertise that would be exceedingly difficult or expensive to develop through the courts.

Agencies can also initiate actions on behalf of the collective interests of large numbers of persons exposed to risks that might be small from the perspective of any individual but large when viewed in the aggregate. The judicial system, on the other hand, depends on private initiatives that may not be forthcoming because of the small economic stake of any individual affected by industrial practices. Furthermore, legislatures are often unwilling or unable to initiate action because of increasingly crowded agendas and relatively fixed decisionmaking capacities. . . .

Given our imperfect world, what contributions (if any) can the courts make towards the advancement of sensible risk management principles when reviewing ad-

ministrative decisions? In addition, what contribution can the courts make when deciding controversies over risk in the first instance? For example, where administrative remedies are unavailable or inadequate, courts may be asked to regulate risk
through injunctive remedies. Even where a system of administrative regulation is
fully operational, agencies generally lack the power to award compensation. Accordingly, courts may be asked to provide such compensation through liability
awards against defendants.

## The Court's Role in Reviewing Administrative Management of Risk

Reviewing courts must first determine the directives contained in the relevant statutes
and ensure that agencies comply with them. This task is especially difficult in the area
of risk management, as many of the statutes rest on false or obsolete premises. For
example, many statutes are based on the view that it is possible to distinguish "safe"
from "unsafe" pollution or exposure levels when, in fact, no clear threshold exists.
Other statutes appear to suppose that it is possible to eliminate or minimize the existing portfolio by imposing maximum feasible control methods simultaneously on
all risks, when, in fact, enormous administrative and economic obstacles block such
a course. Both of these approaches constitute pious fictions in the sense that they ignore the true nature of the risk management problem. They are "pious" in that, presumably, they are well-intentioned; they are fictions in that they deny the trade-offs
and portfolio mixes inherent in the risk management problem.

Courts are not at liberty simply to ignore these pious fictions and to substitute their
own notions of sound policy. Courts cannot, for example, require that standards be
established by weighing costs against benefits where Congress has made clear that
standards are to be based on health considerations alone. There is no reason, however, why health-based standard setting should not proceed from a portfolio perspective, particularly in a world without clear thresholds. Such a perspective would
not only allow, but would also encourage, administrators to ask themselves the following questions when setting standards for a given risk: (a) how serious is the given
risk in relation to other risks; and (b) to what extent will stricter or less stringent regulation of this risk consume administrative and compliance resources that might better be directed against other risks? Courts can thus make a substantial contribution
by exposing the true nature of the risk portfolio problem and by dispelling some of
the erroneous assumptions upon which current statutes are based. . . .

. . . [I]f an industry generates more than one risk—as is usually the case—adoption
of a portfolio perspective will prevent dissipation of resources on the first risk that
happens to be regulated.

The existing statutory scheme does not impose a rigid straitjacket. In most cases
(perhaps all) the statutory language or legislative history allows some room for a
portfolio perspective to operate. With some creativity on the part of administrators

and courts, it should be possible to build elements of a portfolio approach into the existing statutes. In the past, courts have interpreted statutes creatively to promote environmental values. There is no reason in principle why they should not also do so in the area of risk management. Instead, courts have seized all too often on a myopic literalism that takes Congress's pious fictions at face value. Judges may adopt this myopic approach believing it necessary to foreclose executive use of open-ended cost-benefit techniques that could seriously compromise risk reduction goals.

A risk portfolio strategy, however, differs fundamentally from a cost-benefit strategy. Under a portfolio strategy, risk reduction goals are chosen not by cost-benefit analysis but by much broader consideration of relevant social values. In addition, the prioritizing of risks is accomplished, not by an isolated monetary quantification of the costs and benefits of regulating a particular risk, but by a comparison of that risk with other potential candidates in the portfolio. In practice, one can restrict the discretion allowed an agency under a risk portfolio approach, by requiring the agency to justify less than full-fledged regulation of a given risk by showing that such action is consonant with an operative strategy for control of other, more suitable candidates elsewhere in the portfolio. Such a strategy could be embodied in regulations or guidelines.

*Donald T. Hornstein*

# Reclaiming Environmental Law: A Normative Critique of Comparative Risk Analysis (1992)

Comparative risk analysis is the new touchstone for reforming environmental law and policymaking. In 1987 a study group of senior officials at the federal Environmental Protection Agency (EPA or Agency) surveyed thirty-one types of environmental problems within the Agency's jurisdiction, used formal assessment techniques to estimate how much "risk" was posed by each type of problem, and concluded that society should reorganize its approach toward environmental protection by shifting resources from those problems that rank fairly low on the risk index to higher ranked problems. In 1989 EPA commissioned its Science Advisory Board (SAB) to review this conclusion. In what has become a widely referenced report, the SAB in 1990 offered a qualified endorsement; after noting that the data used by scientists to measure environmental risk can be notoriously spotty and that risk-bearing can involve qualitative elements not easily indexed for comparison, the SAB nevertheless supported comparative risk analysis as an "important shift in national environmental policy." The report in hand, EPA Administrator William Reilly announced in early 1991 a major initiative to use risk comparisons as a technique for anchoring Agency decisions more to "the scientific understanding of risk" than to the public's risk "perceptions." Since that announcement, government enthusiasm for the new effort has altogether slipped the bridle of the SAB's qualified endorsement. In February 1991, the Office of Management and Budget (OMB) proposed a "risk reduction pilot project" to determine spending priorities among environmental programs within the Departments of Defense and Energy for fiscal year 1992. Ultimately,

Donald T. Hornstein, Reclaiming Environmental Law: A Normative Critique of Comparative Risk Analysis. This article originally appeared at 92 Colum. L. Rev. 562 (1992). Reprinted by permission.

OMB officials hope, comparative risk analysis will be used to allocate resources *across* environmental programs government-wide.

How are we to judge the legitimacy of this analytic enterprise that forgives us, say, from going the extra mile on oil spill prevention because more risk can be eliminated by attending to the problems posed by global warming? Is it true, as Portia suggests in *The Merchant of Venice*, that judgments are inevitably relative, with our judgments about the acceptability of environmental risk best reached only after comparing all such risks? Or is there too great a danger that comparative risk analysis will rationalize choices we should not make, more in the manner of Ursula the Sea Witch in *The Little Mermaid*, who forces cruel dilemmas on her victims with the smug assurance that "life's full of tough choices, isn't it?" . . .

## The Theoretical Limitations of Comparative Risk Analysis

Comparative risk analysis, if embraced without an eye to its normative weaknesses, may actually undermine environmental law and policymaking rather than deliver the comprehensively rational regime promised by its proponents. For those social scientists who already hold a modest opinion of comparative risk analysis, and view it perhaps as one legitimate decisionmaking factor but not necessarily as a lodestar, this conclusion should seem unsurprising. But increasingly, some social scientists and policymakers argue that rational decisionmaking about environmental issues must be based only (or principally) on risk comparisons. My argument is with the theoretical underpinnings of this "hard version" of comparative risk analysis.

Generally speaking, the hard version is a blend of three views: first, that sound environmental policymaking is mostly an analytic, rather than political, enterprise; second, that environmental risk, measured in terms of expected losses (for example, expected deaths and injuries), is largely the best way for the policy analyst to conceptualize environmental problems; and, third, that different risks, once reduced to a common metric, are sufficiently fungible as to be compared, traded off, or otherwise aggregated by analysts wishing to produce the best environmental policy. That the hard version tends to reflect these viewpoints does not mean that it is an analytical straightjacket, without room for additional analysis or for differences in the degree to which the three common viewpoints may be expressed or applied. Some of the hard version's proponents emphasize the importance of comparing environmental risks only after first translating expected losses into "quality adjusted life years"; others emphasize the marginal costs of risk reduction so as to avoid regulatory programs that might fail cost-benefit criteria. In this spirit, it is possible to envision a more detailed taxonomy of comparative risk analysis that fractures the hard version into numerous (perhaps competing) variations. For the purposes of this Part, however, it is sufficient to describe the hard version as a belief that environmental decisionmaking should focus principally on society's aggregate risk level, and concomitantly that society should base its judgment about the acceptability of any particular environmental risk on comparisons to other risks facing society. . . .

*Expected Utility Theory, Risk, and Comparative Risk Analysis*

Comparative risk analysts are wrong to claim that only their methodology, which focuses on the expected values (losses) of environmental risks, assures a rational approach to decisionmaking. This is because expected value has long been discarded as the sole determinant of rational choice involving risk. Although the founders of probability theory assumed that rational individuals would evaluate a risky outcome only in terms of its expected value (the expected value of a one-in-ten chance of winning $50 is $5), Nicolas Bernoulli demonstrated in 1728 the limits of such a relentlessly actuarialist approach. In the "St. Petersburg Paradox," Bernoulli postulated a gamble by which someone offers to toss a coin until it lands heads and to pay $2 if heads comes up on the first toss, $4 if it takes two tosses to come up heads, $8 if it takes three tosses, and so on. An expected value analysis of this gamble leads to the bizarre proposition that a rational gambler should be willing to pay a *near-infinite* amount of money for the opportunity of a one-shot play, because the gamble offers an *infinitely* large expected value: a 1/2 chance of winning $2 (1/2 × $2 = $1) plus a 1/4 chance of winning $4 (1/4 × 4 = $1) *plus* a 1/8 chance of winning $8 (1/8 × $8 = $1) and so on, continuing to an infinite sum ($1 + $1 + $1 . . .). This proposition, however, attracted no support from professional gamblers.

The solution to the Paradox, offered a few years later by Daniel Bernoulli (Nicolas' cousin), introduced the concept of "utility." Daniel's principal insight involved what modern economists call the marginal utility of money: that the more money you have, the less useful additional dollars are to you (because you will already have used your money to buy those things you value most highly). Applying this insight to the Paradox, Daniel reasoned that a rational gambler would evaluate, say, a $5 bet on the St. Petersburg gamble by the subjective utility *to the gambler* of the overall package of chances offered: a 75% chance of losing money (the odds of a less-than-$5 payoff) coupled with increasingly smaller chances of making money (including the remote chance of making a lot of money). The $5 bet might attract a wealthy gambler who views it as a modest enough price for the opportunity to take a "flyer"; so too, the $5 bet might attract a poorer person who desperately needs a lot of money in a hurry. But because most people are not sufficiently rich nor desperate enough to be attracted to anything costlier than a modestly priced one-shot play, the expected utility of the St. Petersburg gamble is much lower than the gamble's expected *value*.

As expected utility analysis came to dominate most theories of decisionmaking under risk, it led to one of the major difficulties that risk posed to rationality theory: the problem of subjectivity. When substantial risk is involved, most people are risk averse: they tend to avoid gambles that pose the chance of catastrophic loss even when the chances of favorable outcomes are as great (or even greater) than the chances of catastrophic ones. Risk aversion is not in itself irrational, and can vary widely among individuals. This poses a theoretical difficulty: how can one individual's approach to a risky prospect be evaluated if it reflects simply that individual's personal degree of risk aversion (or risk-taking)? The need for theoretical guidance is particularly acute when individuals confront environmental risks—which can involve loss of human life, the extinction of species, and wholesale damage to the biosphere—because individual attitudes toward such risks reflect particularly subjective value judgments. . . .

Comparative risk analysis only superficially mimics expected utility theory. On the one hand, like expected utility theory, comparative risk analysis stresses the need for consistency in order to assure rationality. And, like expected utility theory, comparative risk analysis attempts to achieve consistency by forcing decisionmakers to compare outcomes and make choices. To approach rationally the universe of environmental problems, comparative risk analysts emphasize the advantages of their comparative *methodology* over a less structured political process to address environmental issues.

On the other hand, comparative risk analysis tends to beg the key question of subjectivity that expected utility theory was designed to address. This occurs for two reasons. First, although [John] von Neumann and [Oskar] Morgenstern [in the *Theory of Games and Economic Behavior*] defended expected utility theory as normative for *individual* decisionmaking under risk, they specifically cautioned against using expected utility theory to justify social decisions that would govern people with different subjective utilities. Comparative risk analysis is proposed for making just such societal decisions. Second, although expected utility theory is open theoretically to all of the subjective factors that might influence a decisionmaker's attitude toward risk, comparative risk analysis tends to emphasize aggregate numbers of mortality and morbidity as the principal (or only) factors across which environmental risks should be compared and judged. The critical assumption of the comparative risk analysis, therefore, is that attitudes toward environmental risk are (or should be) evaluated *principally by comparing expected losses, not expected utilities*. By not factoring in the subjective utilities that the von Neumann and Morgenstern methodology was designed to measure, comparative risk analysis provides an analytic structure that simply ignores the key relevance of subjective utility and that assumes, instead, that the utility of a body saved is a body saved is a body saved.

The balance of this part of the Article elaborates on the ways in which comparative risk analysis truncates unduly the analysis of environmental risk.

*Expected Utility Theory and the Problem of Equity: The Failure of Comparative Risk Analysis to Accommodate Equitable Considerations*

Much of environmental law addresses public health risks carried through environmental media, such as the risks posed to human populations by air pollution and groundwater contamination. Typically, comparative risk analysts evaluate these risks according to their expected losses across populations (generally referred to as "population effects" or "population risk"). But in doing so, comparative risk analysts tend to emphasize aggregate effects and to downplay how public health risks are distributed. For example, if the widespread use of chlorine in public drinking water systems causes each year an estimated 400 excess cancers nationwide, an evaluation based on population effects would rank it as a worse cancer risk than that posed by active hazardous waste sites regulated under the Resource Conservation and Recovery Act (RCRA) if air and water pollution from such sites cause no more than 100 excess cancers annually. For the "hard" comparative risk analyst, the evaluation of these risks is simple arithmetic: 400 cancers are worse than 100. This section argues that the full evaluation of these two risks is not so simple.

A system of environmental law must account for equities and inequities in risk-bearing if it is even to purport to incorporate one of the principal goals of any system of justice. Yet, after incorporating considerations of equity, a perfectly plausible case can be made that the risks posed by RCRA sites are "worse" than the risks posed by chlorine by-products in public drinking water: the ex ante chances of developing cancer from RCRA sites are concentrated on relatively few individuals rather than widely shared over the general population; the ex post distribution of actual cancers from RCRA sites is similarly concentrated, and unlike the case of low-level chlorine use, includes the heightened risk of destroying whole families or neighborhoods; and the cancer risks from RCRA sites are disproportionate in relation to the (indirect) benefits from hazardous chemical use enjoyed by the few risk-bearers.

That decisionmakers *might* plausibly reach different evaluations of environmental risks raises what I take to be an important attribute of environmental law: it must be able to reflect and define our values, and not simply count how many of us will suffer. Before this argument is developed, two caveats are in order. First, to accept the significance of equity as a normative goal, it is not necessary to insist that equity must overshadow the aggregate amount of risk to be shared. It may well be defensible that, in an inescapable "match-up" between chlorine and RCRA sites, decisionmakers will give priority to chlorine. My argument, rather, is that it is indefensible for society to make such a choice without appreciating the full dimensions of both risks, especially the equities involved. Not only will a full accounting capture values about which decisionmakers should (and do) care deeply, but it may well lead to a rethinking of policy options that eliminates false conflicts among risks to human life.

Second, to admit equity into the decisionmaking formula does not reject the application of formal risk analysis to environmental problems, but indeed improves the usefulness of such analysis. There is a large difference between "formal" risk analysis and "comparative" risk analysis. Formal risk analysis, like any formal decision theory, professes to be amoral in the sense that it retains flexibility to select whatever objectives and values matter to decisionmakers. At its best, formal analysis accounts for multiple attributes and attempts only to lay out for the ultimate decisionmaker the complexities of problems (and possible solutions) in situations when it is difficult for decisionmakers to proceed solely by intuition. In contrast, many "comparative" risk analysts tend to emphasize one attribute—aggregate effects on population—and view choices based on comparisons of this single attribute as the presumptively "correct" approach. In this respect, comparative risk analysis disserves decisionmakers by masking rather than revealing the full dimensions of public health risks. . . .

*Expected Utility Theory and "Cognitive Error": The Failure of Comparative Risk Analysis to Accommodate Legitimate Public Valuations of Risk*

The attitude of comparative risk analysts toward public participation in policy decisions is mixed at best. "Hard" comparative risk analysts scoff openly at the public's irrationality toward risk, noting with irony that the technologies which have propelled the country to such a high standard of living have also transformed it into a nation of worrywarts. Repeatedly, public rankings of risk are ridiculed when compared to those of experts. . . .

. . . Public-minded experts can point with altruistic alarm at the emerging evidence from cognitive psychology and conclude that comparative risk analysis, even with its faults, is preferable to the random thrashing-about by laypersons who may be sensitive to moral concerns but who systematically misperceive the magnitude and shape of the risks on which to render moral judgment. . . .

Some of the heuristics that have been identified by cognitive psychologists suggest that the lay public tends to err in its assessment of the probability of public risks. The "availability" heuristic, for example, describes the tendency of people to weight the probability of an event by the ease with which some relevant information comes to mind; other information, although relevant, is ignored simply because it does not come to mind so quickly. After the well-publicized crash of a jetliner, many people markedly change their perception of the safety of flying (often by canceling flying plans in the near-term) and ignore the less salient information about the enormous number of routine flights on the same day because that information is not well-publicized, that is, it does not come to mind so quickly. In this vein, some risk analysts complain that the public habitually *over*estimates low public risks, such as commercial nuclear power plants, simply because sensational but statistically unlikely mishaps (Three Mile Island, Chernobyl) happen. For the same reason, these analysts continue, the public *under*estimates large public risks such as the consumption of high-fat diets because the health consequences, although dangerous or fatal to individuals at risk, are diffuse and less sensational. . . .

. . . [A] fully synoptic system of comparative risk analysis would lack legitimacy because its decisions would be despised as undemocratic. The danger is not simply that the public will resent being excluded from decisionmaking processes. It is, in addition, that the cognitive error critique of public participation carries within itself a catch-22 dilemma. If heuristics and framing truly distort the public's view of risk, but experts will be able to make cognitively flawless decisions in the expected-utility tradition, the public will not be pleased. This is because, as prospect theory predicts, the public will not appreciate as fully the statistical gains (in deaths prevented) that comparative risk analysts will claim to deliver *vis-a-vis* the demonstrable deaths that comparative risk analysts must tolerate and that will be much more salient to the public (the availability heuristic). Lecturing the public that it is misperceiving the riskiness of the world will have its limits (the anchoring heuristic). Also, it will surely just be a matter of time before the public's view of risk is magnified by information the scientific community views as irrelevant (the representativeness heuristic), such as when the public learns that the government's risk assessment for a particular chemical was performed by an academician who occasionally does contract work for the chemical's manufacturer.

The dilemma of cognitive error theory highlights the difference between descriptive and normative theories of making decisions involving risk. As a descriptive matter, scholars have defended the legitimacy of expected utility theory as a powerful model that can capture and maximize what people want. Yet if it turns out that when it comes to risk, people do not want what expected utility theory can maximize, then the theory loses its descriptive legitimacy. It is just such a notion that has led economist Kenneth Arrow to note that cognitive error theory is the most "damning criticism" of risk-benefit analysis and to conclude that, "if the implications are as they seem, it is hard to see how any form of benefit-risk analysis can survive." From a descriptive point of view, then, cognitive error theory hardly supports the need to substitute the "scientific understanding of risk" for "public risk perceptions." Indeed, it proves just the opposite.

This raises the question of the normative argument for expected utility theory, that the public should not be trusted with public risk decisions because its cognitive incapacities will produce flawed decisions. This argument, however, underscores the final reason to reject the "cognitive-error" rationale for comparative risk analysis: it is not clear, even with heuristics and framing effects, that public decisionmaking about environmental risks is substantively poor. . . .

*The Failure of Comparative Risk Analysis to Frame Environmental Alternatives*

. . .Comparative risk analysis, to the extent that it fixes the risk baseline in the present among existing risks, proposes a scheme that may often accept, rather than root out, at least some inefficient risk levels. Although it is often propounded as a method to assure cost-effective environmental strategies, comparative risk analysis may in this sense be *less* efficient than current approaches. Consider, for example, the problem of groundwater pollution. A recurring message of the EPA's *Unfinished Business* study and the SAB's *Relative Risk* report is that groundwater pollution, particularly from hazardous waste sites and leaking storage tanks, poses a much less serious risk than global warming, stratospheric ozone depletion, habitat destruction and indoor radon exposure. Assuming that these comparisons accurately reflect aggregate risk levels, it hardly follows that they make an economic case for an across-the-board deemphasis on groundwater protection efforts. There will be innumerable situations in which measures to prevent groundwater contamination will be cost-effective relative to achievable benefits, particularly in areas where groundwater plays an especially important role in the quality of natural ecosystems, as a source of untreated drinking water, or as a source of contaminant-free water for irrigation or industrial processes. In these areas, local risk levels may be inefficient. A global scheme such as comparative risk analysis, to the extent that it ig-nores identifiable inefficiencies in one area out of concern for theoretically "greater" in-efficiencies elsewhere, should at least be approached skeptically. . . .

Comparative risk analysis slows wholesale change by introducing two types of bias into policy formulation. First, rather than addressing the underlying causes of envi-ronmental problems, comparative risk analysis fractures what may be interconnected problems into discrete "risks" and then compares effects. Such a fractured approach misses the chance to craft holistic policies, because decisionmakers are focused on the very visible risk assessments presented to them about different risks, rather than on the more subtle boundary-drawing that made the risks "separate" in the first place. Thus, even the SAB acknowledged that its strategies for addressing thirteen problem areas (for example criteria air pollutants, habitat alteration) could well change if the problem areas were defined differently (for example automobiles, energy-sector ac-tivities). The need to make comparisons, moreover, all but assures that any debates about boundary-drawing will miss what Amory Lovins once called the "infinite regress" of more fundamental questions that are raised when one considers, say, whether to build a big power station: "why a power station? why a big one? why more electricity? why electricity? why more?" By structuring the debate as a choice among existing ways to produce the least amount of risk (as when comparative risk analysts chart the air-pollution benefits of nuclear- over coal-based electricity), comparative risk analysis tends to become merely a blueprint for moving society out of the fire and into the proverbial frying pan. Although the benefits of such incremental improve-ments may be substantial, comparative risk analysis is structured to avoid the oppor-tunity for fashioning more fundamental alternative options (such as a world freed from voracious energy budgets) that may offer even greater benefits.

The shortcomings in policy formulation introduced by this form of bias can be com-pounded by a second form of bias, the tendency of comparative risk analysis to reduce complex environmental problems to simpler ones that are easier to compare. In part, this reductionism is caused when analysts focus only on the first-level effects of envi-ronmental risks, for which there are established data or assessment methodologies, and ignore other first-level effects. And in part, reductionism is also caused when an-alysts flatten the dimensions of environmental risks by simply ignoring second- and third-level effects because these effects involve consequences that cannot be even roughly estimated. As these biases play out, they disadvantage wholesale-level pol-icy options; the more fundamental the change in policy, the more attenuated will be its predicted effects and therefore the more likely to escape ready quantification. . . .

## Reclaiming Environmental Law

. . . For all its ungainliness, the substance of modern environmental law is a com-posite of moral decisions—about the levels of protection to be accorded such non-commodity values as human health, aesthetics, and responsibility toward nonhuman species and ecosystems—and instrumental decisions about the best way to achieve these morally based goals. Modern environmental law is also procedurally dynamic, with the general understanding that states may protect environmental values more strictly than does the federal government and that common-law actions may coexist with regulatory efforts.

Comparative risk analysis seeks simply to substitute one form of approaching risk for the more complex understandings that have been worked out, however imperfectly, in the present legal framework. This raises the indelicate question of the substitution's basic legality as a matter of positive law. Although conclusions cannot firmly be reached until there is a longer track record with the new initiative at EPA, a systematic attempt to sidestep the moral goals set for the Agency statutorily would certainly push the limits of the executive branch's constitutional prerogative and responsibility to faithfully execute the law. . . .

Beyond [this], there lies the more difficult matter of reforming a system of environmental law that is generally ungainly and too often ineffective. Many of the proposals emphasized in the SAB's *Reducing Risk* report—pollution prevention, habitat preservation, and economic incentives—may offer improvements, and have nothing whatsoever to do with comparative risk analysis. Yet even these ambitious suggestions may only touch on the larger problems of human population growth and consumption trends that, increasingly, are being rerecognized as central considerations for environmental policy. As environmental law inevitably addresses these issues, there also arises the possibility that the normative problems that often bedevil environmental law—how safe is safe? to what extent should individual preferences be subordinated to collective decisions—should not and cannot fully be resolved with a set of *a priori* rules. The better answer to the question "how safe is safe?" may be the improved question: "how good is the social dialogue on safety?" . . .

Questions such as these are not addressed simply by calculating, and comparing, expected losses. Yet questions such as these cannot go unanswered if there is to be any hope for social agreement on significant environmental reform. Comparative risk analysis, whatever advantages it may occasionally offer, promises to distract decision-makers and scholars alike from the larger project of reclaiming environmental law.

# Part IV

---

## Global Environmental Concerns and the Future of Environmental Law

*The final chapters of this reader explore the globalization of environmental policy and other important trends that are likely to shape the future of environmental law. The worldwide growth of environmental concern has been one of the most remarkable developments of the last half of the twentieth century. Global concern for the environment has spawned the development of new international institutions and a new regime of international law, which is bringing the nations of the world closer together.*

*In Chapter 12, Lynton Caldwell traces the emergence of international environmental law. This reading is followed by excerpts from the World Commission on Environment and Development's report* Our Common Future, *which outlines the common stake the nations of the world have in protecting the planet's environment. The chapter also includes the joint "Declaration of Principles" on global environmental policy, which was adopted at the Earth Summit in Rio in 1992 by representatives of 178 nations. It then examines why environmental concerns are now playing an important role in world trade negotiations. As global trade mushrooms, the environmental consequences of trade liberalization are becoming a flashpoint for environmental policy disputes. The chapter examines contrasting viewpoints*

*concerning the environmental impact of trade liberalization and its consequences for nations'*
*abilities to adopt and enforce stringent domestic environmental standards. The chapter con-*
*cludes with a statement by the President's Council on Sustainable Development concerning*
*the role of foreign policy in promoting both domestic and international environmental pro-*
*tection.*

*Although it is clear that environmental regulation has made a substantial contribution to*
*improving environmental conditions, there is sharp disagreement concerning future trends*
*and the shape of future policy. Chapter 13 opens with William Ruckelshaus's assessment of*
*the successes and failures of environmental regulation during the last three decades and his*
*call for a fundamental restructuring of the environmental laws. It then considers Gregg East-*
*erbrook's "ecorealist" critique of environmentalism and his optimistic forecast of a remark-*
*ably green future, as well as the Environmental Defense Fund's pointed rebuttal to Easter-*
*brook's claims. Sharply different visions of future policy are then presented in readings from*
*Vice President Al Gore and economist Robert Hahn. The chapter concludes with Christopher*
*Stone's effort to address the question "What sort of planet should this be?" in* **The Gnat Is**
**Older than Man.**

# CHAPTER 12

# International
# Environmental Policy

This chapter reviews the emergence of international environmental policy. It begins with a reading by Lynton Caldwell that discusses the forces that have made environmental policy a new growth area for international law and the new institutions these forces are creating. Although several international treaties addressed environmental subjects early in the twentieth century, the modern era of international environmental cooperation is generally traced to the 1972 Stockholm Conference on the Human Environment. The 133 nations attending this conference approved a joint declaration of environmental principles and agreed to create the United Nations Environment Progamme (UNEP) to help coordinate a global response to environmental concerns.

Caldwell discusses the results of that conference and countries' subsequent difficulties reconciling domestic development goals with international environmental concerns. He notes that nongovernmental organizations have played an important role in generating support for international environmental policy, particularly with respect to successful agreements restricting trade in endangered species and regulating whaling. Multilateral agreements have been remarkably successful tools for addressing issues such as depletion of the ozone layer, because the offending products are being phased out under threat of trade sanctions. Caldwell notes, however, the difficulties of enforcing international environmental law in most other contexts.

In 1982, on the tenth anniversary of the Stockholm conference, the nations of the world gathered in Nairobi for a conference that led to the creation of the World Commission on Environment and Development. Five years later, in 1987, the commission issued a report, entitled *Our Common Future*, which outlined measures for strengthening the growing body of international environmental law. As indicated in the reading drawn from the report, the commission emphasizes the concept of "sustainable development" as the guiding principle for global environmental policy. The report stresses the need to view global environmental challenges as an integral part of the problems of global development. Although it exhorts affluent countries to "adopt life-styles within the planet's ecological means," it also recognizes that it can do little more to promote this end aside from encouraging increased cooperation among nations. The commission also proposed to establish a process to produce a universal statement of principles of environmental protection and sustainable development. The 178 nations gathered at the Rio Earth Summit in 1992 adopted such a declaration of principles, known as the Rio Declaration. While written in highly general terms, the Rio Declaration embodies the most comprehensive and authoritative statement of principles of international environmental law.

As world trade has grown rapidly, environmental issues have become the subject of international trade disputes. The readings in this chapter include opposing positions on the debate over the environmental effects of trade liberalization. Economists Gene Grossman and Alan Krueger argue that trade liberalization ultimately will produce environmental benefits by promoting economic growth that will enable citizens in developing countries to demand increased environmental amenities. Examining air pollution data from various countries, they conclude that levels of air pollution tend to decline once a country's economy produces gross domestic product of between $4,000 and $5,000 per capita. They also argue that trade liberalization helps less-developed countries specialize in economic sectors that cause below-average environmental damage, such as those that are labor-intensive.

Herman Daly, a former senior economist at the World Bank, takes sharp issue with the notion that trade liberalization will be good for the environment. He argues that trade liberalization inevitably reduces a country's ability to control its own environmental policies because labor and capital are mobile across national boundaries. Daly notes that, under a regime of free trade, domestic efforts to internalize environmental costs can more easily be undermined by foreign producers who do not face similar environmental controls. He expresses concern that trade liberalization will disrupt efforts to foster community as local economies are "disrupted by decisions and events over which you have no control, no vote, no voice." Daly maintains that the best hope for achieving sustainable development on a global scale is through imposition of environmental controls at the national level, which trade liberalization will undermine.

In 1996 the secretary of state announced that international environmental concerns would become an integral part of U.S. foreign policy. The reasons for this major policy shift can be found in the chapter's concluding reading from the report of the President's Council on Sustainable Development, *Sustainable America: A New Consensus.* Composed of representatives from a broad cross-section of business, environmental, labor and government organizations, the council released its report in March 1996. Noting that the United States has less than 5 percent of the world's population but consumes nearly 25 percent of the planet's resources, the council concludes that the United States has a responsibility to play a leadership role in international environmental policy. The council finds that global environmental problems directly affect the health, prosperity, and national security of the United States, but that many such problems can be addressed effectively only through multilateral action. The report outlines ways in which the United States can promote more effective international environmental policies.

*Lynton Keith Caldwell*

# International Environmental Policy: Emergence and Dimensions (1990)

The [1972] United Nations Conference on the Human Environment marked the culmination of efforts to place the protection of the biosphere on the official agenda of international policy and law. Specific aspects of the environment had been objects of international negotiations and arrangements, but the concept of collective responsibility of nations for the quality and protection of the earth as a whole did not gain political recognition until the years immediately preceding the Stockholm Conference. Stockholm enlarged and facilitated means toward international action previously limited by inadequate perception of environmental issues and by restrictive concepts of national sovereignty and international interest. In effect, nation-states joined together their sovereignty and jurisdiction to resolve collectively issues that previously would have been definable only within the limits of particular national jurisdictions.

. . . [I]nternational conferences have become major instruments in the development of international policy. They have been both governmental and nongovernmental: nongovernmental meetings often being immediately preceding, or coterminous with, those strictly governmental. Conferences affecting environmental policy have often mixed scientific and political considerations—their outcomes being political, but often informed and modified to some extent by scientific evidence.

Positive elements in these conferences have been (1) stimulation of awareness of issues affecting all or most nations, (2) opportunity for airing grievances and revealing hidden tensions, and (3) obtaining agreement among nation-states sufficient to afford a basis for cooperative action, including research and institutional arrangements.

Negative elements have been (1) opportunities for inflammatory rhetoric and distortion of issues for purposes of propaganda, (2) a tendency to compromise issues to a point of inaction, and (3) uncertainty regarding the ability of governments to honor conference commitments. Particularly for the last reason, some institutionalized follow-up has been essential to the success of most international conferences. . . .

The principal accomplishments of the Stockholm Conference were two-fold: the official recognition of the environment as a subject of general international concern and the institutionalization of that concept in the United Nations Environment Programme (UNEP). . . .

## Environmental Aspects of International Law

International environmental law is not exclusively or even primarily a field of legal practice. There are, of course, international lawyers and litigants, but lawsuits pertaining to environmental issues have been relatively infrequent. In the perspective of international policy, environmental law is perhaps best understood as the collective body of agreements among states regarding mutual rights and obligations affecting the environment. It is embodied in conventions among states (treaties) and, to lesser effect, in international declarations, collective principles, opinions of jurists, and generally accepted practices among states. Enforcement of its provisions, customary or specified by treaty, are usually sought through negotiation (e.g., diplomacy) rather than through adjudication. Its boundaries are definable only in broad terms because new scientific findings of international significance and enlarging perceptions of man-biosphere relationships have continually if unevenly expanded its frontiers.

Emergent aspects of international environmental law include those extensions, codifications, or reinterpretations of rights and obligations among nations that have been long accepted as customary international law. An example is the identification of transboundary air pollution as entailing an obligation of a state to prevent the use of its territory to inflict harm upon its neighbors. There are also new principles and obligations derived from formal agreements, usually treaties, regarding subjects hitherto untouched by the law of nations. Examples may be found in the conventions governing international spaces—notably outer space and the deep sea bed—where technology has at last enabled some nations to establish an operational presence beyond territorial jurisdictional claims. . . .

## Protecting the Biosphere: Methods and Strategies

Although the cumulative record of declared international intent to protect nature and the human environment is impressive, the continuing and growing impact of human activities upon the biosphere leaves the future in doubt. Almost invariably performances fall short of promises. Today the attitude of many people who influence and determine the policies of the world's governments increasingly appears to be divided between a desire to protect the natural world and the quality of the environment and the desire to promote economic growth and ideological political objectives. If international conservation measures are to be realized, the different and often conflicting purposes must be reconciled.

The necessity for reconciliation grows out of the dangers inherent in the policy options available today to many national governments. Some choices in themselves could be severely destructive to the environment, but a risk to environmental conservation is that in an effort toward a reconciliation or balancing of values, the integrity of the biosphere as a whole—its species and ecosystems—may be expendable. For example, values cannot always be balanced by shared or multiple uses of the same area or resource. Some values, such as those inherent in preservation of the great herds of African wildlife, cannot be balanced with the value of agriculture or unlimited tourism in the same place. Some ecological conditions cannot be compromised by incompatible uses and still be preserved. Nations committed by treaty to protection of the environment can be equally committed to policies that make this protection difficult. Even when government experts agree upon the desirability, even necessity, of environmental protection, they may differ fundamentally upon the method or extent of such protection.

Before Stockholm the international environmental movement was a spectrum of many different interests and efforts with little organized interrelationship. The Stockholm Conference set the United Nations Environment Programme (UNEP) in motion, providing an official inter-governmental focus for interaction among organizations concerned with international environmental issues. The UNEP headquarters and secretariat provided a point of convergence for representation of non-governmental environmental organizations through the Environment Liaison Centre. Tendencies toward exclusiveness that once characterized the older NGOs, such as the International Council of Scientific Unions (ICSU) and the International Union for Conservation of Nature and Natural Resources (IUCN), diminished with the growth of opportunities for constructive collaboration. Thus by the 1980s an international network of environmental concern had developed outside the international intergovernmental agencies such as UNESCO and UNEP, and which in fact became necessary in the implementation of these agencies' programs.

It is difficult to assess the strength of the nongovernmental network for environmental policy. Its functioning can be observed in relation to particular issues such as the Convention on International Trade in Endangered Species or protection of whales by the International Whaling Commission. Its influence upon policy is greatest and most critical at national levels in persuading governments to negotiate, ratify, and abide by treaty commitments. The active role of NGOs in promoting the several international environmental treaties endorsed at Stockholm offers at least inferential support for belief in their importance as factors in the development of international environmental policy.

More certain is their importance in inducing an attitude of support for international environmental policy among the people of the world. Environmental protection literally begins at home. Unless environmental quality is valued at local and national levels of society, it is not likely to be a high priority in governmental and international affairs. The scientific, technical, and legal components of international policy are essential to its effectiveness, but without the added human dimension of value commitment policy remains no more than possibility. They afford means to action, but the action depends on human purposiveness. There may already be sufficient information to overcome a great number of the world's pressing environmental problems. But it is not adequately used because environmental quality falls behind other priorities within the power structure of most countries.

National policies and intergovernmental agreements are essential but insufficient to achieve international environmental protection. The basic strategy for global environmental protection must therefore be directed toward popular understanding and evaluation. The need for such effort has been recognized by leaders in the international environmental movement in both governmental and nongovernmental organizations. More by convergence than by conscious design a de facto four-phase strategy has emerged. Its logical components are (1) fact finding, (2) programming, (3) education, and (4) activation. . . .

## Defense of Earth in a Divided World

How to translate . . . the environment-related objectives proposed by various scientific and professional bodies into practical political action is now the critical task of international environmental policy. The legacies of past practice and political indifference are deeply entrenched, and fundamental change in human behavior, in individuals or institutions, is never easy. The conference resolutions, treaties, protocols, programs, and agencies which provide the structure of official international environmental policy also provide the goals of action and often the means. But the energy to realize these intentions derives from personal human commitment intensified through organized, purposive social effort and programmed through government and governmental initiatives. . . .

To defend the environmental future of the earth in a divided world, effective action must be based on a realistic assessment of possibilities. Expectation of an imminent upsurge of worldwide ecological morality would hardly be realistic, but belief in the possibility of a gradual progression toward a universal environmental ethic would find support in actual experience. Such an eventuality is implicit in the many and diverse efforts toward international environmental protection [currently underway]. . . .

To achieve practical results, however, the world must be taken as it is. Its divisions and antagonisms are givens—circumstances that cannot readily be changed. Divisiveness among nations is expressed primarily through their political parties and governments—which are often primary agents of international antagonisms—and not through the people governed. Yet governments must be moved if environmental policy is to be activated. Governments must simultaneously be influenced from within, and induced from without, to work with other governments and international organizations.

Organizations representing transnational environmental interests and values, of which the International Union for Conservation of Nature and Natural Resources

(IUCN) is the notable example, are indispensable means toward energizing the world environment movement. The constituent national member organizations of IUCN represent international environmental concerns within their own countries (but not necessarily the priorities of their governments), avoiding the rejection reflex that frequently characterizes governmental reaction to perceived importunities from without—especially from intergovernmental organizations.

Whatever strengthens and assists nongovernmental international organizations . . . contributes to the prospects for realizing a rational international order of policy and practice for the world environment. In relation to what is needed for effective environmental protection, even at present limits of international receptivity, all programmatic efforts—in research, in education, and in popular activation—are chronically underfunded. How to increase their support is a problem deserving early attention and ingenuity by governments, international organizations, and international philanthropy.

Further, existing institutional arrangements may not be adequate to provide for all aspects of international biospheric protection. At least three areas may be identified which do not appear to be covered by existing institutions or agreements: (1) environmental impacts of international commerce and investment, (2) transnational means to implement environmental protection agreements in the international commons, and (3) means to rehabilitate socio-ecologically bankrupt nations.

No present means adequately protects against environmental damage incident to international investment and resource development. National laws and the policies of some international investment agencies, such as the World Bank, ostensibly provide safeguards against environmentally damaging development. . . . But economic incentives characteristically override environmental considerations. Private investment, especially by multinational corporations, is not easily influenced nor its ramifications easily contained. International resource developers need national collaborators and usually find them. The consequences of this collaboration are not necessarily environmentally damaging, but they have often been so—Daniel Ludwig's Jari Project in the Amazon forest being a case in point. Perhaps nations need some process of mutually agreed upon international review, independent of the inclinations of funding and investment agencies, to assess the national, international, and environmental costs, broadly defined, of international investment proposals and transfers of industrial technologies. The 1982 UNEP Session of a Special Character in its concluding declaration addressed this issue, stating that: "All enterprises including multinational corporations, should take account of their environmental responsibilities when adopting industrial production methods or technologies, or when exporting them to other countries. Timely and adequate legislative action is important in this regard."

As to the second deficiency no solution is presently in sight for an adequate international or transnational arrangement to police environmental protection agreements in the international commons. The history of the United National Conference on the Law of the Sea gives no reason for optimism that an institutional solution to replace and extend present multilateral arrangements can be found in the foreseeable future. And international treaties, such as those relating to endangered species or to whaling, make insufficient provision for collective enforcement. Three developments suggest that this situation may soon change. First, a discussion of Environmental Protection of Extra-Territorial Spaces for Present and Future Generations has been proposed by the government of Malta to the UN General Assembly. Second, a treaty on global climate change seems certain to emerge from the Intergovernmental Panel on Climate Change. And third, there is growing recognition of the need to monitor and report the observance of treaty obligations. Institutions of governance, short of actual government, may be necessary.

The third deficiency in the present international structure for environmental policy is the absence of any institutional arrangement to assist the administration of countries faced with socio-ecological collapse. If there are no countries actually in this state today, some are nearly so. Socio-ecological insolvency means that a state has exhausted its material means of self-support and no longer provides to its people the elementary services of government. Some countries may have already reached this condition, which, however, is masked but scarcely concealed by infusions of foreign monetary aid.

More than a decade ago at an international conference on environment and development I suggested the need for an arrangement under which a severely handicapped nation might voluntarily place itself under some form of international receivership but with a more acceptable name. There would obviously be many difficulties in implementing such an arrangement. But the concept ought not be relegated to the limbo of unthinkable thoughts in a world in which there can be no assurance that a real need for such an arrangement will not arise.

# World Commission on Environment and Development

---

# Our Common Future (1987)

In the middle of the 20th century, we saw our planet from space for the first time. Historians may eventually find that this vision had a greater impact on thought than did the Copernican revolution of the 16th century, which upset the human self-image by revealing that the Earth is not the centre of the universe. From space, we see a small and fragile ball dominated not by human activity and edifice but by a pattern of clouds, oceans, greenery, and soils. Humanity's inability to fit its doings into that pattern is changing planetary systems, fundamentally. Many such changes are accompanied by life-threatening hazards. This new reality, from which there is no escape, must be recognized—and managed.

Fortunately, this new reality coincides with more positive developments new to this century. We can move information and goods faster around the globe than ever before; we can produce more food and more goods with less investment of resources; our technology and science gives us at least the potential to look deeper into and better understand natural systems. From space, we can see and study the Earth as an organism whose health depends on the health of all its parts. We have the power to reconcile human affairs with natural laws and to thrive in the process. In this our cultural and spiritual heritages can reinforce our economic interests and survival imperatives.

This Commission believes that people can build a future that is more prosperous, more just, and more secure. Our report, *Our Common Future*, is not a prediction of ever increasing environmental decay, poverty, and hardship in an ever more polluted world among ever decreasing resources. We see instead the possibility for a new era of economic growth, one that must be based on policies that sustain and expand the environmental resource base. And we believe such growth to be absolutely essential to relieve the great poverty that is deepening in much of the developing world.

From World Commission on Environment and Development, *Our Common Future* (New York: Oxford University Press, 1987). Reprinted by permission of Oxford University Press.

But the Commission's hope for the future is conditional on decisive political action now to begin managing environmental resources to ensure both sustainable human progress and human survival. We are not forecasting a future; we are serving a notice—an urgent notice based on the latest and best scientific evidence—that the time has come to take the decisions needed to secure the resources to sustain this and coming generations. We do not offer a detailed blueprint, but instead a pathway by which the people of the world may enlarge their spheres of cooperation. . . .

## Sustainable Development

Humanity has the ability to make development sustainable—to ensure that it meets the needs of the present without compromising the ability of future generations to meet their own needs. The concept of sustainable development does imply limits—not absolute limits but limitations imposed by the present state of technology and social organization on environmental resources and by the ability of the biosphere to absorb the effects of human activities. But technology and social organization can be both managed and improved to make way for a new era of economic growth. The Commission believes that widespread poverty is no longer inevitable. Poverty is not only an evil in itself, but sustainable development requires meeting the basic needs of all and extending to all the opportunity to fulfil their aspirations for a better life. A world in which poverty is endemic will always be prone to ecological and other catastrophes.

Meeting essential needs requires not only a new era of economic growth for nations in which the majority are poor, but an assurance that those poor get their fair share of the resources required to sustain that growth. Such equity would be aided by political systems that secure effective citizen participation in decision making and by greater democracy in international decision making.

Sustainable global development requires that those who are more affluent adopt lifestyles within the planet's ecological means—in their use of energy, for example. Further, rapidly growing populations can increase the pressure on resources and slow any rise in living standards; thus sustainable development can only be pursued if population size and growth are in harmony with the changing productive potential of the ecosystem.

Yet in the end, sustainable development is not a fixed state of harmony, but rather a process of change in which the exploitation of resources, the direction of investment, the orientation of technological development, and institutional change are made consistent with future as well as present needs. We do not pretend that the process is easy or straightforward. Painful choices have to be made. Thus, in the final analysis, sustainable development must rest on political will.

## The Institutional Gaps

The objective of sustainable development and the integrated nature of the global environmental/development challenges pose problems for institutions, national and international, that were established on the basis of narrow preoocupations and compartmentalized concerns. Governments' general response to the speed and scale of global changes has been a reluctance to recognize sufficiently the need to change themselves. The challenges are both interdependent and integrated, requiring comprehensive approaches and popular participation.

Yet most of the institutions facing those challenges tend to be independent, fragmented, working to relatively narrow mandates with closed decision processes. Those responsible for managing natural resources and protecting the environment are institutionally separated from those responsible for managing the economy. The real world of interlocked economic and ecological systems will not change; the policies and institutions concerned must.

There is a growing need for effective international co-operation to manage ecological and economic interdependence. Yet at the same time, confidence in international organizations is diminishing and support for them dwindling.

The other great institutional flaw in coping with environment/development challenges is governments' failure to make the bodies whose policy actions degrade the environment responsible for ensuring that their policies prevent that degradation. Environmental concern arose from damage caused by the rapid economic growth following the Second World War. Governments, pressured by their citizens, saw a need to clean up the mess, and they established environmental ministries and agencies to do this. Many had great success—within the limits of their mandates—in improving air and water quality and enhancing other resources. But much of their work has of necessity been after-the-fact repair of damage: reforestation, reclaiming desert lands, rebuilding urban environments, restoring natural habitats, and rehabilitating wild lands.

The existence of such agencies gave many governments and their citizens the false impression that these bodies were by themselves able to protect and enhance the environmental resource base. Yet many industrialized and most developing countries carry huge economic burdens from inherited problems such as air and water pollution, depletion of ground-water, and the proliferation of toxic chemicals and hazardous wastes. These have been joined by more recent problems—erosion, desertification, acidification, new chemicals, and new forms of waste—that are directly related to agricultural, industrial, energy, forestry, and transportation policies and practices. . . .

The same need for change holds for international agencies concerned with development lending, trade regulation, agricultural development, and so on. These have been slow to take the environmental effects of their work into account, although some are trying to do so.

The ability to anticipate and prevent environmental damage requires that the ecological dimensions of policy be considered at the same time as the economic, trade, energy, agricultural, and other dimensions. They should be considered on the same agendas and in the same national and international institutions.

This reorientation is one of the chief institutional challenges of the 1990s and beyond. Meeting it will require major institutional development and reform. Many countries that are too poor or small or that have limited managerial capacity will find it difficult to do this unaided. They will need financial and technical assistance and training. But the changes required involve all countries, large and small, rich and poor. . . .

## A Universal Declaration and a Convention on Environmental Protection and Sustainable Development

Building on the 1972 Stockholm Declaration, the 1982 Nairobi Declaration, and many existing international conventions and General Assembly resolutions, there is now a need to consolidate and extend relevant legal principles in a new charter to guide state behaviour in the transition to sustainable development. It would provide the basis for, and be subsequently expanded into, a Convention, setting out the sovereign rights and reciprocal responsibilities of all states on environmental protection and sustainable development. The charter should prescribe new norms for state and interstate behaviour needed to maintain livelihoods and life on our shared planet, including basic norms for prior notification, consultation, and assessment of activities likely to have an impact on neighbouring states or global commons. These could include the obligation to alert and inform neighbouring states in the event of an accident likely to have a harmful impact on their environment. Although a few such norms have evolved in some bilateral and regional arrangements, the lack of wider agreement on such basic rules for interstate behaviour undermines both the sovereignty and economic development potential of each and all states.

We recommend that the General Assembly commit itself to preparing a universal Declaration and later a Convention on environmental protection and sustainable development. A special negotiating group could be established to draft a Declaration text. . . . Once it is approved, that group could then proceed to prepare a Convention, based on and extending the principles in the Declaration, with the aim of having an agreed Convention text ready for signature by states within three to five years. To facilitate the early launching of that process the Commission has submitted for the deliberations of the special negotiating group, a number of proposed legal principles embodied in 22 Articles that were prepared by its group of international legal experts. These proposed principles are submitted to assist the General Assembly in its deliberations and have not been approved or considered in detail by the Commission. . . .

## Strengthen and Extend Existing International Conventions and Agreements

In parallel, governments should accelerate their efforts to strengthen and extend existing and more specific international conventions and co-operative arrangements by:

- acceding to or ratifying existing global and regional conventions dealing with environment and development, and applying them with more vigour and rigour;
- reviewing and revising those relevant conventions that need to be brought in line with the latest available technical and scientific information; and
- negotiating new global and regional conventions or arrangements aimed at pro-

moting co-operation and co-ordination in the field of environment and development (including, for example, new conventions and agreements on climate change,
on hazardous chemicals and wastes, and on preserving biological diversity). . . .

## Avoiding and Settling Environmental Disputes

Many disputes can be avoided or more readily resolved if the principles, rights, and
responsibilities cited earlier are built into national and international legal frameworks and are fully respected and implemented by many states. Individuals and
states are more reluctant to act in a way that might lead to a dispute when, as in many
national legal systems, there is an established and effective capacity as well as ultimately binding procedures for settling disputes. Such a capacity and procedures are
largely lacking at the international level, particularly on environmental and natural
resource management issues.

It is recommended that public and private organizations and NGOs help in these areas by establishing special panels or rosters of experts with experience in various
forms of dispute settlement and special competence on the legal and substantive aspects of environmental protection, natural resources management, and sustainable
development. In addition, a consolidated inventory and referral system or network
for responding to requests for advice and assistance in avoiding or resolving such
disputes should be established.

To promote the peaceful and early settlement of international disputes on environmental and resource management problems, it is recommended that the following procedure be adopted. States should be given up to 18 months to reach mutual
agreement on a solution or on a common dispute settlement arrangement. If agreement is not reached, then the dispute can be submitted to conciliation at the request
of any one of the concerned states and, if still unresolved, thereafter to arbitration or
judicial settlement. This proposed new procedure raises the possibility of invoking a
binding process of dispute settlement at the request of any state. Binding settlement
is not the preferred method for settling international disputes. But such a provision
is now needed not only as a last resort to avoid prolonged disputes and possible serious environmental damage, but also to encourage and provide an incentive for all
parties to reach agreement within a reasonable time on either a solution or a mutually agreed means, such as mediation.

The capabilities of the Permanent Court of Arbitration and the International Court
of Justice to deal with environmental and resource management problems also
should be strengthened. States should make greater use of the World Court's capacity under Article 26 of its Statute to form special chambers for dealing with particular cases or categories of cases, including environmental protection or resource management cases. The Court has declared its willingness and readiness to deal with such
cases fully and promptly.

# United Nations Conference on Environment and Development

# Declaration of Principles (1992)

PRINCIPLE 1
Human beings are at the centre of concerns for sustainable development. They are entitled to a healthy and productive life in harmony with nature.

PRINCIPLE 2
States have, in accordance with the Charter of the United Nations and the principles of international law, the sovereign right to exploit their own resources pursuant to their own environmental and developmental policies and the responsibility to ensure that activities within their jurisdiction or control do not cause damage to the environment of other States or of areas beyond the limits of national jurisdiction.

PRINCIPLE 3
The right to development must be fulfilled so as to equitably meet developmental and environmental needs of present and future generations.

PRINCIPLE 4
In order to achieve sustainable development, environmental protection shall constitute an integral part of the development process and cannot be considered in isolation from it.

PRINCIPLE 5
All States and all people shall cooperate in the essential task of eradicating poverty as an indispensable requirement for sustainable development, in order to decrease

United Nations Conference on Environment and Development, Declaration of Principles, 31 I.L.M. 874 (1992).

the disparities in standards of living and better meet the needs of the majority of the people of the world.

PRINCIPLE 6
The special situation and needs of developing countries, particularly the least developed and those most environmentally vulnerable, shall be given special priority. International actions in the field of environment and development should also address the interests and needs of all countries.

PRINCIPLE 7
States shall cooperate in a spirit of global partnership to conserve, protect and restore the health and integrity of the Earth's ecosystem. In view of the different contributions to global environmental degradation, States have common but differentiated responsibilities. The developed countries acknowledge the responsibility that they bear in the international pursuit of sustainable development in view of the pressures their societies place on the global environment and of the technologies and financial resources they command.

PRINCIPLE 8
To achieve sustainable development and a higher quality of life for all people, States should reduce and eliminate unsustainable patterns of production and consumption and promote appropriate demographic policies.

PRINCIPLE 9
States should cooperate to strengthen endogenous capacity-building for sustainable development by improving scientific understanding through exchanges of scientific and technological knowledge, and by enhancing the development, adaptation, diffusion and transfer of technologies, including new and innovative technologies.

PRINCIPLE 10
Environmental issues are best handled with the participation of all concerned citizens, at the relevant level. At the national level, each individual shall have appropriate access to information concerning the environment that is held by public authorities, including information on hazardous materials and activities in their communities, and the opportunity to participate in decision-making processes. States shall facilitate and encourage public awareness and participation by making information widely available. Effective access to judicial and administrative proceedings, including redress and remedy, shall be provided.

PRINCIPLE 11
States shall enact effective environmental legislation. Environmental standards, management objectives and priorities should reflect the environmental and developmental context to which they apply. Standards applied by some countries may be in-

appropriate and of unwarranted economic and social cost to other countries, in particular developing countries.

PRINCIPLE 12
States should cooperate to promote a supportive and open international economic system that would lead to economic growth and sustainable development in all countries, to better address the problems of environmental degradation. Trade policy measures for environmental purposes should not constitute a means of arbitrary or unjustifiable discrimination or a disguised restriction on international trade. Unilateral actions to deal with environmental challenges outside the jurisdiction of the importing country should be avoided. Environmental measures addressing transboundary or global environmental problems should, as far as possible, be based on an international consensus.

PRINCIPLE 13
States shall develop national law regarding liability and compensation for the victims of pollution and other environmental damage. States shall also cooperate in an expeditious and more determined manner to develop further international law regarding liability and compensation for adverse effects of environmental damage caused by activities within their jurisdiction or control to areas beyond their jurisdiction.

PRINCIPLE 14
States should effectively cooperate to discourage or prevent the relocation and transfer to other States of any activities and substances that cause severe environmental degradation or are found to be harmful to human health.

PRINCIPLE 15
In order to protect the environment, the precautionary approach shall be widely applied by States according to their capabilities. Where there are threats of serious or irreversible damage, lack of full scientific certainty shall not be used as a reason for postponing cost-effective measures to prevent environmental degradation.

PRINCIPLE 16
National authorities should endeavor to promote the internalization of environmental costs and the use of economic instruments, taking into account the approach that the polluter should, in principle, bear the cost of pollution, with due regard to the public interest and without distorting international trade and investment.

PRINCIPLE 17
Environmental impact assessment, as a national instrument, shall be undertaken for proposed activities that are likely to have a significant adverse impact on the environment and are subject to a decision of a competent national authority.

PRINCIPLE 18
States shall immediately notify other States of any natural disasters or other emergen-

cies that are likely to produce sudden harmful effects on the environment of those States. Every effort shall be made by the international community to help States so afflicted.

PRINCIPLE 19
States shall provide prior and timely notification and relevant information to potentially affected States on activities that may have a significant adverse transboundary environmental effect and shall consult with those States at an early stage and in good faith.

PRINCIPLE 20
Women have a vital role in environmental management and development. Their full participation is therefore essential to achieve sustainable development and ensure a better future for all.

PRINCIPLE 21
The creativity, ideals and courage of the youth of the world should be mobilized to forge a global partnership in order to achieve sustainable development and ensure a better future for all.

PRINCIPLE 22
Indigenous people and their communities and other local communities have a vital role in environmental management and development because of their knowledge and traditional practices. States should recognize and duly support their identity, culture and interests and enable their effective participation in the achievement of sustainable development.

PRINCIPLE 23
The environment and natural resources of people under oppression, domination and occupation shall be protected.

PRINCIPLE 24
Warfare is inherently destructive of sustainable development. States shall therefore respect international law providing protection for the environment in times of armed conflict and cooperate in its further development, as necessary.

PRINCIPLE 25
Peace, development and environmental protection are interdependent and indivisible.

PRINCIPLE 26
States shall resolve all their environmental disputes peacefully and by appropriate means in accordance with the Charter of the United Nations.

PRINCIPLE 27
States and people shall cooperate in good faith and in a spirit of partnership in the fulfillment of the principles embodied in this Declaration and in the further development of international law in the field of sustainable development.

*Gene M. Grossman and Alan B. Krueger*

---

# Environmental Impacts of a North American Free Trade Agreement (1991)

The arguments linking trade liberalization with environmental degradation have not been fully articulated. With regard to a [North American Free Trade Agreement,] NAFTA, the environmentalists have expressed a number of reasons for fearing that freer trade and direct investment flows between the United States and Mexico may aggravate pollution problems in Mexico and in the border region. At the least discerning level, some have argued simply that any expansion of markets and economic activity inevitably leads to more pollution and faster depletion of scarce natural resources. A more pointed argument recognizes that pollution already is a severe problem in Mexico and that the country's weak regulatory infrastructure is strained to the breaking point. Under these conditions, it is feared that any further industrialization that results from the liberalization of trade and investment will exacerbate an already grave situation.

Other environmentalists draw their conclusions by extrapolating the experience of the maquiladora sector in Mexico. The maquiladoras are predominantly foreign-owned firms that produce largely for export to the United States under a Mexican policy that allows duty-free imports of foreign components for further processing and re-export. Originally, maquiladoras were required to locate within a 20-kilometer strip along the U.S.–Mexico border in order to qualify for special customs treatment. The sector grew quite rapidly and with little governmental oversight, and now is widely regarded as being a major contributor to the perilous environmental and social conditions in the border region. Environmental groups point to this sector as a prime example of how unregulated expansion in response to trade opportunities can

Gene M. Grossman and Alan B. Krueger, Environmental Impacts of a North American Free Trade Agreement, Discussion Papers in Economics, Woodrow Wilson School of Public and International Affairs, Princeton, NJ, November 1991.

create risks to worker safety and public health. They argue that investments in this sector have been encouraged by the lax enforcement of environment and labor protection laws in Mexico and fear that any further expansion in trade and investment flows between the United States and Mexico will be motivated by firms' desires to avoid the high costs of meeting U.S. regulations.

A further concern of some environmental groups is that a NAFTA may undercut regulatory standards in the United States. Spokespersons have made the political-economic argument that, with freer trade, industry groups in the United States will demand less stringent pollution controls in order to preserve their international competitiveness, so that environmental standards will tend toward a lowest common denominator. The environmentalists worry, moreover, that existing environmental protection laws in the United States may be seen as nontariff barriers to trade in the context of a regional trade agreement. . . .

In this paper we explore some of the empirical evidence that bears on the likely environmental impacts of a NAFTA. . . . We use a cross-country sample of comparable measures of pollution in various urban areas to explore the relationship between economic growth and air quality. After holding constant the identifiable geographic characteristics of different cities, a common global time trend in the levels of pollution, and the location and type of the pollution measurement device, we find that ambient levels of both sulphur dioxide and dark matter suspended in the air increase with per capita GDP at low levels of income, but decrease with per capita GDP at higher levels of income. The turning point comes somewhere between $4,000 and $5,000, measured in 1985 U.S. dollars. For a third measure of air quality, namely the mass of suspended particles found in a given volume of air, the relationship between pollution and GDP is monotonically decreasing. . . .

. . . [Thus], [w]hile [environmental advocacy groups] raise a number of valid concerns, our findings suggest that some potential benefits, especially for Mexico, may have been overlooked. First, a more liberal trade regime and greater access to the large U.S. market is likely to generate income growth in Mexico. Brown, Deardorff and Stern (1991), for example, estimate potential short run welfare gains to Mexico of between 0.6 and 1.9 percent of GDP. We have found, through an examination of air quality measures in a cross-section of countries, that economic growth tends to alleviate pollution problems once a country's per capita income reaches about $4,000 to $5,000 U.S. dollars. Mexico, with a per capita GDP of $5,000, now is at the critical juncture in its development process where further growth should generate increased political pressures for environmental protection and perhaps a change in private consumption behavior. Second, trade liberalization may well increase Mexican specialization in sectors that cause less than average amounts of environmental damage. Our investigation of the determinants of Mexico's trade pattern strongly suggests that the country draws comparative advantage from its large number of relatively unskilled workers and that it imports goods whose production requires intensive use of physical and human capital. The asymmetries in environmental regulations and enforcement between the United States and Mexico play at most a minor role in guiding intersectoral resource allocations. But since it would appear that labor-intensive and agricultural activities require less energy input and generate less hazardous waste per unit of output than more capital and human capital-intensive sectors, a reduction in pollution may well be a side-benefit of increased Mexican specialization and trade.

Our findings must remain tentative until better data become available. We have been unable to use any information about the pollution situation as it currently stands in Mexico, since environmental monitoring there has been unsystematic at best. Furthermore, the kinds of pollutants that we can examine are limited by data availability (e.g., there are no reliable data on emissions of carbon dioxide in different countries). Still, one lesson from our study seems quite general and important. The environmental impacts of trade liberalization in any country will depend not only upon the effect of policy change on the overall scale of economic activity, but also upon the induced changes in the intersectoral composition of economic activity and in the technologies that are used to produce goods and services.

*Herman Daly*

# From Adjustment to Sustainable Development: The Obstacle of Free Trade (1992)

## Why Free Trade Conflicts with Sustainable Development

International free trade conflicts sharply with the national policies of:

(a) getting prices right,
(b) moving toward a more just distribution,
(c) fostering community,
(d) controlling the macroeconomy, and
(e) keeping scale within ecological limits.

Each conflict will be discussed in turn.

(a) If one nation internalizes environmental and social costs to a high degree, following the dictates of adjustment, and then enters into free trade with a country that does not force its producers to internalize those costs, then the result will be that the firms in the second country will have lower prices and will drive the competing firms in the first country out of business.

If the trading entities were nations rather than individual firms trading across national boundaries, then the cost-internalizing nation could limit its volume and composition of trade to an amount that did not ruin its domestic producers, and thereby actually take advantage of the opportunity to acquire goods at prices that were below full cost. The country that sells at less than full-cost prices only hurts itself as long as other countries restrict their trade with that country to a volume that does not ruin

Herman Daly, From Adjustment to Sustainable Development: The Obstacle of Free Trade, 15 Loyola of L.A. Int'l & Comp. L.J. 33 (1992). Reprinted by permission.

their own producers. That of course would not be free trade. There is clearly a conflict between free trade and a national policy of internalization of external costs. External costs are now so important that the latter goal should take precedence. In this case there is a clear argument for tariffs to protect, not an inefficient industry, but an efficient national policy of internalizing external costs into prices. . . .

(b) Wage levels vary enormously between countries and are largely determined by the supply of labor, which in turn depends on population size and growth rates. Overpopulated countries are naturally low-wage countries, and if population growth is rapid they will remain low-wage countries. This is especially so because the demographic rate of increase of the lower class (labor) is frequently twice or more that of the upper class (capital). For most traded goods labor is still the largest item of cost and consequently the major determinant of price. Cheap labor means low prices and a competitive advantage in trade. . . .

(c) . . . [F]ree trade and free capital mobility . . . increase the separation of ownership and control and the forced mobility of labor which are so inimical to community. Community economic life can be disrupted not only by your fellow citizen who, though living in another part of your country, might at least share some tenuous bonds of community with you, but by someone on the other side of the world with whom you have no community of language, history, culture, law, etc. These foreigners may be wonderful people—that is not the point. The point is that they are very far removed from the life of the community that is affected significantly by their decisions. Your life and your community can be disrupted by decisions and events over which you have no control, no vote, no voice.

Specialization and integration of a local community into the world economy does offer a quick fix to problems of local unemployment, and one must admit that carrying community self-sufficiency to extremes can certainly be impoverishing. But short supply lines and relatively local control over the livelihood of the community remain obvious prudential measures which require some restraint on free trade if they are to be effective. Libertarian economists look at *Homo economicus* as a self-contained individual who is infinitely mobile and equally at home anywhere. But real people live in communities, and in communities of communities. Their very individual identity is constituted by their relations in community. To regard community as a disposable aggregate of individuals in temporary proximity only for as long as it serves the interests of mobile capital is bad enough when capital stays within the nation. But when capital moves internationally it becomes much worse. . . .

(d) Free trade and free capital mobility have interfered with macroeconomic stability by permitting huge international payment imbalances and capital transfers resulting in debts that are unrepayable in many cases and excessive in others. Efforts to service these debts can lead to unsustainable rates of exploitation of exportable resources; and to an eagerness to make new loans to get the foreign exchange with which to pay old loans, with a consequent disincentive to take a hard look at the real productivity of the project for which the new loan is being made. Efforts to pay back loans and still meet domestic obligations lead to government budget deficits and monetary creation with resulting inflation. Inflation, plus the need to export to pay off loans, leads to currency devaluations, giving rise to foreign exchange speculation, capital flight, and hot money movements, disrupting the macroeconomic stability that adjustment was supposed to foster. . . .

(e) . . . [P]art of the free trade dogma of adjustment thinking is based on the assumption that the whole world, and all future generations, can consume resources at the levels current in today's high-wage countries without inducing ecological collapse. So, in this way, free trade sins against the criterion of sustainable scale. But, in its physical dimensions the economy really is an open subsystem of a materially closed, non-growing, and finite ecosystem with a limited throughput of solar energy. The proper scale of the economic subsystem relative to the finite total system is a very important question. Free trade has obscured the scale limit in the following way.

Sustainable development means living within environmental constraints of absorptive and regenerative capacities. These constraints are both global (greenhouse effect, ozone shield), and local (soil erosion, deforestation). Trade between nations or regions offers a way to loosen local constraints by importing environmental services (including waste absorption) from elsewhere. Within limits this can be quite reasonable and justifiable. But carried to extremes in the name of free trade it becomes destructive. It leads to a situation in which each country is trying to live beyond its own absorptive and regenerative capacities by importing these capacities from elsewhere. Of course they pay for these capacities and all is well as long as other countries have made the complementary decision—namely to keep their own scale well below their own national carrying capacity in order to export some of its services. In other words, the apparent escape from scale constraints enjoyed by some countries via trade depends on other countries' willingness and ability to adopt the very discipline of limiting scale that the importing country is seeking to avoid.

What nations have actually made this complementary choice? All countries now aim to grow in scale, and it is merely the fact that some have not yet reached their limits that allows other nations to import carrying capacity. Free trade does not remove carrying capacity constraints—it just guarantees that nations will hit that constraint more or less simultaneously rather than sequentially. It converts differing local constraints into an aggregated global constraint. It converts a set of problems, some of which are manageable, into one big unmanageable problem. Evidence that this is not understood is provided by the countless occasions when someone who really should know better points to The Netherlands or Hong Kong as both an example to be emulated, and as evidence that all countries could become as densely populated as these two. How it would be possible for all countries to be net exporters of goods and net importers of carrying capacity is not explained.

Of course the drive to grow beyond carrying capacity has roots other and deeper than the free trade dogma. The point is that free trade makes it very hard to deal with these root causes at a national level, which is the only level at which effective social controls over the economy exist. The adjustment theorist will argue that free trade is just a natural extension of price adjustment across international boundaries, and that right prices must reflect *global* scarcities and preferences. But if the unit of community is the nation—the unit in which there are institutions and traditions of collective action, responsibility, and mutual help—the unit in which government tries to carry out policy for the good of its citizens, then right prices should *not* reflect the preferences and scarcities of other nations. Right prices *should* differ between national communities. Such differences traditionally have provided the whole reason for international trade in goods.

# President's Council on Sustainable Development

## Sustainable America: A New Consensus—International Leadership (1996)

The future of the United States—its security, its prosperity, and its environment—is inextricably linked to the world. American firms and workers compete in a global economy shaped by global trends. The lives of Americans are increasingly affected by global environmental change. In an era of weapons of mass destruction, savage terrorism, and sophisticated transnational crime, national security is tied to conditions and events around the globe. What Americans do and say affect the rest of the world; and changes in the lives of other peoples—whether positive or negative—affect Americans at home.

The United States influences other nations by the force of its example, the power of its economy, and the strength of its arms. The model of American democracy and prosperity has shaped the hopes of many millions of people. The demands of the U.S. markets and the products of U.S. industries influence the economic course of much of the world. With one of the highest standards of living in the world, the United States is the largest producer and consumer in history: with fewer than 5 percent of the world's population, the nation consumes nearly 25 percent of the planet's resources. This high standard of living and huge economy also have made the United States the world's largest producer of wastes and have given the country cause and capacity to become the world leader in the creation and use of innovative technology to reduce wastes and control pollution. Many nations seek to emulate the successes of the U.S. system of environmental protection.

The United States is a world leader—often *the* world leader—whether it chooses to

From The President's Council on Sustainable Development, *Sustainable America: A New Consensus for Prosperity, Opportunity, and a Healthy Environment for the Future* (Washinton, D.C.: U.S. Government Printing Office, 1996).

exercise leadership or not. Other nations hesitate to act to address international issues of security, development, or the environment unless the United States takes the lead. And issues of development, environment, and human security are as surely related globally as they are locally. This country will not prosper, nor will freedom thrive, in a violent and unstable world. Poverty, inequity, and environmental destruction corrode the bonds that hold stability and progress together. The peoples of the world can only achieve their legitimate aspirations for economic betterment within the context of environmental protection and a more equitable distribution of the fruits of that progress. Improvement in people's lives will benefit this country economically, environmentally, and socially by mitigating important sources of global conflict.

There is another reason for U.S. leadership internationally: certain problems can only be addressed through global cooperation. It is easy to understand that the control of nuclear weapons or the creation of conditions for freer trade requires agreement among nations. The same is true of global environmental problems. Previous chapters of this report emphasize the importance of local communities and individual responsibility in moving the United States toward a more sustainable path; some issues affecting individuals and communities can only be solved, however, if nations agree upon common goals and shared responsibilities.

For example, the fisherman of many nations have competed for declining wild stocks of tuna, salmon, cod, and many other fish, a competition that recently flared into violent confrontation and international conflict. The collapse of some fisheries brought misery to communities in the United States and elsewhere. No single nation can by itself limit catches to sustain the fisheries. All nations must agree to abide by the same rules to save the shared resources.

Forests—particularly tropical forests—play a critical role in maintaining the diversity, productivity, and resilience of global ecosystems. Forests are also important national resources subject to sensitive issues of sovereignty. In response both to global markets for tropical hardwoods and domestic demand for land and materials, many countries are rapidly cutting their forests. Individual nations understandably resist calls to preserve their forests to provide global benefits. Only cooperative solutions based on global agreements will work.

Cooperation has worked effectively in structuring a phaseout of chlorofluorocarbons, the human-made gases destroying the ozone layer. U.S. industries responded to clear goals and economic incentives with a flurry of successful innovations that put them ahead of the agreed-upon schedule. The issues that demand international action include not only damage to ocean ecosystems and deforestation, but also—most importantly—changes in the atmospheric chemistry and composition that influence the global climate and loss of biological diversity. Each of these changes is proceeding at an accelerating rate with consequences that are difficult to predict with certainty or precision. Moreover, none of these phenomena can be quickly reversed after their consequences have been fully understood.

The Council heard a set of presentations concerning the science of climate change, the risks, and the uncertainties. Human activities are increasing the concentrations of so-called greenhouse gases. The models used by the Intergovernmental Panel on Climate Change predict a warming of 0.8° F to 3.5°F by the year 2100, although the resulting effects are much less clear.

U.S. emissions of carbon dioxide, the primary greenhouse gas due to human activity, make up approximately 25 percent of global emissions of this gas; the per capita U.S. emissions rate is higher than that of any other major industrialized country and many times that of any developing country. In the future, emissions from the developing world will grow rapidly as their economies grow, and atmospheric concentrations of greenhouse gases consequently will rise. Without change, emissions from developing nations will surpass those from industrial nations—but not for several decades.

It is clear that the United States cannot solve the potential problem of climate change alone. But it is also is clear that unless the industrialized nations demonstrate the benefits of a different development path, there will be little incentive for the rest of the world to follow.

Threats to the global stock of biodiversity represent another global environmental challenge. Although the risks and implications for the United States (as well as its own contribution to the problem) may seem vague and uncertain, the economic and environmental effects could be profound. Economic benefits from wild species make up an estimated 4.5 percent of the U.S. gross domestic product. Fisheries contribute about 100 million tons of food worldwide. One-fourth of all prescriptions dispensed in the United States contain active ingredients extracted from plants, and more than 3,000 antibiotics are derived from microorganisms. Further, nature tourism generates an increasing percentage of tourism revenues worldwide. Yet, for all its value, biodiversity often takes a backseat in many economic development plans. Tropical forests house between 50 and 90 percent of all species on Earth, but because of forest clearing, 5 to 10 percent of the tropical forest species may be faced with extinction within the next 30 years. Around the globe people who depend on the sea for a living are already witnessing a decline in the productivity of many of the world's most valuable fisheries. As with climate change, one nation cannot solve the problem alone, and the potential for economic harm is huge.

In accepting the challenges of leadership posed by its wealth, strength, know-how, and history, the United States must first adopt effective domestic policies to achieve sustainable development so that it can demonstrate that a better path to progress is possible. Falling short of its own goals may signal to the world the ineffectiveness of free institutions to create environmentally sound economic development that equitably distributes the benefits of growing prosperity. If the United States believes that free institutions are the best means for pursuing human aspirations, it must show that these institutions can respond to the great changes taking place.

More than 100 nations have established national councils on sustainable development similar to the U.S. President's Council on Sustainable Development; they seek to create consensus and shape policies to bring together economic, environmental, and equity goals. Some, like the Canadian and Australian Roundtables, began their work several years before the U.S. Council. Most have been organized in response to the 1992 Earth Summit, the United Nations Conference on Environment and Development. Each of the councils is addressing the relationship of human well-being, economic progress, and the environment within the fabric of the conditions, needs, heritage, and politics of its own country. Their council representatives have said—in many different ways—that if the United States fails, they cannot succeed; but if the United States embraces the idea of sustainability, they believe their own nations will as well.

Because the United States is linked to the world by interrelated economic, environmental, and security interests, it cannot simply turn inward. The nation will achieve much that is in its interest by arguing the case for and assisting the transition to global sustainability. It can create markets for U.S. technology, foster equitable conditions under which U.S. industries and workers can compete, and build fair agreements for action to address global problems that affect the United States and its citizens. International engagement for sustainability is a task for government in its relations with other governments, but it is also a task for other parts of society.

For decades, and with considerable success, America has provided aid to nations to encourage development, fight disease, build democracy, and reduce environmental damage. The majority of that aid has come from government, but U.S. philanthropic organizations also have channeled billions of dollars of voluntary contributions into national and global efforts to meet human needs and protect the future. Leading U.S. companies have been influential in moving their industries toward openness and the application of consistent codes of responsible global stewardship. Nongovernmental organizations have helped to spur the creation of strong independent voices in debates on development, environment, and social policies around the world. Both official and unofficial roles are essential to the process of international change.

There must be several elements to this national engagement. One element is having strong and effective bilateral and multilateral development assistance agencies. Through organizations such as the U.S. Agency for International Development, the United Nations, the Global Environment Facility, and the various international organizations charged with helping implement the international environmental accords, the United States can demonstrate its commitment to global development paths that make sense for both this country and the rest of the world. The United States can also continue to play a key role in helping developing countries confront the critical problems this nation has already solved at home, such as the removal of lead from gasoline and the development of environmental assessment techniques. Financial support is one way for the United States to make credible, substantive, and analytical contributions to the work of multilateral institutions and encourage broader participation by other countries.

Second, the United States is a signatory to the international conventions or treaties that are designed to promote common actions to reduce the risks of climate change and biodiversity loss—two of a growing list of international accords to address global environmental concerns. Yet, the United States has not ratified the U.N. Convention on Biological Diversity—the only major industrialized country that has not done so—even though ratification was supported by a broad cross section of U.S. industry and environmental groups. As a result, the United States faces the risk of not being able to participate in the treaty or help shape the treaty's evolution. Further, the United States may forgo potential economic benefits from the import of genetic resources. The international environmental treaties may not be perfect from many different perspectives, but they do offer a framework for nations to use to move forward together when there is little incentive to move alone. America will derive the greatest benefit in support of its economic and environmental interests by participating in these treaties as well as in the full range of international development assistance processes.

Third, this nation must not diminish either the importance of scientific research for domestic and international fronts or the importance of the U.S. role in such research. To develop treaties to deal with new concerns and issues effectively, the scientific understanding of the problems and the possible responses to them must continue to be improved. Therefore, the United States should continue to support research and encourage other nations to participate more in international research on critical issues relevant to health and the environment.

Finally, but no less importantly, this nation should continue to promote and encourage global trading systems that mutually reinforce environmental protection and other social development goals. In recent years, initial steps have been taken to incorporate environmental provisions into regional and multilateral agreements designed to reduce trade barriers and improve equitable access to global markets. These agreements may serve to enhance U.S. economic well-being as well as that of other nations and to promote, in a broader sense, greater global stability. Much still needs to be done, however, in reconciling trade and environmental objectives in an increasingly integrated world economy. This is not just a job for governments, but requires the resources and commitment of the industrial community and the private sector as a whole. Improved economic health and political stability can provide greater resources for environmental protection and a more effective coordinated global approach to the challenges that the nations of the world face together.

# CHAPTER 13

---

# The Future of Environmental Law and Policy

The concluding chapter of this reader takes a critical look at what environmental law has accomplished to date, and its prospects for the future. The chapter begins with the reflections of former EPA Administrator William Ruckelshaus on why he believes that the current system of environmental regulation, despite significant accomplishments, is badly broken and in need of fundamental repair. Ruckelshaus argues that the greatest threats to the environment are no longer the major industrial facilities that environmental law has targeted so heavily. He maintains that the environmental laws have been unrealistically striving for perfection, creating impossible expectations that inevitably erode public trust in the EPA. Ruckelshaus argues that too many important environmental decisions today are made by courts and he recommends that the EPA be given more flexibility to address what it deems to be the most serious environmental problems. He concludes by calling for replacement of the existing welter of environmental laws with a single, unified statute while placing greater emphasis on consensus-building approaches to regulation.

The chapter then considers the debate between Gregg Easterbrook, with his "eco-realistic" view of the future, and the environmentalists whom he criticizes so sharply. Easterbrook maintains that environmentalists have been unnecessarily alarmist and that forces already set in motion guarantee the complete elimination of pollution in the developed world within the next generation or two. The Environmental Defense Fund argues that what Easterbrook decries as "alarmism" is in fact responsible for much of the environmental progress that has occurred. They challenge his assessment of environmental trends, maintaining that it is founded on critical scientific errors.

The chapter then considers different views concerning the shape of future environmental policy, from Vice President Al Gore and economist Robert Hahn. The vice

396 THE FUTURE OF ENVIRONMENTAL LAW AND POLICY

president notes that the twentieth century has witnessed both an unprecedented surge in human population and a sharp acceleration of technological advance. He argues that these developments have caused a fundamental transformation in humans' relationship with nature. Industrial civilization is violently colliding with the planet's ecosystem, according to Gore, and bold action is required to avert catastrophic harm to the global environment. Arguing that environmental protection should become "the central organizing principle for civilization," Gore calls for a "Global Marshall Plan" to save the planet.

Reviewing Gore's book, economist Robert Hahn agrees that a new environmental paradigm is needed which reflects a fundamental rethinking of the relationship of humans to the global environment. However, Hahn believes that the vice president's visionary approach must be complemented by hard-headed policy analysis that asks whether it is worth it to invest massive sums in environmental protection. Hahn suspects that the vice president's proposals would cost hundreds of billions of dollars each year, reducing the material quality of life for most Americans. Thus, he maintains that it is necessary to define more precisely goals and concepts such as "sustainable development," which may yield little more than the long-held understanding of the need to focus on internalizing the external costs of activities that damage the environment.

The book concludes with an excerpt from Christopher Stone's *The Gnat Is Older than Man*, in which Stone reviews the difficulties confronting efforts to construct a truly *environmental* ethic to guide future policy. While admonishing environmentalists that they should view economic analysis as their ally rather than their enemy, Stone explains why economic analysis will not provide the solutions that will truly reconcile environmental policy conflicts. After reviewing various efforts to construct an environmental ethic that is not centered entirely on human welfare, Stone finds that virtually all of them succumb to the pressure to define environmentally "right" choices in terms that will also benefit human welfare. While failing to discern any moral principles that will not be subject to heated dispute, Stone does not leave the reader with a sense of futility, but rather with the excitement of realizing how challenging are the questions raised by environmental policy. What sort of planet should we seek to leave future generations and what policies should we adopt to achieve this end? Ultimately, these are questions for which each of us must supply our own answers.

## William D. Ruckelshaus

# Stopping the Pendulum (1995)

EPA was launched on a huge wave of public enthusiasm. Its programs have had an enormous and beneficial effect on all our lives. The gross pollution we were all worried about 25 years ago is either a memory or under reasonable social control. Why is EPA now the agency everyone loves to hate?

There are four reasons, three built into the very core of EPA, and one that results from the peculiarities of our times.

First, there is the belief that pollution is not just a problem to be worked out by society using rational means, but a form of evil. In the early days of environmentalism this was a plausible idea to many of the people drafting the initial set of laws. Industry at that time didn't take environmental degradation seriously, and there was considerable bad faith—lies, cheating, and so on. But things have changed now. Nearly all major industrial leaders know that environmentalism is here to stay, and so firms wish to avoid charges that they are insensitive polluters, just as they wish to avoid defects in quality. The customers don't like it, and business now realizes that paying attention to the environmental impact of technology or processes benefits the bottom line; environmental protection has become a permanent factor to be weighed by corporate America.

In addition, the most significant threats to our environment now seem to lie, not with major industrial sites, but in the habits of ordinary Americans: we like to drive big, powerful cars, use a lot of electricity, generate a lot of waste, enjoy cheap food, live in grassy suburbs, and collectively send pollution in massive amounts to often distant waterways and airsheds.

The laws, and the enforcement policies that follow them, are still looking for that evil polluter, and in the same place—major facilities. Since the relative threat from these has decreased, EPA is ever more like the drunk looking for his keys under the lamp-post. More effort, more irritation, less achievement to show—and looking awkward at the same time.

William D. Ruckelshaus, Stopping the Pendulum, The Environmental Forum ®, November/December 1995, p. 25.

This phenomenon is directly related to the second major flaw—the commitment to perfection built into the language of our major statutes. In addition to the mistaken belief that absolute safety is both possible and affordable, the theory was that if standards were set extremely high, sometimes on scant scientific evidence, and an extremely tight time frame was set to achieve those standards, then there would be constant pressure on industry and on EPA to make continuous improvements. The nation was committed to a sort of pie-in-the-sky at some future date, a date extended further and further as inevitably EPA missed nearly every deadline set for it. Each time a new generation of clean technology came into use, the response from EPA had to be, "That's great—now do some more," whether that "more" made any sense or not.

It can be argued that the present system has produced significant environmental benefits. True it has; the environment is a good deal less toxic than it once was. But look at the cost. Even though the environment has improved, the agency and the environmental community are pervaded by a sense of failure. In fact, that failure was foreordained by the promise of an unattainable future. In addition, pursuit of perfection inevitably leads to the pursuit of trivialities, which yield more of those famous horror stories. The business of environmental protection devolves into an endless debate about arcane scientific procedures—one in a million or one in a billion. The important moral force of EPA is frittered away, and still we cannot summon the energy to deal with real environmental problems. We cannot direct our attention outward to help the global problems crying out for assistance from the most powerful nation on earth. I do not believe this is what we started out to do in 1970.

The impossible mission of pursuing perfection leads directly to the third quandary — the devolution of all important environmental decisions to the courts. As is well known, nearly every major EPA decision ends up in the judicial system, one result of the determination of the early drafters of our legislation—who were, no surprise here, environmental lawyers—to allow the most liberal provisions for citizen suits. The result has been that most of the environmental protections that are actually (rather than theoretically) put into place are the result not of the deliberations of scientists or engineers or elected representatives or responsible appointed officials, but of consent decrees handed down by judges. . . .

The fourth reason is that peculiar quality of our times, the nearly steady erosion of trust in all public institutions. People don't trust government, but they don't trust business either. At the epicenter of this institutional hell of mistrust is EPA. This is largely because advocates for addressing our environmental problems, and their allies in Congress, feared for the implementation of their program in the event of a hostile administration, and their antidote was to write stringent mandates, restrictions, and timetables into the statutes. But, tying the administrator's hands in this way does not necessarily advance substantive environmental goals; paradoxically, it may even retard them. Promising unachievable perfection simply assures trust-eroding failure. . . .

We have to assume that at some time in the future—probably when this current version of gridlock is more apparent—we will be able to deal seriously with the reform we all recognize is needed. What would that reform look like?

First of all it would have to be *effective.* It must be able to address those problems that a consensus of knowledge and research has identified as the worst environmental risks. This requires an administrative structure capable of marshaling resources to address those problems, in whatever media they occur, and the discretion and flexibility to allocate those resources effectively. This means that Congress is going to have to return to its constitutional role of setting national policy and providing vigorous oversight, and leave the EPA to get on with implementing that policy, free of direct supervision from 535 administrators.

Second, reform has to produce *efficiency.* It has to provide the maximum reduction of risk to human health and the environment per dollar invested in controls or incentives. This implies, first, a vast simplification of environmental rule making. We cannot go on with a system in which the physical volume of the paper necessary to establish a permit approaches the physical volume of the waste to be controlled. Also, some finite, well understood limits should be established for what our society is prepared to apply for a certain level of environmental health, together with some reasonable relationship between what is paid and what we get for it. In other words, environmentalism has to leave the realm of quasi-religion and take its place among the realities of the state, along with national security, social welfare, health, and justice—pretty good company, by the way.

Third, the system must better *reflect the essential democratic values of our society.* The day is past when a dozen or so youngish people can sit in a windowless room in Waterside Mall and, after a year or so, in the last stages of exhaustion, emerge with a set of absolute commands for a major economic sector. We need a system that reflects the real choices of the American people as to what levels of protection they desire locally for local problems, and that builds upon the basic good sense of communities in balancing their environmental and other social values. Needless to say, no one can be allowed to clean up by loading pollution on to a neighbor, and so the new system has to be carefully designed to be consistent with regional, national, and global environmental goals.

Finally, the system has to be *fair.* It cannot impose an undue burden of either risk or expense on any one portion of the population, or allow the transfer of risk from one place to another without fully informed consent. It cannot, for example, expect private landowners to carry the full cost of species protection, nor can it expect farm workers or people living near industrial plants to suffer inordinate risks for the economic benefit of the general population.

It hardly needs saying that no petty adjustment of the current set of laws can easily achieve these objectives. The nation needs a new, single, unified environmental statute supervised by a single authorizing committee and a single appropriations committee in each house of Congress. Not the 12 laws and 70 committees we now have. I am fully aware of the political difficulty of achieving this nirvana, but it is no more vaulted in aspiration than zero cancer risk with a margin of safety below that—an impossible assignment EPA has labored with for decades.

How to get there is, of course, the problem. . . . What one piece of a right answer could look like is slowly emerging from local experiences in this country and from the experience of other nations. It involves a new sort of consensus process, in which all the significant stakeholders are brought together to hammer out a solution to a set of environmental problems. This approach is particularly applicable to problems confined to specific geographic regions. The critical thing about such a process, and the only way to make it work, is that all participants have to understand that the process is the entire and exclusive theater for decisions; therefore Congress and other legislative bodies have to mandate the process. There will be no appeal, and no way to weasel out of the deal. This is critical; no consensus process can survive the idea that one of the parties can get everything it wants, without compromise, in some other forum.

A process of this type has been used successfully by the state of Washington in working through the competing interests of timber companies, environmentalists, Indian tribes, and local communities regarding the cut of timber on state lands. On a larger scale, the Netherlands now runs its entire environmental program out of consensus groups covering every major industry and district. Industries can meet national guidelines in just about any way they choose, but they have to play the game. The Dutch call the national plans developed through such processes government-industry "covenants." They also call them "coercive voluntary agreements."

Whether such a process would work here in a big, mostly empty country, where the tradition is more libertarian, is an open question. But somehow we have to get past this situation where EPA is out there in the boat and everyone else is on the shore jeering as the ship struggles to stay afloat. Somehow, we have to use whatever civic consciousness and sense of community we have left to bring all the interests into the same boat. Because if EPA sinks, we all get pulled under.

*Gregg Easterbrook*

# A Moment on the Earth: The Coming Age of Environmental Optimism (1995)

Ecological consciousness is a leading force for good in world affairs. Without the imperatives of modern environmentalism—without its three decades of unstinting pressure on government and industry—the Western world today might actually be in the kind of ecological difficulty conventional wisdom assumes it to be in. Instead, the Western world today is on the verge of the greatest ecological renewal that humankind has known; perhaps the greatest that the Earth has known. Environmentalists deserve the credit for this remarkable turn of events.

Yet our political and cultural institutions continue to read from a script of instant doomsday. Environmentalists, who are surely on the right side of history, are increasingly on the wrong side of the present, risking their credibility by proclaiming emergencies that do not exist. What some doctrinaire environmentalists wish were true for reasons of ideology has begun to obscure the view of what is actually true in "the laboratory of nature." It's time we began reading from a new script, one that reconciles the ideals of environmentalism with the observed facts of the natural world. Toward that end [I] advance the following premises:

- That in the Western world pollution will end within our lifetimes, with society almost painlessly adapting a zero-emissions philosophy.
- That several categories of pollution have *already* ended.
- That the environments of Western countries have been growing cleaner during the very period the public has come to believe they are growing more polluted.

- That First World industrial countries, considered the scourge of the global environment, are by most measures much cleaner than developing nations.
- That most feared environmental catastrophes, such as runaway global warming, are almost certain to be avoided.
- That far from becoming a new source of global discord, environmentalism, which binds nations to a common concern, will be the best thing that's ever happened to international relations.
- That nearly all technical trends are toward new devices and modes of production that are more efficient, use fewer resources, produce less waste, and cause less ecological disruption than technology of the past.
- That there exists no fundamental conflict between the artificial and the natural.
- That artificial forces which today harm nature can be converted into allies of nature in an incredibly short time by natural standards.
- Most important, that humankind, even a growing human population of many billions, can take a constructive place in the natural order.

None of these notions are now common currency. It is possible to find yourself hooted down for proposing them at some public forums. A few years ago at a speech at a Harvard Divinity School conference on environmental affairs I was hissed merely for saying "People are more important than plants and animals." What better barometer is there of how nonsensical doomsday thinking can become?

But that is a passing situation. In the near future the propositions stated above will be widely embraced by society and even by the intelligentsia. Collectively I call these views *ecorealism*.

Ecorealism will be the next wave of environmental thinking. The core principles of ecorealism are these: that logic, not sentiment, is the best tool for safeguarding nature; that accurate understanding of the actual state of the environment will serve the Earth better than expressions of panic; that in order to form a constructive alliance with nature, men and women must learn to think like nature. . . .

## Is Paradise Paved?

Human sprawl is ubiquitous on planet Earth. Cities both grand and dolorogenic dot six of the seven continents. Autos, trucks, and trains scurry everywhere. Mighty aircraft arc the skies; vessels larger than medieval towns course the seas; chandeliers of technology hang in space. Through human action whole provinces of Earth have been converted from forest or prairie to farms and pasture. Countless rivers have been dammed or diverted. And everywhere are man's machines, from the little motors that power handheld devices to the giant engines known as factories—machines spewing toxic chemicals, respiratory irritants, acids, greenhouse gases, water pollutants, caustic sodas, production slag, agricultural husks, cattle gristle, mineral till, "depleted" uranium, ash, polymer slurries, and products at times hard to distinguish from by-products. In parallel the homes of First World citizens have become little factories in their own right, generating heat or cold, ablaze with lights, pumping out wastes of every variety. . . .

From nature's perspective the picture is surely different. No one could dispute that genus *Homo* affects the Earth more than any other species. Humanity is resourceful and mischievous, assiduously engaged in environmental harm. But is nature really on the run? Several important indexes suggest that it is not.

First, the portion of Earth taken over by humanity is fantastically exaggerated in the popular imagination. The United States is the most growth-obsessed and machine-oriented of cultures. Yet so far only two percent of the U.S. surface area is "built up," according to the U.S. Geological Survey. This figure reflects the concrete footprint of cities, towns, roads, suburbs, homes, offices, factories, airports, and other artificial impositions upon American land. *Two percent.* If lakes formed by dams are thought of as built-up land, the figure rises to slightly over three percent. The comparable figure for Europe is about eight percent built-up. Europe has been in pursuit of the materialist lifestyle for several centuries longer than the United States. Yet even there only a small portion of the biosphere has been seized by people. North and west of New York City and London and Chicago, south of Paris and Bonn, east of San Francisco and Moscow, in all directions around Atlanta and Denver and Warsaw and Madrid, and in many similar locations worldwide, extensive tracts of habitat that have known only occasional human intervention abut centers of mechanistic human excess. . . .

## Trees: Headed Up

An important area in which human and natural perceptions differ is the forest. That portion of the world that remains wooded is a fine proxy for whether nature is in decline; for forests, even the tree plantations of the big lumber companies, are primarily temples of nature, not man.

Today most Americans would surely say that forests are in critical condition. Commentary on the 1990s dispute pitting loggers against the spotted owl in the Olympic forests of Oregon and Washington State was, for example, thick with the words "disaster," "destroyed," "ravaged," and "lost forever" in reference to American forests.

Deforestation is without doubt currently taking a toll on forests in many tropical nations. But in most affluent countries, forest cover has not been declining but expanding for at least several decades. The environmentalist's notion of a forest wipeout in progress is in the Western nations the reverse of the natural reality.

Western Europe today has nearly 30 percent *more* forest area than it had half a century ago, despite the fact that its human population has increased rapidly through that period. In the United States forests reached their nadir in the 1920s, damaged extensively by shoddy logging practices. But as the forestry analyst Roger Sedjo, of the Washington think tank Resources for the Future, has written, sometime around the early 1940s "forest growth nationally came into balance with harvests, and since that time growth has exceeded harvest." The total amount of forest has been expanding in the United States and Western Europe during the postwar era—the very period during which, environmental doctrine says, nature has been put to rout. . . .

At several points in the twentieth century, various environmental problems have seemed to reach a level at which they become irreversible. Forest loss, overuse of bioaccumulative pesticides such as DDT, and stratospheric ozone depletion are three examples. In each case commentators decreed hopelessness. In each case the irreversible problem promptly reversed itself. Forest acres in the developed world are now expanding; DDT was banished and its bioaccumulative effects are nearly gone from the U.S. biosphere; CFCs and other chemicals linked to ozone depletion are already in decline and will go out of production in most countries in 1996, with projections now showing ozone layer replenishment beginning early in the twenty-first century. Yet doctrines of pessimism somehow never get amended as the result of positive experiences.

At this writing two problems widely viewed as irreversible are loss of equatorial rainforests and the artificial greenhouse effect. But what if the developing world executes the same sequence of forest protection seen in the industrial world? A period of unregulated forest loss may be followed by a period of stabilization (deforestation rates have declined sharply in the last three years in Brazil, the country where the problem is worst) and after that a forest recovery. Aforestation of tropical woodlands might begin as soon as the early twenty-first century, a split second from now by the natural stopwatch. And what if nations learn to reduce greenhouse emissions through energy efficiency? That is already underway in many countries. Rather than steadily increasing as commentators consider inevitable, artificial greenhouse gases may begin to decline. Then the specter of global warming will recede as well. . . .

Today we cannot imagine a Western economy based on anything other than a whopping consumption of petroleum. But a century ago no leading intellectual imagined the world running on oil. Just as horses in nineteenth-century cities were certain to yield to some other mode of transportation, what the materialist lifestyle today depends on for its inputs is certain to change repeatedly through the centuries ahead.

Perhaps the most fundamental point of understanding about the biosphere is that it is a *living* system, not static but continuously reacting with itself and its circumstances. Human society is the same, alive and always in transition. If human society attempted to stand still by continuing to gulp petroleum at its current rate, fiasco would follow. But social change will not come to a halt, freezing current trends in place. Through the last 20 years, Western use of petroleum has begun shifting markedly in the direction of conservation. Such changes are partly driven by prices and government policies. But partly they may be seen as organic self-adaptation— society reacting just as nature would to self-correct a resource imbalance.

A Western energy economy based on hydrogen, solar-electric conversion, biomass from vegetation, and similar renewable power is not only not science fiction, it is odds-on to be realized in the lifetimes of some readers of this book. Currently many engineers scoff at the notion that hydrogen and solar-electric conversion will be useful on a commercial scale. But not much more than 100 years ago, gasoline and internal combustion were derided as nonsense. A century ago any sensible economist would have sworn that every dollar of capital in the world would be insufficient to construct the vast infrastructure necessary to create an auto culture: oil fields, refineries, pipelines, ubiquitous gasoline stations, automobile manufacturing facilities, repair shops, and so on. Yet Western society reinvented itself from no cars to all cars in 50 years.

It is well to remember that approaching the turn of the twentieth century, commentators called horse proliferation an "irreversible" peril to society—pasture land would crowd out farms, horse droppings would make cities unlivable, towns would run out of space to bury the horse carcasses, and so on. Just at the moment too many horses seemed an unresolvable environmental threat, the horse population began to drop drastically in response to the arrival of motor carriages. Running out of coal was a common refrain in the 1920s; the U.S. Department of the Interior and the British admiralty, charged with stocking the colliers of the English fleet, were among many authorities to declare coal would soon be gone forever. Within a decade a coal glut began, in response to new coal seam finds occurring at the same time that coal demand fell as the world's infatuation with petroleum commenced. In turn the imminent exhaustion of petroleum was universally decried in the 1970s. Shortly thereafter the price of oil began to plummet.

Here we may proclaim a law of environmental affairs: Whenever all respectable commentators believe a problem cannot be solved, it is about to be solved. Since respectable commentators now consider global warming unstoppable, this law predicts the greenhouse effect is about to become old news. And since respectable commentators now are "sure" that society can never wean itself from fossil fuels, therefore let's predict that the end of the fossil-fuel economy is near at hand.

Though a zero-polluting, renewable-energy economy is not practical at present, no improbably technological leaps are required to bring one into being. Today's fossil-fuel economy is already much closer in structure to a renewable-energy regime than the last century's energy economy was to today's. The Princeton physicists Joan Ogden and Robert Williams have suggested that within a decade or two, cost-effective solar-electric converters will become widely available. Large fields of such devices, placed in deserts where sunshine is intense and there are few living things to disturb, would provide renewable power to separate hydrogen from water. The hydrogen would be piped back to cities for use as a gasoline replacement. In such an energy economy the basic fuel sources would be sunlight and water; the pollution output would be negligible, as hydrogen burns without meaningful air emissions or greenhouse gases.

Once an advanced energy economy is realized, petroleum might still be employed as a chemical feedstock and for other uses, but its political and social significance will conclude. Oil by and large will return to its former status of a murky nuisance that sometimes leaks from the ground; historians will come to consider the Oil Age a curiosity of less lasting significance than the Bronze Age. The industrial way of life may be irksome, but on several important fronts like this it is well ahead of the world's feudal cultures in pursuit of ecological transparency. Nature may love the citizens of the Third World but be rooting for the engineers of the First.

*Environmental Defense Fund*

# A Moment of Truth: Correcting the Scientific Errors in Gregg Easterbrook's *A Moment on the Earth* (1995)

In his book *A Moment on the Earth,* Gregg Easterbrook argues that environmentalists "are surely on the right side of history, but increasingly on the wrong side of the present, risking their credibility by proclaiming emergencies that do not exist." Yet his account of environmental issues is replete with errors and misinterpretations of the scientific evidence. This is especially notable in regard to the four chapters that deal with habitat loss, global warming, ozone depletion, and species extinction, probably the four most serious threats to the natural environment, according to a recent report by the Science Advisory Board of the U.S. Environmental Protection Agency.

We believe that the record should be set straight on Easterbrook's critical scientific errors, for the faulty statements in these four chapters substantially undermine his thesis that many environmental problems have been overstated. . . .

In his chapter on global warming, Easterbrook makes many fundamental errors. He continually confuses global, regional, and local temperature trends, which may differ considerably; he mischaracterizes the results of a poll that was undertaken to determine scientists' views on global warming; and he mistakenly asserts that the sea level has not risen significantly, when it has.

Most flagrantly, however, he erroneously claims that the National Academy of Sciences (NAS) and the Intergovernmental Panel on Climate Change (IPCC), the two most respected scientific authorities on the subject, have substantially lowered their projections of future warming due to a doubling of carbon dioxide in the atmosphere, when they have not. . . .

Environmental Defense Fund, A Moment of Truth: Correcting the Scientific Errors in Gregg Easterbrook's *A Moment on the Earth* (New York: Environmental Defense Fund, 1995). Reprinted with permission.

In [the] chapter ["Radiation, Natural"] and elsewhere, Easterbrook attempts to contrast what he calls the "doomsday" approach to environmental problems with his own so-called "eco-realism," ridiculing, for example, the "idea that relatively tiny amounts of CFCs could trigger an unstoppable progression that strips the entire ozone layer, leaving the biosphere defenseless" (*A Moment on the Earth*, p. 535). Yet this is what, in essence could well have occurred, with very large depletions developing throughout the world, unleashing potentially disastrous consequences for the biosphere, *if* the decision to aggressively limit the use and production of CFC's had not been made.

Moreover, he places himself against the weight of scientific evidence in claiming that UV radiation may not have risen since the emergence of ozone depletion, and that where radiation increases occur, they may have little or no effect. Along the way, he makes elementary errors in relating the history of the discovery of ozone depletion and even suggests, against medical evidence to the contrary, that increases in UV radiation may not be harmful to human health. . . .

The chapter on the northern spotted owl in *A Moment on the Earth* is so full of scientific errors and inaccurate assumptions that its conclusion—that the threat of extinction faced by the owl is overstated—is essentially worthless.

To his credit, Easterbrook is supportive of the Endangered Species Act and the efforts of environmental groups to save species in general. But in opposing the conclusions of independent biologists that the northern spotted owl faced extinction, Easterbrook neglects to cite the voluminous scientific evidence for this position, as contained in numerous peer-reviewed studies. Most importantly, he neglects to mention the definitive findings of the meeting in December 1993, in Colorado, in which biologists and statisticians from throughout the United States and Europe undertook the single largest population study of a bird of prey, and concluded that the northern spotted owl was indeed in rapid decline. . . .

Easterbrook's arguments in his chapter on endangered species are equally problematic. While disputing the conclusions of natural scientists and wildlife biologists that human activities are causing the planet to experience a loss of species of major proportions throughout the globe, he relies on inaccurate assumptions and faulty reasoning.

Moreover, as in the spotted owl chapter, he fails to grasp the difference between the better counting of existing numbers of species with observed trends that show that many of these species are in decline. This is evident when he wrongly dismisses as contradictory the increasing scientific estimates of the total number of species on Earth, and the consensus of biologists that extinction is proceeding at a rate unprecedented since the close of the age of the dinosaurs. . . .

## Conclusion

In *A Moment on the Earth,* Gregg Easterbrook attempts to contrast his own supposedly "eco-realistic" views with the views of those he labels environmental "doomsayers." Yet what the book really does is to set Mr. Easterbrook's own opinions against the weight of scientific evidence, consisting of the findings of hundreds of independent climatologists, atmospheric scientists, and wildlife biologists, working in their respective fields through the world. While continually dismissing the assessments of these experts as overly pessimistic, he caricatures their positions, and incorrectly characterizes their work as part of a biased environmental "orthodoxy." In the process, he impugns the intelligence, judgment, and impartiality of some of the most esteemed scientists of our time, including Rachel Carson, James Anderson, and E. O. Wilson.

Moreover, he repeatedly criticizes scientists whose dire predictions have not come to pass, without fully acknowledging that their forecasts catalyzed changes in laws and policies that forestalled the predictions themselves.

Though the Environmental Defense Fund celebrates the successes of the past, including the banning of DDT and the restrictions on the use of CFC's, and believes that further achievements are within our grasp, we hold that this will be possible only with a realistic assessment of those environmental problems that still remain, based on the best scientific evidence.

Far from being "eco-realistic," Easterbrook's work betrays an exteme naivete concerning the workings of physical processes and natural ecosystems, resulting in an entirely unwarranted optimism that we will easily solve all of our environmental problems in the near future, if we have not done so already. Perhaps he himself should take to heart the advice he offers up so readily to environmentalists: "Learn science and speak logic. Many lesser creatures will thank you" (*A Moment on the Earth*, p. 647).

*Al Gore*

# Earth in the Balance: Ecology and the Human Spirit (1992)

This century has witnessed dramatic changes in two key factors that define the physical reality of our relationship to the earth: a sudden and startling surge in human population, with the addition of one China's worth of people every ten years, and a sudden acceleration of the scientific and technological revolution, which has allowed an almost unimaginable magnification of our power to affect the world around us by burning, cutting, digging, moving, and transforming the physical matter that makes up the earth.

The surge in population is both a cause of the changed relationship and one of the clearest illustrations of how startling the change has been, especially when viewed in a historical context. From the emergence of modern humans 200,000 years ago until Julius Caesar's time, fewer than 250 million people walked on the face of the earth. When Christopher Columbus set sail for the New World 1,500 years later, there were approximately 500 million people on earth. By the time Thomas Jefferson wrote the Declaration of Independence in 1776, the number had doubled again, to 1 billion. By midway through this century, at the end of World War II, the number had risen to just about 2 billion people.

In other words, from the beginning of humanity's appearance on earth to 1945, it took more than ten thousand generations to reach a world population of 2 billion people. Now, in the course of one human lifetime—mine—the world population will increase from 2 to more than 9 billion, and it is already more than halfway there. . . .

Like the population explosion, the scientific and technological revolution began to pick up speed slowly during the eighteenth century. And this ongoing revolution has also suddenly accelerated exponentially. For example, it is now an axiom in many fields of science that more new and important discoveries have taken place in the last ten years than in the entire previous history of science. While no single discovery has had the kind of effect on our relationship to the earth that nuclear weapons have had on our relationship to warfare, it is nevertheless true that taken together, they have completely transformed our cumulative ability to exploit the earth for sustenance—making the consequences of unrestrained exploitation every bit as unthinkable as the consequences of unrestrained nuclear war.

Now that our relationship to the earth has changed so utterly, we have to see that change and understand its implications. Our challenge is to recognize that the startling images of environmental destruction now occurring all over the world have much more in common than their ability to shock and awaken us. They are symptoms of an underlying problem broader in scope and more serious than any we have ever faced. Global warming, ozone depletion, the loss of living species, deforestation—they all have a common cause: the new relationship between human civilization and the earth's natural balance.

There are actually two aspects to this challenge. The first is to realize that our power to harm the earth can indeed have global and even permanent effects. The second is to realize that the only way to understand our new role as a co-architect of nature is to see ourselves as part of a complex system that does not operate according to the same simple rules of cause and effect we are used to. The problem is not our effect *on* the environment so much as our relationship *with* the environment. As a result, any solution to the problem will require a careful assessment of that relationship as well as the complex interrelationship among factors within civilization and between them and the major natural components of the earth's ecological system.

There is only one precedent for this kind of challenge to our thinking, and again it is military. The invention of nuclear weapons and the subsequent development by the United States and the Soviet Union of many thousands of strategic nuclear weapons forced a slow and painful recognition that the new power thus acquired forever changed not only the relationship between the two superpowers but also the relationship of humankind to the institution of warfare itself. The consequences of all-out war between nations armed with nuclear weapons suddenly included the possibility of the destruction of both nations—completely and simultaneously. That sobering realization led to a careful reassessment of every aspect of our mutual relationship to the prospect of such a war. As early as 1946 one strategist concluded that strategic bombing with missiles "may well tear away the veil of illusion that has so long obscured the reality of the change in warfare—from a fight to a process of destruction." . . .

The strategic nature of the threat now posed *by* human civilization to the global environment and the strategic nature of the threat *to* human civilization now posed by changes in the global environment present us with a similar set of challenges and false hopes. Some argue that a new ultimate technology, whether nuclear power or genetic engineering, will solve the problem. Others hold that only a drastic reduction of our reliance on technology can improve the conditions of life—a simplistic notion at best. But the real solution will be found in reinventing and finally healing the relationship between civilization and the earth. This can only be accomplished by undertaking a careful reassessment of all the factors that led to the relatively recent dramatic change in the relationship. The transformation of the way we relate to the earth will of course involve new technologies, but the key changes will involve new ways of thinking about the relationship itself. . . .

Modern industrial civilization, as presently organized, is colliding violently with our planet's ecological system. The ferocity of its assault on the earth is breathtaking, and the horrific consequences are occurring so quickly as to defy our capacity to recognize them, comprehend their global implications, and organize an appropriate and timely response. Isolated pockets of resistance fighters who have experienced this juggernaut at first hand have begun to fight back in inspiring but, in the final analysis, woefully inadequate ways. It is not that they lack courage, imagination, or skill; it is simply that what they are up against is nothing less than the current logic of world civilization. As long as civilization as a whole, with its vast technological power, continues to follow a pattern of thinking that encourages the domination and exploitation of the natural world for short-term gains, this juggernaut will continue to devastate the earth no matter what any of us does.

I have come to believe that we must take bold and unequivocal action: we must make the rescue of the environment the central organizing principle for civilization. Whether we realize it or not, we are now engaged in an epic battle to right the balance of our earth, and the tide of this battle will turn only when the majority of people in the world become sufficiently aroused by a shared sense of urgent danger to join an all-out effort. It is time to come to terms with exactly how this can be accomplished. . . .

With the original Marshall Plan serving as both a model and an inspiration, we can now begin to chart a course of action. The world's effort to save the environment must be organized around strategic goals that simultaneously represent the most important changes and allow us to recognize, measure, and assess our progress toward making those changes. Each goal must be supported by a set of policies that will enable world civilization to reach it as quickly, efficiently, and justly as possible.

In my view, five strategic goals must direct and inform our efforts to save the global environment. Let me outline each of them briefly before considering each in depth.

The first strategic goal should be *the stabilizing of world population,* with policies designed to create in every nation of the world the conditions necessary for the so-called demographic transition—the historic and well-documented change from a dynamic equilibrium of high birth rates and death rates to a stable equilibrium of low birth rates and death rates. This change has taken place in most of the industrial nations (which have low rates of infant mortality and high rates of literacy and education) and in virtually none of the developing nations (where the reverse is true).

The second strategic goal should be *the rapid creation and development of environmentally appropriate technologies*—especially in the fields of energy, transportation, agriculture, building construction, and manufacturing—capable of accommodating sustainable economic progress without the concurrent degradation of the environment. These new technologies must then be quickly transferred to all nations—especially those in the Third World, which should be allowed to pay for them by discharging the various obligations they incur as participants in the Global Marshall Plan.

The third strategic goal should be *a comprehensive and ubiquitous change in the economic "rules of the road" by which we measure the impact of our decisions on the environment.* We must establish—by global agreement—a system of economic accounting that assigns appropriate values to the ecological consequences of both routine choices in the marketplace by individuals and companies and larger, macroeconomic choices by nations.

The fourth strategic goal should be *the negotiation and approval of a new generation of international agreements* that will embody the regulatory frameworks, specific prohibitions, enforcement mechanisms, cooperative planning, sharing arrangements, incentives, penalties, and mutual obligations necessary to make the overall plan a success. These agreements must be especially sensitive to the vast differences of capability and need between developed and undeveloped nations.

The fifth strategic goal should be *the establishment of a cooperative plan for educating the world's citizens about our global environment*—first by the establishment of a comprehensive program for researching and monitoring the changes now under way in the environment in a manner that involves the people of all nations, especially students; and, second, through a massive effort to disseminate information about local, regional, and strategic threats to the environment. The ultimate goal of this effort would be to foster new patterns of thinking about the relationship of civilization to the global environment.

Each of these goals is closely related to all of the others, and all should be pursued simultaneously within the larger framework of the Global Marshall Plan. Finally, the plan should have as its more general, integrating goal *the establishment, especially in the developing world—of the social and political conditions most conducive to the emergence of sustainable societies*—such as social justice (including equitable patterns of land ownership); a commitment to human rights; adequate nutrition, health care, and shelter; high literacy rates; and greater political freedom, participation, and accountability. Of course, all specific policies should be chosen as part of serving the central organizing principle of saving the global environment.

*Robert W. Hahn*

# Toward a New Environmental Paradigm (1993)

To address the problems that lie ahead, we need to move beyond mere platitudes concerning sustainability and improvements in the quality of life and begin to provide a concrete definition of the problems we wish to solve along with a serious analysis of the kinds of tools we might use. For example, if our major concern were preventing global warming, that would imply a very different strategy than if our major concern were reducing the number of people whose lives are not satisfying (in a material or spiritual sense). Vice President Gore says both of these problems are urgent: the "strategic threat, global warming, is the most dangerous of all"; and "the worst of all forms of pollution is wasted lives." Elsewhere, Vice President Gore has identified yet a third problem, hazardous waste, as "the most significant environmental health problem of the decade." Even allowing him some leeway for rhetorical flourish, Gore seems oblivious to the necessity of making trade-offs.

Among the most difficult trade-offs that must be made are between today's environmental problems and those of the future. Buying an "insurance" policy, such as a modest carbon tax, may make sense for addressing climate change, depending on your degree of risk aversion and your views on the theory. It makes no sense if the primary concern is with helping the have-nots who are alive today. Even if the concern is with promoting environmental quality, a strong case can be made for implementing policies that alleviate human suffering and promote economic growth. The challenge is to promote such policies in a way that also improves the local environment. Approximately 1.7 billion people lack access to basic sanitation, leading to widespread disease in children and adults. Problems also arise because of lack of clean water. These are basic human problems, and they are also environmental problems.

Reprinted by permission of The Yale Law Journal Company and Fred B. Rothman & Company from *The Yale Law Journal*, Vol. 102, pages 1719–1761.

Vice President Gore does not lose sight of such immediate problems; he simply fails to make the hard choices. Since the hard choices will be made one way or another, it makes sense to develop a strategy for thinking about them. Here, policy analysis and economics provide a useful guide.

Policy analysis, broadly construed, involves two key components—a description of the state of a system of concern to humans, and a theory that defines the relationship between that system's inputs and outputs. For example, if one were concerned about the impacts of the 1990 Clean Air Act Amendments, one would attempt to measure the state of the "system" before and after the law was implemented. The state of the system could be measured in many ways, including direct measures of environmental quality, the number of regulations, the costs of the regulations, and the nature of the regulations. Thus, policy analysis provides a way of summarizing a complicated system using a few key variables that are of interest to the policy maker. It is thus analogous to a standard accounting system that could be used to summarize the health of a business.

First, one needs to define the nature of the problems that need to be examined. For example, one might consider different ways to operationalize notions of sustainability and different objectives for environmental policy.

A second logical step, in the case of sustainability, would be to explore the strengths and weaknesses of various policies in achieving environmental objectives. It might be useful to know, for example, the cost of a policy to stabilize carbon dioxide emission levels at 1990 levels and its likely effect on the global temperature profile. The focus here should be on "policy-relevant" research rather than the pursuit of science to push back the frontiers of knowledge. While I am a great supporter of both endeavors, the United States government does not always organize its research efforts in ways that produce useful and timely policy insights. With the potentially staggering resources we could spend on reducing greenhouse gas emissions, it is important to have a strategy to spend research dollars in ways that will produce useful insights. It is also important to consider policies in light of the political constraints likely to be imposed on policymakers. Developing "optimal" economic approaches may be of little value to policymakers who are constrained by political forces. Finally, the linkages between policies need to be explored more fully, including the linkages between population growth and resource use, and freer trade and the environment. . . .

After linking objectives and outcomes for various problems, one has to prioritize problems and decide how to proceed. While this prioritization is, of necessity, highly subjective, it can be aided by analysis. Moreover, this prioritization could take place using a number of criteria, which may or may not relate to economic efficiency.

This kind of analytical process is likely to yield several insights that are conveniently glossed over in Vice President Gore's presentation. First, and most important, the Vice President's policy prescriptions are likely to be quite expensive—I suspect they would cost hundreds of billions of dollars annually for the United States alone. Second, while a few of his suggestions may enhance our international competitiveness (read our standard of living), the lion's share of his policies are likely to reduce the material quality of life that most Americans enjoy, at least in the short term. Third, the appropriate or preferred strategy for addressing a particular issue will depend on a variety of factors. Only in rare instances is a kitchen sink approach justified when one considers the costs.

Policy analysis has room for a wide range of perspectives. It includes conventional cost-benefit analysis as practiced by economists, but it is far broader. Thus, people not comfortable with the objectives specified in conventional economic analysis can substitute their desired objectives. Moreover, if we place suitable constraints on the problem, we can include issues related to political feasibility in policy analysis. For example, we could design an energy tax in such a way as to ensure that producers and/or specific consumer groups are likely to be better off than they are now. In the age of personal computers, quantitative policy analysis offers a useful guide for developing and evaluating policies to promote sustainable development.

Vice President Gore's visionary approach to sustainable development is a curious blend of religion, revolutionary zeal, and homespun economics. . . .

I believe a constructive alternative vision can be offered. It is an inclusive vision, acknowledging a wide range of perspectives on complex environmental issues. It is a synthetic vision, melding the strengths of the visionary and the policy analytic approaches. Finally, it is a pragmatic vision, which would portray politics realistically when designing policies to enhance our quality of life.

In a sense, the policy analytic approach and the visionary approach can be viewed as complements. The visionary approach aims primarily to highlight the ramifications of achieving a state closer to Nirvana, however defined. The visionary approach may be best viewed as a way to stimulate discussion by playing on our emotions. The policy analytic paradigm can help ground that discussion in reality. In practice, both may be needed to resolve successfully the major challenges that confront humanity.

While the two approaches can complement each other, they differ in important respects. The policy analytic approach is likely to make concepts of sustainability lose much of their luster. Indeed, I suspect that the policy analytic approach will eventually reduce sustainability to a matter of trying to internalize environmental costs and then hoping for the best. That is, we will never be able to be sure that we are on a sustainable path unless the definition or the analysis trivializes the problem. The policy analytic approach makes a serious attempt to link inputs to outputs, an exercise that is sorely lacking in the Vice President's vision. It does not solve the world's problems, but it does help provide a roadmap for concerned decisionmakers.

Both the policy analytic approach and the visionary approach are highly abstract. They represent different perspectives on the universe—one in which analysis guides the making of decisions which help identify further problems for analysis; and a second, in which the time for analysis has come and gone, and the time for action is long overdue. Both abstractions are useful, but limited. . . .

. . . The reality is that we face serious environmental problems at the local, regional, and global levels. The reality is that we are experimenting with our planet on a massive scale. We do not know very much about what we are doing to the planet; and while so far we seem to have "muddled through," we are not infallible. Mr. Gore sensitizes us to our fallibility.

Vice President Gore correctly points out that we need "a searching reexamination of the ways in which political motives and government policies have helped to create the crisis and now frustrate the solutions we need." At present, we have a limited understanding of how different interest groups—including environmentalists, business, politicians, and bureaucrats—affect the evolution of environmental policy. Research that sheds greater light on these issues would be most useful. I would hope the Vice President promotes public support for such research. It is essential that we understand the forces that shape the status quo to determine the ideas that will be needed to move us in a new direction.

The central theme of this book is that we need a new perspective—particularly in thinking about our relationship to the earth. Mr. Gore uses many examples to demonstrate the importance of perspective, but the one that I found most compelling was the story about artists in ancient Peru who drew figures on the ground that could be recognized only from the air. Looking at things in new ways is one of the trademarks of human intellectual progress.

Over the next century we will be compelled to rethink our relationship to the environment, as well as to one another. The emergence of new technology connects us in ways few could have imagined thirty years ago. The beauty of this book is that it stimulates the reader to take a new perspective. While I do not adhere to Mr. Gore's vision, I do agree that we need to move toward a new paradigm. I hope politicians and scholars seize upon this vision as a starting point for discussion. Who knows? The future of the earth may lie in the balance.

*Christopher D. Stone*

# The Gnat Is Older Than Man: Global Environment and the Human Agenda (1993)

Despite the difficulties of identifying efficient outcomes, the principle is worth remembering: in a world in which so many desires are unfulfilled, and in which there is so much poverty, we cannot regard the environment and its amenities to be infinitely valuable; nor can environmentalists muster political support if they regard each and every response to each and every crisis as equally meritorious.

Hence, the costs and benefits of environmental protection—as best we can estimate them—have to be compared constantly with competing demands. Economic analysis provides the best single way to keep these compromises in view. Indeed, it is a shame that economic analysis is so commonly disparaged by environmentalists, who have somehow gotten the idea that economic thinking and environmental thinking are inherently opposed.

Environmentalists often feel that, by admitting there might be a marketable "right" to pollute, they have given away the store. But some compromises are necessary, and making polluters pay for polluting—thereby reducing the levels—is a whole lot better than allowing them to get away with it for nothing.

The more durable objection is that many environmental values, such as the "values" of noncommercial species, are not captured by markets. As Mark Sagoff has argued so spiritedly, the value placed on preservation has to be set in the political arena, not in markets. "The genius of cost-benefit analysis," Sagoff remarks, is to inhibit "conflict among affected individuals from breaking out into the public realm"—which is exactly where many of them ought to be. But this "market" objection goes only to the most cramped conception of economics. Economic analysis is certainly robust enough to accommodate nonmarket-measured values, although it takes an alliance with the legislature: as a first step, the public bodies can ask citizens what they are willing to pay to preserve a noncommercial species or exotic habitat, and base social decisions accordingly.

Let me illustrate with the question whether to permit or even encourage wolves to reestablish in national parks. Wildlife groups favor their return. The stockbreeders on the fringes of the parks are against it. The ranchers argue that the wolves eat their calves. The conservationists say the ranchers exaggerate; and, anyway, why prefer calves to wolves (or why prefer people eating calves to wolves doing so)? Around Yellowstone there was a virtual standoff—until Defenders of Wildlife came forward with the idea of funding a trust to indemnify the cattlemen for any cattle they lose. In 1992, as a more positive incentive, an additional offer of $5,000 was made to any private landowner whose land hosts a den producing pups allowed to grow to maturity. The compromise solution was an idea that any economist would be pleased to take credit for, and one that showed the potential of "economic instruments" more modestly scaled than global trading.

But closer analysis showed even more. The losses to the state of Wyoming in hunting revenues (stemming from the wolves' predation on moose, elk, and deer) was on the order of $500,000. When people, in particular prospective park visitors, were asked what they would be willing to pay into a hypothetical trust fund to see wolves in the wilds, it turned out that the decision to reintroduce the wolves may have been worth $30,000,000—again, the "right choice" on simple economic grounds, even before we take up the deeper question of an environmental ethic."

Here, the point is simply this. The mutual distrust between economists and environmentalists is unfortunate. I agree with Amartya K. Sen that bridging the gap between economics and ethics would operate to the benefit of each. Economic thinking and economic instruments, with whatever occasional shortcomings in their assumptions about human motivation, keep us continuously vigilant as nothing else does to costs, benefits, alternatives, and opportunities for gains for trade. However, they will not provide us, as much as we would like it, the grand solutions that go right to the heart of our problems. We don't have the data that economics needs, and economics, even broadly understood, cannot arbitrate all of the conflicts we as a community want resolved. In casting about for solutions we should not overlook the contributions that effluent taxes, tradable allowances, and the homier class of tactics exemplified by the wolf fund [could make]. But for all their elegance and promise of apparent simplicity, we will have to look beyond the economic tools to chip away at the problems with a full chest of readier, rougher, more varied, time-proven and modest devices. . . .

. . . [E]ven if we suppose there is some such core of international morality, it does not take us very far. A moderate realist will grant that we can identify familiar moral principles which, by easy extension, condemn as evil the torture of prisoners or the rape of civilians. The problem at hand is much tougher because it lacks any well-chartered foundation in domestic moral literature: for example, in urging protection of the biosphere, to what moral principles can a global moralist refer?

There are, in fact, two distinct types of moral questions relevant to biospheral degradation, each of which raises a fundamental philosophical challenge.

The first task is to identify *a shared international-morality-in-respect-of-the-environment*. To put it simply, if the nations of the world are to cooperate in the reduction of globe-hazarding substances or the protection of species, how are the burdens of those actions to be apportioned?

The second task is no easier: putting aside the conflicts that divide nations from one another: *What are the obligations that humankind, as a whole, owes to the rest of the natural world?*

To illustrate the difference in outlook, the first question could be illustrated thus: If whales are to be protected, have traditional whaling nations any claims for compensation from nations rich in cattle and grain? The second question is the deeper underlying one: Has humankind any duty to whales to begin with? . . .

The difficulties of sorting through . . . competing standards of "fairness" to find the morally right one is frustrating. And that frustration, in turn, provides a major boost for the various market solutions, which advertise the "unseen hand" of the market as rescuing the human mind from hard choices. Various schemes for marketable pollution allowances are a prime example. But most of the market-trading literature deals with the techniques and benefits of trading. It assumes someone else has provided an answer to the threshold question: How shall we assign the original entitlements, the starting point from which the trading begins to operate? Is the right to pollute a personal right of each member of the human species, to be handed out per capita? Or is it a geopolitical right, to be allocated, like a vote in the U.N. General Assembly, evenly among nations? The snag with the first alternative is that it undermines incentives to control population and is theoretically obscure, anyway: Should each person on earth have a pro rata right to the globe's reserves of oil, fish, timber, and farmland? The problem with the second alternative is that to divide pollution entitlements evenly among nations would give the tiniest nation the right to pollute as much as the largest. Do we take the status quo as a starting point, so the rich can fortify the advantage they have gained over the poor, at the poor's expense? And so on.

These are not questions of economics, but, unavoidably, of ethics. Indeed, in any social philosophy, the just distribution of entitlements—of power, wealth, office, opportunity—is among the hardest, most foundational issues. The stakes are all the more momentous when applied on a global scale, but all the more problem-ridden too. Moral philosophers have their hands full warding off skeptics who charge that ordinary moral discourse is at bottom "meaningless." Philosophers who want to apply moral predicates on the international plane—to say that some international acts are "good" and others "evil"—face additional challenge from the realists, above, who maintain that even if moral discourse is intelligible generally, acts of state are beyond its purview. . . .

We have left the hardest for last: the construction of a true environmental ethic. Put aside for a moment the issues that divide nations. How can we arbitrate the conflicts between humankind, on the one hand, and the rest of the natural environment, on the other? Environmentalists incline to downplay the sharpness of the conflict, pointing out that if we foul our nests, strip our forests, and eradicate species, we ourselves suffer, along with Nature. Indeed, many of the main items on the conservationists' agenda, such as protecting the ozone layer and arresting deforestation, need no philosophically exotic justification. We are far from doing what ought to be done, just from traditional considerations of human health and welfare. Similarly with respect to conserving a wide spectrum of plant and animal species: doing so can stand on the grounds of humankind's benefit, since genetic diversity helps insure the resilience of the food chain against the stress of pests, climatic changes, and man-made environmental toxics.

What is the call, then, for a distinctly environmental ethic? First, there is a wide — and I think widening—sentiment that to argue public policy on purely homocentric grounds is unenlightening, even arrogant. Humankind is maturing beyond its need to presume itself the universe's hub. A nonhomocentric foundation for social choice, even if it should support many of the same choices as would ordinary utilitarianism or some other familiar theory, would be more in line with our growing understanding of the grandness and interrelationships of all the natural world.

But the search for an environmental ethic is not just the search for a new rationale to justify the same old ways of life. Humankind's interests and our obligations to Nature may in some sense part ways. Ever since Aldo Leopold, conservationists have been fudging the congruity between conservationism and human welfare. Leopold boldy announced the need for a new "land ethic," but immediately wavered to sound like an enlightened utiliarian, justifying the ethic on the grounds that treating the earth well—understood in some human-independent way—will inevitably redound to humankind's advantage. . . .

The task of constructing a genuine environmental ethic is nothing less crucial than to provide the missing framework. To appreciate why it is needed, and how it would operate in thought, imagine a proposed project for which no one candidly claims warrant in terms of present or even future human welfare, as we ordinarily understand it. The decision to reintroduce wolves into Yellowstone is a good example to pursue. Humans have not acquired a taste for wolf meat, and, even worse for the project's proponents, wolves destroy things humans raise to eat themselves, such as cattle, and other things people like to shoot and mount on their walls, such as moose.

. . . [A]n ingenious (but partial) solution to the problem [is that] [c]onservationists who want to foster the return of the wolves have established a fund to idemnify ranchers for any cattle the wolves destroy. If the fund conservationists can raise continues to prove ample to satisfy the ranchers, then there is no further conflict—and no need to call upon any special, peculiar environment ethic for further guidance. We will just have one group of humans putting up the cash to reach a satisfactory, "efficient" agreement with another group of humans—an agreement in which the wolves are what lawyers call third-party beneficiaries.

The issue becomes tougher if the money that the conservationists are able to raise proves inadequate to cover the costs of reestablishing the wolves. In those circumstances the verdict of ordinary homocentric morality is clear: from a preference utilitarian point of view, humans value the lost steak over the added wolves—and so the wolves must go.

But there is no reason why environmentalists should have to accept that judgment. The modified market solution having brought us as far as conventional economic analysis can travel, the issue could be advanced to the political arena. Should the return of the wolves be subsidized from the public purse, on the grounds of correcting not a "market failure" but a moral one? To pursue this line of thought is to plunge into deep political theory. If one adopts a passive conception of legislative power, in which the representatives restrict themselves to mirroring and making the best "trades" to advance what they presume to be the well-formed desires of their constituents, then there is no justification for the legislators to "overrule." The modified market test already created a strong presumption of what the voters wanted: more cattle, fewer wolves. But Cass Sunstein contrasts this horse-trading, "pluralist conception" of democracy with a more independent and deliberative "Madisonian conception" under which representatives are licensed, indeed, encouraged, to go beyond the question of how to satisfy already well-formed desires and venture into the discovery and evolution of new ones. In other words, the selection of preferences is among the objects of the government process. That view of community underwrites a continuous, representative-led evolution of values including a shift in the balance between the well-being of humans and the flourishing of their environment. The context of the shift would be the legislative discussion of putting a monetary value on the return of the wolves, as it once did on their extinction. The value of the wolves is certainly not going to emerge as infinite—that is, as overriding every conflicting human desire. On the other hand, the legislature need not accept as definitive the prevailing value their electors put on wolves versus cattle, based on their willingness to pay enough into the wolf fund to outbid what the market will pay for lost steak.

The debate would be expected to grope with the rights of the wolves to share in Nature; the significance of the wolves having been here first, the question whether they have not as much right to eat cattle as humankind. Indeed, perhaps the wolves have more right than humankind to the meat the land can support, lacking, as they do, our capacity to make moral choices and our wide-ranging alternatives to select other equally beneficial diets. Some legislator might even quote from Leibniz: "It is certain that God sets greater store by a man than a lion; nonetheless, it can hardly be said with certainty that God prefers . . . a single man to the whole of lion-kind."

Of course, the problem arises when another legislator denies that wolves have rights (or, more likely: "Come back and see me when wolves and lions get the vote"). How do we arbitrate between them? What can either legislator say next to advance his or her point?

It is that exchange which an environmental ethic aims to carry further. The need for such an expanded ethic cuts in wherever, for example, the probable utility benefits of sparing a wilderness area or species, even when the consequences to mankind are intelligently and liberally estimated, do *not* exceed the costs of forgone timber, crops, and living space. In those circumstances, the person favoring preservation, having exhausted appeal to his neighbors' enlightened self-interest, has to invoke *something else* as a warrant for the sacrifice. But that is the nub of the controversy. The skeptic will maintain not merely that it is unwarranted for us to make sacrifices on behalf of species, or even, less plausibly, of inanimate natural objects such as rivers and wilderness areas. More severely, the skeptic will maintain that we cannot even make such a pro-Nature argument *intelligibly.* . . .

In fact, I do not find establishing a prima facie basis for moral considerableness to be the hardest part of the environmental ethicist's task. There are several foundational possibilities to work with, either separately or in combination. But if any of them is going to make much difference in how we think, it has several burdens to contend with.

First, what is being sought is not just a moral viewpoint that accounts for Nature in principle. We need a moral viewpoint rich enough to advance us through the ontological conundrums. By reference to what principles is the moral and legal world to be carved up into those "things" that count and those that don't? Will the unit of our concern be the individual ant, the anthill, the family, the phylum, the genus, or the ant's habitat? One cannot really avoid such quandaries by adopting a holistic or Gaian viewpoint, one that emphasizes the goodness of the planetary whole; that is, if the everything—the whole—is good, what can be bad? How, faced with any human choice, would a holist judge?

Second, suppose that we can do the carving up correctly, that is, identify those objects toward which some prima facie moral regard is justified, for example, perhaps a certain mountain. Even if moral obligations to a mountain are conceded to exist in principle, the question of how they can be discharged remains: How does one "do right by" a mountain?

Third, there are the distributional dilemmas. It is not enough to carve up the world, establishing what is to be of moral considerableness; nor is it enough to agree how that regard translates into prima facie good and bad acts. What are we to do in the case of conflicting indications? For example, suppose that, working with reference to one or another of the various nature-valuing viewpoints, a prima facie case can be made for preserving each of two species of animal—but we cannot preserve both. Do we favor the rare species of lower animal over the less exotic but "higher" one? It is easy to imagine a moral framework whose basic principle is "more life is better than less." One can imagine, too, support for the preservation of a singular unsullied desert. What do we do in the face of an irrigation project that offers to transform the desert into a habitat teeming with life? The general problem is one of a moral judgment's strength. In other words, even if the continued existence of a species, or the state of a river, is granted to be "a good," how do we make adjustments for that moral fact in the face of conflict and of other, competing goods? . . .

. . . [T]o accommodate and allow space for the growth of our intuitions about our relations with Nature, we have not only to choose among competing species, but even prior to that, among competing meta-ethical viewpoints. Do we embrace a moral framework in which all acts are good or bad insofar as they advance or diminish evaluated human welfare? Or are we going to buy into a version of the moral world in which *things* count morally—a version in which the question, "Is the earth the better with a billion more people or a billion more trees?" is a serious issue, not reducible to the average (or aggregate) happiness of hypothetical human populations?

That choice, the selection of an acceptable moral framework, cannot itself be *derived* from any prior moral postulates. It is the answer to the question with which philosophy began—long before the contemporary preoccupation with evaluating acts and (less often) actors: *How ought one to live?* That and what sort of earth are we aiming for are the bedrock issues that lie at the intersection of philosophy and spirit. They are issues that are resolved less by formal choice, in which the mind is governed by appeals to consistency, than by lifestyle choices, in which we open ourselves to provocations of irony and humor, the experience of wilderness, and the echoes of the best traces of our indwelling terrestrial histories. And just a little humility would go a long way: "... *the gnat is older than he.*"

# Contributors

## Individuals

EDWARD ABBEY was a former National Park Service ranger who became one of America's most popular environmental novelists and essayists. He died in 1989.

BRUCE A. ACKERMAN is Sterling Professor of Law and Political Science at Yale University.

VICKI BEEN is a professor at New York University School of Law.

JOEL FRANKLIN BRENNER is a partner at Storch & Brenner in Washington, D.C.

ROBERT D. BULLARD is the director of the Environmental Justice Resource Center at Clark Atlanta University.

LYNTON KEITH CALDWELL is a professor of public and environmental affairs and the director of Advanced Studies in Science, Technology, and Public Policy at Indiana University.

J. BAIRD CALLICOTT is an associate professor in the Department of Philosophy and Religion Studies at the University of North Texas.

RONALD H. COASE is Clifton R. Musser Professor Emeritus of Economics at the University of Chicago Law School.

ROBERT W. COLLIN is an assistant professor of urban and environmental planning at the University of Virginia, School of Architecture.

HERMAN DALY, a former senior economist at the World Bank, is now a lecturer and senior research scholar at the School of Public Affairs at the University of Maryland.

DAVID DONIGER is counsel to the assistant administrator for air and radiation at the U.S. Environmental Protection Agency.

THOMAS R. DUNLAP is a professor of history at Texas A&M University.

GREGG EASTERBROOK is an environmental journalist who has been a frequent contributor to the *New Republic.*

E. DONALD ELLIOTT, former general counsel at the U.S. Environmental Protection Agency, is an adjunct professor of law at Yale Law School and a senior partner at Fried, Frank, Harris, Shriver, and Jacobson.

DANIEL A. FARBER is Henry J. Fletcher Professor and associate dean at University of Minnesota Law School.

CLAYTON GILLETTE is Perre Bowen Professor and Caddell Conwell Research Professor at the University of Virginia School of Law.

AL GORE is vice president of the United States.

H. SCOTT GORDON is a former economics professor at Carleton College in Ottawa, Ontario.

GENE M. GROSSMAN is a professor of economics at Princeton University and the National Bureau of Economic Research.

ROBERT W. HAHN is a resident scholar, American Enterprise Institute, and an adjunct research fellow at the John F. Kennedy School of Government, Harvard University.

SAMUEL P. HAYS is professor emeritus of history at the University of Pittsburgh.

PAUL A. HEMMERSBAUGH is an associate at Sidley & Austin in Washington, D.C.

JAMES A. HENDERSON, JR. is Frank D. Ingersoll Professor of Law at Cornell Law School.

DONALD T. HORNSTEIN is Reef C. Ivey, II, Research Professor and associate dean at the University of North Carolina School of Law.

PETER W. HUBER is a partner at Kellogg, Huber, Horn, Todd & Evans in Washington, D.C.

JAMES E. KRIER is Earl Warren DeLano Professor of Law at the University of Michigan Law School.

ALAN B. KRUEGER is a professor of economics at Princeton University and the National Bureau of Economic Research.

HOWARD A. LATIN is a professor and Justice John J. Francis Scholar at the State University of New Jersey School of Law at Rutgers–Camden.

RICHARD J. LAZARUS is a professor at Georgetown University Law Center.

JAMES P. LEAPE is a senior vice president at the World Wildlife Fund.

ALDO LEOPOLD joined the U.S. Forest Service in 1909. In 1924 he became associate director of the Forest Products Laboratory in Madison, Wisconsin. In 1933 the University of Wisconsin created a chair in game management for him. He died in 1948.

GERALD MARKOWITZ is a professor of history at John Jay College of Criminal Justice, City University of New York.

GEORGE PERKINS MARSH was a widely traveled U.S. diplomat who was an expert on ancient civilizations. He died in 1882.

ARTHUR F. MCEVOY is with the Department of History and the Center for Urban Affairs and Policy Research at Northwestern University.

THOMAS O. MCGARITY is a professor who holds the W. James Kronzer Chair in Trial and Appellate Advocacy at the University of Texas School of Law.

ALAN MILLER is the executive director of the Renewable Energy Policy Project at the University of Maryland.

JOHN C. MILLIAN is a partner at Gibson, Dunn & Crutcher in Washington, D.C.

ARNE NAESS is professor emeritus of philosophy at the University of Oslo, Norway.

RODERICK NASH is a professor of history at the University of California at Santa Barbara.

EUGENE P. ODUM is professor emeritus and director emeritus of the Institute of Ecology, University of Georgia.

RICHARD N. PEARSON is Cone, Wagner, Nugent, Johnson, Hazouri & Roth Professor Emeritus at the University of Florida College of Law.

WILLIAM F. PEDERSON, JR., a former deputy general counsel for the U.S. Environmental Protection Agency, is a partner at Shaw, Pittman, Potts & Trowbridge in Washington, D.C.

ROBERT V. PERCIVAL is a professor of law, Robert Stanton Scholar, and director of the Environmental Law Program at the University of Maryland School of Law.

ROBERT L. RABIN is A. Calder McKay Professor of Law at Stanford Law School.

TOM REGAN is a professor of philosophy and chair of the Philosophy and Religion Studies Department at North Carolina State University.

RICHARD L. REVESZ is a professor at the New York University School of Law.

WILLIAM H. RODGERS, JR., is a professor at the University of Washington School of Law.

CAROL M. ROSE is Gordon Bradford Tweedy Professor at Yale Law School.

DAVID ROSNER is an associate professor of health administration at Baruch College Mt. Sinai School of Medicine, City University of New York.

WILLIAM D. RUCKELSHAUS is the former administrator of the U.S. Environmental Protection Agency.

MARK SAGOFF is with the Institute for Philosophy and Public Policy, University of Maryland.

JOSEPH L. SAX is the House/Hurd Professor of Environmental Law at the University of California at Berkeley School of Law.

CHRISTOPHER H. SCHROEDER is a professor of law and public policy at the Duke University School of Law.

PHILIP SHABECOFF, a former environmental reporter for *The New York Times*, is the executive publisher of *Greenwire,* an environmental news service.

SIDNEY A. SHAPIRO is John M. Rounds Professor at the University of Kansas School of Law.

RICHARD B. STEWART is Emily Kempin Professor of Law at the New York University School of Law.

CHRISTOPHER D. STONE is Roy P. Crocker Professor at the University of Southern California Law Center.

A. DAN TARLOCK is a distinguished professor of law and codirector of the Program on Environmental and Energy Law at the Chicago-Kent College of Law in the Illinois Institute of Technology.

LAURENCE H. TRIBE is Ralph S. Tyler, Jr., Professor of Constitutional Law at Harvard University Law School.

LYNN WHITE, JR., was a professor of history at the University of California, Los Angeles.

GEORGE F. WILL is a syndicated columnist with *The Washington Post*.

EDWARD O. WILSON is Frank B. Baird, Jr., Professor of Science and Curator in Entomology, Museum of Comparative Zoology, Harvard University.

## Conferences and Organizations

THE ENVIRONMENTAL DEFENSE FUND is a national, not-for-profit, research and advocacy organization with over 250,000 members, which seeks practical solutions to a broad range of environmental and human health problems.

THE FIRST NATIONAL PEOPLE OF COLOR ENVIRONMENTAL LEADERSHIP SUMMIT was a four-day conference held in October 1991 that was attended by nearly 600 grassroots and national leaders to develop strategies for addressing environmental problems affecting people of color.

THE OFFICE OF TECHNOLOGY ASSESSMENT was created in 1972 as an analytical arm of Congress. It was abolished in 1995.

THE PRESIDENT'S COUNCIL ON SUSTAINABLE DEVELOPMENT is a group of leaders from government, business, environmental, civil rights, labor, and Native American organizations appointed by President Clinton in 1993 to advise him on sustainable development.

THE UNITED NATIONS CONFERENCE ON ENVIRONMENT AND DEVELOPMENT was an international environmental conference sponsored by the United Nations, which was held in June 1992 in Rio de Janiero. Attended by representatives of 178 nations, the conference featured the largest gathering of heads-of-state in human history.

THE WORLD COMMISSION ON ENVIRONMENT AND DEVELOPMENT was created by the United Nations in 1983, composed of commissioners from 22 nations, and chaired by Gro Harlem Brundtland of Norway.

## Editors

DOROTHY C. ALEVIZATOS is an attorney with Fitzpatrick, Cella, Harper, and Scinto in New York City. She has a J.D. from the University of Maryland School of Law and an M.S. in conservation biology and sustainable development from the University of Maryland at College Park.

ROBERT V. PERCIVAL is a professor of law, Robert Stanton Scholar, and director of the Environmental Law Program at the University of Maryland School of Law.

# Index